I0131909

# Navigating the Blockchain Revolution: Decentralization, Finance, and Beyond

Edited by

## Monica Bhutani, Monica Gupta & Kirti Gupta

*Department of Electronics and Communications*
*Bharati Vidyapeeth's College Of Engineering*
*New Delhi, India*

## Deepali Kamthania

*School of Information Technology*
*Vivekananda Institute of Professional Studies-Technical*
*Delhi, India*

&

## Danish Ather

*Department of IT and Engineering*
*Amity University in Tashkent*
*Tashkent, Uzbekistan*

**Navigating the Blockchain ,Revolution: Decentralization Finance, and Beyond**

Editors: Monica Bhutani, Monica Gupta, Kirti Gupta, Deepali Kamthania & Danish Ather

ISBN (Online): 979-8-89881-150-1

ISBN (Print): 979-8-89881-151-8

ISBN (Paperback): 979-8-89881-152-5

© 2025, Bentham Books imprint.

Published by Bentham Science Publishers Pte. Ltd. Singapore, in collaboration with Eureka Conferences, USA. All Rights Reserved.

First published in 2025.

## BENTHAM SCIENCE PUBLISHERS LTD.
### End User License Agreement (for non-institutional, personal use)

This is an agreement between you and Bentham Science Publishers Ltd. Please read this License Agreement carefully before using the book/echapter/ejournal (**"Work"**). Your use of the Work constitutes your agreement to the terms and conditions set forth in this License Agreement. If you do not agree to these terms and conditions then you should not use the Work.

Bentham Science Publishers agrees to grant you a non-exclusive, non-transferable limited license to use the Work subject to and in accordance with the following terms and conditions. This License Agreement is for non-library, personal use only. For a library / institutional / multi user license in respect of the Work, please contact: permission@benthamscience.net.

### Usage Rules:

1. All rights reserved: The Work is the subject of copyright and Bentham Science Publishers either owns the Work (and the copyright in it) or is licensed to distribute the Work. You shall not copy, reproduce, modify, remove, delete, augment, add to, publish, transmit, sell, resell, create derivative works from, or in any way exploit the Work or make the Work available for others to do any of the same, in any form or by any means, in whole or in part, in each case without the prior written permission of Bentham Science Publishers, unless stated otherwise in this License Agreement.
2. You may download a copy of the Work on one occasion to one personal computer (including tablet, laptop, desktop, or other such devices). You may make one back-up copy of the Work to avoid losing it.
3. The unauthorised use or distribution of copyrighted or other proprietary content is illegal and could subject you to liability for substantial money damages. You will be liable for any damage resulting from your misuse of the Work or any violation of this License Agreement, including any infringement by you of copyrights or proprietary rights.

### *Disclaimer:*

Bentham Science Publishers does not guarantee that the information in the Work is error-free, or warrant that it will meet your requirements or that access to the Work will be uninterrupted or error-free. The Work is provided "as is" without warranty of any kind, either express or implied or statutory, including, without limitation, implied warranties of merchantability and fitness for a particular purpose. The entire risk as to the results and performance of the Work is assumed by you. No responsibility is assumed by Bentham Science Publishers, its staff, editors and/or authors for any injury and/or damage to persons or property as a matter of products liability, negligence or otherwise, or from any use or operation of any methods, products instruction, advertisements or ideas contained in the Work.

### *Limitation of Liability:*

In no event will Bentham Science Publishers, its staff, editors and/or authors, be liable for any damages, including, without limitation, special, incidental and/or consequential damages and/or damages for lost data and/or profits arising out of (whether directly or indirectly) the use or inability to use the Work. The entire liability of Bentham Science Publishers shall be limited to the amount actually paid by you for the Work.

### General:

1. Any dispute or claim arising out of or in connection with this License Agreement or the Work (including non-contractual disputes or claims) will be governed by and construed in accordance with the laws of Singapore. Each party agrees that the courts of the state of Singapore shall have exclusive jurisdiction to settle any dispute or claim arising out of or in connection with this License Agreement or the Work (including non-contractual disputes or claims).
2. Your rights under this License Agreement will automatically terminate without notice and without the

need for a court order if at any point you breach any terms of this License Agreement. In no event will any delay or failure by Bentham Science Publishers in enforcing your compliance with this License Agreement constitute a waiver of any of its rights.

3. You acknowledge that you have read this License Agreement, and agree to be bound by its terms and conditions. To the extent that any other terms and conditions presented on any website of Bentham Science Publishers conflict with, or are inconsistent with, the terms and conditions set out in this License Agreement, you acknowledge that the terms and conditions set out in this License Agreement shall prevail.

**Bentham Science Publishers Pte. Ltd.**
No. 9 Raffles Place
Office No. 26-01
Singapore 048619
Singapore
Email: subscriptions@benthamscience.net

# CONTENTS

PREFACE ............................................................................................................... i

LIST OF CONTRIBUTORS ..................................................................................... iii

**CHAPTER 1 COMPREHENSIVE INTRODUCTION TO BLOCKCHAIN TECHNOLOGY: PRINCIPLES, APPLICATIONS, AND FUTURE PROSPECTS** ................................................. 1
*Nivedita Palia* and *Deepali Kamthania*
**INTRODUCTION** ................................................................................................ 1
**TIMELINE OF BLOCKCHAIN TECHNOLOGY** ................................................. 2
**NEEDS OF BLOCKCHAIN TECHNOLOGY** ...................................................... 4
**TYPES OF BLOCKCHAIN TECHNOLOGY** ...................................................... 4
**BLOCKCHAIN ARCHITECTURE** ..................................................................... 5
    Block Header ........................................................................................................ 7
    Block Body ........................................................................................................... 7
**CHARACTERISTICS OF BLOCKCHAIN TECHNOLOGY** ............................... 8
**AREA OF APPLICATIONS** ............................................................................... 12
**CHALLENGES** ................................................................................................... 14
**CONCLUSION AND FUTURE SCOPE:** .............................................................. 15
**ACKNOWLEDGEMENT** .................................................................................... 15
**REFERENCES** .................................................................................................... 15

**CHAPTER 2 BLOCKCHAIN IN SUPPLY CHAIN MANAGEMENT, TRACEABILITY, TRANSPARENCY, AND PROVENANCE** .................................................. 19
*Prerna Ajmani, Garima Saini* and *Ayush Arya*
**INTRODUCTION** ................................................................................................ 19
**TRACEABILITY AND TRANSPARENCY IN SUPPLY CHAIN MANAGEMENT** ........... 20
    An Insight into Blockchain Powered Traceability Solutions in Supply Chain Management 21
        *Food/Agricultural Supply Chain* ................................................................... 22
        *Pharmaceutical Supply Chain* ..................................................................... 24
        *Courier Express Parcel (CEP) Supply Chain* ............................................... 25
        *Luxury Supply Chain* ..................................................................................... 25
        *Consumer Electronics Supply Chain* ............................................................. 26
        *Manufacturing Supply Chain* ........................................................................ 26
        *Automobile Supply Chain* .............................................................................. 26
        *Textile Supply Chain* ...................................................................................... 26
        *Wood Supply Chain* ........................................................................................ 27
        *Dangerous Goods Supply Chain* .................................................................... 27
**SMART CONTRACTS** ........................................................................................ 27
    Phases for Setting Up Smart Contracts ................................................................ 28
    Benefits of Smart Contracts ................................................................................. 29
    Demerits of Smart Contracts ................................................................................ 31
    Platforms for Smart Contracts .............................................................................. 31
    Blockchain in Asset Tracking & Identity Management ......................................... 33
**CASE STUDIES GIVEN BY REFERENCE** ....................................................... 34
    Case Study 1: A Penalty-Based Blockchain Traceability Solution ........................ 35
    Case Study 2: Cold Chain Management and Blockchain-Enabled Accountability ........ 36
    Case Study 3: Proof of Concept ........................................................................... 37
**CONCLUDING REMARKS** ............................................................................... 38
**REFERENCES** .................................................................................................... 39

**CHAPTER 3  ENHANCING ELECTRONIC HEALTH RECORDS AND PATIENT DATA MANAGEMENT THROUGH BLOCKCHAIN TECHNOLOGY** ................................................ 44

*Prabh Deep Singh, Kiran Deep Singh* and *Harsh Taneja*

INTRODUCTION ................................................................................. 44

    Background and Significance ..................................................... 45

    Purpose and Scope ...................................................................... 46

    Electronic Health Records (EHRs) ............................................ 46

OVERVIEW AND IMPORTANCE ................................................... 47

    Challenges in EHR Management ................................................ 49

BLOCKCHAIN TECHNOLOGY ...................................................... 49

    Fundamentals and Key Concepts ............................................... 51

    Applications in Healthcare ......................................................... 51

INTEGRATION OF BLOCKCHAIN WITH EHRS ........................ 52

    Benefits and Advantages ............................................................ 53

    Technical Implementation Considerations ................................. 55

SECURITY AND PRIVACY IN BLOCKCHAIN-BASED EHRS ... 55

    Encryption and Decentralization ............................................... 56

    Compliance with Data Protection Regulations ......................... 56

CASE STUDIES AND USE CASES ................................................. 58

    Successful Implementations ....................................................... 58

    Lessons Learned ......................................................................... 59

    Future Trends and Implications ................................................. 60

CHALLENGES AND OPPORTUNITIES FOR EHRS AND PATIENT DATA MANAGEMENT ......................................................................... 61

    Potential Innovations ................................................................. 61

    Ethical and Legal Considerations .............................................. 62

SUMMARY ......................................................................................... 62

CONCLUDING REMARKS .............................................................. 63

CONSENT FOR PUBLICATON ....................................................... 63

ACKNOWLEDGEMENT .................................................................. 64

REFERENCES .................................................................................... 64

**CHAPTER 4  BLOCKCHAIN: THE CHALLENGES OF SCALABILITY AND THEIR SOLUTIONS** ..................................................................................... 65

*Amardeep Pandit, Sweeti Sah, Shweta Sharma, Ojasvi Singh, Gaurav Kumar* and *R. Sujithra Kanmani*

INTRODUCTION ................................................................................. 66

LITERATURE REVIEW ................................................................... 66

BLOCKCHAIN SCALABILITY ....................................................... 68

    Block Size and Transaction Throughput ................................... 69

    Network Latency and Propagation ............................................ 70

    Storage and Data Management .................................................. 71

SOLUTIONS OF BLOCKCHAIN SCALABILITY ........................ 72

    Layer 1 Solutions ....................................................................... 72

        *Sharding* .................................................................................. 72

        *Increasing Block Size* ............................................................ 73

        *Updating Consensus Mechanism* ........................................... 73

        *Configuration of Block Size during Transactions* ................. 73

    Layer 2 Solutions ....................................................................... 74

        *Payment Channels* .................................................................. 74

        *State Channels* ........................................................................ 74

    *Sidechains* ............................................................................................ 75
    *Cross-Chain Exchanges* ...................................................................... 75
  Hybrid Solutions ........................................................................................ 75
**CASE STUDIES** .......................................................................................... 76
  Ethereum 2.0 and Sharding ....................................................................... 76
  Bitcoin Lightning Network ........................................................................ 77
  Layer 2 Solutions in Practice: Case Studies ............................................. 78
**METHODOLOGY** ........................................................................................ 79
  Research Framework ................................................................................. 79
  Data Collection ......................................................................................... 80
  Analytical Techniques ............................................................................... 80
  Consensus Mechanisms Analysis .............................................................. 81
  Scalability and Security Assessment ......................................................... 81
  Ethical Considerations .............................................................................. 81
**EXPERIMENTAL RESULTS** ....................................................................... 81
**CONCLUSION** ............................................................................................. 83
**FUTURE SCOPE** ......................................................................................... 84
**REFERENCES** .............................................................................................. 84

**CHAPTER 5  A STUDY ON BLOCKCHAIN ECOSYSTEM SECURITY** ....... 88
*Mukta, Shiksha Kumari, Sherry Verma* and *Mohit Mittal*
**INTRODUCTION** .......................................................................................... 88
**COMPONENTS OF BLOCKCHAIN** ............................................................ 89
  Block ......................................................................................................... 90
  Nodes ........................................................................................................ 90
  Consensus Algorithm ................................................................................ 92
    *Proof of Work (PoW)* ........................................................................ 92
    *PoS* ..................................................................................................... 94
    *Delegated Proof of Stake (DPoS)* ..................................................... 94
    *Proof of Authority (PoA)* ................................................................... 94
    *Byzantine Fault Tolerance (BFT)* ..................................................... 95
    *Proof of Authentication (PoAh)* ........................................................ 95
  Smart Contracts ........................................................................................ 95
  Hash .......................................................................................................... 97
    *SHA-256* ........................................................................................... 98
    *MD5* .................................................................................................. 98
**LITERATURE SURVEY** ............................................................................... 98
**COINS OF BLOCKCHAIN** ........................................................................... 99
  Cryptocurrency ......................................................................................... 99
  Smart Contract ......................................................................................... 100
  Hyperledger ............................................................................................. 100
**APPLICATION OF BLOCKCHAIN** ............................................................ 100
  Supply Chain Management ....................................................................... 100
  Healthcare ................................................................................................ 101
  Financial Services .................................................................................... 101
  Voting Systems ........................................................................................ 101
  Digital Identity ........................................................................................ 102
  Intellectual Property ................................................................................ 102
**SECURITY ISSUES AND CHALLENGES OF BLOCKCHAIN** ................. 102
**ISSUE OF SECURITY FOR ADOPTING BLOCKCHAIN** ........................ 107
**NETWORK WORKING AND SECURITY CHALLENGES** ....................... 107

    MEASUREMENT OF SUCCESS OF BLOCKCHAIN .................................................. 109
    COMPARISON OF HACKING CASES AND SAFE CASES USING BLOCKCHAIN ........ 111
        Performance analysis .................................................. 113
    CONCLUSION .................................................. 115
    CONSENT FOR PUBLICATION .................................................. 116
    ACKNOWLEDGEMENT .................................................. 116
    REFERENCES .................................................. 116

**CHAPTER 6  BLOCKCHAIN-ENABLED ALGORITHMIC TRADING: QUANTITATIVE TECHNIQUES AND REGULATORY COMPLIANCE IN INDIA** .................................................. 121
    *Sonika Malik, Siddharth Bisht, Mumukshu Tyagi* and *Yash Gupta*
    INTRODUCTION .................................................. 121
        Related Work .................................................. 124
        Proposed Work .................................................. 125
        Dataset .................................................. 126
        Mathematical Models and Statistical Metrics Used .................................................. 126
        Additional Strategies Incorporated .................................................. 133
        Implementational Techniques Used .................................................. 136
        Evaluation and Discussion .................................................. 139
    CONCLUSION .................................................. 142
    CONSENT FOR PUBLICATON .................................................. 143
    ACKNOWLEDGEMENT .................................................. 143
    REFERENCES .................................................. 143

**CHAPTER 7  THE CARBON FOOTPRINT OF BLOCKCHAIN: ENVIRONMENTAL IMPACT** .................................................. 146
    *V. Gayathri* and *Tanusri Gururaj*
    INTRODUCTION OF BLOCKCHAIN TECHNOLOGY .................................................. 146
        Key Characteristics of Blockchain Technology .................................................. 147
        Taxonomy of Blockchain Technology .................................................. 147
    ARCHITECTURE .................................................. 148
        Structure of Blockchain .................................................. 149
        Digital Signature .................................................. 150
        Transactional Process of Blockchain .................................................. 150
    APPLICATION .................................................. 151
    ENERGY CONSUMPTION AND $CO_2$ EMISSION .................................................. 153
        Hardware Requirements and PoW Mechanism .................................................. 155
        Non-renewable Resources .................................................. 155
        Carbon Footprint .................................................. 155
    MITIGATION .................................................. 157
    CASE STUDIES .................................................. 158
    FUTURE SCOPE .................................................. 162
    CONCLUSION .................................................. 164
    CONSENT FOR PUBLICATION .................................................. 165
    ACKNOWLEDGEMENT .................................................. 165
    REFERENCES .................................................. 165

**CHAPTER 8  DISSECTING BLOCKCHAIN TECHNOLOGY: AN IN-DEPTH ANALYSIS** .... 168
    *Nikhil Kumar, Richa, Sweeti Sah, Shweta Sharma* and *R. Sujithra Kanmani*
    INTRODUCTION .................................................. 169
    LITERATURE REVIEW .................................................. 169
    METHODOLOGY .................................................. 170

DATA SOURCES ................................................................................................ 172
CONSENSUS MECHANISM ANALYSIS ........................................................ 175
    PoW ............................................................................................................... 176
    PoS ................................................................................................................ 177
SCALABILITY AND SECURITY ASSESSMENT ......................................... 177
    PoW ............................................................................................................... 178
    PoS ................................................................................................................ 178
EXPERIMENTAL RESULTS ............................................................................ 179
    Bitcoin Descriptive Statistics Table ............................................................ 184
CONCLUSION AND FUTURE WORK ........................................................... 186
REFERENCES .................................................................................................... 187

CHAPTER 9 DECENTRALIZED IDENTIFICATION SYSTEMS USING BLOCKCHAIN AND
SOVEREIGN IDENTITY ................................................................................... 190
*Rohan Raj* and *Sachin Gupta*
INTRODUCTION ............................................................................................... 190
    Background and Motivation ......................................................................... 190
    Problem Statement ....................................................................................... 191
    Purpose and Scope ....................................................................................... 192
    Structure of the Chapter .............................................................................. 192
OVERVIEW OF BLOCKCHAIN TECHNOLOGY ....................................... 192
    Introduction to Blockchain .......................................................................... 192
    Key Concepts and Terminology .................................................................. 193
    Benefits and Challenges .............................................................................. 194
    Scope of Blockchain Integration ................................................................. 195
DECENTRALIZED IDENTITY ........................................................................ 195
    Definition and Concepts .............................................................................. 195
    Traditional vs. Decentralized Identity Systems .......................................... 196
    Benefits of Decentralized Identity .............................................................. 197
SELF-SOVEREIGN IDENTITY (SSI) ............................................................. 198
    Principles and Frameworks ......................................................................... 198
    Decentralized Public Key Infrastructure (DPKI) ....................................... 199
    Verifiable Credentials and Digital Identities .............................................. 200
INTERPLAY BETWEEN BLOCKCHAIN AND IDENTITY ........................ 201
    Blockchain as an Enabler for Decentralized Identity .................................. 201
        *Technical Architecture and Components* ................................................. 203
REGULATORY AND ETHICAL CONSIDERATIONS ................................. 205
    Legal and Regulatory Challenges ............................................................... 205
        *Data Protection and Privacy Laws* .......................................................... 206
        *Ethical Implications and Concerns* .......................................................... 206
CASE STUDIES AND APPLICATIONS .......................................................... 207
    Introduction ................................................................................................. 207
        *Real-world Implementations and Examples* ............................................ 208
        *Lessons Learned and Best Practices* ........................................................ 210
DISCUSSION AND FUTURE DIRECTIONS .................................................. 211
    Current Trends and Innovations .................................................................. 211
        *Integration with Emerging Technologies* ............................................... 211
        *Blockchain Interoperability* ..................................................................... 211
        *Improved User Experience* ....................................................................... 211
        *Regulatory and Compliance Solutions* .................................................... 212
    Open Research Questions ............................................................................. 212

      *Massive Adoption* ................................................................................ 212

      *Scalability* ........................................................................................ 212

      *Regulatory Compliance* .................................................................... 212

      *User Privacy and Security* ................................................................ 212

    Potential Future Developments ............................................................ 213

      *Global Standards for SSI* .................................................................. 213

      *New Blockchain-Based Identity Solutions* .......................................... 213

      *Integration with Emerging Technologies* ............................................ 213

      *Improved Interoperability and Usability* ............................................ 213

**SUMMARY** .......................................................................................... 213

**SUMMARY OF KEY FINDINGS** .......................................................... 214

**FUTURE DIRECTIONS** ........................................................................ 214

**CONCLUSION** ..................................................................................... 215

**CONSENT FOR PUBLICATION** .......................................................... 215

**ACKNOWLEDGEMENTS** ..................................................................... 215

**REFERENCES** ..................................................................................... 215

**CHAPTER 10 EXPLORING THE SPECTRUM OF BLOCKCHAIN: PRIVATE, PUBLIC, CONSORTIUM, AND HYBRID AND THEIR APPLICATIONS** ............................ 217

    *Aparna Singh, Jaya Sinha, Tanu Shree* and *Surbhi Sharma*

**INTRODUCTION** .................................................................................. 218

**LITERATURE REVIEW** ...................................................................... 219

**ARCHITECTURE OF BLOCKCHAIN** ................................................. 222

    Blocks ................................................................................................ 224

    Distributed Network and Consensus Protocols ..................................... 224

    Node Types ......................................................................................... 227

    Smart Contracts .................................................................................. 228

**TYPES OF BLOCKCHAIN** .................................................................... 229

**CHARACTERISTICS OF BLOCKCHAIN** ............................................ 232

    Decentralization .................................................................................. 232

    Consistency ......................................................................................... 232

    Security .............................................................................................. 232

    Anonymity .......................................................................................... 234

    Traceability ........................................................................................ 234

    Immutability ....................................................................................... 234

    Transparency and Irreversibility .......................................................... 234

    Smart Contracts .................................................................................. 235

**APPLICATION AREAS OF BLOCKCHAIN** ......................................... 235

    Internet of Things (IoT) ...................................................................... 235

    Finances ............................................................................................. 236

    Healthcare .......................................................................................... 237

    Supply Chain Management .................................................................. 238

    Industrial IoT (IIoT) ........................................................................... 239

**CONCLUSION AND FUTURE SCOPE** ................................................. 240

**CONSENT FOR PUBLICATION** .......................................................... 240

**ACKNOWLEDGEMENT** ...................................................................... 241

**REFERENCES** ..................................................................................... 241

**CHAPTER 11 MEGAETH: A NEW ERA OF REAL-TIME BLOCKCHAIN TECHNOLOGY** ..... 243

    *Kajal Dubey* and *Dhiraj Pandey*

**INTRODUCTION** .................................................................................. 243

WHY ANOTHER BLOCKCHAIN? AN OVERVIEW OF MEGAETH'S ROLE AND
FUNCTION ................................................................................................ 244
    Why is There a Need for New Blockchains? ........................................... 244
    Limitations of Current Blockchain Frameworks .................................... 245
MEGAETH: A SOLUTION TO EXISTING BLOCKCHAIN CHALLENGES ..... 246
    Solving the Straggler Problem .............................................................. 246
    Node Specialization Approach .............................................................. 246
        *Sequencers* ...................................................................................... 246
        *Provers* ............................................................................................ 247
        *Full Nodes* ....................................................................................... 247
        *Advantages of Node Specialization* ................................................. 247
CURRENT SCALABILITY ISSUES IN EVM-BASED BLOCKCHAINS ........... 248
ENGINEERING A REAL-TIME BLOCKCHAIN: MEGAETH'S APPROACH ...... 249
DESIGN PHILOSOPHY AND APPROACH ..................................................... 249
    Measure, Then Build ............................................................................ 250
    Push Hardware Boundaries .................................................................. 250
TRANSACTION EXECUTION IN MEGAETH .................................................. 250
    Overview of the Transaction Process ................................................... 250
        *EVM Performance Challenges* ........................................................ 251
    State synchronization .......................................................................... 252
    Updating the state root ........................................................................ 253
    Block gas limit .................................................................................... 254
    Supporting infrastructure ..................................................................... 255
    Adopting a Comprehensive Strategy for Blockchain Scaling ............... 256
FUTURE RESEARCH AND DEVELOPMENT PROSPECTS ............................ 256
    Key Solutions Developed by MegaETH ................................................ 256
        *Enhanced Parallel Processing Capabilities* ................................... 256
        *Efficient Just-In-Time (JIT) Compilation* ...................................... 256
        *Improved State Synchronization Method* ......................................... 257
        *Adaptive Block Gas Management* ................................................... 257
        *Advanced RPC Node Enhancements* ............................................... 257
    Anticipated Advancements and Their Implications for Blockchain Technology ... 257
        *Boosted Transaction Throughput and Speed* .................................. 257
        *Reduced Latency and Enhanced User Experience* .......................... 257
        *Strengthened Security and Network Resilience* .............................. 258
        *Scalability for Diverse Use Cases* .................................................. 258
    Future Trends ...................................................................................... 258
        *Novel Scalable Consensus Protocols* .............................................. 258
        *Apply of AI and Machine Learning* ................................................ 258
        *Solutions for Cross-Chain Interoperability* ................................... 258
        *Quantum-Resistant Cryptography* ................................................... 259
        *Environmental Sustainability* ......................................................... 259
CONCLUSION ............................................................................................... 259
ACKNOWLEDGEMENT .................................................................................. 260
REFERENCES ............................................................................................... 260

CHAPTER 12 MEGAETH SOLUTIONS FOR SECURE HEALTHCARE TRANSACTIONS ... 266
*Kajal Dubey* and *Dhiraj Pandey*
INTRODUCTION ........................................................................................... 266
BLOCKCHAIN TECHNOLOGY AND ITS RELEVANCE TO HEALTHCARE ........ 267
    Blockchain Architecture: Decentralization, Consensus, and Immutability ... 267

Types of Blockchain Networks: Public, Private, and Consortium ........................... 269
MegaETH's Blockchain Solution for Healthcare ........................... 270
   *Overview of MegaETH Platform* ........................... 270
**REAL-TIME DATA SYNCHRONIZATION** ........................... 272
Ensuring Up-to-Date Information with Instant Data Synchronization ........................... 272
Mechanisms for Real-Time Updates ........................... 272
   *Blockchain-Based Synchronization* ........................... 272
   *Real-Time Data Flow Technologies* ........................... 273
Impact on Patient Care ........................... 273
   *Avoiding Errors and Duplication* ........................... 274
   *Coordination of Care* ........................... 274
Case Studies Demonstrating Improved Outcomes ........................... 274
   *Primary Care and Specialty Coordination* ........................... 274
   *Integration of Telemedicine* ........................... 274
Integration with Existing Systems ........................... 275
   *Compatibility with Healthcare IT Infrastructure* ........................... 275
   *Implementation Strategies* ........................... 275
**SECURITY PROTOCOLS** ........................... 275
Data Encryption Standards ........................... 276
   *Types of Encryption Used* ........................... 276
   *Effectiveness of Encryption* ........................... 276
Authentication and Authorization ........................... 277
   *Multi-Factor Authentication (MFA)* ........................... 277
Incident Response and Recovery ........................... 278
   *Communication and Transparency* ........................... 279
**BENEFITS, IMPACT, AND CHALLENGES** ........................... 279
Enhancing Patient Safety ........................... 279
   *Reducing Errors and Enhancing Decision-Making* ........................... 279
   *Streamlining Operations* ........................... 280
Challenges and Solutions ........................... 280
   *Navigating Healthcare Regulations and Standards* ........................... 281
Strategies for Training and Encouraging Use Among Healthcare Professionals ........................... 281
**FUTURE DIRECTIONS** ........................... 281
Emerging Technologies ........................... 281
Long-Term Vision For Megaeth ........................... 282
   *Scalability* ........................... 282
   *Interoperability* ........................... 282
   *Global Reach* ........................... 282
   *Innovation* ........................... 282
**CONCLUSION** ........................... 283
**ACKNOWLEDGEMENT** ........................... 283
**REFERENCES** ........................... 283
**SUBJECT INDEX** ........................... 289

# PREFACE

Blockchain is among the disruptive technologies of the 21st century owing to its impact on redesigning the systems of data protection, finance, and other distributed architectures. Of the many global significance that this technology has, this is the most important one because of the potential of this technology to change the different sectors, including the banking sector, supply chain management, the health sector, and the government. **Navigating the Blockchain Revolution:** This work aims to present the readers with an understanding of the core concept of blockchain technology, the various possibilities offered by this technology, and the problems that this sector encounters as it navigates into the global market.

First, the book aims to acquaint the reader with the basic idea of blockchain through the process of creating Bitcoin, Ethereum, and smart contracts. The early chapters create the basis for realizing that blockchain is much greater than cryptocurrencies' underlying technology. Further sections show that different sectors explained how blockchains are introduced and used to unmask certain issues—whether to secure the monetary operations, enhance the supply chain traces, or, among others, defend healthcare information.

Being aware of the problems related to the adoption of blockchain, this book also tackles the major concerns of scalability, power usage, and regulations issues. Readers will be able to get a realistic picture of the future of blockchain technology just by analyzing the current solutions and further advancements being made.

Furthermore, this book discusses some of these applications when overlaying blockchain with other promising technologies such as IoT and AI. The last chapters shed light on the future, presenting further developments like blockchain connection and decentralized autonomous organisms, which can change numerous branches and how companies work.

Thus, this book aims to be a source of practical information and inspiration for professionals, academics, and enthusiasts. Regardless of whether you are approaching the subject from scratch or enhancing your prior knowledge, this book is set to offer inspiring perspectives on blockchain's broad and growing applications in our new digital world. Our intention with this guide is to provide the necessary insights for readers to go forward into the continuous advancement of blockchain technology.

**Monica Bhutani, Monica Gupta & Kirti Gupta**
Department of Electronics and Communications
Bharati Vidyapeeth's College Of Engineering
New Delhi, India

**Deepali Kamthania**
School of Information Technology
Vivekananda Institute of Professional Studies-Technical
Delhi, India

&

**Danish Ather**
Department of IT and Engineering
Amity University in Tashkent
Tashkent, Uzbekistan

# List of Contributors

**Ayush Arya** — School of Information Technology, Vivekananda Institute of Professional Studies-Technical Campus, Delhi, India

**Amardeep Pandit** — Department of Computer Engineering, National Institute of Technology, Kurukshetra, Haryana, India

**Aparna Singh** — School of Computer Science Engineering and Technology, Bennett University, Greater Noida, India

**Dhiraj Pandey** — Department Of Information and Technology, JSS Academy of Technical Education, Noida, India

**Deepali Kamthania** — School of Information Technology, Vivekananda Institute of Professional Studies-Technical Campus, New Delhi, India

**Garima Saini** — Institute of Information Technology & Management (IITM), GGSIPU, Delhi, India

**Gaurav Kumar** — Department of Computer Engineering, National Institute of Technology, Kurukshetra, Haryana, India

**Harsh Taneja** — Department of Computer Science and Engineering, Graphic Era Deemed to be University, Dehradun, India

**Jaya Sinha** — Department of Computer Science and Engineering, ITS Engineering College, Greater Noida, India

**Kiran Deep Singh** — Chitkara University Institute of Engineering and Technology, Chitkara University, Rajpura, Punjab, India

**Kajal Dubey** — Department Of Information and Technology, JSS Academy of Technical Education, Noida, India

**Mohit Mittal** — School of Engineering and Technology, Sushant University, Gurgaon, Haryana, India

**Mumukshu Tyagi** — Department of IT, Maharaja Surajmal Institute of Technology, New Delhi, India

**Mukta** — School of Engineering and Technology, Sushant University, Gurgaon, Haryana, India

**Nivedita Palia** — School of Engineering and Technology, Vivekananda Institute of Professional Studies-Technical Campus, New Delhi, India

**Nikhil Kumar** — Department of Computer Engineering, National Institute of Technology, Kurukshetra, Haryana, India

**Ojasvi Singh** — Department of Computer Engineering, National Institute of Technology, Kurukshetra, Haryana, India

**Prerna Ajmani** — School of Information Technology, Vivekananda Institute of Professional Studies-Technical Campus, Delhi, India

**Prabh Deep Singh** — Department of Computer Science and Engineering, Graphic Era Deemed to be University, Dehradun, India

**R. Sujithra Kanmani** — School of Computer Science and Engineering, Vellore Institute of Technology, Chennai, Tamil Nadu, India

| | |
|---|---|
| **Rohan Raj** | Department of Information Technology and Engineering, Maharaja Agrasen Institute of Technology, Delhi, India |
| **Richa** | Department of Computer Engineering, National Institute of Technology, Kurukshetra, Haryana, India |
| **Sweeti Sah** | Department of Computer Engineering, National Institute of Technology, Kurukshetra, Haryana, India |
| **Shweta Sharma** | Department of Computer Engineering, National Institute of Technology, Kurukshetra, Haryana, India |
| **Shiksha Kumari** | School of Engineering and Technology, Sushant University, Gurgaon, Haryana, India |
| **Sherry Verma** | School of Engineering and Technology, Sushant University, Gurgaon, Haryana, India |
| **Sonika Malik** | Department of IT, Maharaja Surajmal Institute of Technology, New Delhi, India |
| **Siddharth Bisht** | Department of IT, Maharaja Surajmal Institute of Technology, New Delhi, India |
| **Sachin Gupta** | Department of Computer Science Engineering (CSE), Maharaja Agrasen Institute of Technology, Delhi, India |
| **Surbhi Sharma** | School of Computer Science Engineering and Technology, Bennett University, Greater Noida, India |
| **Tanusri Gururaj** | Ernst & Young Associates LLP, Gurgaon, Haryana, India |
| **Tanu Shree** | Department of Computer Science and Engineering, Galgotias College of Engineering and Technology, Greater Noida, India |
| **V. Gayathri** | Department of ECE, Bharati Vidyapeeth's College of Engineering, New Delhi, India |
| **Yash Gupta** | Department of IT, Maharaja Surajmal Institute of Technology, New Delhi, India |

# CHAPTER 1

# Comprehensive Introduction to Blockchain Technology: Principles, Applications, and Future Prospects

**Nivedita Palia**[1,*] and **Deepali Kamthania**[2]

[1] *School of Engineering and Technology, Vivekananda Institute of Professional Studies-Technical Campus, New Delhi, India*

[2] *School of Information Technology, Vivekananda Institute of Professional Studies-Technical Campus, New Delhi, India*

**Abstract:** Blockchain is an immutable digital ledger system that eliminates the need for centralized storage and authority, enabling decentralized financial transactions. It is made up of timestamped, immutable information blocks that are managed by a collection of nodes rather than by any one node. Using cryptographic methods, every block is connected and secured. Blockchain provides a secure and transparent solution by redefining faith, possession, and identity in financial systems. This chapter thoroughly reviews blockchain technology, focusing on why we need it. Next, the chapter discusses blockchain technology's characteristics, type, architecture, and work. Further, the chapter presents some areas of application and challenges it faces.

**Keywords:** Blockchain, Blockchain technology, Bitcoins, Cryptocurrency, Decentralization, Public blockchain, Private blockchain, Smart contracts, Security, Transparency.

## INTRODUCTION

In the past few years, the word blockchain has changed from a specialised thing to an enormous transforming power with the potential to revolutionize several sectors. It has transformed contracts, financial transactions, and records into digital form. Blockchain technology (BT) was initiated in 2008 with Satoshi Nakamato's introduction of Bitcoin [1]. It introduces the idea of blockchain and initiates the use of cryptocurrency in financial transactions where previously cash was used. The introduction of smart contracts started 2nd generation of blockchain and provides efficiency, security, and transparency to financial transactions.

---

* **Corresponding author Nivedita Palia:** School of Engineering and Technology, Vivekananda Institute of Professional Studies-Technical Campus, New Delhi, India; E-mail: nivedita134@gmail.com

**Monica Bhutani, Monica Gupta, Kirti Gupta, Deepali Kamthania & Danish Ather (Eds.)**
**All rights reserved-© 2025 Bentham Science Publishers**

Alternatively, 3rd generation depends on areas other than finance where blockchain is used, such as healthcare, government, science, *etc.* We are in the fourth generation of blockchain with Artificial Intelligence. In less than a decade, Blockchain has seen three generations. Fig. (**1**) summarizes the generations of blockchain.

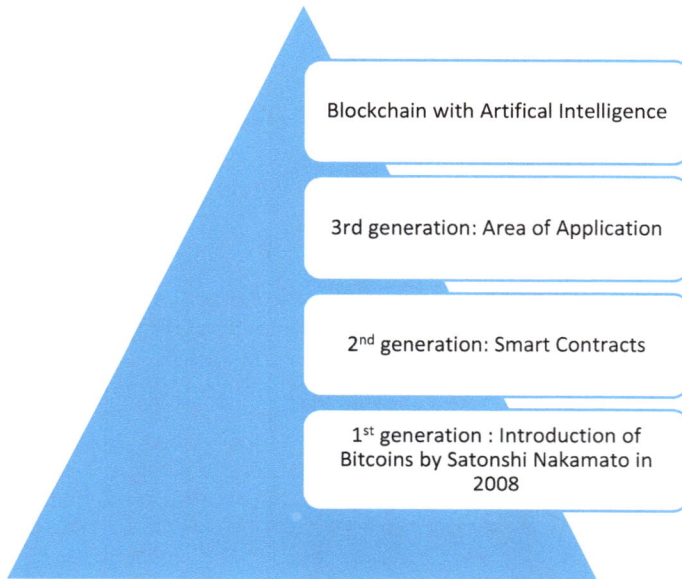

**Fig. (1).** Generations of blockchain technology.

Blockchain has great potential to transform the financial sector digitally, but some pros and cons remain. In this chapter, we provide a brief survey of the BT, its types, the timeline of blockchain, its characteristics, different algorithms used, and areas of application, followed by a discussion of other challenges and future scope.

## TIMELINE OF BLOCKCHAIN TECHNOLOGY

The emergence of the Bitcoin cryptocurrency in 2008 hyped the term "blockchain," but its fundamental ideas and principles have been applied since the 1980s. David Chamu [2] in 1983 proposed the concept of blind signatures for digital transactions. It is a cryptographic technique designed for a safe, automated payment system for enhancing user privacy. Stuart Haber and W. Scott Stornetta 1991 [3] introduced a method for timestamping digital documents by ensuring the validity and integrity of the time of creation. Their pioneering work set the foundation for further development in BT. Reusable Proof of Work (RPoW) was introduced by Hal Finney in 2004 [4] to improve the idea of proof of work, which was initially implemented to combat spam in the digital world. In 2008, Satoshi Nakamoto [1] gave the concept of bitcoin (BTC) in the paper titled "Bitcoin: A Peer-to-Peer Electronic Cash System" defining the decentralized, secure, and transparent transaction system without intervening central authority. On 12th January 2009 [5, 6], the first Bitcoin transaction of 10 BTC occurred between Santoshi Nakamoto and Hal Finney. This historic transaction initiated the era of global cryptocurrency. The world's first bitcoin exchange, "Bitcoin Market" was set up in 2010 [7]. It enables users to transact Bitcoin for U.S. dollars. The first BTC ATM [8] was installed in a Waves Coffee House in Vancouver, Canada, in 2013. It was operated by Robocoin, which allowed users to convert cash for BTC and vice versa. Vitalik Buterin in the year of 2013 presented the idea of a smart contract in his Ethereum white paper [9]. He set up the foundation for the decentralized platform, which can handle decentralized applications (dApps). Officially, in the year 2014, Ethereum launched Blockchain Technology [10]. Concurrently in the same year, the Linux Foundation initiated the Hyperledger project. Free software supports enterprise-grade BT in supply chain management, healthcare, finance, education, *etc* [11]. The establishment of the R3 consortium and the launch of Ethereum's first live release: "Frontier" are the two significant events that took place in the year 2015, which will influence the evolution of BT [12, 13]. The Decentralized Autonomous Organization project was developed on the Ethereum Blockchain and raised US$ 150 million in 2016 [14]. In 2017 Digital Trade Chain platform was announced. Seven European banks collaborated to create the platform. Later it was renamed as we. Trade [15]. Table **1** summarizes the significant events that occurred in the evolution and global spread of BT [1 - 23]. Since 2008, BT has drawn interest from all over the world. Many nations are implementing this technology in various areas such as healthcare, supply chain, finance, agriculture, *etc*. This chapter briefly explained the different aspects of the BT, its area of applications, challenges, and future scope.

**Table 1. Major events occurred [1 - 24].**

| Year | Work Done |
|------|-----------|
| 1983 | Blind signatures for automated payments proposed by David Chaum |
| 1991 | Timestamped documents introduced for securing digital documents |
| 2004 | Reusable Proof of Work (RPoW) introduced by Hal Finney |
| 2008 | The Bitcoin whitepaper was published, outlining a peer-to-peer electronic cash system |
| 2009 | 1st Bitcoin transaction occurred |
| 2010 | World's first Bitcoin exchange, "Bitcoin Market", established |
| 2013 | The first Bitcoin ATM was launched |
| 2013 | Smart contracts in the Ethereum whitepaper proposed by Vitalik Buterin |

*(Table 1) cont.....*

| Year | Work Done |
|------|-----------|
| 2014 | Ethereum blockchain launched |
| 2014 | The Hyperledger project started |
| 2015 | R3 Consortium setup, Ethereum first live release, |
| 2016 | The DAO project, built on Ethereum, subsequently attacked |
| 2017 | A digital trade chain platform announced, Japan acknowledges virtual money. |
| 2018 | Kodak announced that Kodak Coin cryptocurrency, Switzerland, has started paying Bitcoin for taxes. |
| 2019 | Facebook releases the libra |
| 2020 | DeFi Boom, Ethereum 2.0 Phase 0 Launch |
| 2021 | NFT Explosion, Bitcoin All-Time High, China's Cryptocurrency Crackdown |
| 2022 | Ethereum Merge, Adoption of Blockchain in Enterprises |
| 2023 | Central Bank Digital Currencies (CBDCs), Rise of Layer 2 Solutions |
| 2024 | Continued Growth of Web3, Advancements in Interoperability |

## NEEDS OF BLOCKCHAIN TECHNOLOGY

The global financial system regularly handles trillions of cash while serving billions of people. Such ambitious goals come with a various issues that the finance industry has been facing for a long time. These problems consist of the expenditure of several representatives, delays, additional paperwork, and data leakage, causing enormous losses for a company every financial year. BT may be able to resolve these issues faced by the global economic system [25]. Additionally, the cost of the current stock market is driven up due to the existence of regulators, brokers, *etc.* Using the decentralized method, and stock market efficiency can be improved by using smart contracts. For a very long time, the financial sector has faced various challenges. They search for a comprehensive solution that can solve all existing problems. BT has the ability to address all business problems; it executes every investor-company interaction in a decentralized manner without brokers' interference and reduces cost [26].

## TYPES OF BLOCKCHAIN TECHNOLOGY

Blockchain architecture is based on two main aspects: ownership of the data related with joining, such as read, write, and commit. Based on these, BT is categorized into 4 types as shown in Fig. (**2**). Public BT is a non-restricted distributed system. Any user can join the network, authorize the transaction, and access the current and previous records, while Private BT is restrictive in nature and allows selected members to access the network. Consortium and Hybrid BT combine the features of public and private BT. Consortium BT is also known as Federated BT, and it is administered by the group rather than a single member.

Each type of BT has pros and cons, making them fit for different applications. Table **2** provides the comparative analysis for various forms of BT.

Table 2. Comparative analysis for various forms of Blockchain Technology [27 - 29].

| Feature | Public Blockchain | Federated /Consortium Blockchain | Private Blockchain | Hybrid Blockchain |
|---|---|---|---|---|
| **Type** | Distributed | Decentralized | Partially Centralized | Combination of Public and Private |
| **Participation in Consensus** | All miners | Pre-selected nodes | Centralized authority | Selected nodes |
| **Read Permissions** | Public | Restricted to insiders | Administrator consent | Partially public, partially restricted |
| **Efficiency** | Low | High | High | Moderate |
| **Energy Consumption** | Very high | Moderate | Low | Moderate |
| **Immutability** | Impossible to tamper | Could be tampered | Could be tampered | Partially tamper-resistant |
| **Nature** | Permissionless | Permissioned | Permissioned | Permissioned and permissionless |
| **Network Actors** | Unknown | Preselected group | Known | Known and unknown |
| **Speed** | Slow | Moderate | Fast | Faster than public, slower than private |
| **Security** | More secure | Moderately secure | Less secure | More secure than private, less secure than public |
| **Privileges** | No privileges | Equal privileges | Single administrated | Some privileges for certain participants |
| **Examples** | Bitcoin | Hyperledger | MONAX | Ripple |

## BLOCKCHAIN ARCHITECTURE

BT is a distributed, decentralized digital ledger that records transactional data in sequential blocks that are joined by a cryptographic function. Fig. (**3**) given below, shows an example of Blockchain. Every block is linked to the previous block using the parent block hash contained in the block header. The first node in the network is known as Block 0/ Genesis Block, which is a node without a parent node. The internal structure of the blockchain is described in Fig. (**4**). A block is the key element of BT. It is divided into two sections: a block header and a block body [30].

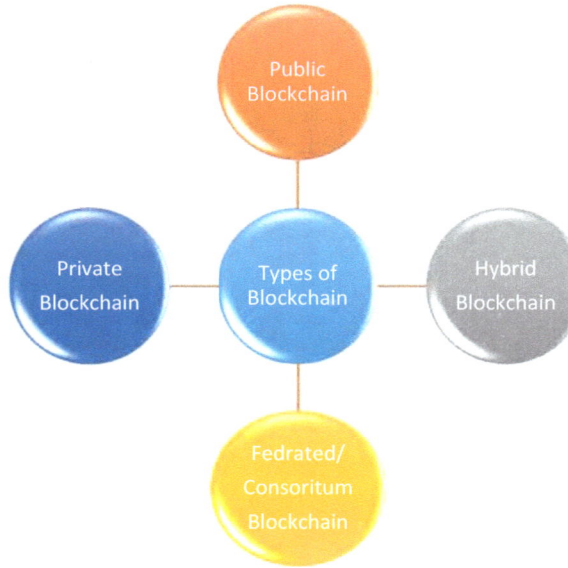

**Fig. (2).** Types of blockchain technology.

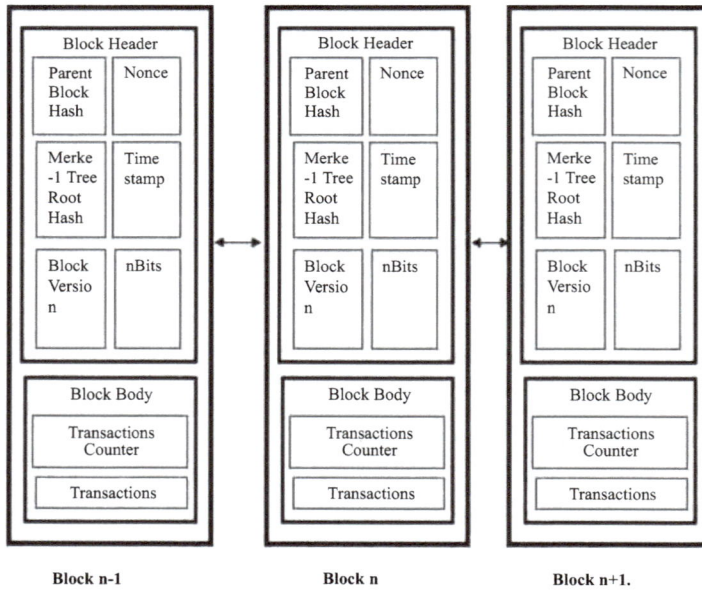

**Fig. (3).** A blockchain example.

```
┌─────────────────────────────────────────┐
│              BLOCK STRUCTURE              │
│  ┌─────────────────────────────────────┐ │
│  │           Block Header              │ │
│  │  ┌────────┐ ┌────────┐ ┌────────┐  │ │
│  │  │ Parent │ │ Time   │ │ Nonce  │  │ │
│  │  │ Block  │ │ stamp  │ │        │  │ │
│  │  │ Hash   │ │        │ │        │  │ │
│  │  └────────┘ └────────┘ └────────┘  │ │
│  │  ┌────────┐ ┌────────┐ ┌────────┐  │ │
│  │  │ Block  │ │ nBits  │ │ Merke  │  │ │
│  │  │ Versio │ │        │ │ -1 Tree│  │ │
│  │  │ n      │ │        │ │ Root   │  │ │
│  │  │        │ │        │ │ Hash   │  │ │
│  │  └────────┘ └────────┘ └────────┘  │ │
│  └─────────────────────────────────────┘ │
│  ┌─────────────────────────────────────┐ │
│  │           Block Body                │ │
│  │  ┌───────────────────────────────┐  │ │
│  │  │     Transactions Counter      │  │ │
│  │  └───────────────────────────────┘  │ │
│  │  ┌───────────────────────────────┐  │ │
│  │  │        Transactions           │  │ │
│  │  └───────────────────────────────┘  │ │
│  └─────────────────────────────────────┘ │
└─────────────────────────────────────────┘
```

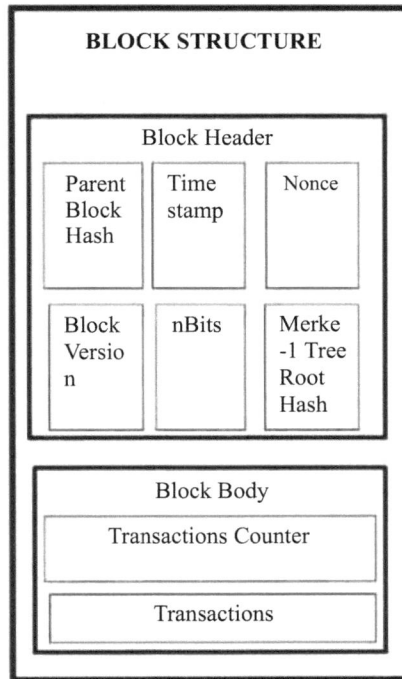

**Fig. (4).**  Structure of a block.

## Block Header

- ***Block Version***: Specifies the version of the software used. It shows the set of guidelines the block follows.
- ***Merkle Tree Root Hash***: A 256-bit hash value summarizes all the transactions.
- ***Timestamp***: It recorded the current time in seconds since 1$^{st}$ January 1970. It helps in sequencing the blocks in chronological order.
- ***nbits***: Represents the difficulty in targeting 32-bit in a format known as target threshold.
- ***The Nonce:4-byte***: Field begins from zero and is used in the Proof of Work (PoW) algorithm, as well as increments for each hash computation.
- ***Parent Block Hash***: 1-byte hash value that indicates the parent block. It is used to link blocks together to form a blockchain.

## Block Body

It consists of a transaction counter and transactions. The count of transactions depends upon the size of the block and transaction size.

# CHARACTERISTICS OF BLOCKCHAIN TECHNOLOGY

BT has the following key characteristics:

**Decentralization**: In traditional systems, every transaction is validated by the central authority, in contrast, blockchain operates through distributed networks while maintaining data consistency.

**Immutability**: Only valid transactions are admitted; a transaction cannot be changed or removed after it has been stored. It guarantees a permanent and un-editable record of every transaction.

**Transparency**: Every participant in the network views each transaction. Details of every transaction are available for audit purposes.

**Security**: Each node/block in the blockchain is connected to the previous node by a cryptographic hash function, which makes the system highly secure.

**Anonymity**: Each participant can interact while remaining pseudonymous with blockchain, which guarantees the privacy preservation of the user.

**Consensus Mechanism**: It is a backbone for any blockchain application. For the proper working of blockchain, it requires some rules and, these rules are provided by a consensus mechanism. The details of some common consensus algorithms are explained below and summarized in Table **3** [31].

***Proof of Work (PoW)***: This consensus mechanism is used by the majority of blockchains. The Bitcoin network uses this strategy [1]. It operates on the criteria that there exists a solution that is easy to verify and extremely difficult to discover. In this mechanism, a new node is added to the network after finding a solution to a complex problem. This process requires a lot of computational resources, using specialized hardware, which leads to high energy usage [32 - 35].

***Proof Stake (PoS)***: It is a consensus mechanism to validate the transaction. In PoW, miners play the same role as the validator in the PoS. The lowest stake value required to become a validator in the Ethereum blockchain is 32ETH. Validators are chosen randomly in the PoS consensus mechanism to construct the new block and verify the other created blocks. In either case, rewards are given to the validators [32 - 35].

***Delegated Proof of Stake***: Daniel Larimer developed the Delegated Proof of Stake consensus algorithm. It moderates the traditional PoS consensus method by preserving an election system by selecting witness nodes for validating the blocks [43 - 46].

***Practical Byzantine Fault Tolerance (pBFT)***: M. Castro and B. Liskov introduced the pBFT consensus algorithm. Zillique & Hyperledger Fabrics both make use of it. It works with high fault tolerance by tolerating one-third of the faulted nodes (Byzantine fault) without hampering the system's integrity [32 - 35].

***Proof of Activity (PoA)***: The PoW and PoS consensus approaches amalgamate in the PoA consensus mechanism. The starting mining procedure is like PoW. After a node is mined, a random set of validators is selected based on the PoS consensus mechanism, which then verify the freshly mined node [32 - 35].

***Proof of Burns (PoB)***: It is more energy-efficient than the PoW consensus mechanism. It is based on the concept of burning "tokens", which indicates removing unspendable addresses from circulation by directing cryptocurrency to them. Miner's mining power in the PoW is determined based on the number of coins burned. The higher the count, the greater the mining power, which ultimately increases energy consumption [32 - 35].

***Proof of Capacity (PoC)***: It is used to validate the blockchain system before deploying a complete system. It finds both technical as well as operational hurdles in the initial stage of the project lifecycle. Using allocated hard drive space, it determines mining rights. This mechanism works in two steps, naming, plotting, and mining [32 - 35].

***Proof of Elapsed Time (PoET)***: It is developed based on the fair lottery method. It decides the mining rights based on a randomly selected waiting time. In this mechanism, every participant node waits for an arbitrary amount of time. It reduces the computational power consumption [32 - 35].

***Delayed Proof of Work***: It provides a security mechanism by enhancing the security of smaller blockchains by exploiting the security of safe and established blockchains [32 - 35].

***Proof of Weight (PoWeight)***: This consensus algorithm was developed to improve the security of blockchain by considering users' weights instead of solely focusing on staking tokens. The weight of the participant is dependent on many factors like data storage, reputation, governance, *etc* [32 - 35].

***Proof of Reputation (PoR)***: This consensus mechanism chooses validator blocks within the network based on reputation. The reputation within the network is built because of trust, previous performance, and their contribution within the network [32 - 35].

***Proof of Space (PoSpace)***: Miners in the PoSpace algorithm prove that they are given a significant memory space on their hard disk to the blockchain network. It is more energy efficient than PoW because it depends on the availability of free storage space [32 - 35].

***Proof of Importance (PoI)***: It finds which participant in the blockchain network is eligible to insert a new node. In the year of 2015, the New Economy Movement introduced it [32 - 35].

***Proof of Stake Velocity (PoSV)***: It promotes ownership and activity in the network. In 2014, Ren proposed it. It uses an exponential growth function to compute coin age instead of a linear function used by PoS [32 - 35].

***Proof of History (PoH)***: It solves the problem of time agreement using cryptographic technique to create a reliable sequence of transactions or events noted in the ledger. PoH allows execution of thousands of transactions instantly [32 - 36].

***Proof of Believability (PoBLV)***: It chooses a validator by considering their previous behaviour and contribution.

***Proof of Time (PoT)***: Verifiable delay functions (VDFs) are used by PoT to select validators. PoT chooses a validator based on each node's fixed stake and ranking score.

***Proof of Existence (PoE)***: It is mainly used for timestamping and authentication. PoE can act as a means to verify a particular piece of existing data instantly, existing without disclosing the data itself. PoE is utilized for certifying documents by guaranteeing their transparency and consistency [32 - 36].

***Proof of Retrievability (PoR)***: It is a cryptographic mechanism developed to verify that memory space providers, like cloud, *etc.*, for storing the entire amount of uncorrupted information and has the ability to access/ retrieve it when required [32 - 36].

***Ouroboros***: It was created to maintain decentralization while handling key issues like security, sustainability, and scalability.

***Stellar Consensus Protocol (SCP)***: The Stellar network uses this protocol for transaction verification. It is created to make decentralized, efficient, and scalable consensus for distributed networks [32 - 36].

**Table 3. Consensus approaches used in Blockchain [32 - 36].**

| Consensus Approach | Principle | Used By |
|---|---|---|
| Proof of Work (PoW) | Solves a computationally intensive problem to create new blocks. | Bitcoin |
| Proof of Stake (PoS) | Validators stake their cryptocurrency to participate in block creation and validation. | Ethereum |
| Delegated Proof of Stake (DPoS) | An election system selects witnesses to verify blocks. | BitShares |
| Practical Byzantine Fault Tolerance (pBFT) | Replicates a state machine to tolerate malicious nodes and ensure consensus. | Stellar |
| Proof of Activity (PoA) | For initial mining and subsequent validation, it combines PoW and PoS. | VeChain |
| Proof of Burn (PoB) | Miners burn cryptocurrency to increase their mining power. | Slimcoin |
| Proof of Capacity (PoC) | The storage space of mining devices determines mining rights. | Burstcoin |
| Proof of Elapsed Time (PoET) | A fair lottery system based on waiting times determines mining rights. | Hyperledger Sawtooth |
| Delayed Proof of Work | Enhances the security of a smaller system by exploiting the established system. | Komodo |
| Proof of Weight (PoWeight) | weight instead of solely focusing on staking tokens. | Algorand |
| Proof of Reputation (PoR) | Selects validators blocks within the network based on reputation. | GoChain |
| Proof of Space (PoSpace) | Energy efficiency depends on the availability of free storage space. | Spacemint |
| Proof of Importance (PoI) | Determines participant eligibility for the addition of a new node. | NEM |
| Proof of Stake Velocity (PoSV) | Uses an exponential growth function to compute coin age. | Reddcoin |
| Proof of History (PoH) | Solves the problem of time agreement using cryptographic technique. | Solana |
| Proof of Believability (PoBLV) | Chooses a validator by considering their previous behaviour and contribution. | IOST |
| Proof of Time (PoT) | Uses VDFs to select validators. | Choronlogic |
| Proof of Existence (PoE) | Used for timestamping and authentication for documents. | HeroNode |
| Proof of Retrievability (PoR) | Ensuring uncorrupted data is retrieved when needed. | PermaCoin |
| Ouroboros | Handled key issues. | Cardano |
| Stellar Consensus Protocol | Decentralized, efficient, and scalable consensus for distributed networks. | Stellar |

## AREA OF APPLICATIONS

This section describes the use of BT in some major areas. Fig. (**5**) given below, summarizes the area of applications.

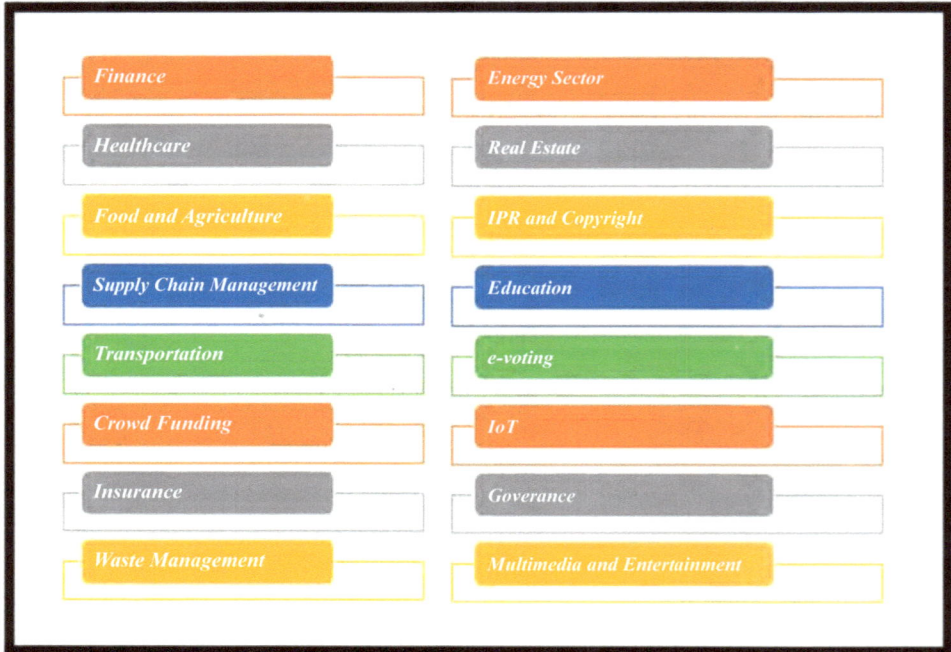

**Fig. (5).** Area of the application blockchain technology [37-52].

**Finance and Banking**: It is used for secure, safe, and transparent transactions. It consists of cross-border financial transactions, smart contracts, share trading and stock marketing, decentralized finance, fraud management, crypto-based banking transactions, and syndicated lending [37].

**Pharmaceuticals & Healthcare**: It is used to store and share patient records electronically and ensures preservation of data privacy. It helps trace and track pharmaceutical supply chain by identifying counterfeit drugs [38].

**Food & Agriculture**: It helps reduce food wastage, tracing and tracking food supply from farms to the table and tracking proper food storage, which helps identify contamination [39].

**Energy Sector**: It allows peer-to-peer energy trading of renewable energy and helps manage and optimize energy consumption and distribution [40].

**Supply Chain Management & Logistics**: It helps trace and track products (raw, intermediate, or finished) from the start to the end user by ensuring transparency and decreasing fraud [41].

**Logistics & Transportation**: Blockchain is used for Autonomous vehicle monitoring, creating opportunities for transportation players, monitoring fuels, and road safety [42].

**Real Estate**: It helps maintain property records accurately by transacting real estate transactions securely and transparently [43].

**IPR and Copyright**: Smart contracts are used to identify the ownership of IPR and copyright in the field of software, arts, music, fashion, literature, *etc* [44].

**Education**: It helps in credential verification and maintains students' identity [45].

**e-Voting**: It provides a secure voting system by verifying the identity of each voter [46].

**Multimedia & Entertainment**: Blockchain can help reduce intellectual property infringement, enhance transparency regarding content ownership, and enable monetizing copyright assets using smart contracts [47].

**Waste Management & Tracking**: Blockchain helps in keeping track of waste from its origin to its disposal location, resulting in an unchangeable and tamper-proof system [48].

**Governance**: Blockchain can revolutionize electronic governance by improving transparency, safety, and efficiency. The government can reduce the cases of corruption and fraud by using blockchain features and able to build trust among its citizens [49].

**Insurance**: Blockchain helps solve key challenges in the insurance sector, such as fraud, inefficient information exchange, reliance on brokers, and manual claim processing using smart contract for automation [50].

**Internet of Things (IoT)**: Architectural flaws in IoT systems made security breaches possible. In a conventional IoT system, all information is stored at centralized locations. Currently, the number of interconnected devices is increasing exponentially, there is a requirement for a decentralized security system such as blockchain [51].

**Crowdfunding**: It is made transparent, secure, and accountable using BT. Blockchain enhances transaction time as well as cost [52].

## CHALLENGES

This section of the chapter presented major challenges [53]. Fig. (**6**) summarizes these challenges.

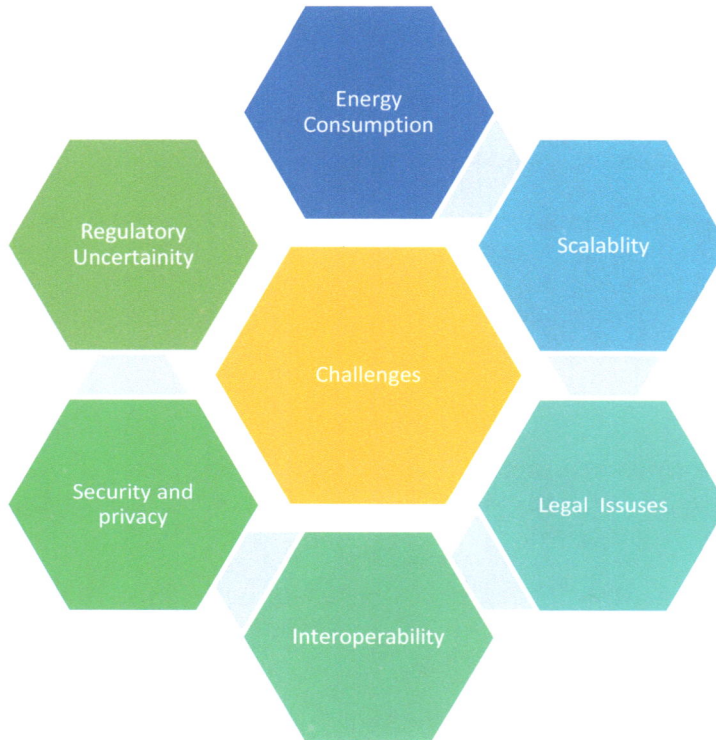

**Fig. (6).** Challenges faced by Blockchain Technology [53].

**Scalability**: As the number of participants increases in the blockchain, transaction processing speed decreases, and it becomes costly, creating difficulties in assisting large-scale applications.

**Energy Consumption**: PoW consensus algorithm is computationally demanding and leads to more energy consumption.

**Regulatory Uncertainty**: Governments are still formulating rules and regulations to govern the use of smart contracts, cryptocurrencies, *etc.*, which develop hesitancy among businesses and developers for their use.

**Interoperability**: The number of blockchain platforms exists, each with different protocols, due to which it is difficult to communicate between networks.

**Security and Privacy**: Blockchain offers individual privacy by hiding its real identity, but cannot provide transactional privacy since the details of all transactions are visible to everyone due to the transparency feature.

**Legal Issues**: Blockchain is still in the development stage, with no clear solution on handling disputes and updating the networks.

## CONCLUSION AND FUTURE SCOPE

Blockchain Technology has grown a lot since its beginning, changing industries and revamping the way digital transactions are executed. Any technology has its own set of benefits and challenges. On one side, its use in the field of cryptocurrencies and other sectors such as finance, education, supply chain management, healthcare *etc.* has shown its capability to improve transparency, decentralization, and security, while on the other side, issues like scalability, energy consumption, cost and efficiency, absence of globally accepted rules and regulation, *etc.* result in uncertainty in the direction of usage of blockchain based solutions. As the technology progresses, improvements in consensus algorithms, defining universal rules and regulatory frameworks will be able to tackle these problems and open new application domains.

## ACKNOWLEDGEMENT

We thank the Vivekananda Institute of Professional Studies-Technical Campus for providing a great environment and resources for doing research work.

## REFERENCES

[1]     S. Nakamoto, *Bitcoin: A peer-to-peer electronic cash system,* 2008. https://bitcoin.org/bitcoin.pdf

[2]     D. Chaum, "Blind signatures for untraceable payments", In: *Advances in Cryptology CRYPTO 82* Boston, USA, 1983, pp. 199-203.
[http://dx.doi.org/10.1007/978-1-4757-0602-4_18]

[3]     S. Haber, and W.S. Stornetta, "How to time-stamp a digital document", *J. Cryptol.,* vol. 3, no. 2, pp. 99-111, 1991.
[http://dx.doi.org/10.1007/BF00196791]

[4]     H. Finney, *Reusable proofs of work,* 2004. http://www.finney.org/~hal/rpow/

[5]     H. Finney, "Twitter post about the first Bitcoin transaction", 2009.

[6]     N. Popper, *Digital Gold: Bitcoin and the Inside Story of the Misfits and Millionaires Trying to Reinvent Money.* HarperCollins: NewYork, 2015.

[7]     https://academy.bit2me.com/en/history-exchanges-bitcoin-trading/

[8]     M. Murugappan, R. Nair, and S. Krishnan, "Global market perceptions of cryptocurrency and the use of cryptocurrency by consumers: A pilot study", *J. Theor. Appl. Electron. Commer. Res.,* vol. 18, no. 4, pp. 1955-1970, 2023.
[http://dx.doi.org/10.3390/jtaer18040098]

[9]     V. Buterin, *Ethereum whitepaper: A next-generation smart contract and decentralized application*

*platform,* 2013. https://ethereum.org/en/whitepaper/

[10]   N. Reiff, *Bitcoin vs. Ethereum: What's the difference?,* 2024. https://www.investopedia.com/
       articles/investing/031416/bitcoin-vs-ethereum-driven-different-purposes.asp#:~:text=Bitcoin%20is%
       20primarily%20designed%20to,%2C%20smart%20contracts%2C%20and%20NFTs

[11]   Linux Foundation, "The Linux Foundation builds the global foundation for open-source enterprise
       blockchain technologies," Linux Foundation Case Studies: Hyperledger, 2022. [Online]. Available:
       https://www.linuxfoundation.org/projects/case-studies/hyperledger

[12]   https://www.r3.com/

[13]   Ethereum Foundation, "The Beacon Chain has launched," Ethereum Foundation Blog, Dec. 1, 2020.
       [Online]. Available: https://blog.ethereum.org/2020/12/01/eth2-beacon-chain-launch/

[14]   D. Siegel, *Understanding The DAO Attack,* 2016.https://www.coindesk.com/learn/understanding-the-
       dao-attack/

[15]   Digital Trade Chain platform rebranded as we.trade, aimed at simplifying trade for SMEs, Finextra
       Research, 2017.

[16]   https://cointelegraph.com/news/japan-officially-recognizes-bitcoin-and-digital-currencies-as-money
       #:~:text=The%20government%20in%20Japan%20is,Japan's%20own%20currency%2C%20the%20Ye
       n

[17]   J. Jolly, "Kodak soars on cryptocurrency plans: Will launch KodakCoin and host ICO", *The Guardian,*
       vol. 10, 2018.

[18]   K. Lyons, and K. McCarthy, "Facebook officially announces its cryptocurrency, Libra", *The Verge,*
       vol. 18, 2019.

[19]   S. Castor, "Ethereum 2.0 goes live as 'world computer' begins long-anticipated upgrade," CoinDesk,
       Dec. 1, 2020. [Online]. Available: https://www.coindesk.com/tech/2020/12/01/ethereum-20-beac-
       n-chain-goes-live-as-worldcomputer-begins-long-awaited-overhaul/

[20]   L. White, "China declares all crypto transactions illegal; bitcoin price falls", *Reuters,* vol. 24, 2021.

[21]   R. Tornow, "2022 Global blockchain survey: New value drivers and opportunities in enterprise
       blockchain adoption", *Deloitte Insights,* vol. 11, 2022.

[22]   A. Rathi, "The rise of Central Bank Digital Currencies (CBDCs) in 2023", *Forbes,* 2023.

[23]   Y. Khatri, "Web3 continues to expand in 2024 with a focus on interoperability and user
       empowerment", *Cointelegraph,* vol. 10, 2024.

[24]   M. Schurtenberger, "Public *vs* Private blockchains: Why public blockchains are the future," 2020.

[25]   Q. Gan, R.Y.K. Lau, and J. Hong, "A critical review of blockchain applications to banking and
       finance: a qualitative thematic analysis approach", *Technol. Anal. Strateg. Manage.,* pp. 1-17, 2021.
       [http://dx.doi.org/10.1080/09537325.2021.1979509]

[26]   S. Karim, M.R. Rabbani, and H. Bawazir, "Applications of Blockchain Technology in the Finance and
       Banking Industry Beyond Digital Currencies", In: *Blockchain Technology and Computational
       Excellence for Society 5.0.* IGI Global, 2022, pp. 216-238.
       [http://dx.doi.org/10.4018/978-1-7998-8382-1.ch011]

[27]   M. Xu, X. Chen, and G. Kou, "A systematic review of blockchain", *Financial Innovation,* vol. 5, no. 1,
       p. 27, 2019.
       [http://dx.doi.org/10.1186/s40854-019-0147-z]

[28]   O. Labazova, T. Dehling, and A. Sunyaev, "From hype to reality: A taxonomy of blockchain
       applications", *52nd Hawaii Int. Conf. Syst. Sci. (HICSS 2019),* pp. 2804-2814, 2019.
       [http://dx.doi.org/10.24251/HICSS.2019.552]

[29]   O.F. Cangir, O. Cankur, and A. Ozsoy, "A taxonomy for Blockchain based distributed storage

technologies", *Inf. Process. Manage.,* vol. 58, no. 5, p. 102627, 2021.
[http://dx.doi.org/10.1016/j.ipm.2021.102627]

[30]    Z. Zheng, S. Xie, H. Dai, X. Chen, and H. Wang, "An Overview of Blockchain Technology: Architecture, Consensus, and Future Trends", *2017 IEEE International Congress on Big Data (BigData Congress), Honolulu, HI, USA,* pp. 557-564, 2017.
[http://dx.doi.org/10.1109/BigDataCongress.2017.85]

[31]    Tripathi, Gautami & Ahad, Mohd & Casalino, Gabriella, "A comprehensive review of blockchain technology: Underlying principles and historical background with future challenges", *Decis. Anal. J.,* vol. 9, p. 100344, 2023.
[http://dx.doi.org/10.1016/j.dajour.2023.100344]

[32]    D. Mingxiao, M. Xiaofeng, Z. Zhe, W. Xiangwei, and C. Qijun, "A review on consensus algorithm of blockchain", *2017 IEEE International Conference on Systems, Man, and Cybernetics (SMC),* 2017 pp. 2567-2572 Banff, AB, Canada.
[http://dx.doi.org/10.1109/SMC.2017.8123011]

[33]    M.S. Ferdous, M.J.M. Chowdhury, and M.A. Hoque, "A survey of consensus algorithms in public blockchain systems for crypto-currencies", *J. Netw. Comput. Appl.,* vol. 182, p. 103035, 2021.
[http://dx.doi.org/10.1016/j.jnca.2021.103035]

[34]    S.M.H. Bamakan, A. Motavali, and A. Babaei Bondarti, "A survey of blockchain consensus algorithms performance evaluation criteria", *Expert Syst. Appl.,* vol. 154, p. 113385, 2020.
[http://dx.doi.org/10.1016/j.eswa.2020.113385]

[35]    L.M. Bach, B. Mihaljevic, and M. Zagar, "Comparative analysis of blockchain consensus algorithms", *41st International Convention on Information and Communication Technology, Electronics and Microelectronics (MIPRO),* 2018 pp. 1545-1550 Opatija, Croatia.
[http://dx.doi.org/10.23919/MIPRO.2018.8400278]

[36]    S.F. Aghili, H. Mala, C. Schindelhauer, M. Shojafar, and R. Tafazolli, "Closed-loop and open-loop authentication protocols for blockchain-based IoT systems", *Inf. Process. Manage.,* vol. 58, no. 4, p. 102568, 2021.
[http://dx.doi.org/10.1016/j.ipm.2021.102568]

[37]    Y. Zuo, "Tokenizing renewable energy certificates (recs)—a blockchain approach for rec issuance and trading", *IEEE Access,* vol. 10, pp. 134477-134490, 2022.
[http://dx.doi.org/10.1109/ACCESS.2022.3230937]

[38]    T. McGhin, K.K.R. Choo, C.Z. Liu, and D. He, "Blockchain in healthcare applications: Research challenges and opportunities", *J. Netw. Comput. Appl.,* vol. 135, pp. 62-75, 2019.
[http://dx.doi.org/10.1016/j.jnca.2019.02.027]

[39]    O.X. B. Almeida, M. Cardenas, T. S. Cobo, E. Ferruzola, and R. C. Cabezas, "Blockchain in agriculture: a systematic literature review", In: *Proc. Technologies and Innovation* CITI 2018 Guayaquil, Ecuador, 2018.
[http://dx.doi.org/10.1007/978-3-030-00940-3_4]

[40]    A. Khatoon, P. Verma, J. Southernwood, B. Massey, and P. Corcoran, "Blockchain in energy efficiency: Potential applications and benefits", *Energies,* vol. 12, no. 17, p. 3317, 2019.
[http://dx.doi.org/10.3390/en12173317]

[41]    M.H. Ali, L. Chung, A. Kumar, S. Zailani, and K.H. Tan, "A sustainable Blockchain framework for the halal food supply chain: Lessons from Malaysia", *Technol. Forecast. Soc. Change,* vol. 170, p. 120870, 2021.
[http://dx.doi.org/10.1016/j.techfore.2021.120870]

[42]    Y. Yuan, and F-Y. Wang, "Towards blockchain-based intelligent transportation systems", *2016 IEEE 19th International Conference on Intelligent Transportation Systems (ITSC), Rio de Janeiro, Brazil,* pp. 2663-2668, 2016.
[http://dx.doi.org/10.1109/ITSC.2016.7795984]

[43]  A. Spielman, Blockchain: digitally rebuilding the real estate industry, 2018.

[44]  N. Jing, Q. Liu, and V. Sugumaran, "A blockchain-based code copyright management system", *Inf. Process. Manage.*, vol. 58, no. 3, p. 102518, 2021.
[http://dx.doi.org/10.1016/j.ipm.2021.102518]

[45]  P. Bhaskar, C.K. Tiwari, and A. Joshi, "Blockchain in education management: present and future applications", *Interact. Technol. Smart Educ.*, vol. 18, no. 1, pp. 1-17, 2021.
[http://dx.doi.org/10.1108/ITSE-07-2020-0102]

[46]  A. Alshehri, M. Baza, G. Srivastava, W. Rajeh, M. Alrowaily, and M. Almusali, "Privacy-preserving e-voting system supporting score voting using blockchain", *Appl. Sci. (Basel)*, vol. 13, no. 2, p. 1096, 2023.
[http://dx.doi.org/10.3390/app13021096]

[47]  Q. Liu, S. Yang, J. Liu, L. Zhao, P. Xiong, and J. Shen, "An efficient video watermark method using blockchain", *Knowl. Base. Syst.*, vol. 259, p. 110066, 2023.
[http://dx.doi.org/10.1016/j.knosys.2022.110066]

[48]  K. Ito, and M. O'Dair, "A critical examination of the application of blockchain technology to intellectual property management", In: *Business Transformation through Blockchain* Palgrave Macmillan: Cham, 2019.
[http://dx.doi.org/10.1007/978-3-319-99058-3_12]

[49]  Y. Liu, Q. Liu, X. Wang, Y. Xie, and Y. Wang, "Advanced naphthalimide-based supramolecular fluorescent self-assembly approach for Fe3+ detection and applications", *Dyes Pigments*, vol. 219, p. 111576, 2023.
[http://dx.doi.org/10.1016/j.dyepig.2023.111576]

[50]  Y. Zuo, "Tokenizing renewable energy certificates (recs)—a blockchain approach for rec issuance and trading", *IEEE Access*, vol. 10, pp. 134477-134490, 2022.
[http://dx.doi.org/10.1109/ACCESS.2022.3230937]

[51]  S. Abed, R. Jaffal, and B.J. Mohd, "A review on blockchain and iot integration from energy, security and hardware perspectives", *Wirel. Pers. Commun.*, vol. 129, no. 3, pp. 2079-2122, 2023.
[http://dx.doi.org/10.1007/s11277-023-10226-5]

[52]  Z. Zheng, S. Xie, H. Dai, X. Chen, and H. Wang, "An overview of blockchain technology: Architecture, consensus, and future trends", *2017 IEEE International Congress on Big Data (BigData Congress), Honolulu, HI, USA*, pp. 557-564, 2017.
[http://dx.doi.org/10.1109/BigDataCongress.2017.85]

[53]  R. Nair, and A. Bhagat, "An application of blockchain in stock market", In: *Transforming Businesses with Bitcoin Mining and Blockchain Applications* IGI Global, 2020, pp. 103-118.
[http://dx.doi.org/10.4018/978-1-7998-0186-3.ch006]

## CHAPTER 2

# Blockchain in Supply Chain Management, Traceability, Transparency, and Provenance

**Prerna Ajmani**[1,*], **Garima Saini**[2] and **Ayush Arya**[1]

[1] *School of Information Technology, Vivekananda Institute of Professional Studies- Technical Campus, Delhi, India*

[2] *Institute of Information Technology & Management (IITM), GGSIPU, Delhi, India*

**Abstract:** Blockchain technology is changing how supply chains work by making things faster, more open, and secure, while also making complicated tasks easier and solving old problems. Blockchain is distributed technology that is safe and secure and once the information is entered into this chain, it cannot be modified. Thus, Blockchain ensures trust and traceability, making it useful for many applications. Blockchain ensures higher security and protects data from any tampering. It also provides the facility of smart contracts for easy workflow. Additionally, Blockchain helps brands show that their products meet industry standards, which builds trust with customers. Overall, this technology is important for making sure goods and services are safe and reliable, while also simplifying how supply chains work. In this chapter, we will explore how Blockchain helps track products in the supply chain, explain smart contracts in detail, and look at some case studies to better understand these ideas.

**Keywords:** Blockchain technology, Cyber threat protection, Decentralized ledger, Efficiency, Process automation, Product provenance, Security, Smart contracts, Supply chain management, Traceability, Transparency.

## INTRODUCTION

Back in 2008, a person who loved technology came up with something new called Blockchain. We do not know who this person is because they stayed anonymous. They made Blockchain to fix some problems with Bitcoin. One big problem was how to send money directly between people without using banks or other middlemen, and another issue was stopping people from spending the same money twice. Today, technology is growing super-fast and helping solve many real-world problems, and Blockchain is one of the ideas that made a big difference.

---

[*] **Corresponding author Prerna Ajmani:** School of Information Technology, Vivekananda Institute of Professional Studies- Technical Campus, Delhi, India; E-mail: prerna.ajmani@vips.edu

**Monica Bhutani, Monica Gupta, Kirti Gupta, Deepali Kamthania & Danish Ather (Eds.)**
**All rights reserved-© 2025 Bentham Science Publishers**

Over time, Blockchain technology gained significant attention from industries, academics, and researchers alike. By 2018, it was recognized as one of the top five emerging technologies. Blockchain has evolved through three major phases. The first generation, Blockchain 1.0, emerged in 2009 with a primary focus on supporting digital currency, particularly Bitcoin. As the technology's potential became clearer, the second generation, Blockchain 2.0, appeared in 2014, emphasizing the use of Smart Contracts in various applications, notably through Ethereum. By 2017, Blockchain 3.0 was ushered in, driven by the Hyperledger initiative, leading to the development of decentralized applications across a wide range of industries.

Today, Blockchain's applications extend beyond finance and cryptocurrency, impacting fields such as education, healthcare, agriculture, the Internet of Things (IoT), and even governance. Additional uses include electronic voting, autonomous vehicles, trading systems, supply chains, smart grids, and networking, among others.

## TRACEABILITY AND TRANSPARENCY IN SUPPLY CHAIN MANAGEMENT

Traceability and "transparency" are two terms that people often mix up in supply chain management, but they mean different things, even though they are connected. Transparency is about how much you can see what's happening in the supply chain. It means that everyone involved can easily get the info they need about a product, without anything missing or getting messed up. According to a study [1], transparency means all the people in the supply chain can quickly and easily find the info they need. Traceability, on the other hand, is more about being able to find specific details about any part of the supply chain [2, 3].

Researchers also interchange the term traceability with tracking [4 - 6]. Tracking is following the product from where it starts to where it ends up while tracing is about going backward and finding where the product originally came from.

A study breaks transparency down into three parts: history-based transparency, operations transparency, and strategy transparency [7]. History-based transparency, which is achieved through tracking and tracing, refers to a complete and verifiable record of a product's journey. In essence, traceability enables transparency by providing the necessary tools for tracking and tracing.

Several studies have integrated traceability into different supply chain scenarios to enhance transparency. For instance, a study [8] developed a system for creating transparency in the meat supply chain. This system allows consumers to trace the history of meat in the market, suppliers to track its movement, and government agencies to monitor its quality. Another example is the introduction of GPS [9]. LAB, a Global Positioning System (GPS)-enabled traceability system designed to ensure transparency in global supply chains by managing production planning and supply chain events.

However, these centralized traceability systems have limitations, particularly when it comes to data manipulation. Centralized systems often struggle with transparency and trust issues [10]. A study describes centralized traceability systems as monopolistic, asymmetrical, and opaque, which can lead to problems like corruption, falsification of data, and system failures [11].

On the other hand, Blockchain technology offers decentralized, immutable, transparent, secure, and auditable ledger [12]. Blockchain's traceability, security and decentralized features make its usage worthier in supply chain management [13]. Any transaction that occurs in the supply chain can be recorded in blocks, that can be arranged in chronological order in the Blockchain. To ensure complete transparency, these records are further verified by all authorized participants of Blockchain. A study suggests that Blockchain serves as a trustworthy, transparent, and verifiable resource for all the stakeholders in a particular supply chain [14].

As compared to a centralized system, in Blockchain, each block is linked cryptographically with others thus abolishing data tampering. Blockchain can be further classified as: public, private, and consortium types [15]. Researchers in a study [16] highlighted that Blockchain can mitigate various supply chain risks such as information delays, lack of transparency, security issues, and IT platform incompatibility. Further, the amalgamation of IoT and smart contracts has increased the acceptance and effectiveness of Blockchain-based traceability supply chain systems [17, 18].

## An Insight into Blockchain Powered Traceability Solutions in Supply Chain Management

Blockchain technology has already been integrated into numerous supply chains to establish traceability, with the goal of enhancing transparency. This section explores various real-world applications of Blockchain-based traceability solutions as reported in academic literature. Each case is examined to understand the purpose of implementing Blockchain for traceability, including its strengths, limitations, and the methodologies used to develop these solutions. Additionally, the supply chain models employed in these solutions are analyzed, specifically in relation to distribution network designs. As noted in a study, there are six key distribution network designs, and the level of order visibility plays a crucial role in determining the most suitable design [19]. Visibility, in this context, refers to the ability to access and share information across the supply chain. A high level of visibility is directly linked to a more transparent supply chain.

Table **1** gives the overview of distribution network design and its impact on order visibility within the six distributions.

Table 1. Overview of distribution network designs and their impact on order visibility.

| Distribution Network Design Type | Order Visibility |
|---|---|
| Direct Shipping from Manufacturer Storage (Drop Shipping) | Essential for customer service, though more difficult to achieve. |
| Direct Shipping from Manufacturer Storage with In-Transit Merging | Faces similar challenges to drop shipping in terms of visibility. |
| Distributor Storage with Carrier-Based Delivery | Easier to manage compared to manufacturer storage. |
| Distributor Storage with Final-Mile Delivery | Less of a concern and simpler to implement than manufacturer storage or distributor storage with carrier delivery. |
| Manufacturer/Distributor Storage with Customer Collection | Difficult to manage but crucial for success. |
| Retail Storage with Customer Collection | Straightforward for in-store orders, but complex and necessary for online and phone orders. |

This section further explores how Blockchain-based traceability solutions can enhance supply chain visibility across different network configurations. Further, an extensive literature review in this context has been provided and arranged thematically below.

### Food/Agricultural Supply Chain

Blockchain traceability solutions have gained significant recognition in the food and agricultural sectors, providing transparency and accountability throughout supply chains.

A study introduced a groundbreaking framework aimed at enhancing the traceability of soybean products, built on the Ethereum Blockchain [20]. This system allows for seamless tracking from seed producers to customers, involving entities like farmers, grain processors, and retailers. By leveraging the Interplanetary File System (IPFS) and standardized identifiers such as Global Trade Identification Numbers (GTIN), the framework improves product tracking and resolves quality issues by pinpointing the origin of any problems. Participants in this supply chain use smart contracts on the Blockchain to update and manage information as it flows through the system.

In a related context, a study proposed a food traceability system using BigchainDB, Blockchain, IoT, and the Hazard Analysis and Critical Control Points (HACCP) methodology to ensure food safety [21]. Similarly, some researchers combined Blockchain with IoT and HACCP to address gaps in centralized traceability systems for halal food [22]. By adhering to Islamic dietary laws and integrating Blockchain, the system helps prevent non-halal products from entering the market. A study further explored the topic with an experimental study on halal meat supply chains, utilizing Hyperledger Fabric [23].

A study developed AgriBlockIoT, a Blockchain-based system for managing agricultural supply chains [24]. A test case, 'farm to fork,' was deployed using Ethereum and Hyperledger, demonstrating how the platform facilitates communication between participants like producers, distributors, and consumers.

Walmart has also ventured into Blockchain-based traceability by partnering with IBM. In a pilot study, a Blockchain solution built on Hyperledger Fabric significantly reduced the time needed to trace mango origins, taking only 2.2 seconds compared to the previous seven-day process [25]. Similarly, a study developed a traceability solution integrating Blockchain with Low Power Wide Area Networks (LPWAN) [26]. Their approach uses traditional Enterprise Resource Planning (ERP) and IoT systems to relay data directly to Blockchain networks, enhancing transparency in smart agriculture.

In the palm oil industry, which faces environmental and social concerns, a study proposed a Blockchain-based traceability system using the Roundtable on Sustainable Palm Oil (RSPO) guidelines [27, 28]. The system tracks the journey of palm oil products from plantations to consumers, ensuring adherence to sustainability standards.

A study introduced a Blockchain solution for transparency in Chinese agro-food supply chains, focusing on fresh produce and meats [30]. This system employs Radio-Frequency Identification (RFID) devices to track products through each stage of the supply chain, offering real-time monitoring and ensuring the involvement of food safety authorities for quality control.

Addressing issues of counterfeiting in the wine industry, a study developed a framework using the multichain Blockchain platform to verify wine authenticity [31]. Each batch and bottle is assigned a unique identifier, allowing stakeholders to trace its history from grape growers to retailers.

Efforts to trace seafood, such as tuna, have also been explored by organizations like Provenance and the International Pole and Line Association (IPLA). A study described how RFID tags are attached to tuna once caught, enabling continuous tracking through the supply chain [32]. When processed, the fish are tagged with QR codes to facilitate further tracking, offering a cost-effective and efficient traceability solution.

Overall, Blockchain traceability systems play a crucial role in preventing food safety hazards by providing real-time tracking and enabling rapid response to potential issues. Customers benefit from enhanced product transparency, while regulatory bodies can monitor supply chain activities more effectively. These systems, supported by smart contracts, contribute to the sustainability, resilience, and efficiency of food and agricultural supply chains.

### *Pharmaceutical Supply Chain*

Authors in a study introduced an Ethereum-based traceability solution aimed at tracking and monitoring events within a pharmaceutical supply chain [49]. This system includes a sender, a receiver, and an IoT-enabled container that gathers data on variables such as temperature, pressure, vibrations, location, and humidity. The collected data is processed using Raspberry Pi 3 hardware, and if a contract condition is breached, the processing unit triggers a function within the smart contract, which then broadcasts the relevant information across the entire Blockchain network. This feature allows for real-time tracking of pharmaceutical products during transit. The system's feasibility was demonstrated through a case study involving a vaccine supply chain.

Similarly, Modum.io, a Swiss start-up, applied Blockchain and smart contracts to monitor temperature in the pharmaceutical supply chain during transport, using sensors and Smart Contracts [50]. The temperature is recorded on the Ethereum Blockchain, and each container is assigned a unique track-and-trace number. The sender can start the temperature tracking using an Android smartphone, while the receiver can access the product's journey history by scanning a QR code. As Blockchain ledgers are tamper-proof, the receiver can verify whether the product was stored in optimal conditions. This solution was tested with a prototype application designed for a distribution network that includes a supplier, wholesaler, and warehouse.

In another approach, a Blockchain-based traceability system is suggested for the pharmaceutical supply chain to combat fraud during distribution [51]. Their system integrates Blockchain technology with an IoT framework known as Global Data Plane (GDP). Each product is assigned a unique hash that tracks its status and prevents replication. When one entity transfers a batch of drugs to another, the transaction details are sent to a controller, which stores the information on a private Blockchain.

Some researchers explored the use of Blockchain in the pharmaceutical industry to prevent counterfeit drugs [52]. Their work focused on developing a mobile application to track the journey of drug products from the manufacturing site to the pharmacy. Every time the ownership of a drug changes, a new transaction is recorded on the Blockchain, preserving the history of the product. This system can track drugs from production to final delivery, and even record the drug's effects on patients for future analysis.

Although these Blockchain traceability solutions for the pharmaceutical supply chain vary slightly in terms of technology and methods, they all share a common goal: tracking the physical movement of medications while ensuring their quality and authenticity. Additionally, these systems offer other potential benefits, such as automatic notifications for the expiration dates of specific brands and batches of medicines. In the context of a pandemic, Blockchain technology could play a crucial role in pharmaceutical supply chains. A consortium Blockchain network involving hospitals, manufacturers, and government agencies could help manage the supply and demand of essential medicines during emergencies.

### Courier Express Parcel (CEP) Supply Chain

Blockchain technology presents significant potential for Courier Express Parcel (CEP) supply chains. Researchers have also explored the possibilities of Blockchain in operations and supply chain management, introducing an innovative system for parcel tracking called the Blockchain-based Logistics Monitoring System (BLMS) [53]. This system allows customers, logistics providers, and other stakeholders to track and trace parcel shipments throughout the supply chain ecosystem. The Ethereum Blockchain was used for implementing and testing the system. While this framework is promising, there is also potential for CEP companies to expand their use by integrating Blockchain for handling customer returns. However, Blockchain solutions for reverse supply chains have yet to be thoroughly addressed in existing research.

### Luxury Supply Chain

Blockchain-based traceability solutions offer significant advantages in luxury goods supply chains. A study highlighted how Blockchain technology, through platforms like Everledger, benefits the trade of jewelry items [54]. These Blockchain Technology Supported (BTS) platforms enhance the certification and authentication of luxury products like diamonds, benefiting both manufacturers and consumers. In traditional retail settings, sales staff often spend considerable time providing customers with product details, and the proof of authenticity is typically paper-based, making it susceptible to tampering. By using BTS platforms for the sale of high-value jewelry, these issues are resolved. Information stored on the Blockchain remains permanently unchangeable, ensuring transparency. Customers purchasing luxury items are especially concerned with the authenticity and quality of their products, making Blockchain an ideal solution for these needs.

### Consumer Electronics Supply Chain

The Consumer Electronics (CE) industry consists of companies involved in designing and manufacturing products like televisions, laptops, and smartphones. In tackling the issue of counterfeit goods, a study highlighted the potential of Blockchain technology within this sector [55]. In the CE industry, the transfer of ownership is a critical process that requires careful monitoring to prevent counterfeit or duplicate products from entering the market. Blockchain can play a crucial role in ensuring the authenticity and traceability of these items throughout the supply chain.

### Manufacturing Supply Chain

A study introduced a Blockchain-based system for the first time to trace manufactured products and their components or ingredients [56]. The system enables the tracking of various input materials used in production and monitors their transformation throughout the manufacturing process. Key participants in the system include suppliers, manufacturers, logistics providers, certifiers, and consumers. To maintain the link between a product and its individual components, the system incorporates the concept of a token receipt. The prototype of this solution was implemented on the Ethereum Blockchain using smart contracts.

### Automobile Supply Chain

A study introduced PartChain, a decentralized application designed for the automotive industry to enhance the traceability of automobile parts, which are produced in different regions globally and distributed through international supply chains [57]. The key players in this system include Original Equipment Manufacturers (OEMs), suppliers, and logistics providers. While the implementation requires significant effort, the application allows for tracking defective parts and mitigating issues without the need to recall entire batches of vehicles. It also helps prevent counterfeit parts from entering the supply chain. Smart contracts were used to integrate business logic within the supply chain.

### Textile Supply Chain

Researchers proposed a Blockchain-based solution to enhance traceability within the textile industry [58]. The system focuses on a case involving various stakeholders, including cotton producers, manufacturers, wholesalers, distributors, customers, registrars, and auditors. This Blockchain traceability solution significantly boosts transparency, allowing customers, retailers, and auditors to track the complete history of a product. By providing this level of visibility, the system can greatly enhance customer trust and confidence in purchasing textile products.

## Wood Supply Chain

In a recent study, a system is presented that integrates RFID technology with Blockchain to track the movement of valuable timber throughout its supply chain, ensuring both its quality and authenticity [59]. The simulation followed the timber's journey from its origin to the final customer as a product. Additionally, a prototype of the proposed Blockchain architecture was developed within the simulated environment. The implementation was carried out using Microsoft Azure Blockchain Workbench.

## Dangerous Goods Supply Chain

Handling the supply chains for hazardous materials, such as explosives, requires heightened security and careful management. A study proposed an innovative Blockchain-based system designed to track and trace dangerous goods during transit [60 - 62]. This system provides relevant information to all stakeholders involved in the supply chain, including regulatory authorities. The manufacturer of hazardous goods establishes a smart contract detailing essential information about the goods being transported. This data is accessible to all network participants, allowing authorities to swiftly respond to emergencies and trace issues by examining the event history. The transparency offered by Blockchain enhances the management of risky situations in hazardous goods supply chains. Similarly, such a system could be applied to weapon supply chains, enabling military organizations to monitor the location and availability of weapons effectively.

This section has explored the diverse applications of Blockchain-based traceability solutions across various supply chains. The upcoming section will further illustrate how these solutions contribute to supply chain transparency.

## SMART CONTRACTS

The introduction of Blockchain technology has sparked significant changes across various industries, particularly with the development of smart contracts. A smart contract is essentially a piece of code that is programmed to carry out an agreement between two or more parties [29]. Once certain pre-known conditions are met, it automates the execution of actions. One of their unique qualities is that they can work on their own, without any human intervention. Traditionally, the contracts required a third-party middleman (like a lawyer or an escrow service), who would look upon or enforce the agreement. But with smart contracts, the entire process is now super simple, as we can now self-execute as soon as the required conditions are met.

One of the biggest advantages of these smart contracts is the assurance or surety they provide to us. Since this contract will be written in the coded format, it'll be executed as it is commanded or programmed, this means there's no chance of its delay or manipulation. This reliability is crucial for everyone who's involved in this, as they can completely rely on the contract itself for interpreting the terms, and there's no need for any third party to mediate in this.

Smart contracts are stored on something called a Blockchain. A Blockchain is like a big online record book that's spread out across lots of different computers (called nodes). This means that the same contract is saved in many places at the same time, so everyone involved in the contract can see it. This makes things more open and honest because everyone can check the details of the contract. And since no one person or company controls the whole Blockchain, it is really hard for anyone to mess with the contract or change how it works. Once the contract is saved on the Blockchain, it is pretty much locked in, so no one can change it without permission, which keeps it safe and builds trust.

Another important thing about these smart contracts is that once they're on the Blockchain, they can not be changed at all. This makes sure that the contract is real and stays the same, so no one can come in later and mess with the rules or details. This helps everyone trust the process, knowing that the contract will happen exactly as it was written from the start [33 - 35].

**Phases for Setting Up Smart Contracts**

Creating a smart contract on a Blockchain is a step-by-step process, and each step is important to make sure everything works properly.

1. **Understanding the Agreement:** The first thing is to figure out what the contract is all about. All the people involved need to know exactly what they agree to, like what each person has to do and what they'll get in return. This is to make sure there is no confusion later. Legal and money-related stuff is also discussed here, so everyone knows what's happening.
2. **Deciding the Rules:** Next, the people involved decide on the rules or conditions of the contract. These are the things that will make the contract kick

in, like a trigger. For example, if there's a rule that says you get a discount if your birthday is near the date of the contract, this can be added as a condition. When the system sees that the condition is true (like it's close to your birthday), it will automatically apply the discount.

3. **Writing the Code:** After setting the rules, the contract is turned into a code. This is like writing a program that tells the contract exactly how to behave. The code is tested to make sure it works correctly and doesn't have any mistakes. It is super important to get this right because if the code is wrong, the contract might not work like it is supposed to.

4. **Choosing a Blockchain:** Once the code is ready, you need to pick which Blockchain to put it on. Some popular choices are Ethereum or Bitcoin, each with its pros and cons. For example, Ethereum can handle more complicated smart contracts. Encryption is also added here to protect the contract, so nobody can mess with it or see private details.

5. **Running the Contract:** After the contract is put on the Blockchain, it starts working. The smart contract will check if the conditions you set earlier are met. If they are, it will automatically carry out the contract, like applying the discount or transferring money, without anyone needing to do anything manually.

6. **Updating the System:** Once the contract is done, the Blockchain gets updated. This means every computer (or node) on the Blockchain network now has the latest information about the contract, like a record of what happened. And that's the end of the contract's life.

By following these steps, smart contracts can work automatically, securely, and without anyone having to do extra work once it's set up!

**Benefits of Smart Contracts**

As stated in a study, smart contracts have a lot of benefits that make them useful for many different industries [29].

1. **Building trust and being open:** Smart contracts help create trust because they are stored on a Blockchain, which everyone can see and verify. In regular contracts, you often need people like lawyers or notaries to make sure everything is fair, but smart contracts don't need these middlemen. Once a smart contract is made, no one can change it unless everyone on the network agrees. This means everyone involved knows the contract is fair and won't be changed secretly.

2. **Faster and more efficient:** Regular contracts take time because you need to do paperwork, talk to lawyers, or wait for approvals. This can slow things down, especially with international deals. But smart contracts are automatic. Once the

terms of the contract are met, it does everything by itself, right away. This means things happen faster because there's no waiting around for people to do things manually.

3. **Very safe and hard to hack:** Smart contracts are super secure because they run on Blockchain technology, which is spread across many computers (decentralized). In regular systems, data is stored in one place, making it easier to hack or change. But with smart contracts, changing anything would be almost impossible because you'd have to change it across all the computers in the network. This makes them a great choice for industries that need strong security, like finance or healthcare [36].

4. **Saving money:** Smart contracts save money by cutting out the middlemen. In regular contracts, you need lawyers, escrow agents, or other people to manage the deal, which costs a lot of money. Smart contracts do this work automatically, saving you the cost of hiring these people. This is especially helpful for small businesses that don't have the money to pay for complex legal processes.

5. **Works on its own and doesn't need a boss:** Smart contracts work on their own once they're set up, without needing anyone to manage them. Regular contracts often rely on one person or group to enforce the terms, but smart contracts don't need a central authority. They're decentralized, meaning they run on a network of computers, so they're not affected if one part of the system goes down. This makes them more reliable than centralized systems.

6. **No mistakes, more accurate:** Human mistakes can cause big problems in regular contracts, especially if there are lots of steps or parties involved. Smart contracts are fully automated and eliminate human error because everything is coded. Once the conditions are set, the contract works with 100% accuracy. This reduces the chance of misunderstandings or mistakes, making things smoother and more reliable.

7. **Easy to use everywhere in the world:** Smart contracts can be used worldwide without the need for complicated legal processes in different countries. Since Blockchain technology is global, you don't need special approval in every country to use a smart contract. This makes international trade or business easier. Plus, as more industries start using smart contracts, they might create standard templates, making it simpler for businesses to work together without long negotiations.

In short, smart contracts are faster, cheaper, more secure, and more accurate than regular contracts. They are a great tool for businesses that want to streamline their processes and reduce the need for human oversight.

## Demerits of Smart Contracts

Smart contracts can be useful, but they also have problems, especially when we try to use them in real life [37].

* **Immutability:** The **immutability** of smart contracts, while beneficial for security, can also be a drawback. Once a smart contract is deployed, it cannot be modified to accommodate unforeseen circumstances. In traditional contracts, parties can renegotiate and amend terms, but with smart contracts, such flexibility is not available [37 - 39].
* **Privacy Concerns:** Although Blockchain promotes transparency, this feature can become a liability in scenarios requiring **privacy**. All transactions are stored on a public ledger, making it difficult to keep sensitive contractual details confidential. Finding the right balance between transparency and privacy remains a challenge [39, 40].
* **Legal Uncertainty:** The legal standing of smart contracts is still unclear in many jurisdictions. Traditional contracts are governed by well-established legal frameworks, but **smart contracts** are relatively new, and their **enforceability** in court is not guaranteed in all cases. This can create complications in the event of disputes [41, 42].

## Platforms for Smart Contracts

There are different Blockchain platforms that let you create smart contracts, and each one works a bit differently:

* **NXT:** NXT is an older platform that lets people make simple smart contracts using templates. You don't need to write a lot of code, which is great if you just want to set up something basic fast. But because it is so simple, you can't create advanced contracts on it. It is good for small things like basic money agreements or property transfers, but not for bigger projects like decentralized finance (DeFi) or games. It's also secure and energy-efficient because it uses a proof-of-stake (PoS) system.
* **Bitcoin:** Bitcoin is the most popular cryptocurrency, but it was not originally made for smart contracts. Over time, people found ways to create simple contracts with Bitcoin's basic programming. Its language is super simple, which helps keep it secure but makes it hard to build anything too complex. You can create things like multi-signature contracts (where more than one person has to approve something), but you can't build complicated apps or services like on other platforms. It's great for basic stuff, but not for more advanced applications [42].

- **Ethereum:** Ethereum is the go-to platform for building smart contracts and decentralized apps (dApps). It is much more flexible than Bitcoin and lets you create complex contracts using a programming language called Solidity. Ethereum can handle pretty much anything if you pay enough in "gas" (which are fees for transactions). This has made it popular for things like DeFi, NFTs (non-fungible tokens), and all sorts of apps. But it has also got problems like high fees and slow speeds when too many people use it, though the new Ethereum 2.0 upgrade is supposed to help with that [34].
- **Hyperledger Fabric:** This one is a bit different. It is made for businesses that need privacy and control, so only approved people can access it. It is good for industries like finance and healthcare, where security and privacy are super important. You can also write smart contracts using popular languages like Java or JavaScript, which is nice for developers. It is also very fast and scalable for companies that need to process a lot of transactions quickly.
- **EOSIO:** EOSIO is built to handle big, decentralized apps (dApps) and is designed for speed and scalability. It uses a system that does not charge fees for transactions, which makes it appealing for apps where lots of small transactions happen, like games or social media. Developers can write smart contracts using languages like C++ or Python, which makes it easier for those who don't know Blockchain-specific coding.
- **Tron:** Tron started focusing on entertainment, but now it is a broader platform for all kinds of decentralized apps. It is super-fast, handling way more transactions per second than Ethereum, and it is cheaper too. Like EOSIO, it uses a system that makes transactions faster and more scalable. You can write smart contracts using solidity, which is great for people who already know Ethereum.
- **Cardano:** Cardano is known for being very careful and research-driven. It is designed to be secure, scalable, and energy efficient. You can write smart contracts using Plutus, which is secure but more complex. Cardano is unique because it uses "formal verification," meaning it can mathematically prove the contracts are safe, which makes it harder for hackers to break in.
- **Tezos:** Tezos is built to change and upgrade itself without needing big updates that disrupt the network. It is great for people who want their platform to grow and adapt over time. Like Cardano, it uses formal verification to make sure contracts are secure. Developers can also vote on changes, which makes it a community-driven platform.
- **NEO:** NEO is sometimes called the "Ethereum of China" and focuses on combining digital assets, identity, and smart contracts. It supports multiple programming languages, which makes it easier for developers to get started without learning new languages. It is good for building large apps and has a system that supports identity verification, making it useful for industries like

finance.

## Blockchain in Asset Tracking & Identity Management

Blockchain can be used for more than just smart contracts. It is also really helpful for things like tracking assets and managing identity.

- **Asset Tracking:**
    - Asset tracking is basically keeping an eye on where goods (physical or digital) are and what's happening to them over time. Normally, this is done with paper records or big databases, but these methods can be mistaken, be changed by people, or be slow. Blockchain fixes this by using a system where every step of an asset's journey is recorded, and nobody can change it without everyone noticing.
    - With Blockchain, you can track an asset from when it's made to when it's delivered. For example, in a supply chain (like how products get from the factory to the store), you can see details like when a product was made, when it was shipped, how it was stored, and when it got to the customer. Each step is time-stamped and secured with cryptography (a fancy word for strong coding), so it is nearly impossible to change the data without being caught. This means businesses and customers can trust the info they get.
    - The biggest benefit of Blockchain for asset tracking is it reduces fraud (cheating). Since the Blockchain is open for all the allowed people to see, if anyone tries to change or mess with the data, it is easy to spot. This helps stop things like fake products, lying about what goods really are, or illegal activities.
    - Another advantage is that it holds people accountable. Every person or company involved in the supply chain must update the Blockchain with accurate info, and if there's a mistake, you can see who made it. This makes everyone more careful and honest, helping build trust.
    - Blockchain is also used for tracking digital things like copyrights, intellectual property, or even digital coins. By using Blockchain, owners of these digital items can make sure no one steals or uses their stuff without permission. Plus, Blockchain does not need middlemen (like lawyers or banks), which saves money and speeds up processes.

- **Managing personal info:**
    - Managing identities (like your ID, driver's license, *etc.*) is becoming more important because we live in a digital world. Normally, our personal information is stored in central places like government databases or social media accounts. But these can be hacked, stolen, or changed. Blockchain offers a safer way to manage identity by spreading out the control of your

data so no one person or company controls it.

○ Blockchain-based identity systems use encryption (super strong coding) to store your data safely. Instead of one company or government having your info, many computers across a network share it, so there is no single point that can be attacked. This makes it much harder for hackers to break in and steal your identity.

○ Also, Blockchain gives you more control over your information. Normally, when you share your info (like with a bank or website), you trust them to keep it safe. But sometimes they lose it, sell it, or use it without asking. With Blockchain, you own your info. You only share the parts you want, like proving your age without showing your whole ID.

○ Blockchain identity systems also make things faster and safer. Once your identity is on the Blockchain, it is easy for trusted people to check it (like banks, governments, or websites), and you do not need to prove who you are repeatedly. This saves time and money.

○ For big organizations like governments or banks, Blockchain helps solve problems like identity theft (when someone pretends to be you). It creates digital IDs that are hard to fake, and it can be used for things like voting, signing up for services, or getting financial help. Blockchain makes identity verification quicker and more reliable, which helps everyone involved.

In short, Blockchain is making both asset tracking and identity management more secure, transparent, and efficient [43 - 47].

## CASE STUDIES GIVEN BY REFERENCE

In recent times, Blockchain technology has become really popular because many companies in different industries want to make things more transparent, especially in supply chains. It's not just small test projects anymore—many businesses are using Blockchain in real life to see how well it can track and show what happens in the supply chain. The goal is to make sure every step is visible and easy to follow [28].

A great example is T-Mining, a start-up in Antwerp. They partnered with the Port of Antwerp under the 'Smart Port' project to build a Blockchain system that makes releasing containers smoother and safer. This system ensures that each step in moving goods is clear and secure. Similarly, Maersk and IBM worked together to create the 'TradeLens' platform, which is a Blockchain tool for sharing shipping information easily. This helps reduce delays and makes everything run more efficiently.

Accenture, a large services company, has also joined in by working with companies like APL, Kuehne + Nagel, and AB InBev to test Blockchain systems for the shipping industry. Their goal is to solve problems and make supply chains more efficient and transparent. UPS, a well-known delivery company, has also added Blockchain to track packages. With this system, every package can be traced from where it starts to its final destination, ensuring proper handling along the way.

In the retail industry, Carrefour, a large French retailer, uses Blockchain to trace food products. This system allows customers to scan a QR code to get detailed information about where the product came from. This transparency helps customers feel more confident and aware of what they're buying. The pharmaceutical industry is also testing Blockchain tools like 'Medi Ledger' and 'SAP Advanced Track and Trace' to ensure that medicines are real and safe, preventing fake drugs from entering the market.

The luxury goods industry, especially jewelry, is also exploring Blockchain. Projects like Tracr, Provenance Proof, and Trust Chain give customers a clear idea of where their jewelry comes from and whether it is genuine. Everledger, a London-based company, is using Blockchain to track fine wines. They're working with a wine expert to make sure that wine can't be stolen or sold as fake.

In the oil industry, the Abu Dhabi National Oil Company (ADNOC) has partnered with IBM to create a Blockchain system that tracks oil from the moment it is extracted to when it reaches the customer. This increases transparency and trust in the process. The fashion industry is also exploring Blockchain solutions. For example, Provenance and fashion designer Martine Jarlgaard developed a system to track how clothes are made, helping customers know if their clothes were produced ethically.

Studies have also shown that Blockchain is becoming more common in supply chains. Researchers like [68] have written about different real-world tests by well-known companies exploring Blockchain's role in future supply chains.

All these projects show how important transparency has become across industries. Blockchain-based solutions can work in many types of supply chains, no matter how complex they are, and they help make processes more visible and trustworthy.

## Case Study 1: A Penalty-Based Blockchain Traceability Solution

Substandard and fake medicines are a big danger to people's health. Substandard medicines are those that do not meet the right quality because of mistakes in how they're made, stored, or transported. Counterfeit medicines are fake ones that are meant to trick people into thinking they're real. Both of these types of medicines, serious health problems are caused, so it is really important to keep a close watch on how medicines are handled, from the factory to the consumer. The World Health Organization (WHO) says substandard medicines (also called "out of specification") are real medicines that don't meet the required quality standards. This can happen at any point during their production, storage, or transport. To stop this, making sure the whole process is clear and open is key.

Medicines, especially those that need to stay cold, are at higher risk. A "cold chain" is a system where medicines need to be kept at a specific temperature while being stored and transported. The problem with old-fashioned cold chains is that they don't always keep track of important things like temperature and humidity during transport or storage. For instance, once the medicine leaves the factory, refrigerated trucks need to keep the medicine at the right temperature the whole time. Also, warehouses where medicines are stored need to meet the same temperature and humidity standards. But with traditional systems, we often don't know if these rules are being followed, which means people might buy medicines that aren't safe [48].

A solution to this is using Blockchain and Internet of Things (IoT) technology. With these two working together, it is possible to keep an eye on the medicines in real time during their entire journey. Blockchain makes sure that no one can change the records, and IoT devices can track things like temperature and humidity. This way, if something goes wrong, like if the temperature gets too high, we can see exactly when and where it happened and who is responsible. There can also be a system where people get fined if they do not follow the rules. This combo of Blockchain and IoT helps make sure the medicines are safe and meet quality standards.

## Case Study 2: Cold Chain Management and Blockchain-Enabled Accountability

In this case study, we are looking at a cold chain process involving five main players: the manufacturer (who makes the medicine), the buyer, two transport companies, and a warehouse. The manufacturer makes a specific type of medicine that needs to be sent to the buyer's facility. The first transport company (Carrier 1) takes the medicine from the factory to a warehouse. The second transport company (Carrier 2) moves the medicine from the warehouse to the buyer's place. The warehouse is just a temporary stop, and both the transport companies and the warehouse are run by third-party companies (separate from the manufacturer and buyer).

At the factory, the manufacturer makes sure the medicine is stored under the right temperature and humidity. But once the medicine leaves the factory, it is important to keep an eye on the conditions during the whole journey. Everyone involved in this process (both transport companies, the warehouse, and the buyer) needs to make sure the medicine stays within the right conditions until it reaches the buyer. After that, the buyer and their other distributors are in charge, following the rules about storing and handling the medicine correctly.

In this situation, a Blockchain system is used to monitor the temperature and humidity during the whole journey. If anything goes wrong, like if the temperature goes too high or too low, it is recorded on the Blockchain, and everyone involved can see it. This helps keep everyone accountable.

For example, the medicine needs to stay between 4°C and 10°C, with a little wiggle room of ±2°C. So, the temperature is fine as long as it stays between 2°C and 12°C. If it goes out of this range during transportation, the transport company responsible gets a penalty. So, if Carrier 1 is moving the medicine and the temperature goes outside this range, Carrier 1 gets blamed. The Blockchain will record this, and penalties are given based on how many times the rules are broken. If there are too many penalties, the buyer can cancel the contract, and the responsible party has to pay for the losses.

This system makes sure everyone does their job right because the payment is linked to how well the medicine is handled. If the medicine gets to the buyer in good condition, the payment goes through. But if the medicine does not meet the standards, the buyer can reject it. This penalty system, using Blockchain, makes everything more transparent and lowers the chances of bad-quality medicine reaching consumers.

## Case Study 3: Proof of Concept

Proof of Concept (PoC) is a way to test if a new idea can actually work, especially when it comes to new technologies like Blockchain. It is like trying out an idea in a small, safe environment before doing it for real. This is really helpful when you are thinking about using Blockchain to manage the supply chain (how things move from one place to another).

In this case, a PoC was done to see if Blockchain could be used to help manage the cold chain, which is the process of keeping things like food or medicine at the right temperature while they are being transported. The goal was to check if Blockchain could help make the cold chain more transparent (everyone can see what's happening), accountable (everyone knows who's responsible), and trackable (you can see where things are at any time).

To test this, a simple app was created that acts like a cold chain management system using Blockchain. People manually entered data like temperature and humidity, which would normally be automatically tracked by special IoT devices (gadgets that collect data in real- time). The app assumes that all the boxes in the shipment are at the same temperature and humidity, and an IoT device keeps an eye on the conditions as the shipment moves.

The app was built using Microsoft Azure Blockchain Workbench, which is a cloud-based tool that makes it easier to create Blockchain apps. It helps developers quickly build apps by providing the necessary tools, like a Blockchain network, a place to store data, and an interface for users. The app used something called the Ethereum-based Proof of Authority (PoA) consensus, which is a way to manage the Blockchain network where all participants (people or companies) are known to each other.

A smart contract was written in solidity (a programming language) to manage the whole cold chain process. The contract starts when the manufacturer sends the shipment, and it tracks every stage, like when the shipment changes hands between carriers or goes into storage. IoT devices monitor the shipment in real time and add data to the Blockchain as it moves along. The smart contract also sets the rules for everyone involved, like what temperature and humidity should be, what happens if those rules are broken (penalties), and how payments should be made. Once the shipment gets to the buyer, they can check the data and decide whether to accept or reject the product.

In the end, this PoC showed that Blockchain can be really useful for managing the cold chain. It makes it possible to track shipments in real-time and keep accurate, transparent records, which can make the whole supply chain process more trustworthy and reliable.

## CONCLUDING REMARKS

This chapter talks about how Blockchain can help track things better. Using Blockchain to follow and trace things can make supply chains much clearer and easier to understand. A review of the available studies indicates that Blockchain-driven traceability systems are becoming widely adopted across various supply chains. Many of these implementations, according to the literature covered in this chapter, are concentrated in the food and pharmaceutical industries. The integration of IoT and smart contracts has notably expanded the scope of Blockchain applications. However, Blockchain technology is not intended to replace existing systems entirely.

To illustrate Blockchain's effectiveness in enhancing supply chain transparency, a framework for cold chain management was developed [28], with a proof of concept carried out using the Microsoft Azure Blockchain Workbench platform. While numerous Blockchain applications are mentioned in the literature, most remain theoretical. Real-world implementations of Blockchain-based traceability systems are still relatively uncommon. There is a growing need for research that provides empirical evidence of the benefits these solutions offer. Small-scale experiments could help demonstrate the quantitative advantages of Blockchain in supply chain management. As Blockchain technology is still in its early stages, further investigation is necessary to develop new traceability applications.

# REFERENCES

[1]     G. J. Hofstede, *Hide or confide? The dilemma of transparency. The emerging world of chains and networks.*, 2004.

[2]     R.R. Pant, G. Prakash, and J.A. Farooquie, "A framework for traceability and transparency in the dairy supply chain networks", *Procedia Soc. Behav. Sci.,* vol. 189, pp. 385-394, 2015.
        [http://dx.doi.org/10.1016/j.sbspro.2015.03.235]

[3]     M.M. Aung, and Y.S. Chang, "Traceability in a food supply chain: Safety and quality perspectives", *Food Control,* vol. 39, pp. 172-184, 2014.
        [http://dx.doi.org/10.1016/j.foodcont.2013.11.007]

[4]     André Jeppsson, and Oskar Olsson, *Blockchains as a solution for traceability and transparency.*, 2017.

[5]     T. Pizzuti, and G. Mirabelli, "The global track and trace system for food: General framework and functioning principles", *J. Food Eng.,* vol. 159, pp. 16-35, 2015.
        [http://dx.doi.org/10.1016/j.jfoodeng.2015.03.001]

[6]     S. Sarpong, "Traceability and supply chain complexity: confronting the issues and concerns", *Eur. Bus. Rev.,* vol. 26, no. 3, pp. 271-284, 2014.
        [http://dx.doi.org/10.1108/EBR-09-2013-0113]

[7]     Geert Hofstede, "Hofstede", *GJ, & Minkov, M,* 2010.

[8]     Huub Scholten, *Enabling transparency in meat supply chains: Tracking & tracing for supply chain partners, consumers and authorities.*, 2014.

[9]     A.S. Girsang, T. Prabowo, "Monitoring system using GPS for logistic's key performance indicator", *Adv. in Sci., Tech. and Eng Sys. J.,* vol. 4, no. 6, pp. 32-37, 2019.
        [http://dx.doi.org/10.25046/aj040604]

[10]    M. El Maouchi, O. Ersoy, and Z. Erkin, "TRADE: A transparent, decentralized traceability system for the supply chain", *Proceedings of 1st ERCIM Blockchain Workshop 2018,* 2018.

[11]    A. Marchese, and O. Tomarchio, "A blockchain-based system for agri-food supply chain traceability management", *Sn Comput. Sci,* vol. 3, p. 279, 2022.
        [http://dx.doi.org/10.1007/s42979-022-01148-3]

[12]    Ilhaam A. Omar, Mazin Debe, Raja Jayaraman, Khaled Salah, Mohammad Omar, Junaid Arshad, "Blockchain-based Supply Chain Traceability for COVID-19 personal protective equipment", *Comput. Ind. Eng.,* vol. 167, p. 107995, 2022.
        [http://dx.doi.org/10.1016/j.cie.2022.107995]

[13]    Mahtab Kouhizadeh, Joseph Sarkis, and Qingyun Zhu, "At the nexus of Blockchain technology, the circular economy, and product deletion", *Applied Sciences 9.8,* p. 1712, 2019.
        [http://dx.doi.org/10.3390/app9081712]

[14]   Don Tapscott, and Alex Tapscott, "Blockchain revolution: How the technology behind bitcoin is changing money, business, and the world", *Penguin,* 2016.

[15]   V.J. Morkunas, J. Paschen, and E. Boon, "How blockchain technologies impact your business model", *Bus. Horiz.,* vol. 62, no. 3, pp. 295-306, 2019.
[http://dx.doi.org/10.1016/j.bushor.2019.01.009]

[16]   Jen-Hung Tseng, "Governance on the drug supply chain *via* gcoin blockchain", *Int. J. Environ. Res. Public Health,* vol. 15, no. 6, pp. 1055-1055, 2018.
[http://dx.doi.org/10.3390/ijerph15061055]

[17]   A. Reyna, C. Martín, J. Chen, E. Soler, and M. Díaz, "On blockchain and its integration with IoT. Challenges and opportunities", *Future Gener. Comput. Syst.,* vol. 88, pp. 173-190, 2018.
[http://dx.doi.org/10.1016/j.future.2018.05.046]

[18]   S. Rouhani, and R. Deters, "Security, performance, and applications of smart contracts: A systematic survey", *IEEE Access,* vol. 7, pp. 50759-50779, 2019.
[http://dx.doi.org/10.1109/ACCESS.2019.2911031]

[19]   Sunil Chopra, Peter Meindl, and Dharam Vir Kalra, *Supply chain management by pearson.,* Pearson Education India, 2007.

[20]   K. Salah, N. Nizamuddin, R. Jayaraman, and M. Omar, "Blockchain-based soybean traceability in agricultural supply chain", *IEEE Access,* vol. 7, pp. 73295-73305, 2019.
[http://dx.doi.org/10.1109/ACCESS.2019.2918000]

[21]   F. Tian, "A supply chain traceability system for food safety based on HACCP, blockchain and internet of things", *2017 International conference on service systems and service management,* IEEE, 2017.
[http://dx.doi.org/10.1109/ICSSSM.2017.7996119]

[22]   A. Rejeb, "Halal meat supply chain traceability based on HACCP, Blockchain and internet of things", *Acta Technica Jaurinensis,* vol. 11, no. 4, pp. 218-247, 2018.
[http://dx.doi.org/10.14513/actatechjaur.v11.n4.467]

[23]   G.R. Chandra, I.A. Liaqat, and B. Sharma, "Blockchain redefining: The halal food sector", *2019 Amity International Conference on Artificial Intelligence (AICAI),* 2019.
[http://dx.doi.org/10.1109/AICAI.2019.8701321]

[24]   Miguel Pincheira Caro, "Blockchain-based traceability in agri-food supply chain management: A practical implementation", *2018 IoT Vertical and Topical Summit on Agriculture-Tuscany (IOT Tuscany),* 2018.
[http://dx.doi.org/10.1109/IOT-TUSCANY.2018.8373021]

[25]   R. Kamath, "Food traceability on Blockchain: Walmart's pork and mango pilots with IBM", *J. Br. Blockchain Assoc.,* vol. 1, no. 1, pp. 1-12, 2018.
[http://dx.doi.org/10.31585/jbba-1-1-(10)2018]

[26]   J. Lin, "Blockchain and IoT based food traceability for smart agriculture", *Proceedings of the 3rd international conference on crowd science and engineering,* 2018.
[http://dx.doi.org/10.1145/3265689.3265692]

[27]   T. Hirbli, Palm Oil traceability: Blockchain meets supply chain., 2018. Available: http://dspace.mit.edu/handle/1721.1/7582.

[28]   J. Sunny, N. Undralla, and V. Madhusudanan Pillai, "Supply chain transparency through blockchain-based traceability: An overview with demonstration", *Comput. Ind. Eng.,* vol. 150, p. 106895, 2020.
[http://dx.doi.org/10.1016/j.cie.2020.106895]

[29]   V. Sharma, P. Ajmani, and C. Iwendi, "Blockchain application with specific reference to smart contracts in the insurance sector", In: *The Application of Emerging Technology and Blockchain in the Insurance Industry.* River Publishers, 2024, pp. 179-208.

[30]   T. Feng, "An agri-food supply chain traceability system for China based on RFID & Blockchain

technology", *2016 13th international conference on service systems and service management (ICSSSM).,* 2016.
[http://dx.doi.org/10.1109/ICSSSM.2016.7538424]

[31]   K. Biswas, V. Muthukkumarasamy, and W.L. Tan, "Blockchain based wine supply chain traceability system", *Future Technologies Conference (FTC),* 2017.

[32]   Candice Visser, and Quentin A. Hanich, *How Blockchain is strengthening tuna traceability to combat illegal fishing.,* 2018.

[33]   V. Buterin, "A next-generation smart contract and decentralized application platform", *White Paper,* vol. 3.37, pp. 2-1, 2014.

[34]   M. Alharby, and A. Van Moorsel, "Blockchain-based smart contracts: A systematic mapping study", *arXiv preprint arXiv:1710.06372,* 2017.
[http://dx.doi.org/10.5121/csit.2017.71011]

[35]   N. Szabo, "Formalizing and securing relationships on public networks", *First Monday,* vol. 2, no. 9, 1997.
[http://dx.doi.org/10.5210/fm.v2i9.548]

[36]   B. Marino, and A. Juels, "Setting standards for altering and undoing smart contracts", In: *10th International Symposium, RuleML 2016* Stony Brook, NY, USA, 2016.
[http://dx.doi.org/10.1007/978-3-319-42019-6_10]

[37]   Merit Kolvart, Margus Poola, and Addi Rull, "Setting standards for altering and undoing smart contracts", *Rule Technologies. Research, Tools, and Applications: 10th International Symposium,* 2016 RuleML 2016, Stony Brook, NY, USA, July 6-9, 2016.
[http://dx.doi.org/10.1007/978-3-319-26896-5_7]

[38]   S. Huckle, R. Bhattacharya, M. White, and N. Beloff, "Internet of things, Blockchain and shared economy applications", *Procedia Comput. Sci.,* vol. 98, pp. 461-466, 2016.
[http://dx.doi.org/10.1016/j.procs.2016.09.074]

[39]   S. Nzuva, "Smart contracts implementation, applications, benefits, and limitations", *J. Inf. Eng. Appl.,* vol. 9, no. 5, pp. 63-75, 2019.

[40]   S. B, A. S. Sh, S. K. E, S. N. K and N. S, "Blockchain industry 5.0: Next generation smart contract and decentralized application platform", *2022 International Conference on Innovative Computing, Intelligent Communication and Smart Electrical Systems (ICSES), Chennai, India,* pp. 1-8, 2022.
[http://dx.doi.org/10.1109/ICSES55317.2022.9914151]

[41]   H.M. Kim, and M. Laskowski, "Toward an ontology-driven blockchain design for supply-chain provenance", *Int. J. Intell. Syst. Account. Finance Manage.,* vol. 25, no. 1, pp. 18-27, 2018.
[http://dx.doi.org/10.1002/isaf.1424]

[42]   M. Vukolić, "Rethinking permissioned Blockchains", *Proceedings of the ACM workshop on Blockchain, cryptocurrencies and contracts,* 2017.
[http://dx.doi.org/10.1145/3055518.3055526]

[43]   A. Jøsang, "Trust requirements in identity management", *Proceedings of the 2005 Australasian workshop on Grid computing and e-research-Volume 44,* 2005.

[44]   G-J. Ahn, and M. Ko, "User-centric privacy management for federated identity management", *2007 International Conference on Collaborative Computing: Networking, Applications and Worksharing (CollaborateCom 2007),* 2007.
[http://dx.doi.org/10.1109/COLCOM.2007.4553829]

[45]   T. Rathee, and P. Singh, "A systematic literature mapping on secure identity management using Blockchain technology", *J. King Saud Univ. – Comput. Inf. Sci.,* vol. 34, pp. 5782-5796, 2022.

[46]   J. Camenisch, "Privacy and identity management for everyone", *Proceedings of the 2005 workshop on Digital identity management,* 2005.

[http://dx.doi.org/10.1145/1102486.1102491]

[47]   S. Suriadi, E. Foo, and A. Jøsang, "A user-centric federated single sign-on system", *J. Netw. Comput. Appl.*, vol. 32, no. 2, pp. 388-401, 2009.
[http://dx.doi.org/10.1016/j.jnca.2008.02.016]

[48]   M. Hulea, "Pharmaceutical cold chain management: Platform based on a distributed ledger", *2018 IEEE International conference on automation, quality and testing, robotics (AQTR)*, IEEE, 2018.
[http://dx.doi.org/10.1109/AQTR.2018.8402709]

[49]   H. Hasan, E. AlHadhrami, A. AlDhaheri, K. Salah, and R. Jayaraman, "Smart contract-based approach for efficient shipment management", *Comput. Ind. Eng.*, vol. 136, pp. 149-159, 2019.
[http://dx.doi.org/10.1016/j.cie.2019.07.022]

[50]   Thomas Bocek, "Blockchains everywhere—a use-case of Blockchains in the pharma supply-chain", *2017 IFIP/IEEE Symposium on Integrated Network and Service Management (IM)*, 2017.
[http://dx.doi.org/10.23919/INM.2017.7987376]

[51]   B.A. Archa, and K. Achuthan, "Trace and track: Enhanced pharma supply chain infrastructure to prevent fraud", *First International Conference, UBICNET 2017*, 2018.
[http://dx.doi.org/10.1007/978-3-319-73423-1_17]

[52]   I. Haq, and O. Muselemu, "Blockchain technology in pharmaceutical industry to prevent counterfeit drugs", *Int. J. Comput. Appl.*, vol. 180, no. 25, pp. 8-12, 2018.
[http://dx.doi.org/10.5120/ijca2018916579]

[53]   P. Helo, and Y. Hao, "Blockchains in operations and supply chains: A model and reference implementation", *Comput. Ind. Eng.*, vol. 136, pp. 242-251, 2019.
[http://dx.doi.org/10.1016/j.cie.2019.07.023]

[54]   T.M. Choi, "Blockchain-technology-supported platforms for diamond authentication and certification in luxury supply chains", *Transp. Res., Part E Logist. Trans. Rev.*, vol. 128, pp. 17-29, 2019.
[http://dx.doi.org/10.1016/j.tre.2019.05.011]

[55]   J.H. Lee, and M. Pilkington, "How the Blockchain revolution will reshape the consumer electronics industry [future directions]", *IEEE Consum. Electron. Mag.*, vol. 6, no. 3, pp. 19-23, 2017.
[http://dx.doi.org/10.1109/MCE.2017.2684916]

[56]   M. Westerkamp, F. Victor, and A. Küpper, "Tracing manufacturing processes using blockchain-based token compositions", *Digit. Commun. Netw.*, vol. 6, no. 2, pp. 167-176, 2020.
[http://dx.doi.org/10.1016/j.dcan.2019.01.007]

[57]   D. Miehle, "PartChain: A decentralized traceability application for multi-tier supply chain networks in the automotive industry", *2019 IEEE International Conference on Decentralized Applications and Infrastructures (DAPPCON)*, IEEE, 2019.
[http://dx.doi.org/10.1109/DAPPCON.2019.00027]

[58]   Tarun Kumar Agrawal, Ajay Sharma, and Vijay Kumar, "Blockchain-based secured traceability system for textile and clothing supply chain", *Artificial Intelligence for Fashion Industry in the Big Data Era*, pp. 197-208, 2018.
[http://dx.doi.org/10.1007/978-981-13-0080-6_10]

[59]   Simone Figorilli, "A blockchain implementation prototype for the electronic open-source traceability of wood along the whole supply chain", *Sensors*, vol. 18, no. 9, p. 3133, 2018.
[http://dx.doi.org/10.3390/s18093133]

[60]   A. Imeri, and D. Khadraoui, "The security and traceability of shared information in the process of transportation of dangerous goods", *2018 9th IFIP International Conference on New Technologies, Mobility and Security (NTMS).*, IEEE, 2018.
[http://dx.doi.org/10.1109/NTMS.2018.8328751]

[61]   M.A. Ali, "IoT and blockchain based smart agriculture monitoring and intelligence security system", *2022 3rd International Conference on Computation, Automation and Knowledge Management*

*(ICCAKM).,* IEEE, 2022.
[http://dx.doi.org/10.1109/ICCAKM54721.2022.9990243]

[62]     T. Hai, "A novel & innovative blockchain-empowered federated learning approach for secure data sharing in smart city applications", *International Conference on Advances in Communication Technology and Computer Engineering,* 2023 Cham.
[http://dx.doi.org/10.1007/978-3-031-37164-6_9]

CHAPTER 3

# Enhancing Electronic Health Records and Patient Data Management through Blockchain Technology

**Prabh Deep Singh[1,*], Kiran Deep Singh[2] and Harsh Taneja[1]**

[1] *Department of Computer Science and Engineering, Graphic Era Deemed to be University, Dehradun, India*

[2] *Chitkara University Institute of Engineering and Technology, Chitkara University, Rajpura, Punjab, India*

**Abstract:** Blockchain technology has the potential to help deliver more efficient health services, improving patients' experience from end to end. In this chapter, a blockchain platform is analyzed, which adopts a protocol that is designed to both regulate access to data and information, digitize health data, and enable an untrusted reader to ask for the execution of arbitrary algorithms on the peer's private databases, whose contents must remain hidden to those who are not authorized to access them, and obtaining an efficient and scalable response. The chapter uses blockchain technology to enhance electronic health records and patient data management. Several standardized technologies and models are available in the market for electronic health records, but the users, *i.e.*, patients and hospitals, trust and believe in those services that provide enhanced security to their data. Blockchain can be utilized for securing EHR by deploying attributes of a public or private blockchain, enabling permission access by hospitals and granting access easily to patients and family members.

**Keywords:** Big health data, Blockchain, Centralization, Chain methods, Electronic health record, Electronic medical record, Encryption, Health care, Medical-chain, Patient data management.

## INTRODUCTION

This research proposes that electronic health records (EHR) and patient data management can be drastically enhanced by adopting public blockchain technology. A public blockchain's innovation overcomes the weak points of every other electronic model in terms of disintermediation, crucial security, ownership, data integrity, and data sharing. It is expected that after the widespread adoption of EHR, large-scale blockchain technology will be deployed to support and

* **Corresponding author Prabh Deep Singh:** Department of Computer Science and Engineering, Graphic Era Deemed to be University, Dehradun, India; E-mail: ssingh.prabhdeep@gmail.com

**Monica Bhutani, Monica Gupta, Kirti Gupta, Deepali Kamthania & Danish Ather (Eds.)**
**All rights reserved-© 2025 Bentham Science Publishers**

enhance this demotion in the health industry. With an open transparent platform, it will also provide a cost-effective secure way for general 'people' to take control of their own health data [1].

The problem of electronic health records (EHR) security, data integrity, secure patient data sharing, and privacy is huge and unsolved. Large-scale data breaches made by hacking, stealing, and insider attacks are increasingly common with EHRs. In addition, corrupted and/or unreliable data in a patient's EHR, the data integrity problem, may result in inappropriate patient care. Furthermore, large-scale data sharing may result in misunderstanding and possible misuse of health information. The new powerful electronic model in management has the potential to address many longstanding and billowing problems, including multi-organization environments, because of its innovative features such as disintermediation and public and private key cryptography.

## Background and Significance

In addition to highlighting the lack of industry standards and policy regulations, research related to the adverse impact of inadequate data and electronic health records (EHR) management has proven valuable for several reasons. EHR typically refers to health-related information based on sharing and storage in the electronic format that is maintained by the patient or an organization. Utilizing the data, such as administrative data, extracted from such an electronic form of patient payment, treatment, and outcomes has facilitated healthcare professionals to improve their decision-making. As these data capture that billing systems have been changing rapidly as a result of their ad hoc basis, many of the current issues are related to security, privacy, and compliance regulations protecting sensitive healthcare data from unauthorized disclosure, particularly as the result of a large amount of data breaches [2]. This has led to organizing data in a more secure manner surrounding the establishment of standards designed to guide the more comprehensive use of electronic health data.

The National Institute of Standards and Technology (NIST) defines blockchain technology as a decentralized digital ledger that records transactions across multiple computers. This allows parties to safely and securely exchange information, including individual user data, through distributed applications. Blockchain has often been equated with Bitcoin, in that it was initially developed to serve as the accounting method for cryptocurrency, but the technology has evolved and come to the forefront as a multi-faceted peer-to-peer and secure technology [3]. The technology's unique characteristics suggest that it could be leveraged, and has the potential to work, to improve data management issues in healthcare and medicine including the inefficiencies and revenue loss related to claim and billing management, slow and cumbersome settlements, and patient data privacy breach [4].

**Purpose and Scope**

The scope of this paper is to analyze the advantages and disadvantages of the current EHR and BD systems and propose a new blockchain-based EHR and data management system in which the patient data is stored in a secure, transparent, and elegantly structured way. It provides control to the patient over their data. It also provides more benefits to the BD managers, such as transparency and security. In addition, it focuses on a Patient Hash tree-based approach with separate data and index distribution to resolve the limitation of using the Merkle tree to generate a large number of hashes. The main scope focuses on comparing the efficiency of current and proposed data on the blockchain and finding the benefits or demerits of the current existing proposed problem. It currently uses IPFS and the medical chain, but many different blockchain-based EHR systems and new EHR networks can also be used. This can also be implemented using other blockchain-based networks. As a result, the proposed system not only brings about the improvement of the patient transaction system but also the storage and control problem of medical blockchain-based EHR problems. Data management is at the heart of this.

In this paper, a patient manages patient transaction information, and a tamper-proof patient data structure is provided. The proposed system adopts IPFS for data storage and management of transaction information. Blockchain (Medical-chain) is adopted to keep patient data and encryption key to be used to generate a Merkle tree. As a result, detailed transaction information is protected in the system. The proposed system not only brings about the improvement of the patient transaction system but also the storage and control problem of medical blockchain-based EHR problems. It is possible to enhance functionality such as revealing others who want to know your information. You will be able to provide protection if you do not want to share your data with others or those who are not authorized. It is expected that patients will help them in a healthier and more effective way to build EHR and BD-based EHR.

**Electronic Health Records (EHRs)**

For data analysis, a tremendous volume of patient data and evidence-based knowledge, *i.e.* clinical practice guidelines, are analyzed to benefit clinical decision-making, and patient treatment, and enable metrics of patient engagement, satisfaction, and treatment outcomes. A central EHR database is centralized with many independent but EHR-aware healthcare applications. They can establish a connection with EHRs by querying EHR-Aware regulations. The processing of large volumes of complex data on clinical and genetic patient variability, clinical practice guidelines, and metrics related to patient treatment can be managed with increased performance. Information management functions of EHR systems cover the collection, storage, retrieval, and modification of medical records, medical images, medical signals, clinical documentation, administrative data, research databases, data for health service planning, drug dictionaries, bibliographic references, clinical guidelines and standards, and resources for educational use. The value of data can be dramatically transformed into information that enables such applications to support patients and medical professionals.

EHR systems fulfill three vital functions: data storage, data management, and data analysis. Data insurers, healthcare providers, medical professionals, regulatory organizations, and individual patients are all stakeholders in the EHR system. Within EHR systems, minimum requirements for data storage include a prescribed universal format and minimum security and integrity of data. They enable various healthcare applications to attach data promptly and efficiently. The format of EHR and the value of data and metadata have to be unaltered since they were stored. The patient retains control over the access to and the utilization of the data and sets up general consent directives in place. The patients own the EHRs and must be able to access, copy, or erase them.

## OVERVIEW AND IMPORTANCE

Electronic health record (EHR) systems are on the brink of fulfilling the promise of big data to the healthcare industry as depicted in Fig. (**1**). Exploiting the insights hidden in patient data allows medical professionals to create personalized treatment plans and deliver individualized care models. Furthermore, secondary analysis of EHR (big health data) promises to revolutionize public health through broader insights into various medical conditions and diseases, and novel techniques for their prevention, diagnosis, and treatment. At their core, EHRs contain real-time and life-long patient health data. Thus, accurate and immediate access to EHRs is crucial in medical decision-making, especially in emergencies.

Healthcare systems globally are undergoing a structural transition. They are evolving to become more aligned with the needs of the end-users, *i.e.*, the patients. This evolution is especially enabled through the advancement of digital information and communication technologies, and eHealth represents one of its manifestations. At the same time, a number of challenges to the adoption and meaningful use of eHealth, especially of electronic health records (EHRs), persist. Central in them is the role of EHRs as centralized systems of medical data where the fine-grained permissions on access and modifications are difficult to implement. This work advances the case that these challenges can be mitigated through the integration of recent advances in distributed ledgers (a class of decentralized and distributed "blockchain" databases) into the fabric of EHR systems.

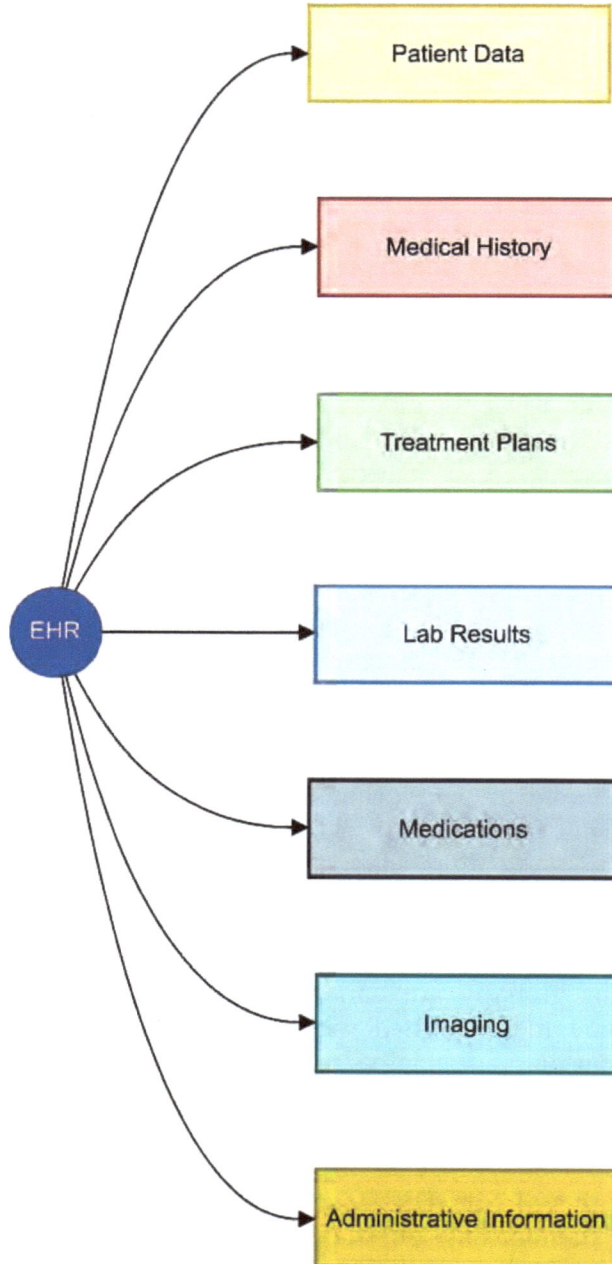

**Fig. (1).** Components of electronic healthcare record.

## Challenges in EHR Management

EHR has been widely promoted by OECD (Organization for Economic Co-operation and Development), in the context of its confidentiality and efficiency. However, the benefits of having patient's data at their fingertips are often outweighed by inherent conflicts and challenges, particularly electronic health data break security problems. It is worth noting that patient medical information is extremely precise, and includes detailed data about patients' illnesses, treatments, and irrelevant habits and activities. In fact, there are associated requirements for confidentiality assurance, around medical and non-medical sponsors and stakeholders' legitimate interests in this information. Experts infer that EHR's two well-known complications are the large number of diverse healthcare providers, payers, and individual patients who contribute to EHR data and how data are accumulated, intended for comprehensive reporting for medical practice, education, supervision, and even research, especially big data analytics. Clearly, without a well-verified authenticity assurance and therefore compliance, all the aforementioned advantages from EHR management unavoidably be eroded and rendered largely ineffective.

When considering efficiency in healthcare, health information technology is generally a consensus for effectiveness. EHR, as a promising stage form of EMR (Electronic Medical Record), provides more information than traditional paper records, giving healthcare providers tools to offer improved care. It is evident that through EHR real-time and secured access, healthcare providers can make better decisions, lower costs, and even deliver better and quicker services. Also, EHR can help spot potential issues more proficiently, stay current with regular updates on treatment, and report accurate and complete information about patients' health. EHR may result in desirable patient health outputs from prompt, efficient, and educated medical treatments. Collectively, EHR-related activities are aimed to make comprehensive improvements in patient care and much more.

## BLOCKCHAIN TECHNOLOGY

Fig. (2) shows the key features of blockchain technology where each chain is made up of a number of blocks. These blocks are linked together across storage volumes at checked intervals. Every time any change is made anywhere in the blockchain, the applications and the users running the applications become aware of the change in less than an hour, usually in a few seconds.

The least of benefits that blockchain produces is a mechanism that provides a high level of error tolerance against common security threats in addition to being a stable and efficient way of maintaining the information about the transaction and lifecycle of a logistics chain in a decentralized environment [5].

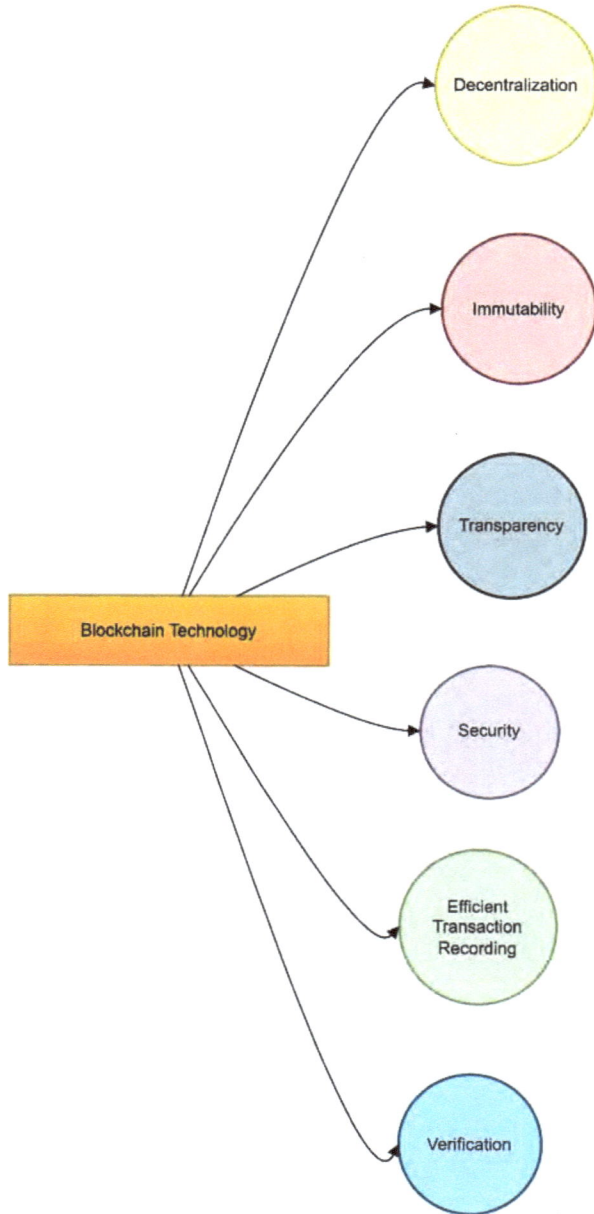

**Fig. (2).** Key features of blockchain technology.

Blockchain is a type of distributed ledger used to maintain a growing list of transactions, known as 'blocks', and like any good transactional database, it can add additional blocks of transactions to an already existing chain of blocks. As the name implies, a blockchain is, in fact, a chain of such 'transaction blocks'. Blockchain is used to store information on the transactions conducted across a particular platform in a secure and efficient manner. For example, in case of logistics and cargo transport protocols, a number of service providers will be part of the distributed ledger. Each time a transaction occurs in the platform that needs to be recorded, the data of that particular transaction will be recorded as a block that carries the transaction information [6]. Blockchain can monitor the lifecycle of an audit certificate by recording the attestation of the consignment. The logs of data from the event will be used to automate the process.

## Fundamentals and Key Concepts

All the conducted transactions are undeniable on the public ledger, also referred to as the block explorer. Thanks to the absence of a centralized body, which would manage and promote the acceptance of relevant records, the distributed ledger is characterized by immutability, belonging to the security and privacy characteristic per se. Moreover, the scope of the conducted smart contract can affect the accuracy and the information value included in the facilitated process. Along the lines of the overall contribution of blockchain technology in electronic health data management can be articulated as the level of implemented blockchain operations between patients and health providers. These operations include registration, ordering, changing, scheduling, (un)docking time of provided healthcare services, as well as facilitation of various financial cryptocurrency modifications.

The blockchain is a peer-to-peer distributed ledger, characterized by security, privacy, immutability, integrity, and traceability. Each node with the blockchain purveys the ledger, which contains a list of conducts, also referred to as blocks. These blocks provide a record of the merged transactions. Furthermore, the blockchain is characterized by security and privacy, traceability, and decentralization in particular. The security and privacy characteristics are guaranteed through the adoption of strong cryptographic techniques. These techniques provide a layered encryption across a pair of contumacious public and private keys. The integrity and traceability characterizations make it impossible to modify or annul any added transactions and run the presence of indexical entry. The decentralization characteristic is a result of the use of a consensus algorithm, which is responsible for approving any added conduct. To proceed with the use of these fundamental fundamentals, any implemented blockchain portrays the ledger structure and asset lifecycle as the key elements.

## Applications in Healthcare

With the popularity of smartphones and wearable devices, users are accustomed to collecting and managing their health-related data in mobile phone apps. These apps are able to connect health data from their corresponding hospitals. Hospital means and access information, such as patient medical records, prescriptions, and laboratory tests, are saved in their databases. Mobile apps will request data from the hospital whenever necessary. App developers must invest much enterprise restorers to improve the hospital database prior to app development, as well as enterprise service platforms to authenticate with the app. However, mobile apps perform medical data sharing through unsecured authentication and message exchanges and become a door for passive data leakage. If the server of mobile health apps is not equipped with strong administrative security mechanisms, it is likely to facilitate data breaches, especially by application developers [7, 8]. In the real world, mobile health apps will violate privacy policies for commercial purposes at the expense of data privacy for users. Thus, there is an urgent need to protect data privacy *via* decentralization and data sharing limitations, provided by smart contracts and immutable storage attributes in blockchain.

The widespread application of blockchain to healthcare data management is currently a popular trend as can be seen in Fig. (**3**). Blockchain technology offers great potential for health data management by providing a reliable platform to securely store, manage, and exchange healthcare data. The consensus algorithm and distribution characteristic of blockchain technology lead to protected electronic health records. In addition, combining blockchain technology with health data can realize fine-grained data sharing and access management. Current academic and industrial researchers have provided many applications for blockchain health data management. Some applications focus on privacy protection, while others focus on data management. These product requirements illustrate the great market demand and further, confirm the potential application of blockchain health data in clinical applications.

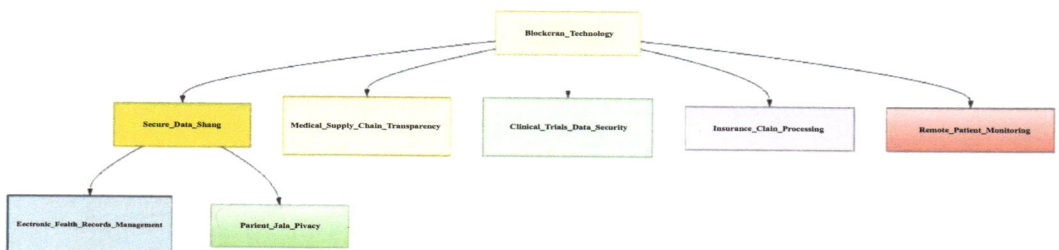

**Fig. (3).** Applications of blockchain in healthcare system.

## INTEGRATION OF BLOCKCHAIN WITH EHRS

Decentralization of Data: The primary purpose of blockchain technology directly addresses the challenge of a distributed ledger of data that is decentralized in terms of the way the data pertaining to the patients are structured. The lifetime medical history of a patient is the lifetime asset of the patient, and no central authority should own the entire patient's health records except the patient. This distributed public ledger trust between the health workers and the patients about the data. Any healthcare provider and patient could connect to the blockchain at any time to retrieve the required data, ensuring that the treated patients' data compliance is accurate. Since the patient-centric data model is stored in a distributed private or public ledger, it leads to a reduction in infrastructure costs, following rules for permissions, third-party costs, security centers since data are fragmented over the peers in the network, and the consensus mechanism makes any tampering of the data practically impossible due to a large number of peers.

The data generated by healthcare institutions is termed electronic health records (EHR), which include patient demographics, laboratory test results, medications, medical history, immunization records, allergies, vital sign measurements, and personal statistics deposited by healthcare institutions or the user itself. Integrating e-health platforms with the underlying blockchain technology, it is expected to result in various terabytes of data and facilitate the development of platforms that would allow patients to trade their existing medical data. The outcome of integrating e-health with a blockchain not only benefits the patients but also the resources, scientific community, hospitals, insurance agencies, and the healthcare industry. The value of EHR on a blockchain not only offers a global scope for the healthcare industry, but changes the way the healthcare industry is getting assisted worldwide, and how patients perceive their health records in an encrypted and immutable state.

The data generated by healthcare institutions is termed electronic health records (EHR) in Fig. (**4**), which include patient demographics, laboratory test results, medications, medical history, immunization records, allergies, vital sign measurements, and personal statistics deposited by healthcare institutions or the user itself. Integrating e-health platforms with the underlying blockchain technology, it is expected to result in various terabytes of data and facilitate the development of platforms that would allow patients to trade their existing medical data. The outcome of integrating e-health with a blockchain not only benefits the patients but also the resources, scientific community, hospitals, insurance agencies, and the healthcare industry. The value of EHR on a blockchain not only offers a global scope for the healthcare industry, but changes the way the healthcare industry is getting assisted worldwide, and how patients perceive their health records in an encrypted and immutable state.

**Benefits and Advantages**

Blockchain technology has the potential to overcome issues related to lack of privacy, security, and trust in the currently used systems and protocols for EHRs.

Smart contracts and oracles can be used to record and automate management functions, access control policies, and the usage of EHRs. They can also overcome the issue by allowing customized access by case-reliant criteria rather than the whole contents of the EHR. The key benefits and advantages of applying blockchain technology for EHRs and patient data management are having control over personal EHR data, no mediators, compatible structured management, clear records for wary and legal purposes, and using blockchain transparency for patient trust in healthcare. Blockchain technology could bring a robust amendment to the security of patients' medical records as it leverages technical, organizational, and authorized mechanisms. This technology has the potential to overcome the missing links in the current systems such as a warranty of immutability, integrity protection, and the recording of an immutable trust path.

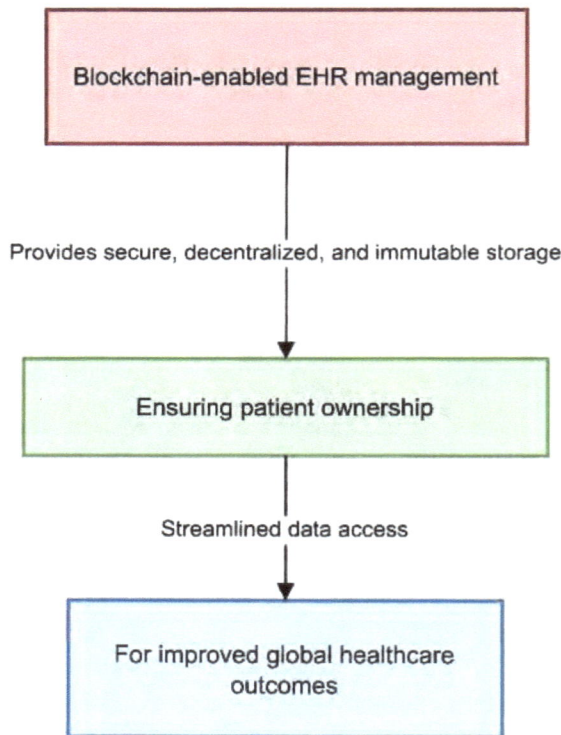

Fig. (4). Blockchain-enabled EHR management in healthcare.

From the first analysis, it is evident that blockchain technology does have the potential to improve the management of EHRs and also optimize patient data management. These are key potential benefits that blockchain technology was identified to bring to EHRs and patient data management. Several advantages of applying this emerging technology are minimized human intervention, enabling the sharing of indisputable data created by authorized nodes that are linked with patients, enhancement in the discretion of patient data, and changing the method of exchanging EHRs and patient data between healthcare professionals and third parties.

## Technical Implementation Considerations

Within such a network, nodes need to exhibit functional properties like high availability, favorable computational capacity, and the ability to store data to support the needs of electronic health records. Merging conventional data storage, processing backend, and blockchain operations can lead to suboptimal performance and efficiency being experienced by core EHR properties like read, write, and query. During the future shift of EHRs from proprietary storage onto blockchains, the need is to anonymize transaction-resolver participation and support efficient massive data transactions in order to honor data processing backends and system inherent throughput requirements. However, despite the enormous volume, transactions of healthcare providers, insurance companies, clinical researchers, and national health policy planners can be operational mainly in batch offline mode [9].

Technical considerations in blockchain implementations for EHRs involve both the specifications of blockchain nodes in blockchain networks for eHealth applications and the data structures and functionality of an EHR application based on blockchain technology. The first aspect concerns the configuration details of nodes in a blockchain network and the second aspect touches on the implications of respective choices of blockchain technologies to the properties of EHRs. Blockchain nodes in eHealth applications are likely to communicate through a well-organized peer-to-peer network with common communication protocols.

## SECURITY AND PRIVACY IN BLOCKCHAIN-BASED EHRS

Health records have become a frequent target of cyberattacks, similar to financial services firms and retail companies, because of the large volumes of personal, private, and financial information that the systems contain. To mitigate these problems related to security and control, a decentralized model of identity is proposed as a middleware network system that prevents triangulation of the patient's identity and therefore keeps it confidential, without losing control. By exploiting cryptographic schemes available on the blockchain, even when granted consent, the results demonstrate acceptable performance of the proposed middleware network system, the actual implementation of the algorithm, and the evaluation of BCT in the medical field. The implementation of the middleware network system could reduce this risk because of the indirection of the patient's data.

## Encryption and Decentralization

Decentralization ensures the lack of need for access to central servers, with information duplicated and consistently distributed across every single network node. Each node then becomes a mirror of the entire database and is capable of accessing and resetting that data. In order for new blocks to be created, a hashing process is executed by a majority of the nodes within the network. Once security and integrity are assessed, these data blocks are joined to the existing blockchain, ensuring that all of the computing power present within the network is required to reach a consensus or approve changes. By requiring approval from the network, the individuals overseeing the servers are incapable of ending control over services and are thereby barred from altering records contained in previous blocks [10]. With blockchain, users can maintain an autonomous level of security control over their own data.

The central concept behind blockchain is the encryption of records, with each block featuring a unique encrypted identification key called a hash, which is linked to the hash of the previous block. This hash code is created through composition from the decrypted form of the data using a hash function. Fig. (**5**) demonstrates the data is encrypted using complex algorithms, only someone possessing the decryption key can view plaintext data. As a result, information within a block cannot be altered without access to either the originating keys or the decryption keys. The linking of the hash key across all records creates a blockchain, interconnecting all of the data spanning the entire network. Once a block has been added to a blockchain, the data it contains is unchangeable unless the majority of the network's nodes collaborate to alter the ledger. This process enhances the security of that data.

## Compliance with Data Protection Regulations

Blockchain technology can guarantee the integrity and confidentiality of patient records, ensuring complete correspondence to the data protection requirements set up by the legislator in the relevant field of EHR management. It can also support data management and administration, decrease the risk of unauthorized actions, and provide mechanisms for the maximization of privacy requirements. Blockchain technology can be a very effective solution in the health service sector — besides the EHR — for securing and safeguarding medical and patient-identifiable data.

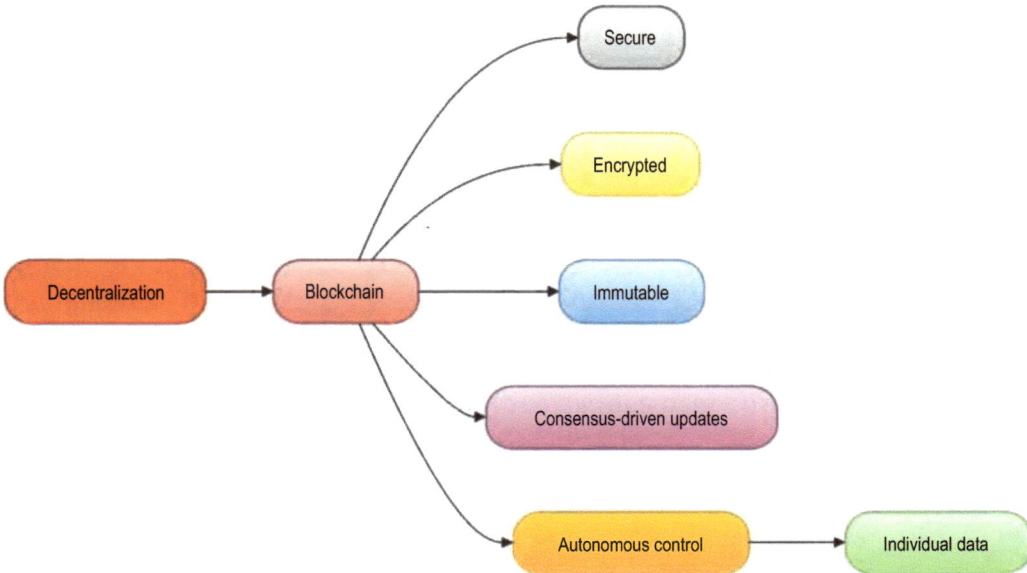

**Fig. (5).** Encrypted and decentralized messenger for iOS and android.

Several blockchain-based personal data management systems (PDMS) have been proposed that offer compliance with data protection regulation through user-managed consent and retention periods. It was also reported that consent must be appropriately obtained and maintained in a broad blockchain network. Tailored to the GDPR, decentralization traits well suit the subject matter, scope, and objectives of the law of the European Union.

Blockchain as an infrastructure can work alongside traditional databases rather than replace them, providing important features like immutability and transparency in compliance with these data protection laws and regulations while not exposing the records to accidental deletions or oversights.

Data management of EHRs and patient databases across the globe requires compliance with both domestic and international data protection laws, such as the General Data Protection Regulation (GDPR) in the European Union, HIPAA in the USA, the Personal Data (Privacy) Ordinance (PDPO) in Hong Kong, and others. These laws expect organizations that are custodians of personal data to take appropriate protective measures such as user consent, adequate security, limited retention periods, and other features.

## CASE STUDIES AND USE CASES

In order to monitor, keep track proof, and disclose the therapy legal conduct record, it is necessary to deploy a file for that. This difficulty came from two perspectives: first, the person who holds the private key can integrate the therapy record behavior in the chain that can be accessible by other stakeholders who have the therapy trace track interest. Second, the holder of the access control key can prevent the private key holder from the abusive use of signing, for example, forging a fake record in case of a disputed medicine effect or an injury issue on using the medicine. But, in blockchain's transparency state, it is challenging to tackle the first perspective problem. Since the main property of blockchain is transparency, it is also a double-edged sword that can make stakeholders less active in integrating the medical behavior or official therapy record in the chain for consideration with external colleague parties who hold the illegal use or ownership gain point.

### Successful Implementations

BitFidence is a second project that tries to mitigate the privacy issues of clinical documents by creating a distributed service that facilitates both sharing and protecting it. The key aspect of BitFidence is the use of links of authenticated data to the hash of the elements from the Ethereum blockchain. Furthermore, the confirmation of modification in the proposed method helps to guarantee that preservation and verification are always used in relation to the initial clinical information. Numerous benefits can be obtained through the use of this kind of method, for instance, singularity and re-usability of executable codes, interoperability, mutability, and sharing of all sorts of data that is related to patient health. The last project presented in this work is MedRec, which is based on the Ethereum statically typed programming language; it aims to provide an infrastructure for the data sharing of medical information between unrelated participants. The system uses a platform for scalable ChainMethods, evidence-based storage in the Ethereum blockchain, but uses IPFS; a file system without a source that is designed for storing and linking version control blocks, by providing a unique cryptographic fingerprint for each unit of storage. The use of the IPFS is to store an actual medical data asset, which enables lower latencies when deploying, but it also provides a higher bandwidth when it comes to more extensive records.

A group of researchers developed a four-layer architecture that provides both transparency and immutability through the use of a new blockchain-enhanced-DNFS technology. The DNFS has predefined template-assisted data sharing and collaborative editing for diagnosis, nursing care, and physical examination information registration and sharing. In the third layer (Action-Click interface), nurses can register or acquire diagnosis, nursing care, and physical examination information with just one click, as it is not necessary to enter a data entry point. The fourth layer is Multi-Source Collaborative-Editing Technology, which provides diagnosis, nursing care, and physical examination information through DNFS, clinical documents, and so forth. Not only do these four layers have standard diagnostic, nursing, or physical examination information data entry points but they also have collaborative editing controlled by multiple collaborative editing methods, such as "one form, multiple platforms; one form, multiple department; one form, multiple people".

## Lessons Learned

- Secure access control, revise policies - The tens of thousands of Direct messaging partners, thousands of virtual care and home health care providers, and hundreds of EHRs, including some of the world's largest for-profit and research hospitals, are a testament to the trust that healthcare companies and organizations place in DirectTrust's secure trust framework for the exchange of health information across the care continuum. Enhancing EHR and patient data management system trust with blockchain for improved access control and policy enforcement is a two-edged sword as it thrashes older, easier practices. To gain the benefits of higher patient trust and participation in research, healthcare organizations will need to carefully establish their policies and revamp their infrastructure to adequately secure their access control, governance, and trust in their data and that of any third parties with whom they may share these data.
- Communicate user benefits of private blockchain - The privacy challenges of Ethereum's public blockchain model are well known, as is the ongoing debate over who should be trusted runner nodes; critical use cases for decentralized applications. Collaborative networked healthcare has the potential to mitigate these concerns by running permissioned, private blockchain implementations for desired network actors, *e.g.*, patients, healthcare organizations, and select, vetted third parties. With highly controlled and governed blockchain access, organizations can greatly reduce privacy concerns, latency, and security risks for blockchain trust transactions that result in added value and mutual benefits to the organizations and the patients. Dedicating both hardware and person-hours to the more select user set would enhance participation and trust. The current HIPAA rules and Business Associate Agreements (which will likely continue to evolve) and the European General Data Protection Regulation may guide some of these decisions for the specific healthcare use cases.
- Be transparent about blockchain consensus-trade-offs - There are technical trade-offs related to "efficiency, level of trust, thresholds, scalability," *etc.*, in

blockchain design and operation. Today's trust in third-party implementations is easier to understand, as is their range of capabilities and incentives. At the same time, healthcare organizations are also aware of the challenges, costs, and data security risks of maintaining modern databases and analytics technologies. Blockchain offers promising features for data protection, user control and analytics, but the entire ecosystem needs to understand and engage in the conversation. The different healthcare use cases may need different blockchain designs.

- Educate users on blockchain trust - Automating data sharing and access management is important, but blockchain is known for its immutable decentralized ledgers that can provide cryptographically secure and tamper-evident recording of every event, transaction, and policy decision. This is an asset that the entire health data ecosystem needs to understand, value, and learn from. Privacy-preserved analytics tools that can analyze patient data to advance personalized medicine goals, sharing insights where warranted, have the potential to revolutionize health care and wellness research but to do so in a manner that users trust and understand, given the sensitivity of encounter and session context data.

## Future Trends and Implications

There is also a high demand for effective mechanisms that support patient data management while meeting the patient's demand for privacy-preserving and secure data exchange. The protection of privacy is paramount. In virtually all cases, keeping personal health information secret is vital. Privacy is strongly tied to these. The importance of the ability to keep healthcare records confidential is due to patients often discussing confidential information with their healthcare provider. This is of essential importance, and the need to ensure alliances with mental healthcare providers will want to guarantee no gimmicks during the diagnosis phase related to scheduling computing. The presence of privacy violations may cause negative repercussions for the patients themselves.

Blockchain's novel features and lack of a central authority open it to specific challenges in privacy and security that need to be addressed for the technology to be effectively used in achieving privacy-preserving information exchange. As it stands, the public nature of conventional blockchain networks poses risks by leaking sensitive information stored in them. This vulnerability is problematic in the field of medicine, where records are highly sensitive and often legally regulated as personal data. Medical data are highly personal and sensitive, often with legal protections. Thus, the wide propagation of a record in decentralized models of storage and management of patient control implies considerable privacy concerns. Because of the many legal and social issues surrounding ownership and privacy in blockchain applications, it is very clear that data privacy continues to be the most significant challenge to be addressed.

## CHALLENGES AND OPPORTUNITIES FOR EHRS AND PATIENT DATA MANAGEMENT

### Potential Innovations

The policy of blockchain technology implementation can be addressed through fully holistic systems for decentralized user-centric EHR systems. Solutions are conceived as part of the electronic identity landscape of decentralization and in addition to traditional digital penitentiaries using pseudonymization, or to the e-justice systems already using online litigation. With the blockchain technology ensuring, next to decentralized identity management and authentication and the connected verifiable credentials and self-sovereign identity service, also a decentralized EHR, the different actors may today store and control their own data, grant access, search for (anonymized) data to third parties, or query the patients/clients whenever it is permitted, invoking the different proximity levels between their real-world data and the generic textual data available on the public chain. In the midst of the recent coronavirus outbreak, the group founding the Blockchain and E-health International Association managed advanced solutions that can increase the speed, security, and quality of information exchanged between healthcare professionals as well as public and private institutions. This approach can represent an authentic collective explosion in various areas of research, such as big data, artificial intelligence, 5G technology, the Internet of Things, and data security. Behind the central management, there would, instead, be a decentralized model with an identity manager using a blockchain-based identity and key to guarantee all the principles necessary for data protection and security of the user's digital identity, including full GDPR alignment, and integration of different authorization protocols, such as UMA 2.0, to control data access and sharing for GDPR compliance purposes.

Many potential innovations are based on the concept of self-sovereign identity management, through which, based on the assumption of mutual trust or common interest in electronic health records (EHRs), complete, partial, or aggregate data arise. In principle, the EHR itself is locked or linked to an access control service that uses blockchain technology, which applies a flexible set of rules, such as access thresholds or bandwidth requirements, to consult sessions, to enable access not only for professionals (such as physicians, pharmacists, others), but also to the individuals themselves and services (such as analytics, research). The basic concept is used with either centralized blockchain-based identity management or fully decentralized solutions, also called decentralized systems or universal identity management. They have important distinctions in problems, such as scalability, specialized use, privacy, or regulation and can also be categorized based on intermediation and third-party services. New functionalities, such as personalized medication or health profile analytics, are merged under the concept of digitomics.

## Ethical and Legal Considerations

Currently, much personal health data are either owned or managed by intermediaries who have the right to decide how personal health data should be used and maintained, often without meaningful oversight or authority from individuals themselves. Unfortunately, the rights currently held by those intermediaries may fall well short of what is required to guarantee authentic, secure, and transparent management of personal health data. This situation worsens sharply when considering the use of personal health data beyond the healthcare organization. Instead of being used only for the primary interests of the patients, personal health data might be exploited for various secondary interests without their consent. For example, personal health data are seen as a valuable source of research data and they are used to construct AI training datasets. However, this type of usage creates value from someone's personal health data without sharing that value with them. The value derived from patients' own personal health data is often not properly recognized, and in many cases, patients even inadvertently pay for the process they incur. Accordingly, blockchain technology can provide an assurance mechanism and a platform offering a transparent and trustworthy solution to help individuals take back control of their personal health data, manage their data more securely, and access universal compensation that is meant to benefit all those involved in maintaining the data collectively.

The recent privacy scandal involving the use of personal health data, which were originally stored in a popular electronic health recorder, raises concerns about the widespread adoption of electronic health recorders. It is imperative for stakeholders of blockchain-enhanced EHR to appreciate various ethical and legal considerations to guard against misuse. At the heart of the issue is control, which includes who should own, manage, and have control over personal health data, as well as how to protect sensitive health information. In other words, the question is how personal health data are being used and maintained, and the fairness and transparency people can expect about what happens to their data.

## SUMMARY

This study surveys the key facets of blockchain technology and thoroughly discusses the challenges of existing EHRs and potential remedies proposed from prior research on integrating blockchain technology into EHRs. Blockchain provides two primary types of records: a block and a blockchain. With the support of cryptography and digital signatures, the patient has exclusive control over their health record management. A smart contract, as an electronic program or contract, can be implemented on blockchain to enforce the function of coding and thereby boost the support of healthcare blockchain applications. Blockchain technology provides an efficient and useful mechanism of health data management, where patients can permit for electronic health data recording, tracking, and monitoring through secure and trusted access. This approach has the potential to empower patients to govern their personal healthcare information under a defined data control policy. Future trends of applying blockchain technologies to healthcare data management are discussed to form reflective discussions and assist healthcare administrators, practitioners, or researchers who desire to know more about blockchain technologies for EHRs.

The key facets of blockchain technology in addressing various EHR-related issues and proposing a future direction for enhancing EHR systems are highlighted. One of the key factors attributing to the inexorable growth of several technology realms is the convergence of technologies. Blockchain and EHRs are established, yet independent technologies in their own right and are applicable to entirely different industries. The proposition of studying the application of blockchain technology to EHR systems and researching it at such an early stage is certainly novel. Healthcare professionals have individually suggested a few potential healthcare scenarios in which the collaboration of blockchain with health data management could pose a technological breakthrough.

## CONCLUDING REMARKS

In conclusion, the adoption of blockchain technology in healthcare, particularly in the management of electronic health records, offers a promising solution to existing challenges related to data security, privacy, and access control. By integrating blockchain protocols, healthcare providers can ensure that patient data is managed efficiently while maintaining its confidentiality. This decentralized and secure approach will foster greater trust among users, ultimately improving the quality of healthcare services.

## CONSENT FOR PUBLICATON

The authors confirm that written consent has been obtained from all participants mentioned in this study for the publication of their information, where applicable.

## ACKNOWLEDGEMENT

The authors would like to express their gratitude to all contributors who assisted in the research and development of this work. Special thanks to the healthcare institutions and blockchain experts whose insights greatly contributed to the chapter's findings.

## REFERENCES

[1]    M. Hölbl, M. Kompara, A. Kamišalić, and L. Nemec Zlatolas, "A systematic review of the use of blockchain in healthcare", *Symmetry (Basel),* vol. 10, no. 10, p. 470, 2018.
[http://dx.doi.org/10.3390/sym10100470]

[2]    T. McGhin, K.K.R. Choo, C.Z. Liu, and D. He, "Blockchain in healthcare applications: Research challenges and opportunities", *J. Netw. Comput. Appl.,* vol. 135, pp. 62-75, 2019.
[http://dx.doi.org/10.1016/j.jnca.2019.02.027]

[3]    Teli, Tawseef & Masoodi, Faheem, "Blockchain in healthcare: Challenges and opportunities", *SSRN Electron. J.,* 2021.
[http://dx.doi.org/10.2139/ssrn.3882744]

[4]    S. Namasudra, G.C. Deka, Ed., *Applications of blockchain in healthcare.* Springer: Singapore, 2021.
[http://dx.doi.org/10.1007/978-981-15-9547-9]

[5]    M.S. Arbabi, C. Lal, N.R. Veeraragavan, D. Marijan, J.F. Nygård, and R. Vitenberg, "A survey on blockchain for healthcare: Challenges, benefits, and future directions", *IEEE Commun. Surv. Tutor.,* vol. 25, no. 1, pp. 386-424, 2023.
[http://dx.doi.org/10.1109/COMST.2022.3224644]

[6]    M. Prokofieva, and S.J. Miah, "Blockchain in healthcare", *AJIS Australas. J. Inf. Syst.,* vol. 23, 2019.
[http://dx.doi.org/10.3127/ajis.v23i0.2203]

[7]    H. Taneja, H. Mangal, and N. Agarwal, "Detection of Covid-19 using cough sounds", *Full Length Article,* vol. 7, no. 2, pp. 79-99, 2022.

[8]    A. Kathar, S. Iyer, H. Taneja, and Y. Jadhav, "Early prediction of heart failure by using stacking classifier", *2024 MIT Art, Design and Technology School of Computing International Conference (MITADTSoCiCon),* pp. 1-8, 2024.
[http://dx.doi.org/10.1109/MITADTSoCiCon60330.2024.10575846]

[9]    P.D. Singh, G. Dhiman, and R. Sharma, "Internet of Things for sustaining a smart and secure healthcare system", *Sustain. Comput.,* vol. 33, p. 100622, 2022.
[http://dx.doi.org/10.1016/j.suscom.2021.100622]

[10]   P.D. Singh, R. Kaur, G. Dhiman, and G.R. Bojja, "BOSS : A new QoS aware blockchain assisted framework for secure and smart healthcare as a service", *Expert Syst.,* vol. 40, no. 4, p. e12838, 2023.
[http://dx.doi.org/10.1111/exsy.12838]

# CHAPTER 4

# Blockchain: The Challenges of Scalability and Their Solutions

**Amardeep Pandit¹, Sweeti Sah¹·\*, Shweta Sharma¹·\*, Ojasvi Singh¹, Gaurav Kumar¹** and **R. Sujithra Kanmani²**

*¹ Department of Computer Engineering, National Institute of Technology, Kurukshetra, Haryana, India*

*² School of Computer Science and Engineering, Vellore Institute of Technology, Chennai, Tamil Nadu, India*

**Abstract:** Blockchain technology offers incredible value and opportunity in delivering secured, decentralized transactions but faces significant challenges as it relates to scalability, which hinders adoption and use. As in the maturation of blockchain technology, challenges related to its scalability are important for latest technologies as they can affect scalability and efficiency. These types of challenges to scalability generally emerge through increased user and transaction volumes and cause losses in performance and efficiency as they pertain to a congested network, storage of data, and speed in processing time. Additionally, traditional consensus mechanisms, like proof of work, seamlessly create challenges as they pertain to amounts of computational power, and other resources allow allocation associated with work completion. As we can imagine, potential solutions have already emerged that help to mitigate overcoming these challenges. Solutions related to Layer 2 scaling, such as side chains or payment channels, add an alternative layer to the transaction applications and, theoretically, increase throughput and financially through decreased network congestion. Sharding, which splits the blockchain into smaller, more manageable segments, also improves operational efficiency. Moreover, advancements in consensus algorithms, including Proof of Stake and hybrid models, aim to boost scalability while optimizing resource use. This research explores the primary scalability challenges faced by blockchain systems. It reviews the cutting-edge solutions being developed to improve their performance, ensuring that blockchain technology can effectively support the increasing demands of a decentralized digital world.

**Keywords:** Architecture, Blockchain, Consensus, Decentralization, Ethereum, Forking, Interoperability, Latency, Ledger, Management, Network.

---

\* **Corresponding authors Sweeti Sah and Shweta Sharma:** Department of Computer Engineering, National Institute of Technology, Kurukshetra, Haryana, India; E-mails: sweetisah3@nitkkr.ac.in; shweta.sharma@nitkkr.ac.in

**Monica Bhutani, Monica Gupta, Kirti Gupta, Deepali Kamthania & Danish Ather (Eds.)**
**All rights reserved-© 2025 Bentham Science Publishers**

# INTRODUCTION

Blockchain, an increasingly popular form of decentralized innovation, has a bright future ahead of it. The concept of the blockchain data structure was introduced by Haber and Stornetta and received serious consideration when Nakamoto developed a light bulb idea concerning a cryptocurrency-based payment system in 2008 with Bitcoin [1, 2]. Blockchain technology has been proven to be a transformative force within various industries by offering decentralized, secure, and transparent transaction mechanisms. Even after numerous plus pointers, there too exist some of the major hindrances, one of which is scalability challenges. These challenges have been marked out to be very common during the expansion in user base and transaction volume. This work brings views on the scaling challenges that slow down blockchain performance, specifically focusing on transaction throughput, latency, and storage capacity.

The "Blockchain Trilemma" represents one of the major challenges for cryptocurrencies and their widespread use and acceptance. It is a trade-off presented by a blockchain that attempts to achieve an ideal balance of decentralization, security, and scaling at the same time [3]. Blockchain technology is distinguished by several fundamental features that collectively ensure its security, transparency, and reliability. The most prominent feature is data immutability, which guarantees that once data is documented on the blockchain, it cannot be changed without the unanimous agreement of all nodes in the network. This is because each node retains an entire copy of the ledger, making any unauthorized changes practically impossible. The decentralized qualities of blockchain further reinforce its security, as there is no central authority, government, or individual controlling the system. Instead, a network of nodes collectively manages all transactions, ensuring that the system remains robust and resistant to manipulation [4]. Fig. (1) depicts the characteristics of blockchain.

# LITERATURE REVIEW

As blockchain technology grows in importance, addressing its scalability challenges becomes crucial. Key issues such as data storage, throughput, and monetary costs are central, with off-chain methods emerging as promising solutions to enhance performance. The impact of consensus methods and blockchain types on scalability is significant, while privacy and security remain critical factors that influence both scalability and system efficiency, highlighting the need for further research in these areas [5].

| Faster Settlement | Census | Distributed |
|---|---|---|
| Decentralized | Immutable | Unanimous |
| | Secure | |

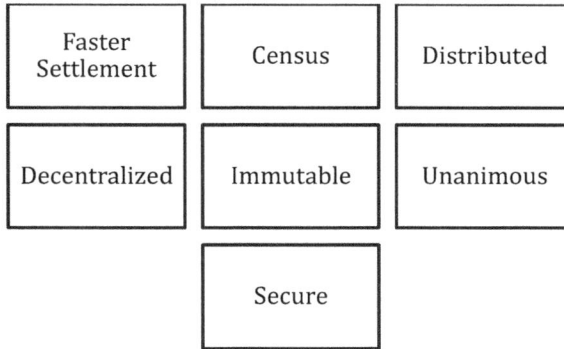

**Fig. (1).** Characteristics of blockchain.

Blockchain technology has the potential to transform peer-to-peer (P2P) energy trading but faces challenges related to scalability, security, and decentralization. While blockchain offers several advantages, issues such as complex smart contracts, infrastructure changes, and regulatory hurdles complicate adoption. Economic concerns, including cryptocurrency volatility, add further challenges. Collaboration among energy companies, regulators, and technology providers, along with the development of regulatory frameworks, is essential for secure and scalable blockchain-based energy trading. Recent advancements in blockchain technology have focused on optimizing performance metrics [6]. A notable approach has achieved a 40% deduction in transaction verification times and a 60% advancement in throughput through efficient Delegated Proof of Stake (DPoS) consensus, Interplanetary File System (IPFS), and sharding. The model also illustrated cost-effectiveness with a 30% deduction in gas prices and a 25% decline in ether consumption. Scalability has been improved by 70% as compared to traditional Proof of Work (PoW) systems. Future improvements focused on refining consensus mechanisms, advancing cryptography, and implementing dynamic sharding. Cross-chain interoperability could further enhance the interconnectedness of decentralized ecosystems [7].

The amalgamation of blockchain and AI in healthcare holds transformative potential for improving data efficiency and patient care. However, challenges persist in scalability (19%), interoperability (24%), and power consumption (28%). Sharding appears promising for scalability, despite its complexity and potential security risks, while forking could lead to network fragmentation. Future research focused on improving consensus mechanisms to enhance transaction performance and power efficiency, sustaining the broader adoption of blockchain technology in healthcare [8]. As blockchain networks expand, managing data size and storage becomes increasingly challenging. Techniques such as design modification, pruning, sharding, ephemeral, zk-SNARK, off-chain, and historical data repositories address different needs. Ephemeral and light client solutions are well-suited for resource-constrained devices while sharding and pruning are effective for specific data management and security requirements. Successful implementation depends on matching these techniques to the blockchain's demands. Future research aims to develop frameworks that utilize machine learning or context-aware methods to automatically choose the most appropriate data management techniques [9]. Scalability is a challenge for blockchain technologies like Bitcoin and Ethereum, which impact performance due to long transaction times and excessive effort. Various solutions are being sought to address these issues. Some solutions may use data science technologies such as distributed computing and parallel processing, which can distribute and process large data across multiple systems. Blockchain can also be combined with AI to increase scalability [10]. Integrating blockchain and IoT faces some problems, such as blockchain technology like Ethereum can process transactions 12 to 15 per second, while IoT devices need more time. Another challenge is privacy since blockchain data distribution is public. We can use zkLedger as a solution because it is established on zero-knowledge cryptography [11]. The major scalability issue in blockchain technology is due to the use of consensus algorithms to ensure the total order of the chain of blocks. However, a much high scalable blockchain technology can be acquired if a more relaxed order can be manipulated.

Setchain - a novel distributed concurrent data type may greatly improve scalability. Some results show that Setchain is orders of magnitude faster than consensus-based ledgers. Setchain executes a grow-only set with epochs and tolerates Byzantine server nodes [12]. The core problem that blockchains are still struggling to provide the same level of latency and throughput as centralized financial systems lies in the inefficiency of consensus protocols. Layer 2 protocols can be a solution to this. Layer 2 protocols may process micro-transactions with sub-second latency and reduced fees, which may allow blockchains to scale [13]. An innovative approach to address the problem of scalability of blockchain technology can be an adaptive restructuring of Merkle trees. Merkle trees are the fundamental components of blockchain architecture. They are reliable for providing data integrity and fostering efficient assurance processes. By this adaptive restructuring of these trees, we can significantly reduce the path length for validation processes, which will enhance the efficiency and scalability of blockchain systems [14].

## BLOCKCHAIN SCALABILITY

Scalability for blockchain denotes the ability of a blockchain-based network to process a high volume of transactions within a reasonable timeframe. In addition, as blockchain networks evolve, they must contend with scalability where not only the system can scale with an increased volume of users, transactions, and nodes but also in decentralized ecosystems, which necessarily and inherently violates centralization with the transactional processing distributed amongst multiple nodes. Further, in case of distributed and decentralized systems, the transaction processing is distributed between multiple nodes, which introduces multiple levels of scalability challenges and issues since, inherently, scalability challenges exist in decentralized blockchain architectures. For a centralized system processing transactions, a managed authority governs the system in itself to process transactions; however, for blockchain-based systems, a consensus process is utilized, which includes party consensus from everyone involved in the transaction to agree on the validation and documentation of a transaction. Often, the communication and consensus requirements to validate and document these transactions can take time and financial resources.

## Block Size and Transaction Throughput

A core performance metric for blockchain systems is transaction throughput, expressed as Transactions Per Second (TPS). As the count of users and transactions grows; typically, the throughput of the network decreases or degrades the efficiency of processing these transactions. For instance, Bitcoin has a TPS of about 7, whereas Ethereum has one of about 15. The slow TPS performance is rooted in the consensus used and limitations such as block size that are built into these systems [15]. In case of Bitcoin, scalability concerns have arisen over whether or not Bitcoin should use a larger block size to accommodate more transactions. The increase of a block size will lead to a greater TPS due to more transactions being accommodated within a single block, while network-wide use will tackle centralization when smaller nodes are unable to regularly mine blocks that lead to compensation, which is an integral part of the Bitcoin ecosystem. The diminishing TPS of Bitcoin and enormous space-related problems can potentially be solved—the potential scalability burden handled through distributed decentralized peer-to-peer (P2P) distribution of files as well as the use of the Twin-Ledger—allowing us to decisively deal with scaling. To be explicit, we can utilize the PoW consensus to simultaneously deal with aspects of scalability and large consensus, decentralized consensus, and security without compromise [16].

Bitcoin, the largest cryptocurrency, faces challenges with extended verification times and high transaction fees, hindering its adoption. To address this, a new optimization problem aims to increase transaction count per cycle by adjusting block size and creation time without compromising network stability. A learning framework using machine learning, specifically Extreme Gradient Boost (XGB), has been developed to predict optimal block sizes based on nine Bitcoin network attributes. The XGB has achieved 63.41% accuracy in predicting block sizes, leading to improvements: a 12.29% increase in block size, a 13.45% rise in transaction fees, and a 14.88% boost in transaction support rate and count, thus reducing wait times and improving adoption [17].

**Network Latency and Propagation**

Network latency refers to the delay in communication between nodes in a blockchain network. As the count of nodes increases, the time required to propagate transactions and blocks across the network also increases. High latency can lead to forks, where different parts of the network temporarily disagree on the state of the blockchain, reducing overall efficiency.

Latency can also be a lag in an instruction or signal. There can be a lag in either the processing of data or its transmission. Another form of latency is disk latency and network delay. Latency in a network is the portion of time it takes for data to travel from its origin to its conclusive destination [18]. Users don't want to wait and will leave a service the moment they start experiencing delays. The same holds true for Web3 and the metaverse. In fact, time-to-finality is even additional critical for the metaverse as real-time, immediate interactions are a condition for an immersive user experience. While TPS may be utilized for estimating the performance of a blockchain, it is only one-half of the equation. Comparable to how Internet connections need both high bandwidth and low latency to deliver speedy services. Likewise, blockchain platforms require both high throughput and low transaction latency to do the identical; for example, Bitcoin. While it is stated to have 7 TPS, the lowest time it takes for a transaction to be achieved is 10 minutes, as one block is constructed every 10 minutes on Bitcoin; for *e.g.*, if only the person performing a transaction on the Bitcoin network, it would still take 10 minutes for the transaction to be documented on the chain. Likewise, Ethereum sits at around 20 TPS, but its latency is around 12 seconds [19].

Blockchain technology is increasingly used across various sectors due to its capability to meet diverse necessities. Evaluating the performance and attributes of blockchain platforms is essential before deployment, and blockchain simulators are a key tool for this. However, existing simulators face limitations in scalability, event scheduling, time control, and simulation accuracy.

To manage these issues, this chapter introduces a new Blockchain Simulator established on Event-Layered Architecture (BSELA). BSELA features a modular design with an event-driven scheduling mechanism that enhances efficiency, stability, and maintainability in simulations. It also includes a time improvement mechanism based on event rounds to improve accuracy and handle real-time demands. Validation of BSELA through comparisons with existing simulators and experimentations on network connectivity, block propagation, and INV message propagation shows significant improvements in data transfer efficiency and security. The simulator's flexibility and scalability are confirmed, making it a valuable tool for blockchain research [20].

## Storage and Data Management

With developing hardware requirements comes the need for specialized tasks to run blockchain nodes as a provider. Infura and Alchemy are two main tasks keeping nodes for Web3 protocols and developers. However, they centralize blockchain records inside the hands of specialized service vendors, developing a single point of failure (SPOF) and privacy risks [21].

As blockchain networks grow, the measure of the blockchain ledger also improves. Storing and managing this ever-growing amount of data poses challenges for nodes with limited storage capacity. If the ledger becomes too large, it may discourage new users from joining the network, leading to centralization and reducing the prevailing security of the blockchain.

The combination of blockchain technology with cloud storage and also the Internet of Things (IoT) complicates data management in Decentralized Applications (DApps). Because blockchain is not efficient at handling large quantities of data, efficient management of both on-chain and off-chain data will become important. Space reservation methods in cloud storage are a reasonably inexpensive approach, and off-chain data replication can help mitigate single points of failure. In addition to all of these considerations, optimizing data management in Blockchain-based Internet of Things (BIoT) environments has not been fully analyzed yet. Our work organizes a model of the BIoT environment by utilizing cloud storage as well as blockchain on a peer-to-peer network. It employs the asynchronous benefit actor-critic algorithm alongside data packing, space reservation, and data reproduction, resulting in a rapid convergence algorithm and improved performance. The proposed approach will enhance the process of scaling up, create a more secure and reliable blockchain IoT network, and develop a system that will manage data efficiently [18].

The Internet of Medical Things (IoMT) directs the computing ability or capability of connecting smart medical devices and medical applications to healthcare systems through the Internet, and it opens up a wealth of challenges on privacy, security, scalability, and data accessibility. This chapter addresses the challenges outlined within a proposed blockchain model for Secure Data Management Framework (SDKMDF) to enhance user trust, secure sharing, and communication of patient data accessibility and scalability. The BSDMF framework handles assured data management in part by employing blockchain data management across private servers, implantable medical devices (IMDs), and a cloud-based server. Experimental data indicates that the BSDMF framework achieves notably high-performance metrics, an average of 97.2% accuracy, and a moderate trust value of 98.3%, exceeding previous approaches to sharing and communicating patient data [22].

## SOLUTIONS OF BLOCKCHAIN SCALABILITY

Blockchain's decentralized nature ensures peer-to-peer transactions without central control but results in slower speeds compared to centralized systems. Two main scaling approaches are used to address this. Various solutions have been suggested and implemented to manage the scalability challenges in blockchain technology. These solutions can be extensively categorized into Layer 1 (on-chain) and Layer 2 (off-chain) solutions. Layer 1 scaling enhances the base blockchain protocol but faces challenges such as high storage costs and latency. Layer 2 solutions, including roll-ups and payment channels, handle transactions off the mainnet, significantly boosting throughput and efficiency. This chapter explores both Layer 1 and Layer 2 scaling methods, emphasizing that Layer 2 protocols offer superior performance in managing blockchain transactions [23].

### Layer 1 Solutions

Layer 1 blockchain functions as the base layer, enabling the flow of decentralized interactions without the need for centralized authority. Examples include Bitcoin, which introduced decentralized ledgers, and Ethereum, which provides smart contracts and decentralized applications, to Solana, which was designed for scalability with increased throughput and low latency. Layer 1 protocols provide a consistent execution and interaction layer of basic activity on-chain and serve as the foundation to enable decentralized activities [23]. Layer 1 solutions implicate making adjustments to the blockchain protocol itself to enhance scalability. Significant Layer 1 solutions include the following:

### *Sharding*

Sharding is a procedure of splitting up the blockchain network into slighter partitions called shards that allow for processing transactions at the same time which dramatically increases throughput. For example, Ethereum 2.0 is an example of a blockchain network that utilizes sharding to attain better scalability. Sharding partitions splits up a blockchain into smaller, parallelized pieces of data termed shards. In a traditional blockchain, every node hosts and processes the entire blockchain. Meanwhile, in sharding, the node host processes a specific portion of the blockchain data that belongs to its assigned shard exclusively. Therefore, through this process, the holistic burden placed on every node is reduced - thus increasing transaction throughput for better network optimization as a whole [30]. Cryptographic primitives: Layer 1 blockchains utilize cryptography algorithms to layer both protection and transparency. Data stored on layer 1 blockchains are hosted across millions of subscribed nodes - the practical application of cryptography permits the ability to balance security with transparency in regard to trust in that type of ecosystem. One example is in Bitcoin, where a use case is made based on a private key and a public key. Each user of Bitcoin has its private key that is transformed into a public key through a cryptographically reversible, meaning only the user who possesses the private key can sign and send funds to other public addresses, while the public key is used to send and make Bitcoin transactions [24].

## Increasing Block Size

Employing an increased block size of the blockchain increases the count of transactions per block and hence improves the throughput or volume of transactions. An example of transaction throughput of blockchain technology is Bitcoin, which has a block size of about 1 MB, or around 2000 transactions. However, if the block size is increased to around 8 MB, throughput would also increase to about 16,000 transactions in parliament [24].

## Updating Consensus Mechanism

A consensus mechanism can be changed to an energy-efficient consensus mechanism. An example of this would be Ethereum's updated protocol, which changed from a PoW consensus mechanism to an energy-efficient PoS, improving the transaction process [25].

The inclusion of new consensus algorithms specifically the Proof of Authority (PoA) and Byzantine Fault Tolerant (BFT) algorithms used within the structure of blockchain technology for effective purposes essentially reduces the time and resources required to reach consensus and do this more efficiently. More effective consensus algorithms will allow for more scalability, as they have abundant throughput and much less wait time [26].

## Configuration of Block Size during Transactions

Some blockchains are configured in such a way as to create the users experience a more dynamic consensus mechanism, specifically a dynamic block size, essentially allowing users to change the block size, increasing throughput when transaction volume requires it. Essentially, users, *i.e.* other networks, can have the capacity or configuration to increase transaction volume during high transaction volume and lower configuration during less transaction volume [27].

## Layer 2 Solutions

Layer 2 solutions are solutions that are constructed on top of pre-existent blockchain protocols so that the solutions may perpetuate transactions off-chain while yet benefiting from the protection and distributed nature of the blockchain protocol. Layer 2 allows scalability and privacy improvements to blockchain applications while preserving the security and decentralization assumed in blockchain protocols. Layer 2 operates off-chain, indicating that Layer 2 processes blockchain transactions outside of the Layer 1 blockchain while using the blockchain's secure, correct, and auditable account of transactions. Moreover, Layer 2 solutions seek to enhance performance metrics, such as transaction throughput and latency, without a loss of attack resilience obtained originally from the blockchain. Layer 2 solutions are landmark innovations that seek to ameliorate the scalability and effectiveness of blockchain networks exploited initially for Bitcoin and Ethereum [34]. By transporting tasks from a primary blockchain (Layer 1) to an external layer (Layer 2), Layer 2 can process transactions quickly, reduce costs, and produce the value inherent in the network, *i.e.*, security and decentralization. Some examples of Layer 2 solutions are:

Off-chain computations entail offloading extensive resource tasks to applications outside of the blockchain environment while retaining only the resulting verification within the blockchain accounting, often with proofs of integrity supporting the results. This can reduce calculation and storage needs by restricting these functions to off-chain environments. Rollups serve as an illustrative example, whereby transactions take place off-chain and are only minimum evaluations/summaries of collectively assessed transactions, *i.e.* a full list of transactions becomes a pre-development score on the blockchain. Optimistic rollups assume without argument correctness except in problem cases, while ZK uses cryptographic proofs as evidence of end result validity [26].

### *Payment Channels*

Payment channels allow users to conduct numerous off-chain transactions after locking funds on the blockchain. Only the beginning and ending balances are recorded on the blockchain, reducing fees and transaction times. These channels can form networks, enabling payments through intermediaries for a fee. The Lightning Network for Bitcoin and Raiden Network for Ethereum are key standards of this solution.

### *State Channels*

State channels enable parties to perform multiple transactions off-chain, with the final state being recorded exclusively on the blockchain. This decreases the load on the main blockchain and enriches transaction throughput. The Lightning Network for Bitcoin and the Raiden Network for Ethereum are illustrations of state channel implementations [27].

## *Sidechains*

Sidechains run parallel to a main blockchain, connected *via* a two-way peg that allows asset transfers between chains by locking and unlocking funds. This enhances scalability by offloading specific tasks to the sidechain. The Liquid Network, anchored to Bitcoin, and Polygon, a framework for building Ethereum sidechains, are prominent examples. Polygon also supports its cryptocurrency, MATIC. State channels improve blockchain scalability by enabling off-chain interactions for smart contract updates, reducing the need for frequent on-chain transactions. Inspired by payment channels, which handle off-chain payments, state channels extend this concept to arbitrary state transitions while maintaining blockchain security [27].

## *Cross-Chain Exchanges*

Cross-chain exchanges facilitate asset transfers between different blockchains without central intermediaries using methods like atomic swaps or specialized protocols. Cosmos and Polkadot are leading examples, with Cosmos using zones connected *via* the Inter Blockchain Communication (IBC) protocol and Polkadot employing a central relay chain and the Cross-chain Message Passing protocol (XCMP). Both sustain their native cryptocurrencies, ATOM and DOT, respectively. Cross-chain communications facilitate the transfer of data and assets between different blockchains without relying on central intermediaries. This is achieved using methods like atomic swaps and specialized protocols. Key aspects of these communications include cross-chain consensus, which ensures that information from one blockchain is trusted by another, and properties like safety, liveness, and atomicity, which guarantee that transactions are valid, processed eventually, and either fully completed or rolled back [28].

## Hybrid Solutions

A hybrid blockchain model proposed in recent research combines the strengths of both Layer 1 and Layer 2 approaches. This model is particularly beneficial for banks and e-commerce platforms. It features personal blockchains for user privacy and a global blockchain for server-to-server communication. Private miners, controlled by business policies, handle the addition of new blocks and hashing, significantly reducing power consumption and enhancing efficiency. By integrating centralized and decentralized elements, this hybrid solution offers the simplicity of traditional systems with the scalability and fault tolerance of blockchain technology. Hybrid combines the elements of both. For example, Ethereum's evolution to Ethereum 2.0 involves a combination of sharding (Layer 1) and rollups (Layer 2) to achieve greater scalability [29].

Fig. (**2**) illustrates the key features of each phase in the Ethereum 2.0 upgrade process, emphasizing the layered approach from the initial Casper FFG activation to the final scaling enhancements [5].

**Phase 0**
- Casper FFG activation
- Beacon Chain Launch

**Phase 1**
- Deployment of 64 PoS Shards
- Ethereum 1.0 Integration

**Phase 2**
- Enabling Smart Contract Execution
- Cross-Shared Communication

**Hybrid**
- Personal Blockchain and Global Blockchain
- Enhanced Efficiency

**Fig. (2).** Flow chart showing the major features of each phase.

## CASE STUDIES

This section explores real-world case studies of blockchain networks that have implemented scalability solutions. By analyzing the successes and challenges faced by these networks, we can achieve insights into the effectiveness of different scalability approaches.

### Ethereum 2.0 and Sharding

Ethereum 2.0 represents a new development in the competency of Ethereum, adopting blockchain technology to solve some of the problems that have affected the efficiency of the network, including scalability. Sharding was the main remedy that was realized in Ethereum 2.0. It is a method that partitions the blockchain into shorter but feasible sections comprehended as "shards." Since sharding enables the network to parallelize the transactions, it recreates an important role in the enhancement of the throughput of the network [30].

As a matter of fact, sharding is being carried out in phases. The first one is called Phase 0, which includes the Beacon Chain, which helps control the shards and consensus. The subsequent phases relate to the execution of shard chains and the PoW to PoS shifts [31].

An example of sharding is test networks, most of which include Medalla and Pyrmont test networks. Both these test nets have been proven to do sharding by processing hundreds of thousands of transactions per second, while the first version of the Ethereum network could only process tens of transactions per second. The use of such solutions is not without difficulty and includes cross-shard communication and network security [30, 32].

The raising of Ethereum to Ethereum 2.0 has already witnessed some level of accomplishment; the initiation of the Beacon Chain in December 2020, jointly with the continual growth of the validators involved in the network. It is still ongoing even today that all of these aspects are in the process of being implemented. Wide-ranging as the advances are being made, it is the steps that have been accomplished so far that offer a positive look into the future of scalable blockchain networks [32]. After moving to PoS, the energy usage was lowered by 99.95%, and decreased average block times to 12 seconds [33].

Fig. (**3**) displays the estimated energy consumption in TWh/yr for Ethereum for several products and industries [34].

## Bitcoin Lightning Network

The best Layer 2 solution is the Bitcoin Lightning Network, which aims to contribute to the solution of the Bitcoin scalability problem by means of off-chain processing of fast and low-cost transactions. In contrast to the ordinary on-chain operations, making the execution of each activity in the BTC network recorded on the blockchain, several operations, when performed under the Lightning Network protocol, are combined and completed off-chain, which also minimizes the load on the primary Bitcoin chain [34].

Bitcoin inception includes a low TPS throughput; as a network, Bitcoin can manage only about 7 TPS. This has a limitation of congestion in the network and high transaction fees, particularly when traffic is very high, and hence, it can hamper the growth of Bitcoin as an open system of payment across the globe. The Lightning Network solves these problems in a way that payment channels are made between users where transactions can happen instantly and at a very minimal fee. But, for each of these Pairwise Payment Paths, only the Open and the Closed states are logged on the Blockchain and not the individual transactions within the channels constituted by such states [34, 35].

There has been growth in the public and businessmen's awareness of the use of the Lightning Network as an efficient solution to Bitcoin's scalability issues. However, there are still some barriers in front of BCs, such as the security in the network and the liquidity. The factors that require constant attention include the amount of money needed in the channels to perform operations and ensure the channels against attacks. Nonetheless, it is pertinent to note that Lightning Network can likely be regarded as a breakthrough in Bitcoin's scalability problem, which opens more opportunities for inexpensive and fast transactions worldwide [34, 35].

## Layer 2 Solutions in Practice: Case Studies

Second-tier solutions like the Bitcoin Lightning Network have many advances in the rehabilitation of the scalability problem in blockchain networks. The proposed solutions, specifically state channels, sidechains, and roll-ups, serve as layers on top of already-existing blockchain networks that aggregate and settle simultaneously, resulting in increasing transactions and decreasing latency while preserving security and decentralization. There are many solutions that can be effectively compared to Raiden Network, a solution that operates off-chain on the Ethereum network as a scaling solution for micropayments. Like Lightning Network's off-chain solution for Bitcoin, Raiden Network utilizes payment channels to enable instant and low-cost settlements. As a result of performing the transaction operations from the Ethereum Network, the Raiden Network helps in increasing the TPS and decreasing the latency time. In this case, Raiden has been most applicable in decentralized applications that demand large numbers of transactions, specifically gaming and DeFi applications. However, similar to the LN, the Raiden Network also has issues concerning security, liquidity, and usage [26, 36].

The Optimistic Rollups and ZK-Roll Ups use cases on Ethereum are another key example. Many of these roll-up solutions consolidate a number of transactions and provide a bundle that is put on the main blockchain. It reduces the frequency with which participants must transact on the Ethereum network, which increases the Ethereum network's overall throughput without compromising its current security and decentralization. Optimistic Roll-Ups can be used, for instance, as the scalability solution for various DeFi platforms; however, they need to undergo the challenge phase to check the reality of the transactions. ZK-Rollups, as opposed to this, employ zero-knowledge proofs to verify the transactions in real time and are even more secure and faster [28, 29]. The two cases clearly illustrate how Layer 2 solutions solve the scalability issues that occupy the implementation of blockchain networks. However, each of these solutions also has its disadvantages and problems, but the further evolution and implementation of these technologies are vitally important for the practical introduction of blockchain in different spheres.

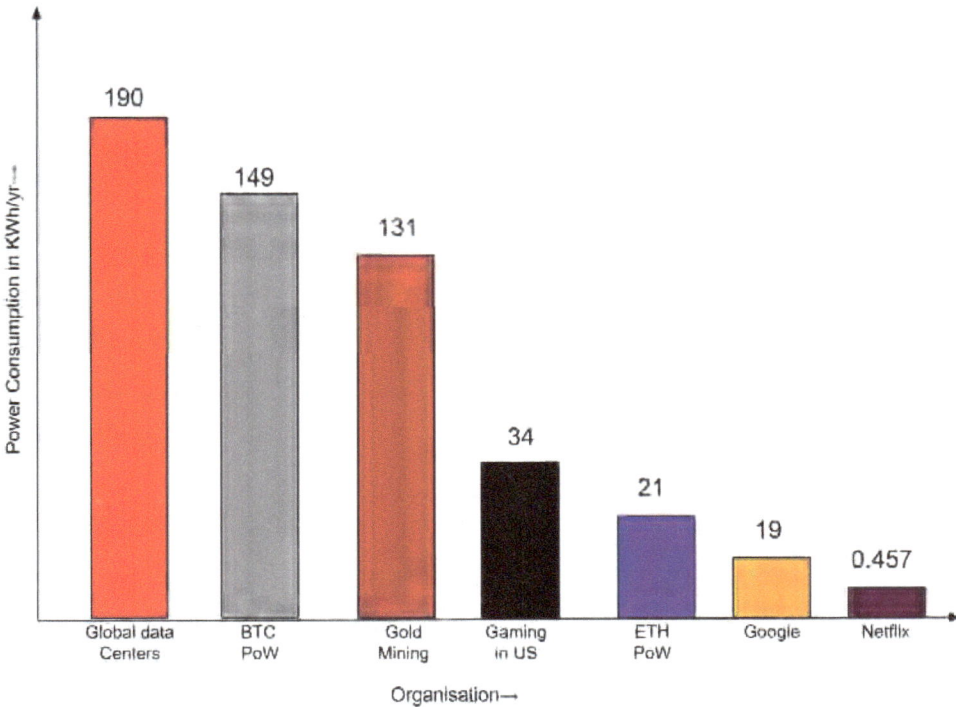

**Fig. (3).** Annual energy consumption in TWh/yr.

## METHODOLOGY

In this section, we clarify the methodology applied in this research study, including the design of the research, data sources, and analysis process, to better understand the elements that comprise blockchain technology and the consensus mechanisms behind decentralized and autonomous organizations. Our aim is to be as participatory and transparent as possible and to show how we collaborated with and engaged existing research in this area.

### Research Framework

We conducted a comparative analysis of Bitcoin and Ethereum, chosen for their widespread use and distinct consensus mechanisms – Bitcoin's PoW and Ethereum's PoS. The mixed-methods approach combined qualitative and quantitative analyses to explore each platform's social, economic, and environmental impacts, as well as network efficiency. Fig. **(4)** shows the workflow of the proposed work.

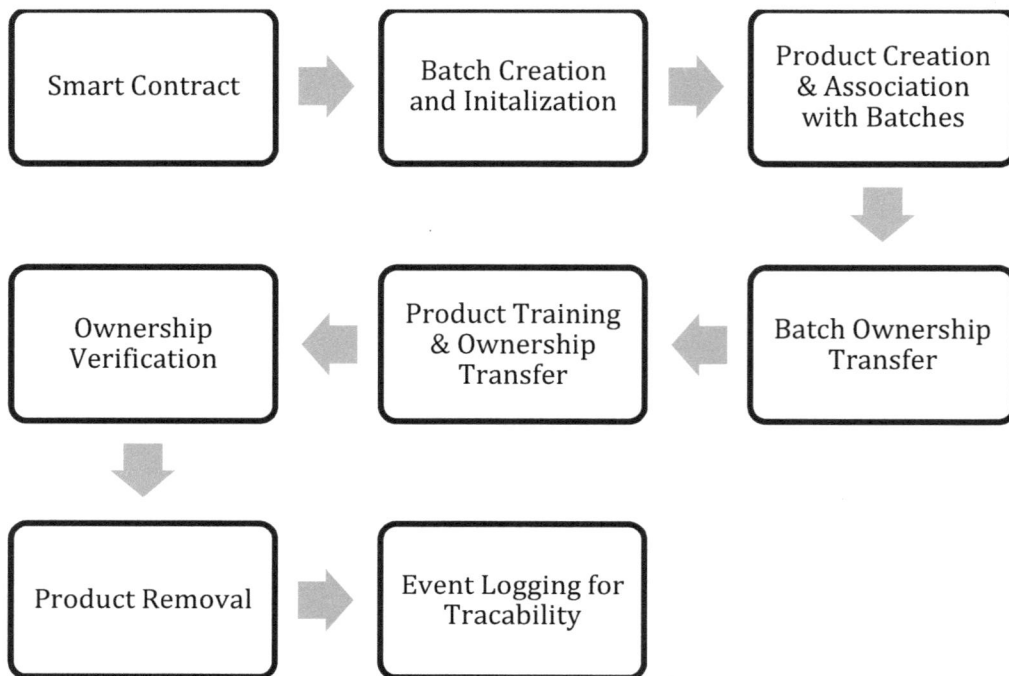

**Fig. (4).** Flowchart structure with scalability integration.

## Data Collection

Data is gathered from Blockchain Explorers, where platforms like Blockchain.info and Etherscan provide detailed transaction and block data. The second source is Public Dataset, where historical data from Kaggle and GitHub offered transaction timestamps and block sizes. Also, Application Programming Interface (APIs) where real-time data was sourced from Bitcoin Core and Ethereum JSON-RPC APIs for current transaction processing times and network conditions [22, 17].

## Analytical Techniques

Descriptive Statistics: To summarize average block sizes, transaction volumes, and processing times.

Comparative Analysis: To contrast Bitcoin's PoW with Ethereum's PoS on metrics such as validation times and energy consumption.

Performance Benchmarking: To assess scalability and security through transaction times, network load effects, and simulated attacks.

## Consensus Mechanisms Analysis

PoW: Analysing block sizes, mining rewards, and environmental impact for Bitcoin.

PoS: Evaluating validator performance, block validation times, and staking rewards for Ethereum.

## Scalability and Security Assessment

Transaction Processing Times: Under varying network conditions.

Security: Through smart contract audits and simulations of common attack vectors.

## Ethical Considerations

Our study focused on publicly available data, emphasizing data integrity and objective reporting to ensure valid and unbiased findings.

## EXPERIMENTAL RESULTS

Baseline blockchains have low TPS, high latency, and high storage needs due to each node maintaining the entire blockchain history. Sharding improves TPS and reduces storage per node by splitting the network into parallel shards, though latency remains moderate due to inter-shard communication. State channels achieve very high TPS, as shown in Table **1**, and very low latency by processing transactions off-chain with minimal on-chain storage requirements. Sidechains offer high TPS and moderate latency with their independent blockchains but require moderate storage as each sidechain maintains its ledger. Overall, state channels excel in TPS, and latency, sharding, and sidechains provide significant improvements over baseline blockchains, and the latter suffers from the highest storage demands and latency. Table **2** shows the average gas cost before and after optimization techniques.

Hence, it can be concluded that the findings of the experimentation indeed prove that the proposed blockchain-based supply chain management system can indeed scale efficiently while indeed being cost-optimized and stable. Various aspects implemented in the current system's design and relevant optimizations allow the system to expand scalability to accommodate growing quantities of transactions and, therefore, make it applicable to large-scale SCM.

**Table 1. Impact of Scalability solutions on the performance of blockchain.**

| Scalability Solutions | TPS (Transaction Per Second) | Latency (Seconds) | Storage Requirement (GB) |
|---|---|---|---|
| Baseline Blockchain | 10 | 60 | 100 |
| Sharding | 1000 | 10 | 200 |
| State Channels | 500 | 1 | 50 |
| Sidechains | 200 | 30 | 80 |

**Table 2. Average gas cost before and after optimization techniques.**

| Smart Contract Functionality | Average Gas Cost (Pre-Optimization) | Average Gas Cost (Post-Optimization) |
|---|---|---|
| Token Transfer | 50,000 | 21,000 |
| Simple NFT Minting | 100,000 | 60,000 |
| Complex DeFi Interaction | 500,000 | 300,000 |

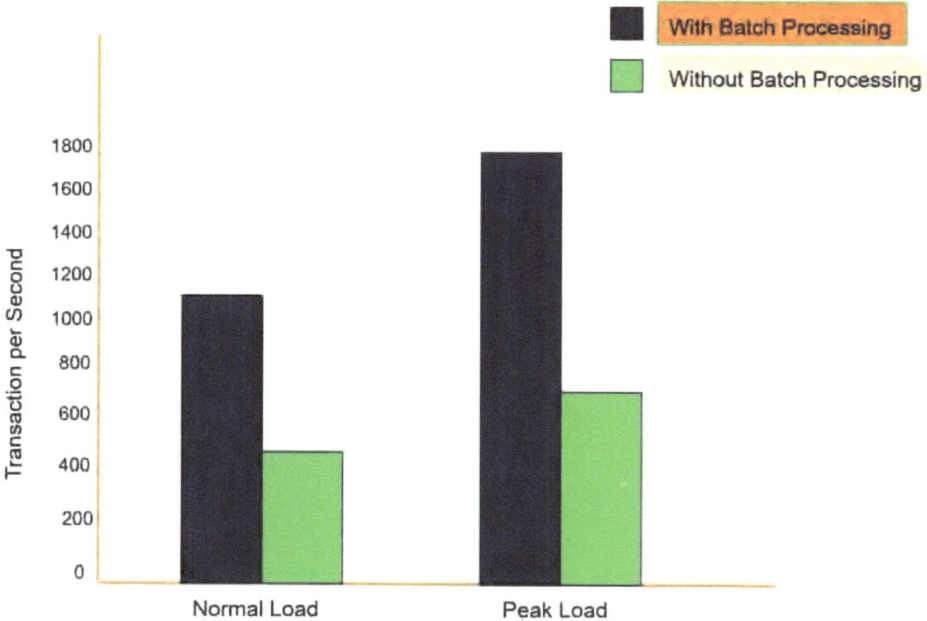

**Fig. (5).** Throughput improvement with batch processing.

The combination of batch processing and parallel transaction handling can significantly increase the throughput of a system in high-demand situations, as shown in Fig. (**5**). In batch processing, many transactions are analyzed together and aggregated into a single batch, minimizing the per-transaction overhead, and resulting in better utilization of system resources. The batch processing technique enables quicker assessment of transactions, especially of larger volume batches, through reduced latency rates and maximizing processing efficiency. Parallel transaction processing identifies workloads and distributes transaction processing across various units or threads, allowing transaction workloads to be executed simultaneously across as many systems as demand requires, which mitigates the latency and overhead present in sequential transaction processing. Overall, these two techniques allow transaction volume to increase dramatically while providing more versatility in structure, and transacting operations in a robust and low-latency context during heavy demand.

## CONCLUSION

As a blockchain network grows and the user and transaction volume increase, it must expand additional resources on transaction processing and validation while still maintaining throughput in the long run. Unlike conventional systems of significant scale, blockchain networks are never intended to be capable of fully scaling while also preserving decentralization and security. In this chapter, we have examined the previous situation of the two biggest covered blockchain systems of Bitcoin as representative of PoW blockchains, while Ethereum had made the transition to PoS blockchain systems. Through considerations of transaction processing times, time to validate the block, and the environmental concerns with PoW and PoS systems, the significance collectively showed the advantages, disadvantages, and trade-offs of PoW and PoS systems.

The abundant and relevant data accessible through blockchain explorers, public datasets, and real-time APIs enabled a comprehensive assessment of the efficiency, scalability, and security of the network. By employing descriptive statistics, comparative analysis, and performance benchmarks, it was possible to analyze the differences in both PoW and PoS advantages and disadvantages under different situations. Layer 2 options, such as Lightning Network or Plasma, are another viable approach that applies scalability as they allow users to transact off-chain as well as interrupt the blockchain into many sequential, smaller pieces that can process transactions in parallel. This transaction speed is on the transaction streams but it does not fully alter the base blockchain transaction stream. However, it tends to add complexity with some risk of centralization. A blockchain secure system has not been fully developed at this point; even with evolving consensus mechanisms as well as PoS that can maintain security to some degree while simultaneously using less energy, full scaling in a secure way is still a work in progress. Advancing and financing the new technologies will reveal how developments may reach utilization in many different industries and domains that follow social constructs of decentralization and transparency. While blockchain may provide opportunities for benefit in some cases, a sustainable balance of outcome-effectiveness, scalable environment, and secure technology must occur before scaling is used.

## FUTURE SCOPE

The future of blockchain scalability lies in the continued development and adoption of innovative technologies. This means that further improvements and applications of blockchain scalability will occur in the future as well. The following points explore some of the emerging shifts and potential future for blockchain scalability.

**Quantum Computing:** Even though quantum computing is relatively new, it may change the way that blockchain scalability can be addressed due to better problem-solving capabilities compared to classical computers.

**Cross-Chain Interoperability:** Given the chance of new many-blockchain formation, the smooth interaction between these different networks will be essential for scalability. Such projects as Polkadot as well as Cosmos are among the pioneers of creating protocols for inter-chain communication.

**DeFi and Layer 3:** In combination with DeFi applications, there is an increasing need to continue decentralizing as much as possible. To accommodate more complicated DeFi communities, Layer 3 solutions that are based on Layer 2 are currently being discussed intensively.

## REFERENCES

[1]     C. Warmke, "What is bitcoin", *Inquiry (Oslo),* vol. 67, no. 1, pp. 25-67, 2024.
        [http://dx.doi.org/10.1080/0020174X.2020.1860123]

[2]     D. Khan, L.T. Jung, and M.A. Hashmani, "Systematic literature review of challenges in blockchain scalability", *Appl. Sci. (Basel),* vol. 11, no. 20, p. 9372, 2021.
        [http://dx.doi.org/10.3390/app11209372]

[3]     G.M.A. Al-Kafi, G. Ali, and J.T. Faiza, "SHBF: A secure and scalable hybrid blockchain framework for resolving trilemma challenges", *Int. J. Inf. Technol.,* vol. 16, pp. 3879-3890, 2024.

[4]     Siva Raja Sindiramutty, Noor Zaman Jhanjhi, Chong Eng Tan, Navid Ali Khan, Abdalla Hassan Gharib, and Khor Jia Yun, "Applications of blockchain technology in supply chain management", *Cybersecurity Measures for Logistics Industry Framework,* pp. 248-304, 2024.

[5]     M. Rashid, I. Rasool, N.A. Zafar, and H. Afzaal, "Formal modeling and verification of justification and finalization of checkpoints in ethereum 2.0 beacon chain", *IEEE 1st Karachi Section Humanitarian Technology Conference, Tandojam,* pp. 1-6, 2024.
        [http://dx.doi.org/10.1109/KHI-HTC60760.2024.10481930]

[6]    S. Alam, M. Shuaib, W.Z. Khan, S. Garg, G. Kaddoum, M.S. Hossain, and Y.B. Zikria, "Blockchain-based Initiatives: Current state and challenges", *Comput. Netw.,* vol. 198, p. 108395, 2021.
[http://dx.doi.org/10.1016/j.comnet.2021.108395]

[7]    P.M. Dhulavvagol, S.G. Totad, A.M. Anagal, S. Anegundi, P. Devadkar, and V.S. Kone, "ShardedScale: Empowering blockchain transaction scalability with scalable block consensus", *Procedia Comput. Sci.,* vol. 233, pp. 432-443, 2024.
[http://dx.doi.org/10.1016/j.procs.2024.03.233]

[8]    S. Garg, R. Kumar Kaushal, N. Kumar, and E. Boonchieng, "Exploring research challenges of blockchain and supporting technology with potential solution in healthcare", *Int. J. Comput. Digit. Syst.,* vol. 15, no. 1, pp. 487-507, 2024.
[http://dx.doi.org/10.12785/ijcds/160138]

[9]    Y.I. Alzoubi, and A. Mishra, "Techniques to alleviate blockchain bloat: Potentials, challenges, and recommendations", *Comput. Electr. Eng.,* vol. 116, pp. 109216-109216, 2024.
[http://dx.doi.org/10.1016/j.compeleceng.2024.109216]

[10]   Manjula K Pawar, Prakashgoud Patil, "Logistic regression for enhancing scalability of blockchain system", *Procedia Comput. Sci.,* vol. 252, pp. 146-153, 2025.
[http://dx.doi.org/10.1016/j.procs.2024.12.016]

[11]   A. Dhar Dwivedi, R. Singh, K. Kaushik, R. Rao Mukkamala, and W.S. Alnumay, "Blockchain and artificial intelligence for 5G-enabled Internet of Things: Challenges, opportunities, and solutions", *Trans. Emerg. Telecommun. Technol.,* vol. 35, pp. 1-19, 2021.

[12]   M. Capretto, M. Ceresa, and A. Antonio Fernández Anta, "Russo, and César Sánchez", *Improving Blockchain Scalability with the Setchain Data-type,* vol. 3, pp. 1-27, 2023.

[13]   T.A. Alghamdi, R. Khalid, and N. Javaid, "A survey of blockchain based systems: Scalability issues and solutions, applications and future challenges", *IEEE Access,* vol. 12, pp. 79626-79651, 2024.
[http://dx.doi.org/10.1109/ACCESS.2024.3408868]

[14]   O. Kuznetsov, D. Kanonik, A. Rusnak, A. Yezhov, O. Domin, and K. Kuznetsova, "Adaptive Merkle trees for enhanced blockchain scalability", *Internet of Things,* vol. 27, pp. 101315-101315, 2024.
[http://dx.doi.org/10.1016/j.iot.2024.101315]

[15]   J. Xu, S. Peng, C. Wang, and X. Jia, "PuffChain: A dynamic scaling blockchain system with optimal effective throughput", *IEEE Trans. Netw. Sci. Eng.,* vol. 11, no. 3, pp. 3199-3212, 2024.
[http://dx.doi.org/10.1109/TNSE.2024.3363880]

[16]   S. Reno, S.H. Priya, G.M.A. Al-Kafi, S. Tasfia, and M.K. Turna, "A novel approach to optimizing transaction processing rate and space requirement of blockchain *via* off-chain architecture", *Int. J. Inf. Technol.,* vol. 16, no. 4, pp. 2379-2394, 2024.
[http://dx.doi.org/10.1007/s41870-023-01685-x]

[17]   M. Monem, M.T. Hossain, M.G.R. Alam, M.S. Munir, M.M. Rahman, S.A. AlQahtani, S. Almutlaq, and M.M. Hassan, "A sustainable Bitcoin blockchain network through introducing dynamic block size adjustment using predictive analytics", *Future Gener. Comput. Syst.,* vol. 153, pp. 12-26, 2024.
[http://dx.doi.org/10.1016/j.future.2023.11.005]

[18]   Y.P. Tsang, C.K.M. Lee, K. Zhang, C.H. Wu, and W.H. Ip, "On-chain and off-chain data management for blockchain-internet of things: A multi-agent deep reinforcement learning approach", *J. Grid Comput.,* vol. 22, no. 1, p. 16, 2024.
[http://dx.doi.org/10.1007/s10723-023-09739-x]

[19]   H. Xiaoge, Y. Hongbo, C. Bin, W. Yongsheng, C. Qianbin, and Z. Jie, "Joint optimization of energy consumption and network latency in blockchain-enabled fog computing networks", *China Commun.,* vol. 21, no. 4, pp. 104-119, 2024.
[http://dx.doi.org/10.23919/JCC.fa.2023-0488.202404]

[20]   B. Cui, and Y. Hu, "BSELA: A blockchain simulator with event-layered architecture", *Future Gener.*

*Comput. Syst.,* vol. 151, pp. 182-195, 2024.
[http://dx.doi.org/10.1016/j.future.2023.09.034]

[21]  J.W. Heo, G.S. Ramachandran, A. Dorri, and R. Jurdak, "Blockchain data storage optimisations: a comprehensive survey", *ACM Comput. Surv.,* vol. 56, no. 7, pp. 1-27, 2024.
[http://dx.doi.org/10.1145/3645104]

[22]  A. Abbas, R. Alroobaea, M. Krichen, S. Rubaiee, S. Vimal, and F.M. Almansour, "Blockchain-assisted secured data management framework for health information analysis based on Internet of Medical Things", *Pers. Ubiquitous Comput.,* vol. 28, no. 1, pp. 59-72, 2024.
[http://dx.doi.org/10.1007/s00779-021-01583-8]

[23]  I.S. Rao, M.L.M. Kiah, M.M. Hameed, and Z.A. Memon, "Scalability of blockchain: a comprehensive review and future research direction", *Cluster Comput.,* vol. 27, no. 5, pp. 5547-5570, 2024.
[http://dx.doi.org/10.1007/s10586-023-04257-7]

[24]  A. Hafid, A.S. Hafid, and M. Samih, "Scaling blockchains: A comprehensive survey", *IEEE Access,* vol. 8, pp. 125244-125262, 2020.
[http://dx.doi.org/10.1109/ACCESS.2020.3007251]

[25]  J. Xie, F.R. Yu, T. Huang, R. Xie, J. Liu, and Y. Liu, "A survey on the scalability of blockchain systems", *IEEE Netw.,* vol. 33, no. 5, pp. 166-173, 2019.
[http://dx.doi.org/10.1109/MNET.001.1800290]

[26]  J. Eberhardt, and J. Heiss, "Off-chaining models and approaches to off-chain computations", *Proceedings of the 2nd Workshop on Scalable and Resilient Infrastructures for Distributed Ledgers,* pp. 7-12, 2018.
[http://dx.doi.org/10.1145/3284764.3284766]

[27]  L.D. Negka, and G.P. Spathoulas, "Blockchain state channels: A state of the art", *IEEE Access,* vol. 9, pp. 160277-160298, 2021.
[http://dx.doi.org/10.1109/ACCESS.2021.3131419]

[28]  Y. Yang, F. Bai, Z. Yu, T. Shen, Y. Liu, and B. Gong, "An anonymous and supervisory cross-chain privacy protection protocol for zero-trust IoT application", *ACM Trans. Sens. Netw.,* vol. 20, pp. 1-20, 2023.
[http://dx.doi.org/10.1145/3582555]

[29]  H. Marar, and R. Marar, "Hybrid blockchain", *Jordanian Journal of Computers and Information Technology,* vol. 6, no. 0, pp. 1-9, 2020.
[http://dx.doi.org/10.5455/jjcit.71-1589089941]

[30]  V. Buterin, "A next-generation smart contract and decentralized application platform", *Ethereum White Paper,* vol. 3, pp. 1-36, 2014.

[31]  G. Wood, "Ethereum: A secure decentralised generalised transaction ledger", *Ethereum Project Yellow Paper,* vol. 151, pp. 1-32, 2014.

[32]  R. Vinayakumar, M. Alazab, K.P. Soman, P. Poornachandran, A. Al-Nemrat, and S. Venkatraman, "Deep learning approach for intelligent intrusion detection system", *IEEE Access,* vol. 7, pp. 41525-41550, 2019.
[http://dx.doi.org/10.1109/ACCESS.2019.2895334]

[33]  H. Berenjestanaki, Mohammad, H. R. Barzegar, N. El Ioini, and C. Pahl, "An investigation of scalability for blockchain-based e-voting applications", *International Congress on Blockchain and Applications,* vol. 778, pp. 134-143, 2023.
[http://dx.doi.org/10.1007/978-3-031-45155-3_14]

[34]  V. Pawar, and S. Sachdeva, "ParallelChain: a scalable healthcare framework with low-energy consumption using blockchain", *Int. Trans. Oper. Res.,* vol. 31, no. 6, pp. 3621-3649, 2024.
[http://dx.doi.org/10.1111/itor.13278]

[35]  E. Blockchain, "Ethereum Blockchain," *Kaggle Datasets,* 2020. Available from:

https://www.kaggle.com/datasets/bigquery/ethereum-blockchain (Accessed on: June 2024).

[36]   Available from: https://github.com/bitcoin/bitcoin

# CHAPTER 5

# A Study on Blockchain Ecosystem Security

**Mukta[1,*], Shiksha Kumari[1], Sherry Verma[1]** and **Mohit Mittal[1]**

*[1] School of Engineering and Technology, Sushant University, Gurgaon, Haryana, India*

**Abstract:** Blockchain Technology is one of the leading technologies nowadays. Its unique characteristics such as decentralized, trackable, temper-resistant, reliable, and secure nature make the blockchain popular from the traditional database. Blockchain has a wide range of applications, not limited to the financial sector but also includes healthcare, education, supply chain management, smart cities, and the transportation sector, providing more features and resilience. Various academic and industry sectors have adopted this technology for the past few years due to its secure nature. However, due to its wide range of applicability in both sectors, security has become one of the major issues that need to be addressed. This article focused on the security in the blockchain ecosystem containing the various components integrating to form the blockchain network. The study includes security regarding blockchain protocol, smart contracts, nodes, wallets, decentralized applications, and collaboration between the different elements of the blockchain ecosystem.

**Keywords:** Block, BlockChain attacks, Blockchain, Consensus algorithm, Cryptocurrency, Cryptography, Hacking, Hyperledger, Intellectual property, Ledger, Weaponization.

## INTRODUCTION

Satoshi Nakamoto coined the term Bitcoin having its underlying technology blockchain. Bitcoin is the first cryptocurrency used for funds transfer between the two parties without the involvement of any centralized authority. The blockchain ecosystem is growing faster with the rapidly growing technology. Blockchain is a distributed ledger that records all the transactions and provides transparency, trust, and security to all the transactions. Blockchain [1] is a more secure and resilient technology, making it popular in diverse applications, but it is not completely secure and cyber-attack proof.

Industries are adopting this technology for the future perspective to attract more customers and other business enterprises, but security is a major concern that

* **Corresponding author Mukta:** School of Engineering and Technology, Sushant University, Gurgaon, Haryana, India; E-mail: mukta.mittal2006@gmail.com

**Monica Bhutani, Monica Gupta, Kirti Gupta, Deepali Kamthania & Danish Ather (Eds.)**
**All rights reserved-© 2025 Bentham Science Publishers**

needs to be focused on. People participating in blockchain networks can be faulty leading to a serious impact on security which violates the law and regulations of the country. Blockchain technology has many applications, including the financial area, the Internet of Things (IoT), education, supply chain management, transportation, and the medical sector. It is more secure and resistant compared to traditional databases having features such as, **i)** there is no single point of failure, which makes this network more resilient; **ii)** the consensus algorithm ensures the security and integrity of the network on the same state of the network; **iii)** provides the immutability and integrity due to permanent storage of the data in the ledger. Having a lot of benefits of using blockchain technology, still it suffers from various security challenges [2] that need to be addressed: 51% of attacks are one type of attacks in which the attacker gains access to more than 50% of computational power; another one is the smart contract, which a self-executing code runs on the blockchain leading to security threats due to bugs or flaws in the code. Moreover, blockchain uses cryptographic techniques to secure data thus poor key management is also one of the security threats. This article highlights the security threats and challenges of the blockchain ecosystem.

## COMPONENTS OF BLOCKCHAIN

With the advent of technology and the internet, several methods were proposed and used for storing data. However, each had limitations of security and accountability in case of fraud or data leakage. Blockchain ecosystem on the other hand is a combination of several interconnected entities that collaborate in providing the most secure and decentralized way of storing critical information. All the components work together to ensure the coherence of the data. It has transformed the mode of financial transactions in the most secure, unanimous way, especially in an untrustworthy medium. Additionally, transparency adds a trust factor amongst the users of this niche technology. One needs to understand the participants of this complex yet safe network to harness the power of this new-age approach. Fig. (**1**) depicts the composition of the blockchain network.

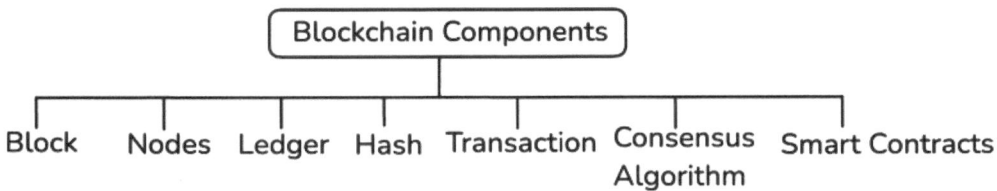

**Fig. (1).** Blockchain ecosystem [3].

## Block

It is a kind of immutable data structure that stores records of several transactions. Every block has a unique ID called hash and it also stores the previous block's hash, thereby creating a chain of blocks we address as blockchain. Each block consists of a body and a block header. The body has records of transactions. The header is the very crucial part of the block. It has metadata comprising a Merkel root, a predecessor block hash, a timestamp, and nonce. This metadata ensures linear and cryptographic linkage of blocks in the chain. Merkle root [4] is a single hash value for all the transactions in the block. It is created by pairing and hashing all the transactions. This process ensures that tampering in any transaction will result in a different hash value and Merkle root for the block. Therefore, any tampering in the transaction can be easily detected. It makes the integrity and verification of all transactions simpler by not requiring every single transaction to be checked. The timestamp tells the time the block was created. Fig. (2) depicts the chain of blocks along with the structure of the individual block. The hash of the predecessor block is used to compute the current block's hash by hashing the metadata present in the header of the block. The first block has no parent block and is called a genesis block.

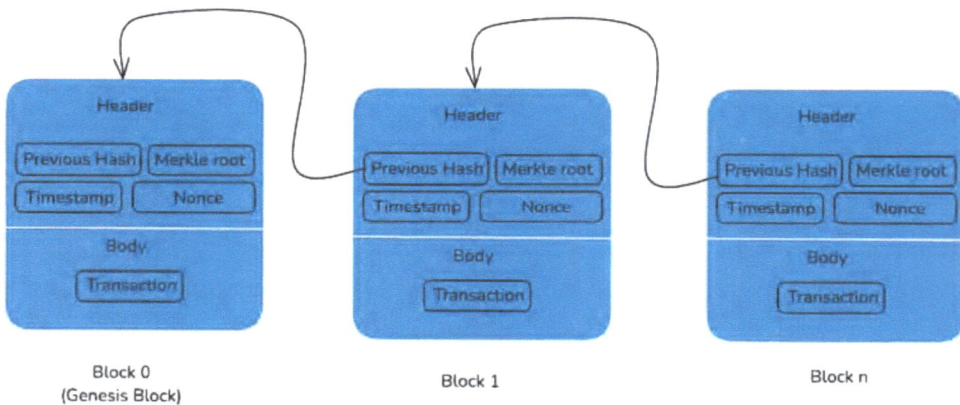

**Fig. (2).** Structure of block in blockchain [5].

## Nodes

They are the most basic structure of the network. Nodes are the devices that run specialized blockchain software and record the transactions' history as digitized and secure ledgers. The fundamental responsibility of the node is to authenticate the legitimacy of each group of transactions called block. They are also accountable for assigning unique identification to each transaction, making them different. It further shares the transaction history or the ledger with other nodes to enforce transparency and decentralization in the system. Without the nodes, this network will have functionality like that of a centralized secure system, which is still vulnerable to attacks without any accountability [6].

Different nodes have different functionalities as per the system's requirements. Some nodes store the entire copy of the chain of blocks, whereas some only store records. The nodes storing all the chain blocks are termed full nodes. They have a robust mechanism for validating and verifying all the transactions in the blockchain. They can accept or reject a transaction based on some consensus algorithms.

The Bitcoins network has full nodes. Full nodes can be categorized into miners, validators, and authority nodes. Miners are the nodes that need to solve complex mathematical puzzles to validate a transaction using the Proof-of-Work consensus algorithm. On the other hand, the validators are the nodes that keep their money at stake to validate the transaction and get rewarded for it. They work under the Proof-of-Stake consensus algorithm. The authority nodes are full nodes with the task of authorizing new nodes in the blockchain. On the other hand, light nodes or simplified verification nodes store only the header and Merkel root information of the blocks, reducing the storage requirement and making them more computationally efficient than full nodes. These nodes interact with the full nodes to get the details of transactions. Their use cases are found in the system having limited bandwidth like mobile wallets. Fig. (**3**) shows the main types of nodes in the blockchain network.

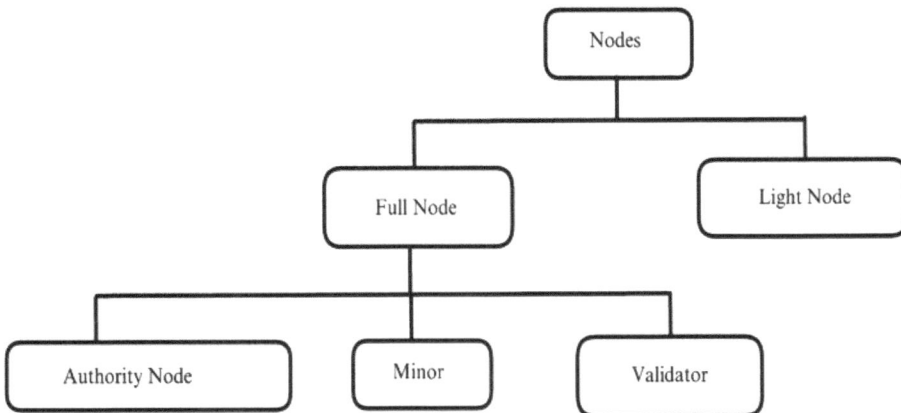

**Fig. (3).** Types of node.

## Consensus Algorithm

The centralized systems have a single point of authority to whom all the network participants should agree. This results in a lack of transparency and a prone system. In the blockchain ecosystem, which is inherently a decentralized network, a mechanism is required for each participating peer to agree on the state of the digitized and distributed ledger. Such a mechanism is termed a consensus algorithm through which every party in the network reaches a consensus on the status of the blockchain. The main objective of these algorithms is to ensure consistency of the values in the network. Each node in the distributed system should see the blockchain's most updated and current value. The consensus method also ensures that peers have equal authority and control over the ecosystem. The network remains tamper-proof and resilient to failures due to several consensus mechanisms. Fig. (**4**) shows one of the most widely used consensus algorithms [7].

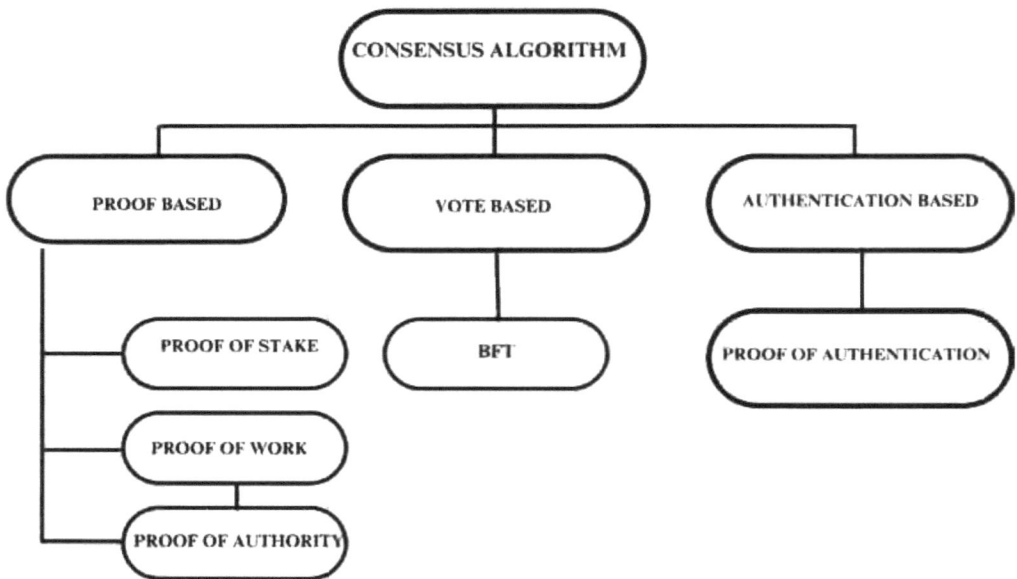

Fig. (**4**). Consensus algorithm.

## *Proof of Work (PoW)*

Proof of work is the blockchain ecosystem's original and most fundamental consensus mechanism. It was first proposed in 1993 [8] and then by the originator of blockchain, Satoshi Nakamoto who also created Bitcoin [9]. In Pow, the nodes were primarily termed miners. Miners compete with each other to solve a complex mathematical problem called the hash. The one who solves it broadcasts it amongst the peer miners for approval. Once validated, the winning node can add a block to the network. The winning node also gets rewarded with recently produced cryptocurrency. The difficulty level of solving the hash keeps increasing dynamically according to the number of blocks mined. PoW involves users' initiation of transactions. The network nodes validate these transactions based on the valid digital signature, the permissible amount of money, *etc.* Once the transactions are verified, the miners (nodes) club them into blocks. After this, the competing miners follow the hit-and-trial method to find a random nonce value. They keep trying with different nonce values and hash it with other information of the block to generate a hash. The hashing is done by using a cryptographic hash function. Once the miners find a hash that matches the difficulty level, they broadcast the newly created block into the group. If the block gets the maximum voting, it gets added to the blockchain. In return, the rewards are given to the miner. Fig. (**5**) demonstrates the working of PoW. This approach ensures decentralization, security, and coherence of the data. However, it is not computationally efficient as it requires more computation power to solve the complex puzzle. More sustainable and energy-efficient approaches were suggested later.

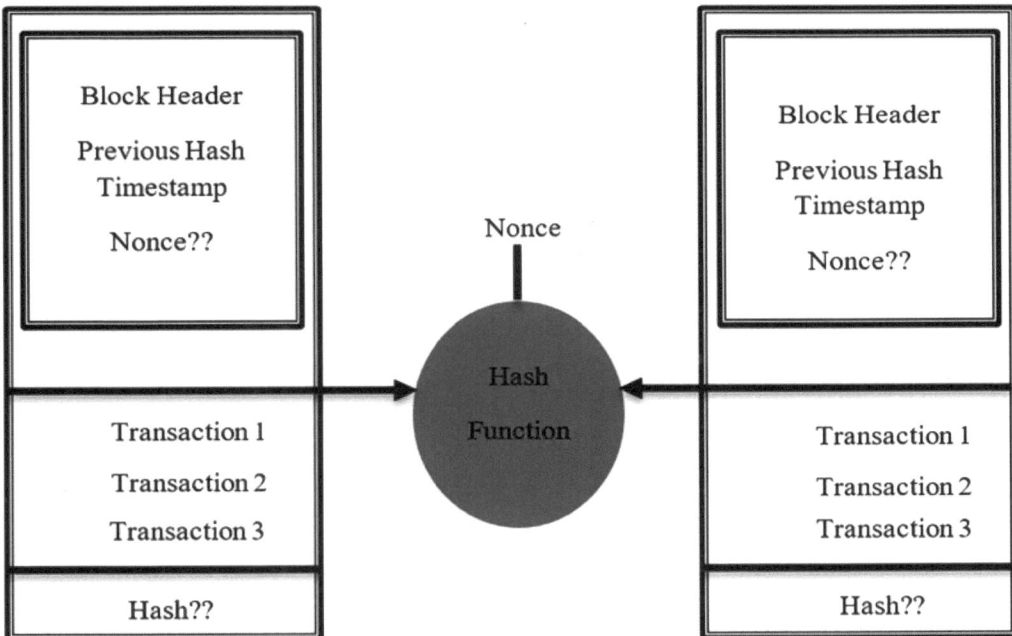

**Fig. (5).** PoW (Proof of Work).

## PoS

Proof of Stake is an energy-efficient and scalable alternative to PoW. It was first proposed by King and Nadal in 2012 [10]. In this approach, the nodes often termed validators put their cryptocurrency at stake to validate the transactions and propose the addition of a new block. It does not require computationally heavy mining work as in the case of proof of work. The system picks up the validator based on random selection and the money they have put on stake. This approach incentivizes the validators as their stake is at risk if they act maliciously. Once the validators are chosen, the new block is proposed. Other validators then validate this block. If the proposed block gets a reasonable number of consensuses, it gets added to the blockchain. The validator in turn gets rewarded with the transaction fee. The next block then contains the current block's hash, continuing the blockchain chain. This approach ensures security and integrity as the validator risks losing his stake if he allows fraudulent transactions. So, he acts honestly. However, PoS can result in a centralized system if the validators have much to put at stake and the ones who do not have anything have a lesser chance to participate in this consensus algorithm. Ethereum 2.0 implements PoS.

## Delegated Proof of Stake (DPoS)

Delegated proof of stake is a variant of PoS primarily proposed to address the drawback of PoS [11]. This approach does not require all the validators to participate rather few nodes termed delegates or witnesses engage in the process. The delegates must propose a new block, which is then broadcast amongst other token holders or shareholders. If most shareholders approve, the delegate earns its reputation in the network and thus gains shareholder votes. If a delegate approves a fraudulent transaction or tries to attack the network, it will lose its reputation, and shareholders will withdraw their votes, thereby replacing it with another delegate. This mechanism ensures decentralization and is faster and more efficient than the Proof of Stack (PoS). However, the limited number of delegates can later pose a risk of centralization. Also, vote buying can be another concern as delegates are purely elected based on the votes they get from token holders. It is also susceptible to one point of failure [12].

## Proof of Authority (PoA)

Proof of Authority is a consensus mechanism that has a predefined small set of nodes that can append a block in the blockchain and approve transactions [13]. These handfuls of nodes are trusted validators who are not incentivized because of their cryptocurrency but their identity and reputation. It is beneficial for enterprise or private blockchain systems as these networks require a more controlled way of validating and updating the digital ledger and securing the blockchain network. It requires less computation power and is not time-consuming. Further, it is faster than PoW and PoS. However, it is still vulnerable to attacks.

## Byzantine Fault Tolerance (BFT)

The Byzantine Fault Tolerance consensus method was proposed to deal with the Byzantine General's Problem [14]. This problem states that for any system to work, all the components should agree on the designed strategies. However, few of them are not in favor of it and may act maliciously. BFT enables the blockchain ecosystem to achieve a consensus on validating transactions and security even in adverse situations. A higher level of trust is required from many nodes to authenticate transactions. If these nodes disagree, then the transaction is rejected. Its drawback is its high dependency on many nodes for approval. If these nodes act suspiciously, the blockchain will not reach an agreement, hampering the network's integrity. There are a few variations that address the limitations of this approach. PBFT (The practical Byzantine fault tolerance) breaks down the validation process into several steps, ensuring that different nodes participate in each step [10]. Each node must validate the transaction before passing them for the next steps. If the network has "3f+1" nodes, then this approach can handle "f" dubious nodes. This robust approach ensures systems integrity even when few nodes are compromised.

## Proof of Authentication (PoAh)

Proof of Authentication is an extended and better version of PoA in terms of governance and security [15]. In this approach, a hierarchy of validators is defined. Higher-level validators are responsible for handling complex tasks and have more roles than lower-level validators. This approach adds an extra layer of security, scalability, and trust in the network. Any suspicious act by lower-level nodes can be checked by validators on the upper level.

## Smart Contracts

Smart contracts are self-executing agreements that are signed and stored as transactions in the blockchain network [16]. The terms and conditions of agreements are coded within this digital contract. The pre-conditions are in the form of if-then-else. They are executed automatically once the pre-defined instructions are fulfilled. They are coded in the specialized language as per the blockchain system. For example, Ethereum uses Solidity to create smart contracts. The participating parties must agree to this contract's conditions before its creation. Once agreed upon, the contract is made using any network-specific language and published on the blockchain, like any other transaction, for validation. Once approved, it becomes part of a digitized and distributed ledger.

These contracts are triggered when the pre-coded criteria are met like payment will be initiated as soon as some delivery is done. Their self-executing nature bypasses the need for third parties like banks for digital currency transfers. This paper contract reduces both the time and cost associated with traditional contracts. Furthermore, publishing them on blockchain decentralizes them, ensuring security and transparency. The tamper-proof features of blockchain ensure that they are immutable and less prone to fraud. Smart contracts are categorized into several categories based on their complexity and functionality. Fig. (**6**) depicts the types of smart contracts.

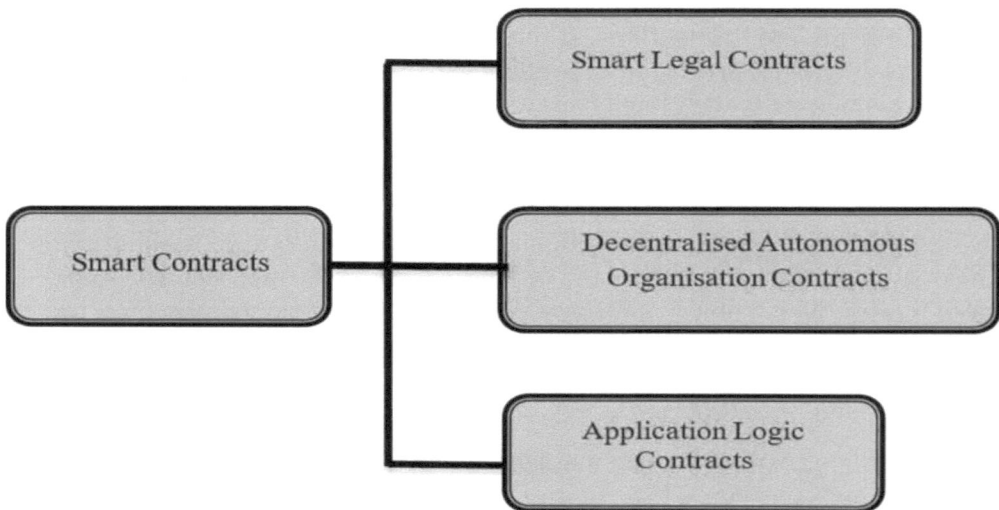

**Fig. (6).** Types of smart contract.

SLC (smart legal contracts) incorporates the legal structure into the code and ensures their autonomous enforcement without third-party intervention. The participants execute this contract through their digital signatures. Such agreements are executed once the pre-defined condition is fulfilled. If the party involved doesn't abide by the legality they may face legal actions. This kind of agreement has several use cases in legal and real estate areas, supply chain management, finances, insurance, and healthcare [17, 18]. DAO (Decentralized autonomous organization contract) is a unique contract that forms a group and makes decisions on its behalf. It provides voting rights to its members and there is no hierarchy in this blockchain-owned group. It has applications in domains where collective and collaborative decision-making is paramount.

Non-governmental organizations, investment fund groups, *etc.* are a few applications of this contract. Application logic contracts (ALC) are a special kind of contract signed between machines and other contracts [19]. They have application-based code that works with decentralized applications like decentralized gaming apps. The code syncs with other contracts and devices like the Internet of Things.

Despite several use cases and features of smart contracts, they still are vulnerable to security threats. A strong correlation between them and cryptocurrency makes them more vulnerable to attacks [18]. Its immutable nature makes it difficult to locate and fix the bug. They might need to interact with external sources also, and if in case that source turns out to be malicious, it can result in huge financial losses. Authors have reported losses amounting to $50 million in a decentralized autonomous organization contract breach. By 2022, 30 security breaches in smart contracts were reported. Recently in July 2024 Wazrix, a cryptocurrency platform suffered from losses of $235 million due to a cyberattack. These increasing trends of cyber-attacks highlight the need for a robust security system to be implemented in the blockchain ecosystem.

**Hash**

These functions make the blockchain data encrypted and thus secure. They take some data as input and convert it into a fixed-length hexadecimal number. They are robust, therefore, no two input values can have the same hash value. Also, breaching the hash to get the original data is complicated. Different types of hash functions are being used depending on the security level and efficiency required. Fig. (**7**) shows the most commonly used hash [20].

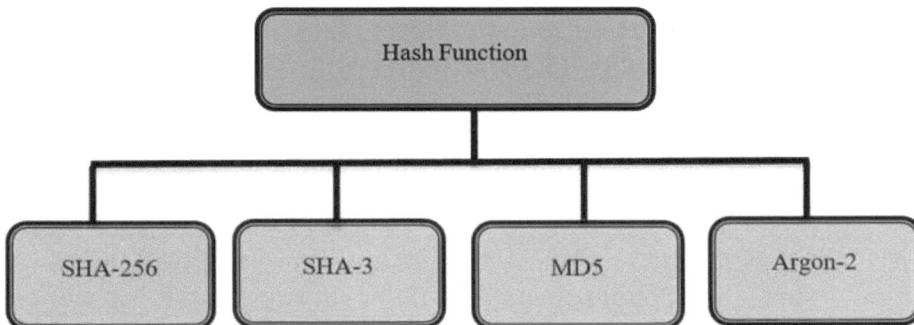

**Fig. (7).** Types of hash function [21].

## SHA-256

Is the most widely used cryptographic function across blockchain networks. It produces a 32-byte hexadecimal hash value and is used across PoW consensus algorithms. And SHA-3 is one of the secure hash algorithms released by NIST. It was designed to provide better security and robustness against attacks. Compared to SHA-256, it can produce variable length output depending on which variant is used.

## MD5

Message digest algorithm 5 produces a 16-byte hash value for any input given to it. It was proposed by Ronald Rivest to replace MD4. It was primarily designed to hash passwords, but it suffered from several collision attacks where the same hash value was produced for two different inputs. Argon-2 is a more secure hash algorithm that requires a significant amount of RAM to produce a hash value. This feature makes it more secure from attacks.

## LITERATURE SURVEY

Hassija *et al.* [22] made an attempt to identify security issues in drone applications. Additionally, the paper explores four emerging technologies: blockchain, software-defined networking, machine learning, and fog computing. However, a key limitation of this study is the lack of a comparative analysis.

The study conducted by the telecommunication engineering center [23] has highlighted the major risks associated with blockchain technology like 51%, DoS, Wallet management, Cybil attack, and eclipse attack. However, it does not offer any solution to mitigate these risks.

Thavasimuthu *et al.* [24] attempted to develop a blockchain-based architecture for various IoT applications, including industrial systems, smart factories, healthcare, medical data, smart grids, energy consumption, multi-WSN authentication systems, and blockchain for VANETs. However, the paper notes several issues with blockchain implementation in these applications and lacks a comparative analysis.

Li *et al.* [25] studied different types of blockchains and their associated security challenges, such as double-spending, 51% attacks, and smart contract exploitation. The authors proposed solutions to mitigate these risks using technologies like Hawk, Smart Pool, a quantitative framework, OYENTE, and Town Crier.

Loi *et al.* [26] proposed a smart pool system that leverages blockchain's efficiency, reduces intermediaries, and ensures the system is tamper-proof and auditable.

Loi *et al.* [27] introduced the symbolic analysis tool OYENTE for detecting bugs in Ethereum smart contracts in another paper. This research highlights how smart contracts can be adapted to predefined conditions to create a secure environment that prevents bugs or malicious attacks and explores how oracles can be integrated to connect smart contracts with off-chain data.

Moosavi *et al.* [28] discussed how blockchain technology can enhance security in IoT devices, healthcare, industry, and energy systems.

Taylor *et al.* [29] examined the application of blockchain in IoT, networks, and data storage, along with the associated risks. This paper also delves into the cryptographic methods used in IoT devices and related security concerns but does not provide solutions for integrating blockchain with other devices.

This paper evaluates seventeen types of IoT applications, focusing on blockchain-based security and privacy [30]. It assesses security requirements such as traceability, identity privacy, location privacy, non-repudiation, authentication, and system resilience against attacks using techniques like BAN logic, game theory, theoretical analysis, and the AVISPA tool.

Jiang *et al.* [31] have performed a comparative analysis of security in traditional transactions and blockchain by combining the AES cryptography algorithm and IPFS, applying verification methods like two-way authentication or zero-knowledge proof. It does not provide a verification solution for non-plaintext data.

## COINS OF BLOCKCHAIN

### Cryptocurrency

Blockchain applications are not only related to cryptocurrency; they can play into various sectors, offering businesses stability, and improving time management and cost savings. These applications can be categorized into different sectors, such as finance and healthcare. In the financial sector, cryptocurrency is the center of the blockchain application. Bitcoin, the first decentralized cryptocurrency, was introduced by Satoshi Nakamoto in 2009. It uses distributed data storing technology with immutability features named blockchain technology to build its data structure and transaction system, without relying on physical currency.

Transactions always need encryption. Cryptocurrency [32] transactions utilize highly secure encryption techniques to enable direct exchanges between buyers and sellers without third-party involvement. In these transactions, the sender digitally signs the message, which is then transmitted to the network and the receiver retrieves this message by the receiver's public key. Other users in the network verify the transaction.

## Smart Contract

Smart contracts [33] are programming code self-executing according to agreements between buyers and sellers, residing on a decentralized blockchain network. These contracts are particularly beneficial in business collaborations and maintain trust and stability between the parties without knowing each other. It also allows agreements to be embedded in the system, providing all facilities to all participants without third-party involvement. Ethereum, an open-source blockchain platform, hosts these smart contracts and provides a decentralized virtual machine to execute them using its native digital currency, ETH.

## Hyperledger

Hyperledger [34] is a private blockchain type. It is an open-source platform developed by a collaborative effort that includes leaders from finance, banking, supply chain, IoT, manufacturing, and technology. The Linux Foundation hosts it. Hyperledger does not rely on cryptocurrency; only authorized members can access this network. The transaction procedure in Hyperledger is a managed agreement written in the form of chain code (smart contracts). When a user initiates a transaction request in Hyperledger Fabric, it is processed with network validation and initiating chain code in a designated channel. The Hyperledger Fabric is used in client applications. To ensure privacy, the transaction process within the network is conducted through isolated channels, protecting the interactions between participants.

## APPLICATION OF BLOCKCHAIN

## Supply Chain Management

In supply chain management [35], tracking the movement of goods from their origin to their destination is essential. Blockchain facilitates this by providing a distributed ledger that ensures transparency and traceability, while also reducing fraud through a tamper-proof record of each step in the process.

Additionally, the smart contract feature on the blockchain is a valuable tool, automating various processes in the supply chain, such as releasing payments.

Furthermore, blockchain's immutable nature aids in supplier management by verifying suppliers' credentials and performance history, and it supports efficient auditing and reporting.

## Healthcare

In healthcare, blockchain offers a safe and secure environment for storing and sharing patient records. Its inherent design ensures that patient data cannot be altered without authorization, protecting the integrity of the information and limiting access to authorized individuals only. The distributed nature of blockchain allows for interoperability between different healthcare systems, enabling doctors to make better-informed decisions by having access to a patient's complete medical history.

Moreover, blockchain's immutability feature helps reduce fraud in the pharmaceutical industry by enabling continuous monitoring of records over time. Additionally, the smart contract functionality automates processes like insurance claims, streamlining operations and reducing the need for manual intervention.

## Financial Services

Security is the most critical aspect of any transaction, and blockchain provides a secure environment for financial services [36]. Blockchain facilitates various financial services, such as cross-border payments, settlement services, and payment clearing, in a smart, secure, cost-effective, and time-efficient manner. The smart contract feature of blockchain automates financial agreements, enhancing trust between parties even if they do not know each other. Every transaction on the blockchain is recorded in an encrypted format, and each block is linked to the previous one, with hashing based on the previous block's hash number. This creates a fraud-resistant environment with a high level of security. Blockchain also offers a safe environment for using digital assets, promotes globalization, reduces the cost of currency creation, and minimizes fraud in taxation.

## Voting Systems

A voting system [37] requires safety, security, transparency, voter anonymity, real-time vote counting, and the ability to audit the entire election process. Blockchain technology can provide all of these capabilities. Digital identity with encryption ensures secure voter identification and maintains voter anonymity. Blockchain's immutability feature creates a safe and secure voting system, while its distributed ledger technology enables real-time vote counting and transparent auditing of the election process.

## Digital Identity

Blockchain's distributed ledger technology provides a secure platform for storing digital identities [38], allowing individuals to own and manage their identities directly on the blockchain. This self-sovereign identity model empowers users by eliminating the need for third-party organizations to manage or validate their identity. Through cryptographic techniques, blockchain enables verification without revealing personal data, preserving privacy while ensuring security [39]. The data stored on the blockchain is immutable, making it reliable for multiple purposes. Additionally, this technology offers an efficient and cost-effective platform for identity management.

## Intellectual Property

Blockchain's distributed ledger technology offers a platform for securely storing property-related documents, such as trademarks, patents, and copyrights, in an immutable format along with their registration dates [40]. By implementing smart contracts, processes like licensing and receipt generation can be automated, enhancing efficiency. The distributed ledger also increases transparency, and traceability, and provides proof of authenticity for these assets. Additionally, cryptographic techniques ensure the security of the stored data.

## SECURITY ISSUES AND CHALLENGES OF BLOCKCHAIN

To complete a transaction in a blockchain network, the process involves several phases: transaction creation, broadcasting the transaction, network verification, including the transaction in a block, block propagation across the network, and applying a consensus mechanism to validate the newly added block. Once consensus is achieved, the block is added to the top of the blockchain. Fig. (**8**) shows the architecture of transactions.

Throughout this process, there are multiple potential loopholes. In this process, a data packet is created when a transaction is initiated, a data packet contains a header and a payload. A header contains the preamble frame delimiter, frame check sequence, destination MAC address, Source MAC address, and ether type. Packet definition is approximately the same as IPV4 or IPV6. Fig. (**9**) depicts the Ethernet Packet Structure.

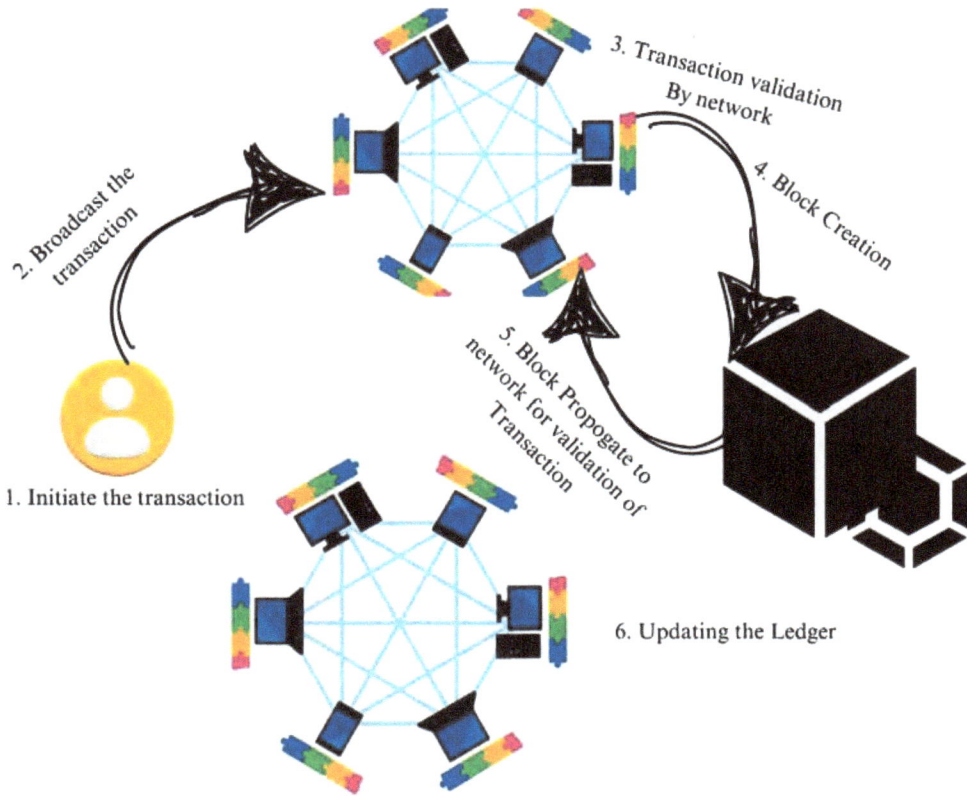

**Fig. (8).** Architecture of transaction.

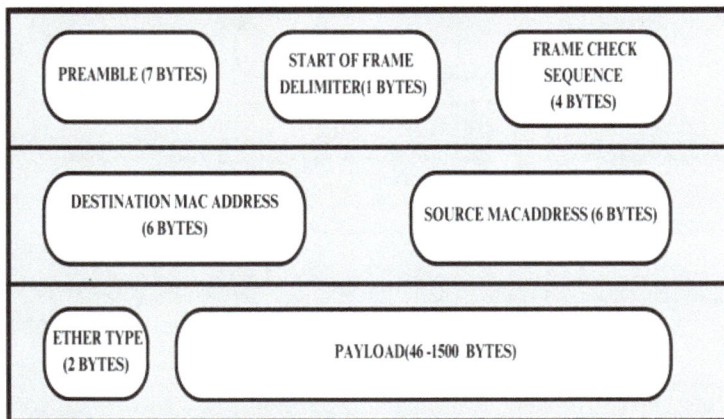

**Fig. (9).** Structure of ethernet packet.

And every packet requires encryption using mechanisms like ECC or RSA. Fig. (**10**) summarizes the encryption mechanism used in transactions. If a phishing or malware attack compromises a node, there is a risk of the private key being leaked. An attacker can create fraudulent transactions if a user's private key is compromised.

After the transaction is created, it needs to be transmitted across the network using a peer-to-peer protocol. However, if an attacker floods the network with fake nodes, known as a Sybil attack, it can disrupt the transmission of legitimate transactions. Once the transaction is transmitted, the next step is verification by the network. The peer-to-peer protocol has been initiated to reach each node of the network.

Fig. (**11**) represents all the P2P protocols used in achieving the node. Each node uses a public key to verify the transaction, but this verification takes time. During this period, there is a risk of double spending or racing conditions occurring. Following verification, the transaction is grouped into a block by miners. The consensus mechanism, such as Proof of Work (PoW), Proof of Authority, or Proof of Stake (PoS), determines which node will create the block. If a node controls more than 50% of the network's computational power, there is a risk of a 51% attack, where the node could manipulate the blockchain. After creating a block, it must be verified and propagated throughout the network. During this stage, there is a risk of block withholding or selfish mining attacks, where a node delays broadcasting a block to gain an unfair advantage. As nodes reach consensus on the validity of the newly added block, there is a chance of consensus mechanism attacks.

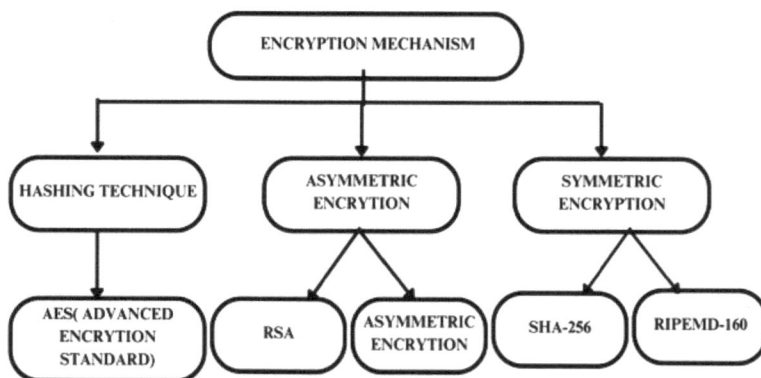

**Fig. (10).** Types of encryption mechanism.

PEER TO PEER PROTOCOL

- GOSSIP PROTOCOL(USED IN BITCOIN AND ETHERIUM)
- DISTRIBUTED HASH TABLE(USED IN INTERPLANATORY FILE SYSTEM)
- KADEMLIA (USED IN SWARM)
- RAFT AND PAXOS(USED IN HYPERLEDGER FABRIC)
- WHISPER PROTOCOL(USED IN COMN BETWEEN DAPPS)
- LIBP2P(USED IN POLKADOTS)

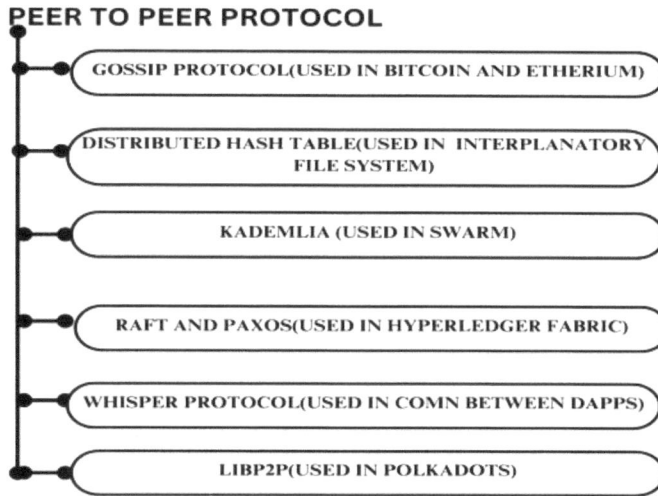

**Fig. (11).** Types of peer-to-peer protocol.

Finally, when the block is added to the chain, the network could be vulnerable to reorganization attacks, especially if the network has lower hash power or stake, allowing attackers to potentially rewrite the blockchain's history. Whenever the term cryptocurrency is mentioned, several risks need to be considered, including market risk, smart contract exploitation risk, key theft risk, liquidity risk, credit risk, operational risk, bank disintermediation risk, and capital flow risk. Table **1** depicts the most concerning risk that can happen during transactions from initiation to ledger updation.

**Table 1. Attacks in network.**

| Attack | Description | Events |
|---|---|---|
| **Validation Attack** | | |
| 51% Attack [41] | When more than 50% of nodes make the wrong decision, they are allowed to manipulate the transaction. | In January 2019, 51% of attacks were on the Ethereum Classic blockchain, resulting in double-spending transactions worth over $11 lakh. |
| Sybil Attack [42] | When a hacker creates fake identities and has a large influence over the network, a single node controls a significant number of nodes which affects the decentralization also. | The Bitcoin network suffered from the Sybil attack in 2015. |

*(Table 1) cont.....*

| Attack | Description | Events |
|---|---|---|
| **Validation Attack** | | |
| Selfish Mining Attack [43] | Miners create a strategy where they keep discovered blocks as private blocks to gain an advantage over the network, which can create a new fork. | Till now, none has reported about selfish mining. |
| **Transaction Attack** | | |
| Double-Spend Attack [42] | When the same cryptocurrency is spending more than one time due to the latency of updating on the block. | In November 2020, Bitcoin Gold (BTG) suffered from a double-spend attack, thus a loss of $70,000 worth of BTG. |
| Routing Attack [45] | When hackers try to manipulate the routing data across the network. Like border gateway protocol hijacking, route leaks, Distributed denial of service attacks, and Traffic interception [44]. | In 2014, the proposed attack was acknowledged by researchers in 2014. |
| Finney Attack [44] | This is a type of double-spending attack where the miner is the attacker, acts as a normal miner, and ends the transaction to himself without broadcasting. | Theoretical concept. |
| Time Jacking Attack [46] | In these attacks, hackers alter the node's network timestamp, forcing it to accept alternative networks. | Bitcoin Timejacking Vulnerability, 2011. |
| Bribery Attack [45] | Offers incentives to miners to act against the network interest, like ignoring transactions. | Bribery attack against EOS Governance, 2018. |
| Replay Attack [47] | At the time of forking the network, it reuses a valid data transmission maliciously or fraudulently. | This attack came into existence when The Ethereum and Ethereum Classic split into two different parts in 2016. |
| **Coding Attack** | | |
| Smart Contract Exploit | Exploits vulnerabilities in smart contracts, such as reentrancy bugs, to steal funds or manipulate contract behavior. | The DAO Hack, 2016, losses $60 million. |
| Flash Loan Attack | Takes advantage of flash loans to manipulate markets or drain funds from protocols within a single transaction. | In 2020, due to the manipulation of oracles and lending protocols, the DeFi protocol suffered a flash loan attack, losing nearly $1 million. |
| **Network attack** | | |
| Node Hijacking | At the time of data flow, a node can disrupt the data flow and can create obstacles in communication. | Ethereum Classic Node Hijacking, 2019, with losses of $1.1 million. |
| Eclipse Attack [44] | It targets a specific node by isolating it from the rest of the network, allowing the attacker to manipulate the node's view of the blockchain. | Demonstrated attack that was mentioned by Researchers from Boston University and the University of Pittsburgh in 2018. |

*(Table 1) cont.....*

| Attack | Description | Events |
|---|---|---|
| **Validation Attack** | | |
| Token Hijacking [48] | Involves taking over a token contract, often exploiting vulnerabilities in the contract's code or management processes. | In 2021, the Poly Network was hacked, causing a loss of $610 million. |
| Denial of Service (DoS) Attack [46] | Overloads the network or specific nodes with excessive requests, disrupting normal operations. | Bitcoin Gold DoS Attack, 2018. |
| Phishing Attack [46] | It targets the node through luring communications to steal private keys or other secret information. | Coinbase Phishing Attack, 2019. |
| Dusting Attack [49] | Strategy to trace the transaction and deanonymize user by sending tiny amounts of cryptocurrency to wallets. | Bitcoin Dusting Attack, 2019. |
| Consensus Attack [44] | Consensus is a type of protocol where the weak protocol can be a cause of an attack, such as weaknesses in the proof of stake or delegated proof of stake. | Ethereum Classic 51% Attack, 2020. |

## ISSUE OF SECURITY FOR ADOPTING BLOCKCHAIN

Several challenges hinder the widespread implementation of blockchain technology. One major issue is the lack of standardization, which leads to compatibility problems across different regions and platforms. With many blockchain platforms available, each with its own set of rules, achieving uniformity is difficult. Blockchain operates on distributed networks where every node contains all information to ensure security and transparency. However, as the network grows, handling large volumes of transactions quickly and efficiently becomes increasingly challenging [50].

Maintaining the blockchain requires consensus mechanisms, which in turn demand significant energy consumption. Another major obstacle is the absence of consistent government regulations for blockchain adoption, especially in areas like digital currencies. Different regions have their own rules and regulations, and there is no unified framework for governments to classify and regulate blockchain-based assets. Additionally, blockchain technology requires specialized knowledge and skills to develop, implement, and maintain, making it difficult for organizations to adopt without the necessary expertise. Hode *et al.* [51] have mentioned four issues administrative, technical, functioning, and community.

## NETWORK WORKING AND SECURITY CHALLENGES

A traditional network, commonly used in corporate and home environments, operates through a series of well-defined steps from physical connection to packet delivery. These steps include network setup and configuration, packet creation, encryption, routing, sending the packet, delivery, and decryption, each of which presents its security challenges. During network setup, devices such as routers, switches, and firewalls are used, and IP addresses are assigned to manage device identification, with DNS and DHCP configured for address and naming management. It can create some security risks like misconfigurations, default settings, and unauthorized physical access can lead to attacks like DHCP Spoofing. Once the network is set up, packet creation involves encryption, which relies on algorithms that may have vulnerabilities, potentially exposing the network to Side-Channel Attacks. As packets are transmitted across the network, routers direct them using protocols like TCP/IP for reliable transmission, which can be susceptible to risks such as packet sniffing, Man-in-the-Middle (MitM) attacks, and routing attacks.

To access the network, authentication mechanisms are required for both users and devices, but this process can be compromised by Phishing Attacks and Insider Threats. The internet is a network of interconnected networks, often segmented to limit attacks and managed with software like firewalls. However, improper network segmentation and VLAN Hopping can still pose risks. Upon packet delivery, additional challenges arise in data storage, such as Ransomware Attacks and issues related to cloud storage. In VPN networks, VPN Misconfiguration and Remote Access Exploits can occur, while web services are vulnerable to Denial of Service (DoS) Attacks and unpatched vulnerabilities. Table 2 depicts the description of the attacks mentioned above.

**Table 2. Attacks in traditional network [52].**

| Attack | Description |
|---|---|
| Distributed Denial of Service (DDoS) Attack | When an attacker overwhelms the traffic lead to cause service disruption and network congestion, creating chances for financial losses and increasing the packet delivery time. |
| Man-in-the-Middle (MitM) Attack | When an attacker tries to intercept two parties' communication can lead to data breaches and unauthorized access to sensitive information. |
| Phishing Attack | When attackers give luring to users by email, website, or message users get trapped in it, resulting in the leakage of crucial information. |
| SQL Injection Attack | When attackers inject malicious SQL queries for the retrieval of sensitive information or deletion of databases that can lead to unauthorized access to databases and losses of information. |
| Ransomware Attack | When the attacker writes a program, it encrypts the user's data and demands a ransom for decrypting. |
| Brute Force Attack | When the attacker tries to get the password by checking all combinations of passwords. |

*(Table 2) cont.....*

| Attack | Description |
|---|---|
| Zero-Day Exploit | When a software developer is an attacker and fixes patches in software at the time of development. This vulnerability can cause significant security risks. |
| Insider Threat | When trusted individuals try to steal the organizational information for their personal benefit. |
| Session Hijacking | There are many mechanisms in the network to give the chance to node to initiate the transaction, in this phase, if the attacker gets the token of another's node known as session hijacking. |
| ARP Spoofing/Poisoning | An ARP packet contains a target hardware address and a target protocol address, an attacker can modify these addresses can block traffic. |
| DNS Spoofing | When an attacker redirects the DNS record to a malicious website. |
| Malware Attack | When an attacker injects malicious software into the system. |
| Packet Sniffing | When attackers capture the data packet and analyze it to steal the packet information. |

## MEASUREMENT OF SUCCESS OF BLOCKCHAIN

The aim of writing this article is to measure how blockchain use in applications gives a more success rate than failure. This part determines the percentage of success rate of blockchain technology. The success and failures of blockchain security largely hinge on cryptography, which plays a crucial role in safeguarding data by linking block hashes between the current and previous blocks. The effectiveness of blockchain security is influenced by several factors, including the strength of the consortium, robust governance policies, operational practices, data privacy measures, consensus mechanism, network decentralization, and compliance with regulatory environments. However, default blockchain security measures are often insufficient to fully protect against threats, especially those related to payment processors, smart contracts, and third-party vendors, which may have weaker security protocols on their applications and websites. Several attacks are already mentioned in Table **1**. Consequently, hackers have exploited vulnerabilities in the design, implementation, and execution of these networks to steal funds from blockchain platforms. Fig. (**12**) describes the hacking strategy used by hackers. The main aim of hackers is to earn money. Hacking can be done for two purposes: data hacking and transaction hacking. But the purpose is the same. The hacking process typically begins with reconnaissance, where the hacker gathers information about the target, such as block addresses, domain names, and network topology. This information helps the hacker determine the best procedure to identify potential vulnerabilities or entry points. Vulnerabilities can be in the network, smart contract, or in the associated platform.

**1.Reconnaissance**:
Gathering
information on the
target.

**6. Covering Tracks**:
Removing evidence
of the attack.

**2. Vulnerability
Scanning**: Identify
potential
weaknesses.

**5.Transferring
Funds**: Stealing or
moving
money/assets.

**3. Weaponization**:
Preparing the
necessary tools or
malware.

**4. Creating a
Connection**: Link
between the hacker
and the target.

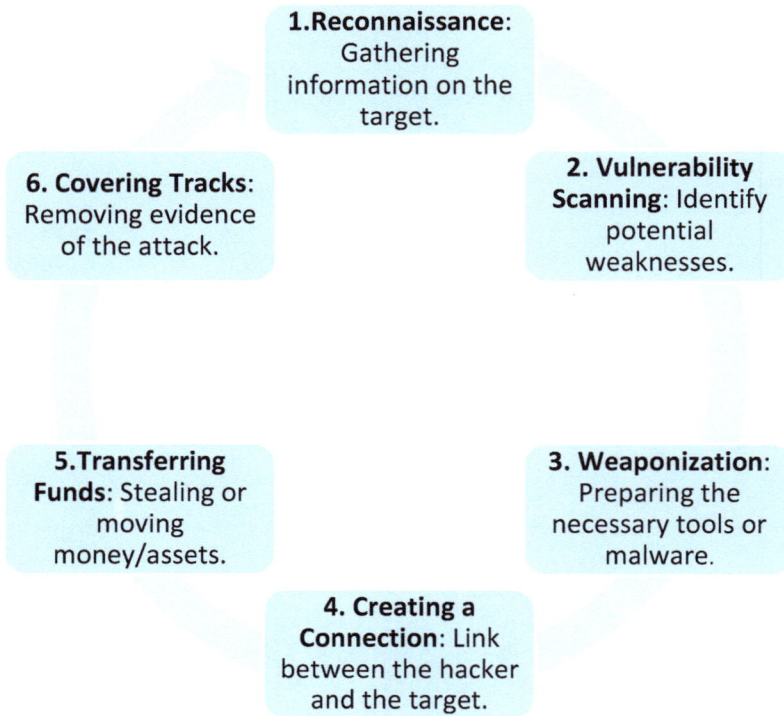

**Fig. (12).**  Hacking strategy.

After collecting the necessary data, the hacker moves to the scanning and enumeration phase to detect loopholes in the target's systems that can be exploited. Loopholes can be created or detected by using any means like private key theft, phishing, social engineering, smart contract exploitation, and 51% attack.

Once vulnerabilities are identified, there are many methods represented in Fig. (**13**) that can be used by hackers to proceed to gain access. After gaining access, the hacker typically attempts to escalate privileges within the system, moving from a lower-level user account to one with administrative rights. Following this, the hacker focuses on maintaining access by installing backdoors or rootkits to ensure continued control over the system. This may involve creating fake user accounts or modification of smart contracts, malicious node deployment, compromised private key management, manipulation of consensus protocols, code injection in DApps, exploiting cross-chain bridges, backdoors in third-party integrations, or creating rogue updates or forks. Finally, the hacker moves to the covering tracks phase, where they attempt to erase any evidence of their intrusion to avoid detection and possible retaliation. This may include splitting and distributing funds across numerous transactions, coin mixing, and tumbling services, or using dark web services.

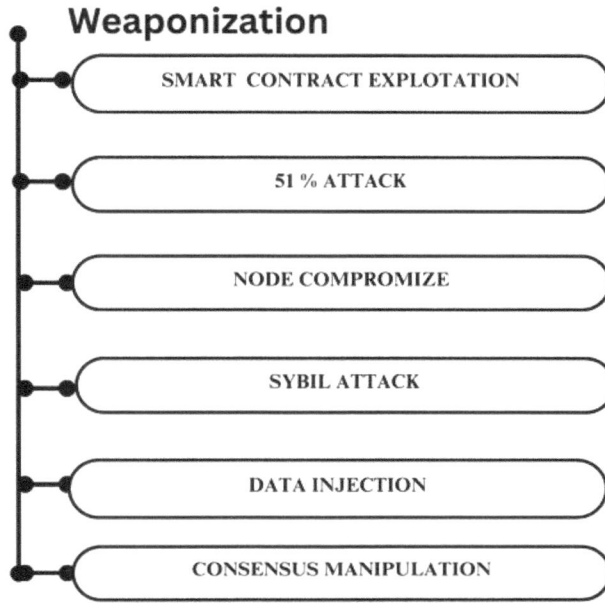

**Fig. (13).** Method of weaponization.

## COMPARISON OF HACKING CASES AND SAFE CASES USING BLOCKCHAIN

There is no established audit strategy available in the market, so precise data for comparison is lacking. However, based on information from the website, some hacking events according to the crypto crime report [53] from the year 2018 to 2023 are listed in Table **3**.

**Table 3. Hacking events from 2018 to 2023.**

| Year | Hacking Event | Fund Stolen (in Millions) | Vulnerability Used |
|------|---------------|---------------------------|--------------------|
| 2018 | Coinbase [54] | $534 | Private Key exploitation |
| | Bitgrail [55] | $195 | Software vulnerability |
| | Bethumb [56] | $31 | Phishing attack |
| | Bancor [54] | $23.5 | Smart contract exploit |
| | Verge | $1.7 | 51% |

(Table 3) cont.....

| Year | Hacking Event | Fund Stolen (in Millions) | Vulnerability Used |
|------|--------------|--------------------------|---------------------|
| 2019 | Upbit [54] | $49 | Phishing and unauthorized access |
| | Binance [57] | $40 | API key compromise |
| | GateHub | $1 | Phishing and exploit of wallet vulnerability |
| | Cryptopia [54] | $16 | Unauthorized access and insider involvement |
| | EOS gambling app hacks [58] | $24 | Smart contract vulnerabilities |
| 2020 | KuCoin [68] | $280 | Private Key |
| | bZx | $8.1 | Smart contract Exploit |
| | Harvest Finance [59] | $34 | Flash Loan attack |
| | Eterbase [60] | $5.4 | Phishing and unauthorized access |
| | Balancer Pool [61] | $0.5 | Flash loan attack and smart contract exploit |
| 2021 | Poly Network [62] | $610 | Cross-chain bridge exploit |
| | PancakeHunny [63] | $1.9 | Flash loan attack |
| | Liquid Exchange [64] | $97 | Unauthorized access and private key compromise |
| | Cream Finance [64] | $130 | Flash Loan attack |
| | BadgerDAO [66] | $120 | Front-end phishing attack |
| 2022 | Ronin Network [68] | $625 | Private Key compromise |
| | Beanstalk Farms [67] | $182 | Governance Exploit |
| | Nomad Bridge [68] | $200 | Cross-chain bridge exploit |
| | Wintermute [69] | $160 | Private key compromise and API vulnerability |
| | FTX Exchange [55] | $477 | Unauthorized access following insolvency |
| 2023 | Euler Finance [70] | $197 | Flash loan attack and smart contract exploit |
| | Atomic Wallet [65, 71] | $100 | Private key compromise |
| | Multichain | $126 | Bridge exploit |
| | Horizon Bridge | $100 | Cross-chain bridge exploit |
| | GDAC Exchange | $13 | Phishing and unauthorized access |

Various motives, including financial gain, corporate espionage, hacktivism, revenge, political motivation, curiosity/challenge, data theft, disruption/chaos, cyber warfare, and intellectual property theft often drive hacking. These activities are generally categorized into two main types: data breaches and financial breaches. These breaches are a type of crime that can be any type such as, CSAM Human Trafficking, Ransomware, Stolen Funds, Sanction, Terrorism Financing, Scam, Cyber Criminal Administration, Fraud shop, or darknet market. Hackers sometimes demand ransom for stolen data, while other times they directly access accounts to steal money. It is relatively easy to determine financial losses in cases of transaction hacking, but analyzing financial losses due to data breaches is more complex. According to website knowledge, numerous hacking incidents occurred between 2019 and 2023, Table **4** depicts how much financial losses happened in terms of whole transactions within a single network from 2019 to 2023.

**Table 4. Financial losses in the whole transaction in a single network from the year 2019 to 2023.**

| Year | Number of Safe (In Billion) | Notable Hacking Incidents | Funds Stolen (in million) | Attack Method |
|------|------|------|------|------|
| 2019 | ~2.5 | Upbit [72] | $49 | Phishing attack and unauthorized access |
| 2020 | ~3 | Ethereum DAppHacks [73] | $47 | Smart Contract Vulnerabilities |
| 2021 | ~3.5 | Poly Network Hack [62] | $610 | Cross-chain bridge exploit |
| 2022 | ~4.2 | Ronin Bridge Hack [68] | $625 | Private key compromised |
| 2023 | ~5.0 | Euler Finance [74] | $197 | Flash loan and smart contract exploit |

It is important to note that no precise mathematical formula exists to calculate the exact data.

## Performance analysis

According to the Crypto Crime Report, the financial losses from the year 2018 to 2023 associated with using blockchain in real-world applications are minimal compared to safe transactions in blockchain. Our blockchain technology offers a higher success rate of security.

However, some discrepancies noted in Table **5** are because of the fact that smart contract technology is purely based on codes. Codes can have bugs. Verification is purely based on the nodes' consent and that can be biased. The world does not widely adopt this technology. Attack vulnerability is still to be found. The consensus mechanism adopted by blockchain can be poor. These vulnerabilities help hackers to get into the in-network and steal money. When Table **5** is analyzed, it is noted that less than half the percentage of total transactions in a network is vulnerable. Fig. (**14**) illustrates the statistics of hacking incidents across various blockchain platforms over the course of one year. Fig. (**15**) below represents the statistics of total transactional amount *vs.* hacking amount from the year 2018 to 2023.

**Table 5. Safe transaction *vs.* total transaction from 2018 to 2023.**

| Year | Safe Transaction | Total Transaction |
|------|------------------|-------------------|
| 2018 | $4.60 | $938.78 |
| 2019 | $12.50 | $657.89 |
| 2020 | $9.40 | $2186.05 |
| 2021 | $23.20 | $19333.33 |
| 2022 | $39.60 | $16500 |
| 2023 | $50.66 | $14900 |

The possible solution of attacks in the blockchain technology, while innovative, is not immune to vulnerabilities, with various attacks posing risks to its security. A notable threat is the "51% attack," which can be mitigated by increasing network decentralization, making it difficult for any single entity to dominate. Additionally, implementing checkpoints to limit the number of transactions within a specified period can further safeguard the network. To combat Sybil attacks, requiring nodes to invest resources in their creation and ensuring that each node has a unique, resource-validated identity can help reduce the risk of fake nodes. Double Spending attacks can be addressed by employing a strong consensus mechanism that mandates validation from over 90% of the network's nodes. For smart contract exploitation, regular code audits and formal verification processes are essential. Diversifying connections and ensuring nodes connect to a broad range of peers can prevent eclipse attacks, while multi-homing, or connecting to multiple ISPs or networks, can protect against routing attacks. Enhancing block propagation speed and implementing a fair block reward mechanism can deter selfish mining, with penalties imposed on nodes found guilty of such behavior. Additionally, blockchain protocols like PoS and PoW, which have their vulnerabilities, may benefit from hybrid mechanisms and regular updates to stay resilient against long-range and time-jacking attacks. Finally, social engineering attacks can be mitigated through user education, multi-factor authentication, and the use of cold storage to secure significant amounts of cryptocurrency.

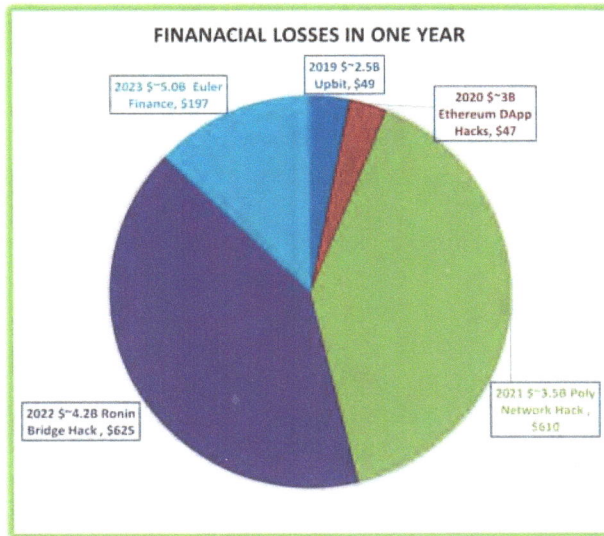

**Fig. (14).** Hacking percentage in a network during one year.

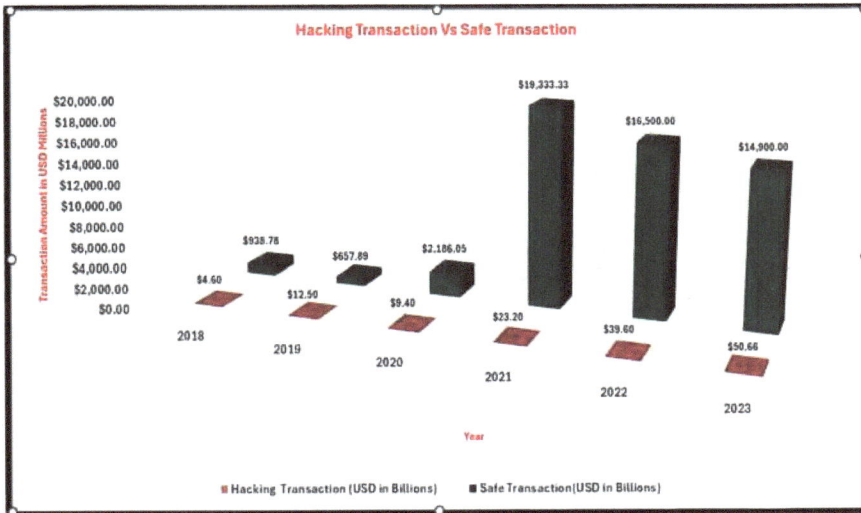

**Fig. (15).** Crypto currencies transaction *vs* hacking transaction statistics (2018-2022).

## CONCLUSION

This article presents a comparative analysis of the hacked incidents with safe incidents in the blockchain by examining a particular application event during whole-year transaction from 2018 to 2023. It concludes that blockchain technology is a significantly more secure system. The analysis covers various cybersecurity hacking incidents in blockchain networks, discussing transaction processes, and hacking methods, and developing a taxonomy for blockchain attack issues. These issues stem from concerns related to blockchain conceptualization, network implementation, smart contract functionality, mining processes, and consensus mechanisms. However, the article acknowledges that blockchain technology is not without vulnerabilities. It explores potential solutions for these weaknesses. Additionally, the article catalogs real cybersecurity incidents within blockchain systems, providing guidance for designers and implementers on creating more secure blockchain systems. The article also suggests directions for future research, emphasizing the need for enhanced cryptography, improved access control systems, smart contract regulation at regular time of intervals, the mechanism of faster transactions, and an implementation mechanism to provide a time slot for updating the block.

## CONSENT FOR PUBLICATION

We hereby grant permission for the use and publication of our work presented in the research paper "A Study on Blockchain Ecosystem Security" submitted for publication to Bentham Books.

## ACKNOWLEDGEMENT

We want to express our sincere gratitude to our Institutes for supporting us throughout the development of this research paper titled "A Study on Blockchain Ecosystem Security".

## REFERENCES

[1]   Available from: https://www.investopedia.com/terms/b/blockchain.asp (accessed 29 june 2024).

[2]   S. Singh, A. S. S. Hosen, and B. Yoon, "Blockchain security attacks, challenges, and solutions for the future distributed IoT network", *IEEE,* vol. 1, no. 1, pp. 99-99, 2021.
[http://dx.doi.org/10.1109/ACCESS.2021.3051602]

[3]   S. Aggrawal, and N. Kumar, "Blockchain components and concepts", *Elsveir,* vol. 121, pp. 387-398, 2021.

[4]   Y-C. Chen, Y-P. Chou, and Y-C. Chou, "An image authentication scheme using merkle tree mechanisms", *Future Internet,* vol. 11, no. 7, p. 149, 2019.
[http://dx.doi.org/10.3390/fi11070149]

[5]   Available from: https://www.geeksforgeeks.org/blockchain-structure/

[6]   R. Michalski, D. Dziubaltowska, and P. Macek, "Revealing the character of nodes in a blockchain with supervised learning", *IEEE,* vol. 1, no. 1, pp. 99-99, 2020.
[http://dx.doi.org/10.1109/ACCESS.2020.3001676]

[7]   A. Azbeg, Kebira, Ouchetto, ouail, J. andaloussi, Said and F. Laila, "An overview of blockchain consensus algorithms: Comparison", *Challenges and Future Directions,* 2020.

[8]   C. Dwork, and M. Naor, Pricing *via* processing or combatting junk mail, *Advances in Cryptology—CRYPTO'92* Heidelberg, Berlin, 1993.

[http://dx.doi.org/10.1007/3-540-48071-4_10]

[9]     Available from: https://bitcoin.org/en/

[10]    S. King, and S. Nada, *Ppcoin: peer-to-peer crypto-currency with proof-of-stake,* 2012.

[11]    F. Schuh, and D. Larimer, "Bitshares 2.0: Financial smart contract platform", *Blakesburg,* 2015.

[12]    Tangem Team, "What is delegated proof-of-stake (DPoS)?", *Tangem,* 2023. Available from: https://tangem.com/en/blog/post/delegated-proof-of-stake-dpos/ (accessed 8 August 2024).

[13]    S. Fahim, S.M. Katibur Rahman, and S. Mahmood, "Blockchain: A comparative study of consensus algorithms PoW, PoS, PoA, PoV", *Int. J. Math. Sci. Comput.,* vol. 9, no. 3, pp. 46-57, 2023. [http://dx.doi.org/10.5815/ijmsc.2023.03.04]

[14]    G. Zhang, F. Pan, Y. Mao, S. Tijanic, M. Dang'ana, S. Motepalli, S. Zhang, and H-A. Jacobsen, *Reaching consensus in the byzantine empire: a comprehensive review of BFT consensus algorithms.* Distributed, Parallel and Cluster Computing, 2023.

[15]    D. Puthal, S.P. Mohanty, P. Nanda, E. Kougianos, and G. Das, "Proof-of-authentication for scalable blockchain in resource-constrained distributed systems", In: *IEEE Int. Conf. Consum. Electron. (ICCE)* Las Vegas, NV, USA, 2019. [http://dx.doi.org/10.1109/ICCE.2019.8662009]

[16]    M. Bartoletti M and L. Pompianu, "An empirical analysis of smart contracts: Platforms, applications, and design patterns", *International Conference on Financial Cryptography and Data Security,* 2017.

[17]    R. Casado-Vara, P. J., FD, and J. Corchado, "How blockchain improves the supply chain: Case study alimentary supply chain", *Procedia Comput Sci,* pp. 393-398, 2018.

[18]    S. N. Khan, F. Loukil, and C. Ghedira-Guegan, "Blockchain smart contracts: Applications, challenges, and future trends", *Peer-to-Peer Network,* pp. 2901-2925, 2021.

[19]    M. Brezitska, "Blockchain smart contracts: Implementation & best practices", *Binariks,* 2023. Available from: https://binariks.com/blog/smart-contracts-blockchain-examples/ (accessed 9 august 2024).

[20]    H.A.H. Hasan, "A review of hash function types and their applications", *Wasit J. Comput. Math. Sci.,* vol. 1, no. 3, pp. 120-139, 2022.

[21]    *WazirX suffers security breach; $235 million worth of funds moved.* Economics Times: India, 2024.

[22]    V. Hassija, V. Chamola, A. Agrawal, A. Goyal, N.C. Luong, D. Niyato, F.R. Yu, and M. Guizani, "Fast, reliable, and secure drone communication: A comprehensive survey", *IEEE Commun. Surv. Tutor.,* vol. 23, no. 4, pp. 2802-2832, 2021. [http://dx.doi.org/10.1109/COMST.2021.3097916]

[23]    T. Loozen, "Smiling young woman looking at smartphone in funfair at night", *Building a better working world,* 2024. Available from: https://www.ey.com/en_pl/telecommunications/top-10-riss-for-telecommunications

[24]    R. T, S.B. S v, S. S, and A. T, "A study on blockchain technologies for security and privacy applications in a network", *Int. J. Electron. Commun. Eng.,* vol. 10, no. 6, pp. 69-91, 2023. [http://dx.doi.org/10.14445/23488549/IJECE-V10I6P107]

[25]    X. Li, P. Jiang, T. Chen, X. Luo, and Q. Wen, "A survey on the security of blockchain systems", *Future Gener. Comput. Syst.,* p. 107, 2017.

[26]    L. Luu, Y. Velner, J. Teutsch, and P. Saxena, "SmartPool: Practical decentralized pooled mining", *26th usenix Security symposium,* 2017. Available from: https://www.usenix.org/conference/usenixsecurity17/activities (accessed 9 August 2024).

[27]    L. L, C. D.H, O. H, S. P, and H. A, "Making smart contracts smarter", *Proceedings of the 2016 ACM SIGSAC Conference on Computer and Communications Security,* vol. 24, pp. 254-269, 2016.

[28]   N. Moosavi, and H. Taherdoost, "Blockchain technology application in security: A systematic review", *Blockchains,* vol. 1, no. 2, pp. 58-72, 2023.

[29]   P.J. Taylor, T. Dargahi, A. Dehghantanha, R.M. Parizi, and K.K.R. Choo, "A systematic literature review of blockchain cyber security", *Digit. Commun. Netw.,* vol. 6, no. 2, pp. 147-156, 2020.
[http://dx.doi.org/10.1016/j.dcan.2019.01.005]

[30]   M.A. Ferrag, and L. Shu, "The performance evaluation of blockchain-based security and privacy systems for the internet of things: A tutorial", *IEEE Internet Things J.,* vol. 8, no. 24, pp. 17236-17260, 2021.
[http://dx.doi.org/10.1109/JIOT.2021.3078072]

[31]   Y. Jiang, G. Sun, and T. Feng, "Research on data transaction security based on blockchain", *Sch. Comput. Commun.,* vol. 13, no. 11, 2022.
[http://dx.doi.org/10.3390/info13110532]

[32]   P.D. DeVries, "An analysis of cryptocurrency, bitcoin, and the future", *Int. J. Bus. Manag. Commer.,* vol. 1, no. 2, pp. 1-9, 2016.

[33]   S.N. Khan, F. Loukil, C. Ghedira-Guegan, E. Benkhelifa, and A. Bani-Hani, "Blockchain smart contracts: Applications, challenges, and future trends", *Peer-to-Peer Netw. Appl.,* vol. 14, no. 5, pp. 2901-2925, 2021.
[http://dx.doi.org/10.1007/s12083-021-01127-0] [PMID: 33897937]

[34]   M. Krstić, and L. Krstić, "Hyperledger frameworks with a special focus on Hyperledger Fabric", *Vojnotehnicki glasnik,* vol. 68, no. 3, pp. 639-663, 2020.
[http://dx.doi.org/10.5937/vojtehg68-26206]

[35]   C. Bentaher, and M. Rajaa, "A literature review and research framework", *Supply Chain Management 4.0,* vol. 7, no. 1, pp. 117-127, 2022.

[36]   A. A. M. Fairoh, N. N. Hussin, N. A. A. Jamali and M. M. Ali, "The impact of blockchain in financial industry: A concept paper", *Inf. Manag. Bus. Rev. AMH Int.,* vol. 16, no. 1, pp. 190-196, 2024.

[37]   M. H. Berenjestanaki, "Blockchain-based e-voting systems: A technology review", *Adv. Blockchain Technol. Appl.,* vol. 13, no. 1, 2024.

[38]   Z. Chen, and S. Wu, "Research on digital identity authentication technology based on blockchain", *J. Phys. Conf. Ser.,* vol. 1802, 2021.
[http://dx.doi.org/10.1088/1742-6596/1802/3/032091]

[39]   Z. Song, G. Wang, Y. Yu, and T. Chen, "Digital identity verification and management system of blockchain-based verifiable certificate with the privacy protection of identity and behavior", *Security and Communication Networks,* vol. 2022, 2022.

[40]   B. Singh, and A.K. Tripathi, "Blockchain technology and intellectual property rights", *J. Intellect. Prop. Rights,* vol. 24, pp. 41-44, 2019.

[41]   E. Resure, and S. Kvihaug, "51% attack: Definition, who is at risk, example, and cost", *Investopedia,* 2024. Available from: https://www.investopedia.com/terms/1/51-attack.asp (accessed 8 August 2024).

[42]   M. Iqbal, and R. Matulevicius, "Exploring sybil and double-spending risks in blockchain systems", *IEEE Access,* vol. 9, no. 1, pp. 76153-76177, 2021.
[http://dx.doi.org/10.1109/ACCESS.2021.3081998]

[43]   N. Madhushanie, S. Vidanagamachchi, and N. Arachchilage, "Selfish mining attack in blockchain: a systematic literature review", *Int. J. Inf. Secur.,* vol. 23, no. 3, pp. 2333-2351, 2024.
[http://dx.doi.org/10.1007/s10207-024-00849-5]

[44]   S. Aggarwal, and N. Kumar, "Attacks on blockchain", *Adv. Comput.,* vol. 121, pp. 399-410, 2021.
[http://dx.doi.org/10.1016/bs.adcom.2020.08.020]

[45]   Available from: https://www.immunebytes.com/blog/routing-attacks-in-blockchain-security/ (accessed

5 August 2024).

[46]   F. Johnand and C. Luciano, "Blockchain security: Common vulnerabilities and how to protect against them", *Hacken Anniversary*, 2023.

[47]   R. Jacalynn, "What is a blockchain replay attack?", *Certik*, vol. 3, p. 9, 2022.

[48]   Token mechanism – an overview, ScienceDirect Topics, Elsevier. [Online]. Available: https://www.sciencedirect.com/topics/computer-science/token-mechanism

[49]   E. Rasure, and M. Reeves, "Bitcoin dust: Overview, disadvantages, and example", *Investopedia*, 2024. Available from: https://www.investopedia.com/terms/b/bitcoin-dust.asp#:~:text=Bitcoin%20dust%20 refers%20to%20the,in%20a%20wallet%20or%20address

[50]   M. A. Ferrag and L. Shu, "The performance evaluation of blockchain-based security and privacy systems for the Internet of Things: a tutorial", *IEEE Internet of Things Journal*, vol. 8, no. 24, pp. 17236-17260, 2021.
[http://dx.doi.org/10.1109/JIOT.2021.307807]

[51]   D. J. Ghode, "Recent advances in industrial production", pp. 157-165, 2022.

[52]   N. Mangrulkar, A.R.B. Patil, and A.S. Pande, "Network attacks and their detection mechanisms: A review", *Int. J. Comput. Appl.*, vol. 90, no. 9, 2014.
[http://dx.doi.org/10.5120/15606-3154]

[53]   C. Team, "Funds stolen from crypto platforms fall more than 50% in 2023, but hacking remains a significant threat as number of incidents rises", *Chainlaysis*, 2024. Available from: https://www.chainalysis.com/blog/crypto-hacking-stolen-funds-2024/ (accessed 8 August 2024).

[54]   C. I. Team, "The 10 biggest crypto hacks in history", *Crystal*, 2021. Available from: https://crystalintelligence.com/investigations/the-10-biggest-crypto-hacks-in-history/ (accessed 7 August 2024).

[55]   D.Z. Morris, "BitGrail cryptocurrency exchange claims $195 million lost to hackers", *Fortune Crypto*, 2018. Available from: https://fortune.com/crypto/2018/02/11/bitgrail-cryptocurrency-claims-hack/

[56]   W. Zhao, "Bithumb $31 million crypto exchange hack: What we know (and don't)", *CoinDesk*, 2018. Available from: https://www.coindesk.com/markets/2018/06/20/bithumb-31-million-crypto-exch-nge-hack-what-we-know-and-dont/

[57]   N. De, "Hackers steal $40.7 million in bitcoin from crypto exchange binance", *CoinDesk*, 2019. Available from: https://www.coindesk.com/markets/2019/05/07/hackers-steal-407-million-in-bi-coin-from-crypto-exchange-binance/

[58]   D. Canellis, "Hacker exploits eos smart contract to steal $200k from gambling app", *TNW*, 2018. Available from: https://thenextweb.com/news/eos-gambling-app-hacked (Accessed 3 Aug 2024).

[59]   Harvest finance fund theft incident – Oct 26, 2020 – Detailed Analysis, Immunebytes, 2020. [Online]. Available: https://www.immunebytes.com/blog/harvest-finance-fund-theft-incident/

[60]   F. Truta, "Cryptocurrency exchange eterbase loses $5.4 million to hackers overnight", *Bitdefender*, 2020. Available from: https://www.bitdefender.com/blog/hotforsecurity/cryptocurrency-exchang--eterbase-loses-5-4-million-to-hackers-overnight/ (accessed 25 july 2024).

[61]   1inch Network, "Balancer Pool with STA deflationary token incident," 1inch Blog, Jun. 29, 2020. [Online]. Available: https://blog.1inch.io/balancer-hack-2020/

[62]   U-Lun Chen, Yung Ting Chang, J. Jimmy Yang, "Cryptocurrency hacking incidents and the price dynamics of bitcoin spot and futures", *Finance Res. Lett.*, vol. 55, p. 103955, 2023.
[http://dx.doi.org/10.1016/j.frl.2023.103955]

[63]   Available from: https://coinmarketcap.com/currencies/pancake-hunny/

[64]   Elliptic, "Liquid exchange hacked: $94 million stolen," Elliptic Blog, 19 Aug. 2021. Available from: https://www.elliptic.co/blog/liquid-exchange-hacked-94-million-stolen#:~:text=According%20to%20

Elliptic's%20analysis%2C%20just,such%20as%20Uniswap%20and%20SushiSwap [Accessed 24 aug 2024].

[65]  Immunefi, "Hack analysis: Cream finance oct 2021," Medium, Nov. 9, 2022. [Online]. Available: https://medium.com/immunefi/hack-analysis-cream-finance-oct-2021-fc222d913fc5

[66]  Chainalysis, "$2.2 billion stolen from crypto platforms in 2024, but hacked volumes stagnate toward year-end," Chainalysis Blog, Dec. 19, 2024. [Online]. Available: https://www.chainalysis.com/blog/crypto-hacking-stolen-funds-2024/ (accessed 1 August 2024).

[67]  S. Kesslar, "Attacker drains $182m from beanstalk stablecoin protocol", *CoiDesk,* 2022. Available from: https://www.coindesk.com/tech/2022/04/17/attacker-drains-182m-from-beanstalk-stablecoin-protocol/

[68]  S. Meshchenko, "Hacks of cefi and blockchain bridges", *H-X,* 2022. Available from: https://www.h-x.technology/blog/top-blockchain-incidents-involving-hacking-attacks.

[69]  M. Singh, "Crypto market maker wintermute loses $160 million in defi hack", *TechCrunch,* 2022. Available from: https://techcrunch.com/2022/09/20/crypto-market-maker-wintermute-loses-160-million-in-defi-hack/#:~:text=Wintermute%2C%20a%20leading%20crypto%20market,industry%20to%20suffer%20a%20breach.

[70]  D. Chmiel, "Crypto hacking losses halved in 2023: A surprising turn", *Finance Magnets,* 2024. Available from: https://www.financemagnates.com/cryptocurrency/crypto-hacking-losses-halved-in-2023-a-surprising-turn/

[71]  H. Partz, "Atomic wallet faces lawsuit over $100m crypto hack losses: Report", *Cointelegraph,* 2023. Available from: https://cointelegraph.com/news/crypto-atomic-wallet-faces-class-action-over-100m-crypto-hack-losses

[72]  web3author, "Upbit hack: What, when, and how?", *Medium,* 2023. Available from: https://medium.com/web3coda/breaking-down-the-upbit-heist-everything-you-need-to-know-556617c31c22 (accessed July 2024).

[73]  Hacken, "Biggest defi hacks of 2020 report", *Hacken.* Available from: https://hacken.io/discover/biggest-defi-hacks-of-2020-report/ (Accessed 19 Oct 2022).

[74]  C. Nightingale, "How did the euler finance hack happen? - full hack analysis", *Cyfrin,* 2024. Available from: https://www.cyfrin.io/blog/how-did-the-euler-finance-hack-happen-hack-analysis#:~:text=Euler%20Finance%20was%20hacked%20for,including%20a%20proof%20of%20concept.&text=%E2%80%8DEuler%20Finance%20was%20hacked,in%20their%20EToken%20smart%20contract (accessed 29 August 2024).

# Blockchain-Enabled Algorithmic Trading: Quantitative Techniques and Regulatory Compliance in India

**Sonika Malik**[1,*], **Siddharth Bisht**[1], **Mumukshu Tyagi**[1] and **Yash Gupta**[1]

*[1] Department of IT, Maharaja Surajmal Institute of Technology, New Delhi, India*

**Abstract:** Indeed, this paper will discuss various strategies, and approaches of algorithmic trading with a view to making profits through data analysis. It introduces the way of operations in terms of mathematical models and logical approaches to gather and evaluate the information about investment potentialities. Hence, another contribution of this study is the analysis of these models and techniques in the context of the Indian market with regard to SEBI regulation. The paper also expands on the role of adopting blockchain technology within algorithmic trading to reduce opacity, increase security, and optimize its running. This study informs on how blockchain can transform trading strategies in India's regulatory environment when used through smart contracts, DEXs, tokenization of assets, write-once ledgers, and real-time clearing. The results highlight the radical evolution of applying algorithmic trading coupled with blockchain to the new generation of more complex financial platforms for India.

**Keywords:** Algorithmic trading, Backtesting, Blockchain technology, CAGR, Calmar Ratio, Delta variations, Data analysis, Data scrubbing, Derivative market, Risk-to-reward ratio.

## INTRODUCTION

Traders and investors have traditionally relied on securities and stock market assets to achieve financial gains. The fundamental principle guiding these activities has often been to "Buy Low, Sell High," a strategy that underpins many conventional trading approaches. That said, as both the theory and practice of financial markets have become more intricate, this rather straightforward approach has been augmented, and in some cases, overshadowed by vehicles of greater complexity. This shift leads us to the topic of our study: To be precise, it involves Quantitative Trading as well as Algorithmic Analysis. Today's traders whether small or big investors are using sophisticated tools and techniques for the

---

* **Corresponding author Sonika Malik:** Department of IT, Maharaja Surajmal Institute of Technology, New Delhi, India; E-mail: sonika.malik@msit.in

**Monica Bhutani, Monica Gupta, Kirti Gupta, Deepali Kamthania & Danish Ather (Eds.)**
**All rights reserved-© 2025 Bentham Science Publishers**

investment so as to make perfect decisions for maximum profit. Quantitative trading is one of the drives that mark significant progress in this endeavor. It refers to the involvement of mathematical models and computational tools as well as applying them in order to perform a huge number of transactions of stocks and any other sorts of financial assets. Quantitative trading, on the other hand, can be defined as an advanced form of trading that differentiates between 'buy' and 'sell' based on some established algorithms rather than employing conventional instinct and subjective judgment of the market trends. This change has made quantitative trading even more achievable, making more institutional investors approach this method of trading in addition to the availability of new technologies and tools needed for quantitative trading, individual traders can now easily obtain them, which were originally widely used only in large financial businesses [1, 2]. The main feature of quantitative trading complemented the statement made above is that data is used quite extensively. Gain charts identify that accurate quantitative traders work with computer languages and even numerical methods to gather and assay previous records of the stock exchange. This information is then employed in the construction of theoretical and prognostic modes of operation with the goal of predicting market shifts. The reliability of these models to a large extent, is predicated on the veracity of the data that have been entered into the system in the past. Credible historical data help the trader understand trends in the market that can help him in his trading. Basically, backtesting is one of the most important aspects used in quantitative trading. Backtesting is the process of analyzing the current market to historical data in order to devise a trading strategy. Such a process affords a way for traders to assess their techniques free from risk environment as well as validate their credibility before using them under real trading conditions. Looking at how the strategy would have operated in the past creates a way through which the trader can evaluate the possibility of its success and make changes as deemed necessary. Backtesting is a process that lets out possible loopholes in the strategy and modifies facets to increase its strength and efficiency. It can therefore be concluded that the role of the regulation has been pivotal in defining the prospects of algorithmic trading in India. In India, the Securities and Exchange Board of India (SEBI) was quite active in regulating algorithmic trading with a perspective of keeping the market as clean as possible and would not allow algorithmic trading in case it presented a threat of disrupting the market [3].

First, SEBI enacted rules to standardize the market because developers are using third-party algorithms with custom APIs access. This shift intended to control the market and the lack of it, concerning such algorithms as uncontrolled and not having a head moderator who would create and introduce them. The year under review has also witnessed severe disruption due to the COVID-19 pandemic affecting various aspects of the economy and business regulation. Earlier, SEBI had imposed certain stringent norms and after a decade of implementation, SEBI eased some of these norms to provide more flexibility and choice to traders regarding algorithmic trading tools. Significantly, the allowed rate of transactions per second changed from 20 to 120, which stoked new opportunities for the traders to work out and apply the self-coded algorithmic platforms. This relaxation was in light of the increased popularity of algo-trading in India as well as the changing dynamics of the market that required an amendment to the rules to suit the traders and investors. The possibility of translating blockchain into the growing field of algorithmic trading brings more prospects for increasing its transparency and security, as well as optimization of its work. Quantitative trading can benefit from blockchain technology as follows. Some of the advantages of the concept of blockchain include: the ability to provide accuracy and security on data that is analyzed quantitatively from historical records. This feature is very essential for the preservation of trading models and the appropriate decision-making to be based on valid data. One interesting feature of the actualization of trading strategies that can be derived from smart contracts, which are widely used in the sphere of blockchain technology, is the possibility of automatization of trades provided that certain conditions are met. Such automation reduces the number of third-party participants in trading and lowers the interval between the actions thus improving the effectiveness of trading transactions. Smart contracts can be used to develop trading algorithms that allow certain trades to be carried out in a precise way without any human interference. This capability is especially useful in trading that occurs frequently in a manner with high velocity.

Other innovations made possible by blockchain technology are decentralized exchanges also known as DEXs. DEXs enable decentralized trading where individuals are able to deal directly with others without the assistance of a central clearinghouse. This approach strengthens security because there is a lower tendency for exchange hacks and brings out the aspect of minimization of the chances of manipulation. There is also increased efficiency in trading transactions as they occur on public ledgers that can be checked to be accurate [4].

Thus, blockchain as an enabler of asset tokenization may be considered a breakthrough in the financial market. Tokenization is a process whereby traditional assets are created in a digital form only to be traded in blockchain markets. It makes it possible to invest in portions of expensive and illiquid commodities, besides making it possible to buy and sell stakes in such properties. In addition, tokenization gives the following benefits: Trading can be conducted at any time, making trading highly liquid; there is also an option for more algorithms to trade. Through the processes of constant trading and ownership in small shares, the tokenization of assets contributes to the overall accessibility and liquidity of the market to open more opportunities for investment and trading.

This paper aims to review this development, particularly the application of blockchain technology in algorithmic trading in the Indian market under SEBI regulations. In this paper, we investigate how the measures of quantity have made it possible to outline justifiably how blockchain can revolutionise trading strategies through the analysis of models, techniques, and regulations to foster a secure and efficient trading space.

## Related Work

Algorithmic trading and various quantitative methods are further analyzed in the context of the adoption of blockchain technology, which improves the very nature of trading and minimizes possible risks. A study evaluates a trader's portfolio based on different measures such as risk and return measures [5, 6]. These evaluations form the basis for the subsequent performance analyses that we intend to perform in the context of the blockchain-based information storage system. Some authors specifically analyzes the concept of technical analysis's ability to be a trading tool by considering theoretical and empirical research work [7]. This review aims to discuss how blockchain can enhance reliability and transparency in technical analysis interfaces for verifiable trading decisions. A study focuses on High-Frequency Intraday Trading Strategies while citing statistics that make it easy to compare with the implementation of blockchain [8]. The given facts indicate how the technology can optimize the processes of high-frequency commerce risk-free and in the shortest time possible. Another study covers the aspects of trading based on fundamental and technical characteristics and applies blockchain as a tool for storing records that provide higher accountability in the quantitative analysis of stock [9]. All in all, this approach enhances the reliability of trading decisions that stem from the fundamental and technical analyses carried out. A study refers to stock exchanges and their patterns of operation with a focus on efficiency, data credibility, and openness that comes with the application of blockchain technology [10]. As a result of this study and by adopting blockchain, the paper identifies the opportunities of using statistical models and mathematical tools with enhanced credibility and protection. In COVID-19, a study performs an analysis on the shares of dominant industries that use blockchain for real-time updating, and authentic data management, due to market fluctuations [11]. This work also emphasizes that blockchain can uphold reliability and integrity, especially in turbulent times. Another study examines the Reversal Trading Strategy and applies blockchain technology to give undisputable statistical yields [12]. This research adds to the understanding of how blockchain can increase the audibility of trading strategies, and thus enhance the transparency of the market, to enhance the confidence of all members. All of these together give the advancement of algorithmic trading and quantitative analysis by means of blockchain integration. Specifically, researchers believe that through the implementation of blockchain technology, including applications of distributed ledger and smart contracts, trading will become more secure, and transparent and will allow for the development of more efficient approaches and generally improve the quality of trading markets. Z. Zheng *et al*. provide a comprehensive survey on the challenges and opportunities associated with blockchain technology in their paper "Blockchain Challenges and Opportunities: The survey is titled "A Survey" [13]. It addresses broader issues of blockchain such as its benefits and drawbacks. More specifically it is important for understanding how blockchain can help develop actual trading systems since it presents the reader with actual cases that show how blockchain can be effectively integrated in trading applications. Their arguments formed the basis for assessing the application potential and value of Blockchain in financial markets. The paper by T. Hendershott *et al*. ''Does Algorithmic Trading Improve Liquidity? '' focuses on algorithmic trading's effect on the nature of markets [14]. It is relevant to their work to develop insights to make sense of how various trading strategies such as those based on blockchain impact markets. The evidence presented helps to assess the advantages and issues emerging when applying blockchain in current trading platforms.

## Proposed Work

The design to develop a high degree of modularity is critical to the design and execution of the project as described in the proposal. There can also be an ability to make individual parts of the system to be separately released, modified or improved. For instance, upon having better-differentiated data, the system can comfortably incorporate these new resources into the model, enhancing its overall efficiency and precision without requiring a new development. Furthermore, this capability decouples other components critical to the work, including the GUI or the strategy algorithms necessary for the functioning of the system. As time passes or as new technology emerges or new methodologies are introduced, it may be realized that some of the parts have outlived their effectiveness. The modularity, which is proposed in the concept will allow for the replacement or enhancement of these components without necessarily affecting the overall system. This flexibility is vital for keeping the system vital with proper technological updates for achieving sound and precise results in the future. Besides flexibility, the modular structure also enables the continuous development of new products in the area. It allows the team to experiment with and incorporate cutting-edge tools and techniques as they emerge, ensuring that the system remains at the forefront of technological advancements. This approach not only future-proofs the project but also positions it to continuously deliver high-quality results that align with evolving industry standards and user expectations.

## Dataset

Data collection has to be from reliable and accurate sources, to provide a fundamentally sound basis for our analyses. In order to work with a specific stock exchange, we would require access to information like spot data for options for nifty companies . While National Indices like the NSE can provide helpful data, it is important to identify third-party sources, as they can string together data- dating back to multiple years with the necessary metrics, and summary reports, that we can work upon to develop a strategy. Here, spot data is the data that has recorded the minute-by-minute variations in the underlying stocks of options. And options are contracts that allow investors to profit off successful predictions, by paying a premium. Note if the investors' predictions are wrong, they can opt not to buy the stock, however, the premium paid is non-refundable and leads to losses. And the whole purpose of our study is to create profitable decisions. While data can be collected relatively easily by large entities, they have to be worked upon and formatted so that they can be readily processed by our various tools to generate strategies. For the associated project that we made with this paper, that is - the implementation of our study that we aimed for a relevant and accurate dataset spanning over a large enough time period to ensure reliability in our analysis reports. The data was acquired from third-party sources and spanned over 4 years. The data included spot data and daily summary reports regarding the stock in question over the described timespan. The acquired data was then cleaned and then pre-processed into a suitable format. Thereafter we created modules of different technical indicators and mathematical models, which we chose for their technical performance, and applied them to the given data we have pre-processed.

## Mathematical Models and Statistical Metrics Used

- **Black-Scholes Model-** The Black-Scholes-Merton (BSM) model is a foundational mathematical framework used to evaluate and price European-style options. Developed by Fischer Black, Myron Scholes, and Robert Merton, this model revolutionized the financial world by providing a method to calculate the theoretical price of options, enabling more informed trading decisions. The BSM model finds widespread application in the European markets, where options can only be exercised at maturity. Nonetheless, its usage can be confined to the American market due to the fact that American options enable early exercise that is not considered by the BSM model. This limitation limits its applicability to other such markets, where early exercise is a key factor [15].

Hence in the light of the contingency of characteristics of Indian options with European style options, the BSM model is very much applicable in the Indian context. In the Indian market, exercising options can be done only on the due date regarding the specifications under which the BSM model was derived. Therefore, the BSM model can be easily implemented in pricing options in the Indian stock market since it possesses the characteristics mentioned above; however, the assumptions and constraints of this model should be fully understood to incorporate modifications where needed. For instance, the BSM model assumes that volatility is fixed and the risk-free rate is known and fixed while in real markets, these variables may change. However, when coupled with some form of compensations that take into consideration movement in market factors such as volatility, the BSM model can still be used effectively in the pricing of options in the Indian market. The following are some of the greatest assumptions used by the BSM model in its working. These include the assumptions that no dividends are paid out in the lifetime of the option, that the market is unpredicted and behaves in a random manner, and also, that the cost incurred when buying and exercising the option is zero, and lastly that the risk-free interest rate and the variance of the underlying stock are constant and known. Also, the model presupposes that the prospect of the underlined asset is normally distributed. These assumptions while useful for the formulation of the model may occasionally cause the model to diverge from reality [16]. Although it is not without its limitations, it is an essential concept in today's world of financial study and it is of explicit use to most traders and analysts who use it to price options contracts, assess the risks involved, and design their future trading strategies. That is why the main advantages of the BSM model include its ability to take many input variables such as the current price of the underlying asset, the option's strike price, time to expiration, risk-free rate, and volatility and produce a theoretical option price out of them. The price plays a central role in a trader's evaluation of a particular option to see whether fairly priced or overpriced or underpriced. Besides, the model's operation is flexible and thus can be adjusted and expanded in order to fit different market situations, which makes it a rather practical tool for analyzing financial data. Despite the fact that the BSM model was initially designed for European-style options, when adjusted and used with proper precautions, the new model is also relevant for other markets, including the Indian market, which makes it a crucial part of the options pricing theory [17].

The first communication Black and Scholes used is the mathematical notation and this is expressed in Eq. (**1**) below:

$$C = SN(d_1) - Ke^{-rt}N(d_2) \tag{1}$$

Where,

$$d_1 = \frac{\ln_k^s + (r = \frac{\sigma_v^2}{2})t}{\sigma_s \sqrt{t}} \text{ and } d_2 = d_1 - \sigma_s \sqrt{t}$$

And,

C = Call Option Price,

S = Current Stock (or other underlying) price,

K = Strike Price,

r = Risk-free interest rate,

t = Time to maturity,

N= A normal distribution.

- **Merton's Model** – Merton's Model is a relatively more elaborate model derived from the Black Scholes Merton (BSM) model, which attempts to evaluate a company's credit risk by valuing the company's equity as a call option on its assets. What the model does is assess the probability that a given firm will be unable to meet its debt obligation through a comparison of its current value of assets against the value of debt. In the case that the asset value is lower than the debt level, the company will be in a position of default. Thus, this approach provides a more extended and methodologically sound view of credit risk and appears to be far more suitable when it comes to large-scale firms as it integrates market data and assets' variability. Out of the examinations made on the applicability of this theory to the Indian market condition, Merton's Model has been found to be more suitable to be applied, though it was primarily developed to be used on European-styled options. The fact that the model was developed for a financial market similar in structure to the current Indian financial market, and the conditions at which the said model was developed also makes it a good fit for use in India with regard to companies listed in the NSE. Despite the flaws, including the assumption of constant volatility and market efficiency, it generally serves the purpose for investors and risk managers to measure credit health since it is more precise than other methods in determining the default risk [18, 19].

The representation of Merton's model can be stated in the following mathematical notations as given in Eq. (**2**).

$$E = V_1 N(d_1) - Ke^{-r\Delta t} N(d_2) \qquad\qquad (2)$$

Where, and

$$d_1 = \frac{\ln\frac{V_t}{K} + (r + \frac{\sigma_v^2}{2})\Delta t}{\sigma_s\sqrt{\Delta t}}$$
$$d_2 = d_1 - \sigma_s\sqrt{\Delta t}$$

and, E = Theoretical value of a company's equity,

$V_t$ Value of the company's assets in period t,

K = Value of the company's debt,

t = Current time period,

T = Future Time period,

r = Risk-free interest rate,

N = Cumulative standard normal Distribution,

e = Exponential term (*i.e.*, 2. 7183...),

σ = Standard Deviation of Stock Returns.

- **Black Scholes Model and Merton's Model in the context of the Indian Market-** The Black-Scholes Model (BSM) and Merton's Model are two well-known models prevalent in the financial markets, which involve the determination of options' value besides credit risk evaluation. A study conducted on six major Indian companies—Aurobindo Pharma Ltd., Eicher Motors Ltd., Infosys Ltd., Mindtree Ltd., Sun Pharmaceutical Industries Ltd., and Mahindra and Mahindra Ltd.—provides valuable insights into the applicability and effectiveness of these models within the Indian market context. The study revealed that while there are differences between the results produced by BSM and Merton's Model, these differences are minimal, ranging from 0.02% to 0.24%. This slight variation suggests that neither model has a decisive advantage over the other, indicating that both models are highly capable and relevant in the Indian market. The study further indicated that certain Indian corporations demonstrated a preference for one model over the other in terms of accuracy and consistency. For instance, BSM was more appropriate for a company such as Aurobindo Pharma Ltd. and Eicher Motors Ltd. This preference can be explained by the fact that some of these firms may fit in the financial characteristics and behavior of the BSM model– constant volatility and a lognormal distribution of the asset prices. While it can be seen that there was a bias towards higher MD & A for the sample of firms, companies such as Infosys Ltd., Mindtree Ltd., Sun Pharmaceutical Industries Ltd., and Mahindra and Mahindra Ltd. favored closer to Merton's Model. To some extent, it might be due to the fact that Merton's Model allows credit risk to be incorporated, whereby a firm's equity is considered to be equivalent to a call option on its assets which may be useful for such firms' financial structures and risk profile.

Contrary to that world; in the present study, it was revealed that there is a slight superiority of Merton's Model with regard to its accuracy and consistency while at the same time stressing the fact that the disparity between the two models is negligible. Thus, there is a slight advantage of Merton's Model, but before choosing between BSM and Merton's Model, one should consider the company in question. The limitations inherent in both models are equally important especially in a real-life situation where factors such as market structure deviate from the theoretical standards assumed in the respective models. So, the practitioners have to apply these models with the knowledge of their limits and potential probably by complementing the understanding derived from each model to get a better understanding of a firm's financial performance and its strategic competitive standing [20]. The study also highlights an important consideration: both models, despite their sophistication, will invariably produce some variations in results when applied to real-world data. This variability underscores the need for caution when relying solely on these models for decision-making. Financial analysts and risk managers should complement these models with other tools and qualitative assessments to account for factors that may not be fully captured by BSM or Merton's Model. This integrated approach can help ensure more accurate and reliable outcomes when evaluating options and assessing credit risk in the Indian market [21].

- **Portfolio Drawdown-** Drawdown is a helpful metric for assessing the potential and overview of the stock. It finds the downward variance in pricing from the peak before it retraces back to the peak. It stands as an accurate measure of volatility and can allow us valuable insights and help in our decision-making.

The volatility of the stock is one of the characteristics that we must fully gauge, to decide its feasibility for investing. And if feasible for investing, what sort of strategies or techniques would be the most suitable to be used? The main defining aspect is the maximum drawdown (MDD), gathered from past historical data, which can allow us to get an estimation to avoid it when we decide to conduct transactions. Keep in mind the MDD is not set in stone and may deviate more in the future, but barring unforeseen circumstances or external factors, the drawdown will remain stable for the short-term periods in question that we are concerned with.

The drawdown while influencing our selling decisions, can also factor in the buying decision as well, as it can be characterized as a risk metric as well. The drawdown will provide us with both the measure of variance in the pricing differential as well as the time taken to fully recover back to the previous or a new peak. While an additional point of emphasis is that drawdowns do not necessarily equate to losses, in most real-world market scenarios even concerning the most stable stock pricing, drawdowns will occur in almost every circumstance [22, 23].

Beta is a useful analytic measurement means to express the relation between stock and index returns. Understanding past progressions and their concurrent variance is something that allows us and other traders who are so concerned as well to gauge and assess those particular companies' volatility with a definitely defined technical metric, allowing us to adopt certain strategies that will generate maximum profits. The beta will assess systematic risks by describing movement in a stock or a portfolio's return concerning the market return. The overall conclusion is that Beta is useful for comparing the relative systematic risks for a particular stock, enabling us to make the necessary decisions in a particular informed manner. The quantitative metrics at hand provide additional insights and allow us certain objectivity in making the aforementioned decisions, in relation or context to a company or a group of companies [24].

- **Calmar Ratio-** The Calmar ratio, also known as the Drawdown Ratio is a measurement index to access risk-adjusted returns for investments. Its naming comes from California Managed Accounts Reports, whose owner Terry W. Young came up with the Calmar Ratio as a superior alternative to the Sterling Ratio, by using the latest 36 months' average rate of return to drawdown and quantifying it on a monthly basis instead of yearly basis. This allows for a gradual progress/regression of the plotted graph that smoothens the sharp swings and turns in the plotted trace of the graph [25].

The trace of the Calmar Ratio for a given investment is more gradual as compared to other similar ratios. This gradual change allows for a better understanding and evaluation of our investment's increase/decrease in worth in real-time value. The gradual trace also allows for a more detailed study of the investment in question.

The Calmar Ratio can be expressed as shown in Eq. (3).

$$Calmar(T) = \frac{Returnover[0.T]}{Max\ Drawdown\ over[0.T]}$$  (3)

$$T = Time$$

Were,

T = Time Period

A possible improvement upon the existing Calmar Ratio that has been proposed is the "Normalised Calmar Ratio", where the Calmar Ratio is linked to the Sharpe Ratio for comparison of drawdowns between two portfolios [26]. Because the usage of the Sharpe Ratio is an additional advantage because it yields maximum returns in a significant majority of a study's sample size, and additional improvements over the Calmar ratio as an optimization parameter [27]. In Table 1, the optimal ratios for better results for various industries in various circumstances have been mentioned. From it, we can largely infer the better applicability of the Sharpe Ratio and gather why the usage of the Normalised Calmar Ratio is preferable. We also see the Sortino ratio outperformed, but that seems to only be the case for Consumer Durable Industries [28].

Table 1. Summary results for the best ratio (out of calmar, sortino, and sharpe ratio) for various industries [27].

| Sector | Highest Cum Return Port | | Max Sharpe Ratio | Max Sortino Ratio | Max Calmar Ratio |
|--------|------|------|------|------|------|
| | Trg | Test | | | |
| Cons Dur | Sortino | Sortino | 1.7979 | 1.5635 | 0.8017 |
| Pvt Banks | Sharpe | Sharpe | 0.9483 | 1.0046 | 0.5940 |
| PSU Banks | Sharpe | Sharpe | -0.1384 | - 0.1655 | 0.0376 |
| Oil & Gas | Sharpe | Sharpe | 1.4019 | 1.0801 | 0.5970 |
| Pharma | Sharpe | Sharpe | 1.3962 | 1.3230 | 1.1404 |

- **CAGR-** which Stands for Compound Annual Growth Rates, is a metric to assess the progression of our combined investments, with a negative value indicating the depreciation of our assets. One of the evergreen trading strategies of trading is that of "Diversification".

This is done so that while external factors and unforeseen circumstances can greatly impact the stock pricing of a company in a negative way, we can assume partial insulation from such incidents. External factors and unforeseen circumstances are generally localized- to a certain company, industry, or even geographical location, but if we do not put all our eggs in a singular basket, we can avoid losses, because our investments are insulated from each other. Investments will be usually done in segregated companies, which are disparate and so separated that happenings in one will not affect another [29].

CAGR will summarize the overall growth of our portfolio, and act as a quantitative means to measure the annual average rate of growth of our compounded interests for a specific period or duration of time. While certain investments may have suffered a loss, others may have netted large enough gains to cover our losses as well as provide us with profits. Keep in mind while CAGR may look like an attractive catch-all metric to judge the soundness of our investments, it is important to study and pay attention to individual investments as well, so the poor-performing ones can be liquidated at an opportune moment. That is because CAGR is only suitable for the overview of our portfolios, rather than giving in-detail summaries of our individual/specific investments and assets that are contributing overall to the larger portfolio [30].

**Additional Strategies Incorporated**

While mathematical and statistical models can provide us with a measure of assured accuracy, they invariably come with drawbacks and restraints that affect their real-world application and reliability. This makes it all the more important for us to incorporate strategies to act as failsafe and to compensate for and overcome the limitations posed by the various models used. This improves the overall analyses that we do and increases the overall completeness of our final results. Another advantage of using defined strategies is adding objectivity to subjectivity. Most decision-making processes by investors can be understood in terms of fundamental and technical analyses, with the fundamental representing the subjective details, the technology does the same for objective and other statistical details [31]. The strategies belong to the realm of fundamental analyses, and their defined aspect will allow for certain consistency and predictability in the results.

- **Square Off-** Square off is a common day trading strategy where traders aim to capitalize on intraday market movements by completing all transactions within the same trading day. In this approach, traders buy and sell stocks in rapid succession, seeking to profit from the price fluctuations that occur throughout the day. The strategy is rooted in the understanding that financial markets are inherently volatile and subject to rapid changes, driven by a multitude of factors including news events, economic data releases, and market sentiment. Traders who engage in squaring off leverage this volatility by identifying short-term opportunities to buy low and sell high within the span of a few hours. Executing a square-off trade requires not only a keen understanding of market dynamics but also the support of substantial capital and advanced trading tools. Large-scale investment backing allows traders to take significant positions, amplifying potential profits from even small price movements. Additionally, sophisticated trading platforms and analytical tools are essential for monitoring real-time market data, identifying trends, and executing trades at optimal moments. These tools often include technical analysis indicators, algorithmic trading systems, and real-time news feeds, all of which help traders make informed decisions quickly [32, 33].

The squaring-off strategy is characterized by its emphasis on short-term gains rather than long-term investment. Traders typically enter the market during a drawdown, when stock prices dip, with the intention of selling the acquired stocks later in the day when prices rebound. The key to success in squaring off lies in timing—traders must accurately predict when to enter and exit their positions to maximize profits. However, this approach also carries significant risks, as market conditions can change rapidly and unpredictably. If the market moves against the trader's position, there may be little time to recover losses, making it crucial to have a well-defined exit strategy.

Despite the risks, squaring off remains a popular strategy among day traders due to its potential for generating quick profits. By closing all positions by the end of the trading day, traders avoid the overnight risk associated with holding positions, where stock prices might change drastically due to after-hours news or events. This strategy is particularly appealing in highly liquid markets, where traders can easily buy and sell large volumes of stocks without significantly impacting the price. While squaring off requires a disciplined approach and a thorough understanding of market behavior, it offers a structured way for traders to navigate the complexities of day trading and capitalize on the fleeting opportunities that arise from market volatility.

- **Short Strangle-** The short strangle is a sophisticated option and a trading strategy designed to generate profits in a low-volatility market environment. Unlike many other trading strategies that rely on significant price movements to yield returns, the short strangle benefits when there is little to no movement in the underlying asset's price. This makes it an attractive alternative for traders looking to capitalize on stable market conditions where price fluctuations are minimal. In a short strangle, the trader simultaneously sells an out-of-the-money call option and an out-of-the-money put option on the same underlying asset, with the same expiration date. The strategy profits from the premiums received from selling these options, under the assumption that the asset's price will remain within a specific range until the options expire. If the price of the underlying asset remains stable and does not breach the strike prices of either the call or the put option, both options will expire worthless, allowing the trader to keep the entire premium as profit [34].

However, while the potential for profit in a short strangle is capped at the total premiums received, the risk is theoretically unlimited, which is a critical consideration for traders. If the underlying asset's price moves significantly in either direction—either rising above the call option's strike price or falling below the put option's strike price—the trader faces substantial losses. This is because the trader may be forced to buy the asset at a higher price than the market value (in case of the call option) or sell it at a lower price (in the case of the put option). Therefore, the short-strangle strategy should only be employed when the trader has a strong conviction that the asset will experience minimal price movement and that the market will remain stable [35].

Because such a strategy is very risky, short strangles are more advisable for those traders who deal with large quantities of contracts and who may need large capital to fund the considerable margins that may be necessary to sustain the position. These traders are not sensitive to the costs as far as large premiums are concerned and can hedge the risk by means of stop losses and or Delta hedges. Notably, the short strangle is well-known among traders who have adequate knowledge of the asset's price and market conditions in which it is being traded to decide when and how this strategy should be applied. Therefore, the short strangle is a special strategy that can serve as an additional tool to earn money in low volatility conditions. Although it provides the possibility of receiving passive income from option premiums, the strategy implies significant risk if the market does not evolve according to expectations. Thus, it can be classified as a rather risky strategy which is the most effective when used in combination with other strategies and it is recommended only for traders having a significant amount of money and a necessary amount of knowledge regarding options and markets [36].

**Diversification of Strategies-** The application of different strategies for mathematical models and portfolio diversification is also applied in investment portfolios as well as the use of methods for the analysis and forecasting of financial assets. Like variability in the portfolio that manages risks in the various investments, variability in the calculation techniques reduces the "risk" of using one particular mathematics that is possibly imperfect or inadequate. Every individual model – like Black-Scholes-Merton (BSM), Forward Testing, and Drawdown analysis – has basic assumptions, factors, and key performance indicators, on which the results are calculated. However, these models can be effective when used separately though they have flaws and contain bias as they are based on some specific inputs and assumptions. Combining several models and techniques is another way in which analysts can get the best from each method while at the same time minimizing the demerits that accompany the approach. For example, BSM might be able to tell something about the prices of options, Forward Testing will be able to make sure that certain trading strategies have favorable results as observed on historical data, and the Drawdown analysis will be useful in understanding losses that can be experienced in future trades. Combined, all these methods provide a broader perspective of the market, or the asset in focus is analyzed. This approach extends the range of possible inputs, including a number of measures, variables, and factors; thus, promising enhanced reliability and stability of the forecast or evaluation.

Besides, cross-verification is also possible through the employment of various strategies in the various models. If one or another model or technique can deliver almost the same results, it brings benefits and credibility to the result. On the other hand, if there are significant differences between the results of one model to another, then this divergence may inform an analyst that there is something wrong. Such differences may indicate certain problems like outliers' existence or upgraded model performance demands that could have otherwise remained unnoticed when using any of the two methods on its own. This comprehensive approach not only improves the accuracy of predictions but also enhances the ability to make informed decisions, thereby increasing the likelihood of successful outcomes in financial markets.

## Implementational Techniques Used

This paper is not the exclusive part of our study, an associated project was created by its authors to showcase and prove the credibility and reliability behind the concepts and strategies that we rely on for our technical analyses. The implementation of the proposed model will require the creation of software with adequately programmed scripts to work with various mathematical models. The models will be included in a module, that can evaluate those models on metrics and will run on the collected dataset, to see the results of our predictive models.

- **Data Collection-** As previously outlined in the dataset information, the data acquisition process involved sourcing data from third-party vendors, which was predominantly provided in CSV (Comma-separated Values) format. While CSV is a widely used format, it presents challenges when working with Python-based tools due to its inefficiencies in handling large datasets and the need for repetitive parsing and conversion processes. Given the scale and complexity of our data, working directly with CSV files would have resulted in significant processing overhead, slowing down our analytical workflows. Therefore, immediately after the acquisition, it became necessary to reformat the CSV files into a more efficient and accessible format that would integrate seamlessly with our Python-based ecosystem.

After careful evaluation, we opted to convert the CSV files into pkl (pickle) format, a native Python object serialization format. The pkl format offers several advantages: it allows for the efficient storage of complex data structures, is directly accessible by Python scripts and libraries, and eliminates the need for repeated conversions, thereby streamlining our data processing pipeline. To facilitate this conversion, we developed a custom Python script that automates the transformation of CSV files into pkl format, ensuring consistency and accuracy throughout the process. The primary objective of our data collection strategy was not only to acquire a sufficiently large and representative dataset but also to ensure that this data was readily usable for subsequent analysis and evaluation. By converting the data into pkl format, we have optimized our operations, enabling faster data access and processing, which is critical for the timely and accurate execution of our analytical models and evaluation modules. This approach ensures that our system can handle large datasets efficiently, laying a solid foundation for further processing, analysis, and decision-making activities.

**Evaluation Modules-** The development of evaluation modules marked a critical phase in our process, following the acquisition, cleaning, and transformation of the requisite data into a suitable format. These modules, crafted using Python, were designed to rigorously evaluate the selected stocks using the processed data as input. Central to this evaluation is a range of sophisticated metrics and models, including the Black-Scholes Model, Compound Annual Growth Rate (CAGR), Drawdowns, and Delta variations. These tools collectively provide a comprehensive assessment of potential investment opportunities, enabling us to analyze the risks and benefits associated with each option in detail. The Black-Scholes Model aids in pricing options, while CAGR offers insights into the stock's growth over time. Drawdowns help in understanding the risk of substantial declines, and Delta variations allow us to measure the sensitivity of the option's price to changes in the underlying asset. Together, these evaluation modules form the backbone of our analytical framework, ensuring that every investment decision is grounded in thorough and precise quantitative analysis.

- **GUI-** The GUI was developed to provide an intuitive and user-friendly interface, enabling users to interact seamlessly with the underlying features of our system. This interface allows users to input their desired upper and lower bounds for put and call options, tailored to the specific data that has undergone back testing. By offering customizable parameters, the GUI empowers users to fine-tune their options strategies according to their individual risk tolerance and investment objectives. This flexibility ensures that users can adapt the model's recommendations to align with their preferences, leading to more informed and personalized decision-making. Additionally, the GUI simplifies complex data interactions, making advanced trading strategies accessible even to those with limited technical expertise, while still maintaining the robustness needed for experienced traders.

- **Back Testing-** Backtesting is a crucial metric for assessing the credibility of our technical analyses by applying them to historical data to evaluate their performance. By selecting a specific period from the past, we generate predictions and plots based on this data and then compare them with the actual historical developments of the stock. This process allows us to gauge the accuracy and reliability of our models, revealing how closely our predictions align with real market movements. Although some discrepancies are inevitable due to market anomalies, backtesting provides valuable insights into the strengths and weaknesses of our strategies, helping us refine our models for better performance in live scenarios. This method not only validates our approaches but also enhances our ability to manage risk and adapt to changing market conditions.

- **Forward Testing-** While most studies have relied on pure statistical efforts to adjudicate their metric's merit over others, we rely on real-life testing and complete strategies to guarantee consistency in results along with credibility. Forward testing is an added measure to test the reliability of our technical analyses. In Forward testing, the entire dataset is inputted into our evaluation module, and the predictive plots are generated for future changes in the stock prices, and the matching of our outputted and real-life changes is done in real-time and manually to fully gauge the accuracy of our technical analyses. Essentially it is a practice of simulated trading, where transactions are set up on paper only, not executed physically, eliminating the risk aspect. Then these mock trades are matched with the real-life changes in the market, to infer whether our decision-making process was sound or not [37, 38].

- **Utility of the Back Testing and Forward Testing-** The goal is to reject and fix failures quickly before the expenses and time-based effort pile up. We should be able to back-test against our hypothesis and output cases. Our testing mechanism should permit us to locate problems in a timely manner and take necessary actions to compensate for and fix those problems along with any others that may arise [39, 40]. Another key objective in our testing strategies has been the exclusion of "look ahead biases", *i.e.*, our backtesting models do not under any circumstance refer to events that have happened after the sample size for their technical evaluation. This when combined with other practices like excluding data mining bias, eliminating data snooping, *etc.* allows for the most optimal and accurate testing models, completely bereft of any bias and systematic error induction in our results [41].

## Evaluation and Discussion

The diversified approach to mathematical models in financial analysis reveals significant improvements in the reliability, accuracy, and robustness of predictions. By integrating multiple models such as BSM, Forward Testing, Drawdown analysis, and others, analysts can cross-validate results, effectively mitigating the limitations inherent in any single model. This multifaceted strategy allows for a more comprehensive assessment, as it accounts for a broader range of variables and scenarios. The convergence of results across different methods enhances confidence in the findings, while any discrepancies prompt further investigation, ensuring that the outcomes are well-founded and credible. Furthermore, the ability to identify and eliminate anomalies through cross-comparison strengthens the overall analysis, providing a complete and more reliable picture of the financial landscape. This approach underscores the importance of diversification, not just in investment portfolios but also in the application of analytical tools and models, ultimately leading to more informed and effective decision-making.

- **Comparative Returns with other strategies-** To gauge the viability of our results, let us first see the real-life result of our model. Table **2** shows the summarized report over 4 years as an aggregate and cumulative of each of the previous years for the native model/strategy proposal that was worked into a functional one by the author(s).

**Table 2. Summary results for our transactions over an annual period.**

| Parameter | Value |
|---|---|
| Overall Profit | 361073 |
| Maximum Drawdown | -18714 |
| Maximum Day Loss | -11287 |
| Maximum Day Profit | 8607 |
| Maximum Win Streak | 15 |
| Maximum Loss Streak | 5 |
| Calmar Ratio | 5.02 |
| Annual Return % | 62.57 |
| Maximum Drawdown % | -12.48 |
| Cost | 1838 |

*(Table 2) cont.....*

| Parameter | Value |
|---|---|
| Win Rate % | 68 |
| Loss Rate % | 32 |

In Table **3**, we can see the comparison in terms of results of various strategies, including the one that was created by us which utilized the various mathematical models and technical metrics to deliver results.

**Table 3. Technical comparison with other studies and strategies.**

| Strategy | Percentage of Returns | Remarks |
|---|---|---|
| Native Strategy | 62.67 | Aggregated from a period of 4 years (2019-2022). |
| HFT Strategy [4] | 52.05 | Aggregated from a period of 9 years (2007-2015). |
| RTS [8] | 49.05 | Aggregated from a period of 6 years (2015-2020). |
| Other Strategies | NA | Other literary works explored various technical metrics but did not publish definitive results that could be compared from a statistical point of view. |

To get a better understanding of our strategy's performance, we must see its yearly performance in terms of returns over the period for which the model was run. In Fig. (**1**), we can see the yearly returns from our strategies that could have been yielded if physical trades were executed.

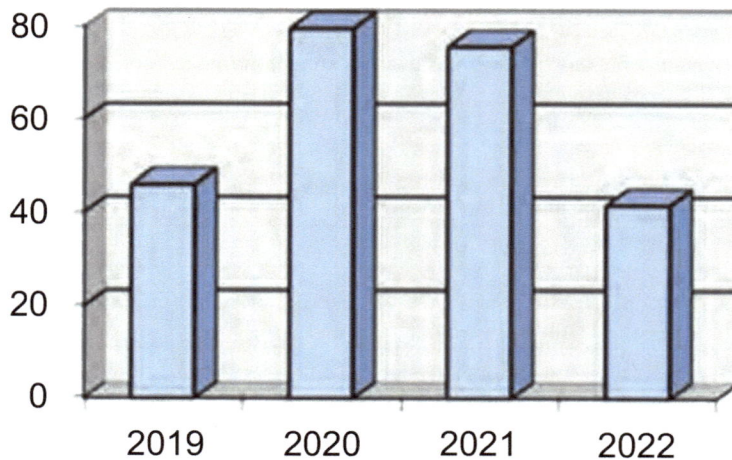

**Fig. (1).** Graphical progression of yearly returns in percentage throughout 2019-2022.

We have been able to gain profits of 62.57% as a standardized average. This number has been aggregated over 4 years as seen in Fig. (**1**). Now let us compare it with other strategies. Graphically it has been done in Fig. (**2**). To understand the returns on a comparative basis, we see this trader's opinionated strategies never crossed the 25% return mark [5]. A study on high-frequency trading strategies which is perhaps the most similar to ours was able to achieve annual returns ranging from 52.05% to 55.77%, which allows us to infer a high degree of consistency, but still lower than our mark (that of 62.57%) [8]. While RTS (Reversal Trading Strategy) shows a maximum annual return rate of 97.50%, the results are highly skewered with the lower range of 30.17% with an average return of 49.04% annually, which is impressive but still allows our results to edge over [12].

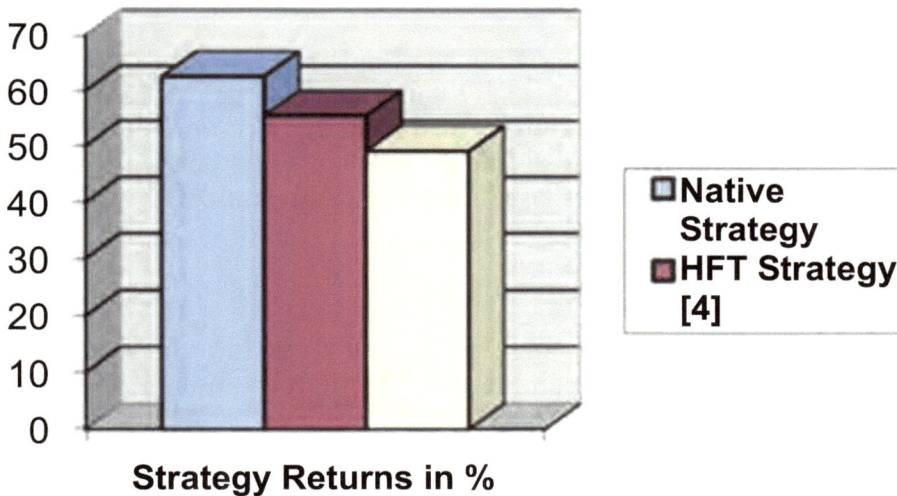

**Fig. (2).** Graphical comparison of various trading strategies as a measure of percentage returns.

- **Evaluation-** To gauge the viability of our results, let us first see the real-life result of our model. The study has evaluated various models, metrics, and strategies to beat the return through fixed bank deposits, the scope for improvement is always there. While the analyses have leaned towards using a technical basis for making decisions, the human link has been left out. The emotional part of decision-making is viewed by some as adverse; we should keep in mind the emotional part can also keep investors away from happenstance pitfalls that befall investments done with purely technical analyses.
- The defining characteristic of our study has been to use a large enough sample case to accurately predict consistency and reliability in our results.
- The second one has been to guarantee ensured profit generation by adopting

varying strategies meant to cater to the varying market conditions, from stable conditions to extreme volatility over both the short and long term.

- Thirdly, while multiple means are available at hand, their existence has been existent for a considerable amount of time, thus allowing for their dissection and analyses by scholars for a sustained period of time, which has invariably exposed vulnerabilities and flaws in them, which occurs in case of all mathematic models, metric, strategies and other technical means available at hand.
- The fourth defining characteristic has been to increase credibility by incorporating both backtesting and forward testing, which instills credibility and reliability concerning our results. Additional steps were taken to strengthen the approaches taken in our testing strategies, to remove flaws and errors, and to induce accurate and consistent results, compatible with varying arrays of input datasets.
- And finally, the fourth one has been the implementational framework. While most studies in the relevant fields have been done by much more knowledgeable authors and researchers, the authors of this study have utilized their technical background, to outlay a technical framework to incorporate the models, metrics, and strategies into a software-based tool, that can be utilized by other investors to from a purely theoretical point of view.

## CONCLUSION

The models and strategies presented in this study aim to provide investors with enhanced decision-making capabilities in algorithmic trading. While we have leveraged various mathematical models, metrics, and strategies to bolster the reliability of our analyses, there remains a continual need for refinement and adaptation in response to evolving market realities. Traditional trading techniques have been adapted to meet modern market challenges, yet the incorporation of fundamental analyses alongside objective and technical metrics underscores the complexity of market dynamics.

Blockchain technology emerges as a pivotal advancement in addressing these challenges by ensuring data integrity, transparency, and security. Through decentralized ledgers and smart contracts, blockchain enhances the auditability and trustworthiness of trading strategies. Moreover, progress in models using artificial intelligence allows for the practical implementation of real-time data and other external factors, enhancing generative insights of techniques and orientations according to the flow of changes in the market. This integrated approach needs to equip the evaluators with strong adequate analytic tools and models that consider proper simulation of market trends in order to equip the investors with proper guidance to engage the global financial markets.

The research that remains for the future should be targeted at the improvement of the integration of various models and approaches within the mathematical framework, and in particular, on creating more efficient algorithms that would be sensitive to the changing conditions of the market. Such improvements may involve the use of machine learning and artificial intelligence to improve model flexibility and accuracy. Thus, increasing the variety of models employed in diversification and specialized for emerging markets and assets could potentially add more value. Such models will have to be updated constantly in order to address the changing financial environment and to make sure that specific strategies are valid and effective in different situations.

## CONSENT FOR PUBLICATON

I, Dr. Sonika Malik, on behalf of all contributors to the chapter titled "Blockchain-Enabled Algorithmic Trading: Quantitative Techniques and Regulatory Compliance in India" confirm that all contributors have given their full consent for its publication. All contributors have reviewed the final version of the chapter and agree with its content and submission. We affirm that the chapter is original and does not infringe on any third-party rights, with all necessary permissions obtained.

## ACKNOWLEDGEMENT

The authors would like to express their sincere appreciation and thanks to the reviewers for their careful and thorough critical appraisal of the paper.

## REFERENCES

[1]     S. Arora, *Evolution of Algo Trading and Its Future in India,* 2017.

[2]     P. Chan, *Quantitative trading: How to build your own algorithmic trading business.* Wiley Finance, 2009.

[3]     Securities and Exchange Board of India (SEBI), "Report on the regulation of algorithmic trading", 2020. Available from: https://www.sebi.gov.in

[4]     A. Catalini, and J.S. Gans, "Some simple economics of the blockchain", *NBER Working Paper No. 22952,* 2016. Available from: https://www.nber.org/papers/w22952
[http://dx.doi.org/10.3386/w22952]

[5]     "Demystifying Trading Strategy Returns", *NumXL,* 2012. Available from: https://numxl.com/blogs/demystifying-trading-strategy-returns/

[6]     Goforth, "The rise of blockchain: Legal and regulatory perspectives", *J. Financ. Regul. Compliance,* vol. 26, no. 3, pp. 358-373, 2018.
[http://dx.doi.org/10.1108/JFRC-09-2017-0084]

[7]     M. Masry, "The impact of technical analysis on stock returns in an Emerging Capital Markets (ECM's) country: Theoretical and empirical study", *Int. J. Econ. Finance,* vol. 9, no. 3, pp. 91-107, 2017.
[http://dx.doi.org/10.5539/ijef.v9n3p91]

[8]     McGroarty, F., Booth, A., Gerding, E., "High frequency trading strategies, market fragility and price spikes: An agent based model perspective", *Ann Oper Res,* vol. 282, pp. 217-244, 2019.
[http://dx.doi.org/10.1007/s10479-018-3019-4]

[9]     Gurung, Aashir & Chaturvedi, Sanyam, "A study on analysis of stock prices of selected industries", 2022.
[http://dx.doi.org/10.13140/RG.2.2.18095.82085]

[10]    D. Spahija, and S. Xhaferi, "Fundamental and technical analysis of the stock price", *Int. Scientific J. Monte,* vol. 1, no. 1, pp. 27-36, 2019.

[11]    G. Nandini, and R. Samal, "Technical analysis of selected industry leaders of indian stock market under the cloud of Covid-19", *Gedrag Organisatie Rev.,* vol. 33, no. 3, pp. -, 2020.
[http://dx.doi.org/10.37896/GOR33.03/473]

[12]    "RTS Strategy", *MarketScanner,* 2021. Available from: https://marketscanner.in/mrt-webinar/

[13]    Z. Zheng, S. Xie, H.N. Dai, X. Chen, and H. Wang, "Blockchain challenges and opportunities: a survey", *Int. J. Web Grid Serv.,* vol. 14, no. 4, p. 352, 2018.
[http://dx.doi.org/10.1504/IJWGS.2018.095647]

[14]    T. Hendershott, C.M. Jones, and A.J. Menkveld, "Does algorithmic trading improve liquidity?", *J. Finance,* vol. 66, no. 1, pp. 1-33, 2011.
[http://dx.doi.org/10.1111/j.1540-6261.2010.01624.x]

[15]    F. Black, and M. Scholes, "The pricing of options and corporate liabilities", *J. Polit. Econ.,* vol. 81, no. 3, pp. 637-654, 1973.
[http://dx.doi.org/10.1086/260062]

[16]    E.F. Fama, and K.R. French, "Common risk factors in the returns on stocks and bonds", *J. Financ. Econ.,* vol. 33, no. 1, pp. 3-56, 1993.
[http://dx.doi.org/10.1016/0304-405X(93)90023-5]

[17]    S. Black, M. Scholes, and J.T. Merton, "The theory of option pricing", *J. Polit. Econ.,* vol. 81, no. 3, pp. 637-654, 1973.
[http://dx.doi.org/10.1086/260062]

[18]    R.C. Merton, "On the pricing of corporate debt: The risk structure of interest rates", *J. Finance,* vol. 29, no. 2, pp. 449-470, 1974.
[http://dx.doi.org/10.1111/j.1540-6261.1974.tb03058.x]

[19]    D.B. Keith, "Corporate debt pricing and the merton model", *J. Fixed Income,* vol. 13, no. 2, pp. 55-63, 2003.
[http://dx.doi.org/10.3905/jfi.2003.319836]

[20]    S. Ghosh, and A.S. Chatterjee, "Application of option pricing models in indian financial markets: An empirical analysis", *J. Indian Bus. Res.,* vol. 11, no. 1, pp. 58-76, 2019.
[http://dx.doi.org/10.1108/JIBR-05-2018-0091]

[21]    A. Sethi, and N. Nilakantan, "Applicability of black-scholes model in indian capital markets", *JBIMS Research Conf.,* 2016.

[22]    M. M. Ali, and S. S. K. Rahman, "Portfolio drawdown analysis: A comprehensive review", *J. Financ. Plan.,* vol. 29, no. 4, pp. 68-79, 2016.
[http://dx.doi.org/10.1002/jpln.2016.29.4.68]

[23]    M.J. Clark, and B.M.T. Miller, "Managing portfolio risk: The role of drawdown analysis", *Risk Manage.,* vol. 12, no. 2, pp. 101-115, 2010.
[http://dx.doi.org/10.1057/rm.2010.2]

[24]    R.N. Prabhu, "Risk & return analysis of nifty stock in Indian capital market", *Risk,* vol. 5, no. 3, 2018.

[25]    X. Zhang, Z. Zhang, and Q. Liu, "Performance measurement of hedge funds: A comparative study of

the calmar ratio and other risk-adjusted metrics", *J. Financ. Res.,* vol. 43, no. 1, pp. 65-82, 2020.
[http://dx.doi.org/10.1111/jfir.12181]

[26]   J. Jonathan, "High frequency strategies", 2018. Available from: http://jonathankinlay.com/2018/12/high-frequency-trading-strategies/

[27]   J.A. Sen, *Comparative Study on the Sharpe Ratio.* Sortino Ratio, and Calmar Ratio in Portfolio Optimization, 2022.

[28]   J.B. Lee, and S.H. Kim, "Re-evaluating hedge fund performance: The calmar ratio *vs.* other performance metrics", *J. Altern. Invest.,* vol. 22, no. 2, pp. 38-50, 2020.
[http://dx.doi.org/10.3905/jai.2020.22.2.038]

[29]   A. Kumar, and V.M. Patel, "A study of compound annual growth rate (CAGR) in evaluating long-term investment performance", *J. Financ. Plann.,* vol. 34, no. 2, pp. 59-71, 2021.
[http://dx.doi.org/10.1002/jpln.2021.34.2.59]

[30]   M.B. Robinson, and H.K. Turner, "Assessing investment returns using CAGR: Recent advances and applications", *Financ. Anal. J.,* vol. 77, no. 1, pp. 83-97, 2021.
[http://dx.doi.org/10.1080/0015198X.2021.1872934]

[31]   D.B. Varshini, Vikas, and C. CM, "Equity research using technical analysis", *Int. J. Res. Innov. Social Sci.,* vol. III, no. VII, 2019.

[32]   M.A. Davis, and K.L. Harris, "The impact of square-off strategies on day trading performance", *J. Financ. Mark.,* vol. 47, pp. 1-15, 2022.
[http://dx.doi.org/10.1016/j.finmar.2022.100483]

[33]   T.L. Becker, and J.C. Williams, "Evaluating short-term trading techniques: The effectiveness of square-off strategies", *Quant. Finance,* vol. 21, no. 4, pp. 529-545, 2021.
[http://dx.doi.org/10.1080/14697688.2021.1892821]

[34]   L. Chen, J.Y. Zhang, and Z.H. Xu, "The effectiveness of short strangle strategies in volatile markets", *J. Deriv.,* vol. 29, no. 2, pp. 31-45, 2022.
[http://dx.doi.org/10.3905/jod.2022.29.2.031]

[35]   R.C. Miller, and K.T. Reynolds, "Advanced options trading: Analyzing the risk and return of short strangle strategies", *Financ. Anal. J.,* vol. 77, no. 3, pp. 92-107, 2021.
[http://dx.doi.org/10.1080/0015198X.2021.1913450]

[36]   S.P. Shivaprasad, E. Geetha, R. Kishore, and M. Rajeev, "Choosing the right options trading strategy: Risk-return trade-off and performance in different market conditions", *Invest. Manage. Financial Innov.,* vol. 19, no. 2, pp. 37-50, 2022.

[37]   A.M. Johnson, and T.K. Williams, "Evaluating algorithmic trading strategies through forward testing: recent advances and applications", *J. Financ. Mark.,* vol. 54, pp. 105-120, 2023.
[http://dx.doi.org/10.1016/j.finmar.2023.100589]

[38]   L.S. Chen, and R.A. Patel, "Forward testing of trading algorithms: A comprehensive review of techniques and best practices", *Quant. Finance,* vol. 22, no. 1, pp. 45-63, 2023.
[http://dx.doi.org/10.1080/14697688.2020.1788219]

[39]   P.J. Anderson, and H.G. Kim, "The utility of backtesting and forward testing in algorithmic trading: A comparative study", *J. Comput. Finance,* vol. 28, no. 3, pp. 77-92, 2023.
[http://dx.doi.org/10.21314/JCF.2023.498]

[40]   M.R. Adams, and N.P. Clark, "Assessing the effectiveness of backtesting and forward testing in financial models: Recent insights", *Quant. Finance,* vol. 23, no. 2, pp. 127-144, 2023.
[http://dx.doi.org/10.1080/14697688.2022.2079385]

[41]   A.G. Peterson, *Developing & backtesting systematic trading strategies.* DV Trading, 2015.

# CHAPTER 7

# The Carbon Footprint of Blockchain: Environmental Impact

**V. Gayathri**[1,*] and **Tanusri Gururaj**[2]

[1] *Department of ECE, Bharati Vidyapeeth's College of Engineering, New Delhi, India*

[2] *Ernst & Young Associates LLP, Gurgaon, Haryana, India*

**Abstract:** Blockchain technology is a distributed digital ledger, which is a sequence of interconnected blocks comprising secure and transparent peer-to-peer transaction records. It is a combination of blocks with shared memory, each of which is uniquely identified by a hash value. The distinctive nature of these blocks makes them resistant to falsification and builds trust and resilience in technology. This chapter provides an overview of blockchain technology, its architecture, and diverse applications. It explores the carbon footprint of blockchain technology and examines its environmental impacts through case studies on Bitcoin mining, Ethereum, Chia network, food supply chain, Tezos blockchain, and geothermal energy. It also endeavors to analyze energy consumption and Carbon dioxide ($CO_2$) emissions and eventually understand high-power usage, which has led to environmental impacts. The carbon footprint, which is the total greenhouse gas (GHG) emitted (including $CO_2$ and methane), is released at high levels and significantly affects habitats because of its ability to trap atmospheric heat. With the emissions of GHGs at high levels, this chapter also focuses on the mitigation process, namely, renewable energy. The chapter in the conclusion underscores the importance of continued efforts to make blockchains more environmentally sustainable.

**Keywords:** Bitcoin mining, Carbon footprint, Chia network, Consensus mechanism, Defi, Energy consumption, Environmental impact, Ethereum, Food supply chain, Geothermal energy, GHG, KlimaDAO, Non-renewable sources, Nordic energy market, Tezos blockchain.

## INTRODUCTION OF BLOCKCHAIN TECHNOLOGY

Information has always been a vital component of our lives, and today, the most significant portion is digitally maintained. Indeed, this is so as the switch to 'digital storage' offers dire consequences, where any mishap can be the public revelation of millions of personal aspects open to abuse. Privacy and security

* **Corresponding author V.Gayathri:** Department of ECE, Bharati Vidyapeeth's College of Engineering, New Delhi, India; E-mail: ythi.kkl007@gmail.com

**Monica Bhutani, Monica Gupta, Kirti Gupta, Deepali Kamthania & Danish Ather (Eds.)**
**All rights reserved-© 2025 Bentham Science Publishers**

issues in recent years have led to the search for better solutions. They established that blockchain technology provides a good solution for these challenges. Unlike most conventional systems that operate in a hierarchy with a major control center, blockchain works as an open ledger digital system that updates correspondingly with all nodes in the network, while maintaining similar data. The data stored in a block can hardly be changed, and any change requires the consensus of the majority [1]. Every block holds information and comes with the digital signature of the preceding block, thereby connecting it. This chain structure also means that if the information in one of these blocks were to be altered in any way, the whole chain would be affected, making the blockchain very secure against such an alteration. Thus, the use of blockchain reduces instances of forgery attempts to minimize bias and enhance data safety.

## Key Characteristics of Blockchain Technology

1. ***Decentralized Peer-to-peer Network:*** Unlike traditional systems, in which there is a client and server, a blockchain consists of nodes or peers that communicate directly with each other without the requirement of a central authority [2, 3].
2. ***Security and Transparency:*** Every transaction is recorded in a public ledger or database that is accessible to all nodes. The system is secure because each block stores the hash value of the previous block [2, 3].
3. ***Smart Contracts:*** These are digital agreements stored in a blockchain network and executed when specific conditions are satisfied. For example, a 10th- or 12th-grade mark sheet/certificate can be stored in a blockchain and issued once a person's identity and other details have been verified [2, 3].
4. ***Proof of Work (PoW):*** A new node cannot be added to the blockchain without approving the transaction. Therefore, participants (miners) in the network contended to solve a type of computational challenge. The first person to solve it gets to add the new block and earns cryptocurrency as a reward [2, 3].

## Taxonomy of Blockchain Technology

1. ***Public Blockchain***: This is a permissionless open network. This implies that anyone can join or become a member. To add a block to the network, a consensus mechanism must be followed, such as a PoW [2, 3], shown in Fig. (**1a**).
2. ***Private Blockchain***: This is also known as a closed network because members can only be part of it through an invitation. They are typically faster and more secure than public networks [2, 3], as shown in Fig. (**1b**).
3. ***Hybrid Blockchain***: This offers transparency and privacy by combining the features of both private and public blockchain networks [2, 3], as shown in Fig. (**1c**).

4. ***Consortium Blockchain***: This is a type of network that, instead of being managed by one organization, is managed by multiple organizations. This means that various organizations can collaborate in a shared ledger [2, 3], as shown in Fig. (**1d**).

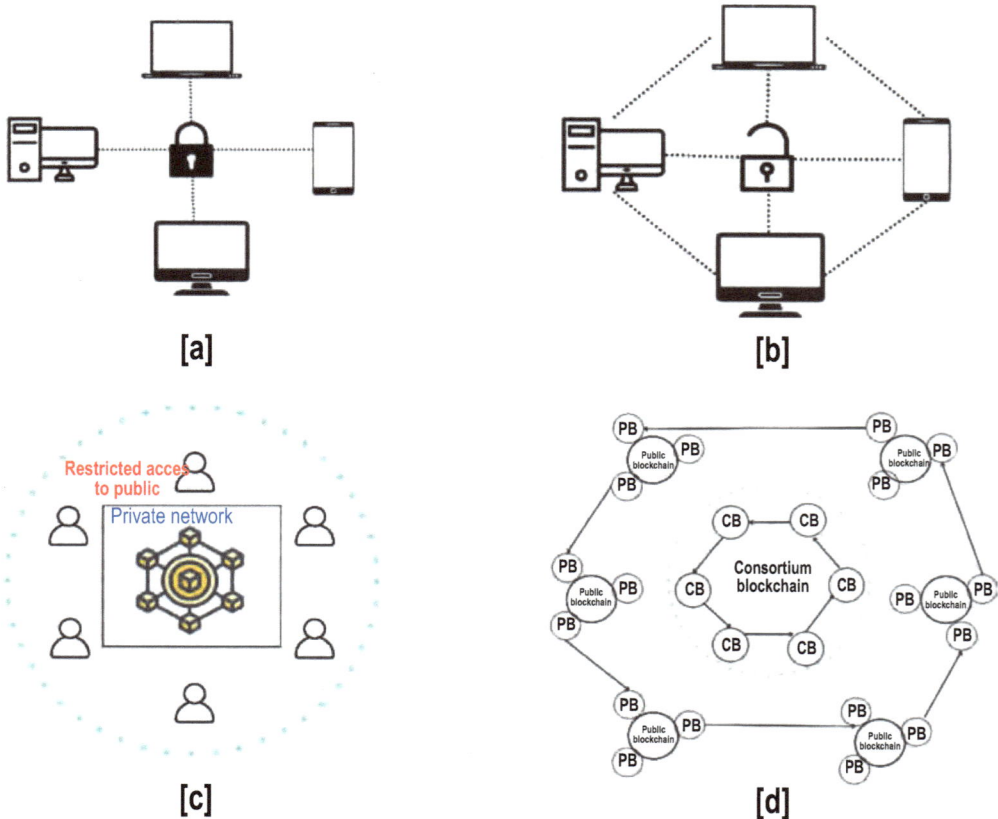

**Fig. (1).** Taxonomy of blockchain technology; (**a**) Private blockchain; (**b**) Public blockchain; (**c**) Hybrid blockchain; (**d**) Consortium blockchain.

## ARCHITECTURE

A blockchain is an order of blocks. This involves maintaining a database of all transactions, similar to a conventional account book. It is a transactional inventory that is immutable, decentralized, secured, consensus, and unanimous. Therefore, a blockchain is a combination of blocks and shared memory. These blocks are the basic structural units of the blockchain systems. A detailed overview of this architecture is provided below [4].

## Structure of Blockchain

A blockchain is a combination of several interconnected blocks. The first block of the system is the genesis block. In this technology, each block points to a previously available block, thereby creating a chain. The link is created using a reference value known as the hash value. Hash values are used to connect to the previous block, which is known as the parent block. Each block contained only one parent block. The genesis block is the first in the chain; it has no parent block and the hash value is zero. This also implies that the genesis block does not point to any other block.

The interior of a block (Fig. **2**) [2] is divided into two sections: the header and the body.

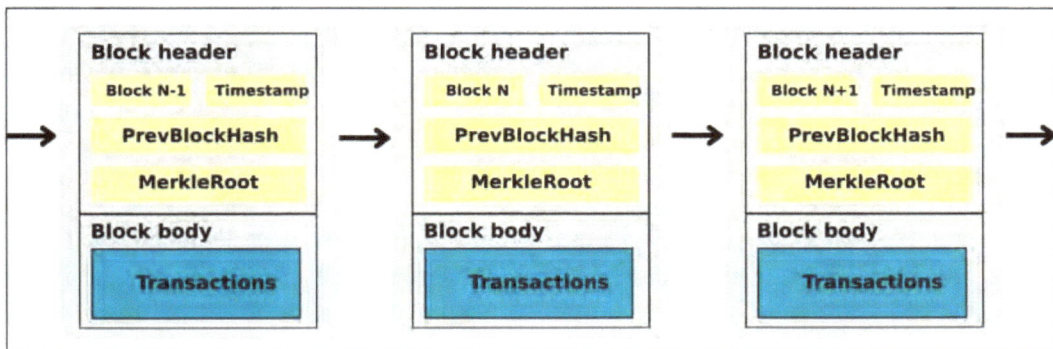

**Fig. (2).** Composition of a blockchain.

- The header section involves:
  1. **Block Version:** This represents a set of validation rules that must be followed when a chain is formed.
  2. **Parent Block Hash:** This is a 256-bit hash value pointing to the previous block.
  3. **Merkle Tree Root Hash:** This is the hash value of all transactions in a block.
  4. **Timestamp:** This is the current universal time in seconds since January 1, 1970.
  5. **nBits:** Target threshold of a valid block hash in a compact format.
  6. **Nonce:** This is a 4-byte field that usually starts with zero and increases for every hash calculation. This information was used in the creation and verification of the blocks.
- The body section of the block is comprised of transaction counters and records [2]. The maximum number of transactions that a block can contain depends on

the block size and the size of each transaction.

## Digital Signature

Digital signatures in blockchains are mathematical schemes used to prove the ownership of electronic coins and verify the integrity and authenticity of digital messages. This is similar to the case of handwritten signatures or stamps. The generation of an electronic signature by the sender involves specialized signing software and verification of the sign by the recipient. Digital signatures use asymmetric key cryptography, which is also known as public-key cryptography. It involves a private key (secret key) and a public key (shared with anyone) to encrypt and decrypt the data. Digital signatures were generated in two phases [3].

1. **Signing phase:** Creation of digital signatures by the sender. Specialized signing software was used to create a hash value for the data to be signed using a one-way hash function. The sender then encrypts the hash value using a private key, which creates a digital signature using a hash algorithm. Finally, encrypted hash values and messages are sent.
2. **Verifying phase:** Verification of digital signature by the receiver. The receiver obtains the message and hash value from which the sender's public key is extracted, which helps decrypt the digital signature to obtain the original hash value. The receiver then calculates the hash of the transaction data if the decrypted hash matches the computed hash value and confirms the integrity and authenticity of the transaction.

Electronic signatures in blockchain technology help solve the problems of manipulation and impersonation because they are valid only if the document remains unchanged. If a message is damaged or changed after signing, the authentication process fails. Thus, digital signatures are proof of data integrity, authenticity, and non-repudiation.

## Transactional Process of Blockchain

The addition of blocks to the blockchain is executed shown in Fig. (**3**) as follows [5]:

1. *Transaction Initiation:* A transaction enters a blockchain network using a hash function for verification. The hashed data are then encoded using the private key of the user to provide user validation, and the encoded result is known as the digital signature of the transaction. Data with signs are then broadcast to the network.
2. *Verification:* Once a transaction enters the network, all nodes check for validity

to ensure that an adequate balance is available to conduct the transaction. Each in the system validates the record by performing user authentication using a public key and data integrity by hashing and comparing the decoded signature. Subsequently, an authentic transaction was broadcast in the network.

3. *New Block Formation:* The block size should not exceed a pre-established capacity; therefore, transactions are grouped together. Verified and legitimate transactions are added only to the mempool. These verified transactions form a mempool at a node, and several mempools form a block.

4. *Consensus Algorithm:* Nodes use a consensus mechanism to add a block to the blockchain network. This mechanism ensures that the new block added is the only version of the valid block because every node is allowed to add blocks, which disrupts the blockchain network. The consensus algorithm is used to create a hash value for the block required to add the block. The node used to add a block is known as the miner.

5. *Addition of Block:* A new block is cryptographically added to the open end of the blockchain using the hash value of the previous block.

6. *Successful Transaction Completion:* The successful addition of a block marks transaction completion, and details of the complete transaction are stored unalterably in the network. These details are available to everyone.

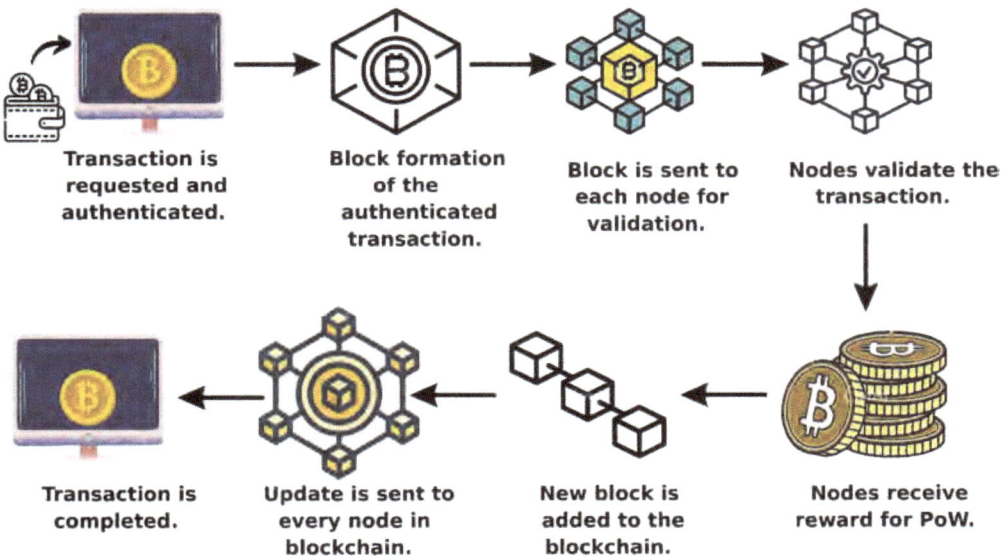

**Fig. (3).** Transaction process of a blockchain.

## APPLICATION

Blockchain technology's capacity to securely manage and preserve the authenticity of information has significantly contributed to its success in various applications as shown in Fig. (**4**) [6].

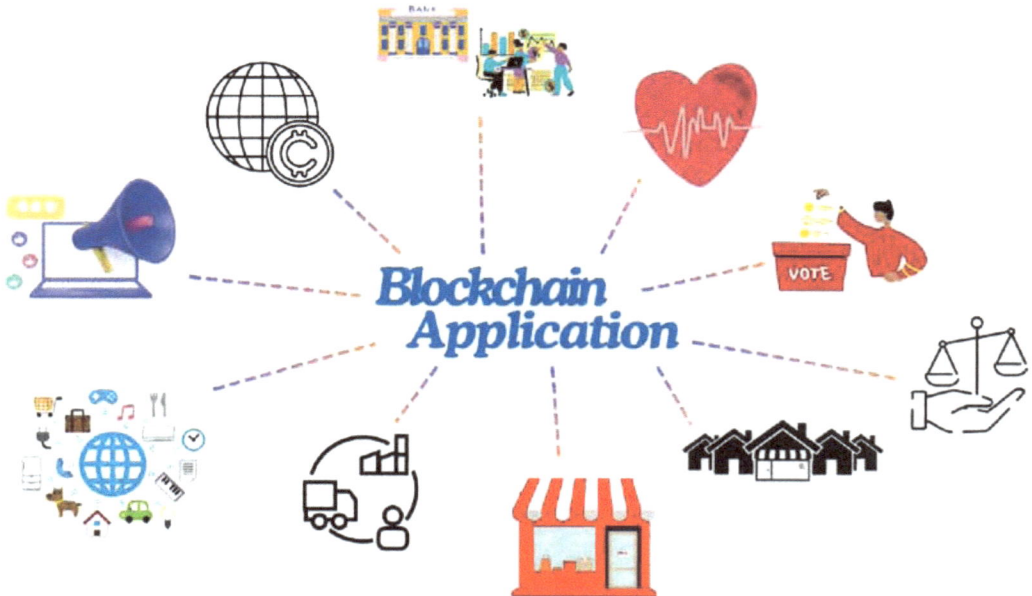

**Fig. (4).** Use cases of blockchain technology.

1. **Cryptocurrency:** Within cryptocurrency, the blockchain keeps transaction records secure and transparent and maintains them in order. These records were shared across the network, thereby building trust among all participants.
2. **Finance and Banking:** In this sector, blockchain is useful in wire transfers, digital verification, and smart contracts, to mention a few. This contributes to decreasing time and expenses and increasing the safety and availability of services.
3. **Healthcare:** In the sector of medical applications, blockchain is beneficial for the management of people's records. It also confirms that medicines are genuine and follow their journey, which minimizes fake drugs. The preservation of patient data and guarding everyone's privacy is also a crucial part of this.
4. **Voting and Governance:** Blockchain offers a secure, transparent, and tamper-proof method to manage voting and ensure the integrity of the election process.
5. **Real Estate:** This helps to maintain records of properties, land registries, contracts, and the buying and selling of estate. This system ensures a reduction in fraud and in intermediary costs. Smart contracts are used to automate and enforce real estate agreements.
6. **Retail:** Blockchain technology helps manage inventories, track stocks, monitor

supply chain transparency, and reduce the risk of counterfeit goods.

7. **Supply Chain and Logistics:** This helps track goods from production initiation to delivery and monitors logistics. Blockchain technology ensures honesty in the supply chain, reduces fraud, and increases trust.
8. **Internet of Things (IoT):** This aids in automating transactions between devices, managing digital identities, enhancing security, and minimizing data tampering.
9. **Media and Advertising:** Blockchain technology is used to monitor content/ad performance, eliminate piracy, and track content usage. This ensures that the payment related to the content/ad is fairly distributed by observing viewers' engagement.

## ENERGY CONSUMPTION AND $CO_2$ EMISSION

As technology advances daily and brings out various innovations in different fields, the automation of tasks makes human lives easier by saving important resources, particularly time. These technological advancements have led to a significant increase in device production. By 2022, an estimated 29 billion connected devices contributed to this surge [7]. With the increase in the use of these devices, energy and electricity demands have also increased, which has had a significant adverse effect on the environment.

Within this broader digital expansion, blockchain technology, particularly cryptocurrency mining, has emerged owing to its significant energy demand shown in Fig. (**5**) [8]. Blockchain technology, with attractive features of decentralization, high security, and transparent transactional records, has also majorly contributed to the production of high energy consumption and consequent $CO_2$ emissions. However, these unique features of blockchain technology have inclined towards energy-intensive models that utilize non-renewable resources. In this section, the reasons for the high energy consumption and $CO_2$ emissions are explained.

To know more about the effects of the blockchain on the environment one needs to turn to look at the aspects that influence the consume of energy. PoW consensus algorithm contributes to it significantly; it is used by popular cryptocurrencies like Bitcoin. It is an innovative technique that involves solving complex mathematical puzzles to validate transactions and ensure the security of the blockchain network and consequently, consumes a lot of computational resources. This includes various cryptographic problems, which require high computational power and servers that remain working and vying for blocks of rewards all the time [9]. Therefore, energy usage has been known to increase significantly, and this has been attributed to the increased energy consumption in the world.

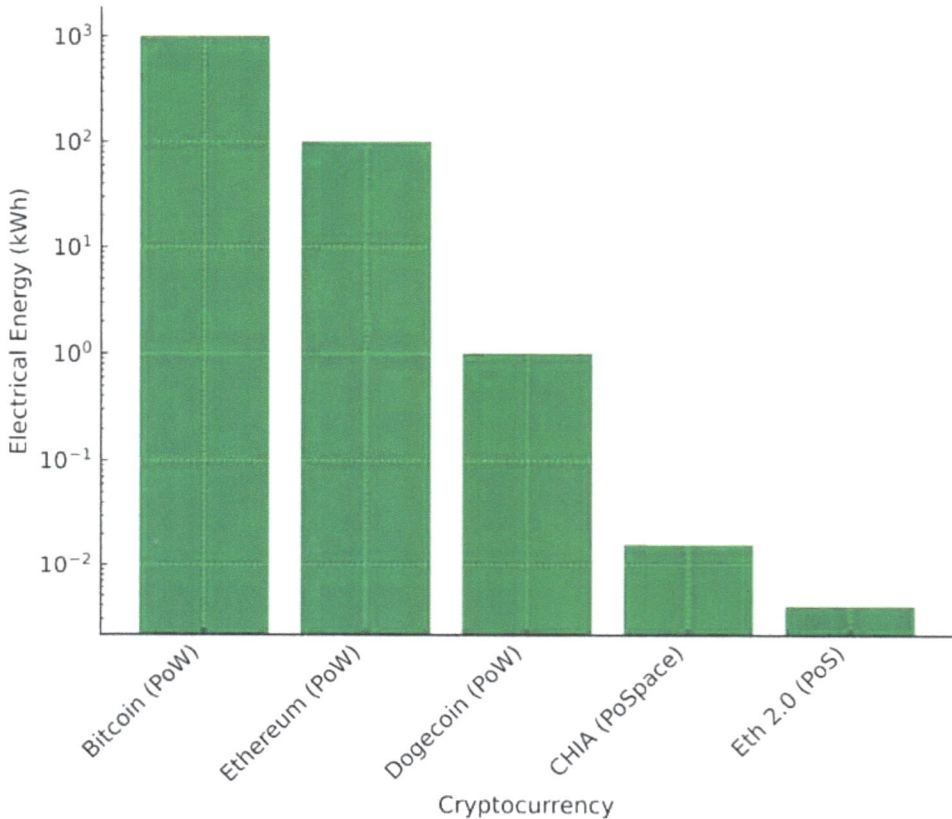

**Fig. (5).** Cryptocurrencies consensus mechanism *vs* Energy consumption.

Further, the demands of hardware for the mining operations are another consideration. Application Special Integrated Circuit (ASIC) and Graphics Performance Units (GPUs) used in the machinery require large quantities of power [10]. These devices require frequent upgrades given the complexity of the algorithms used in mining, multiplying both, the electronic waste and the carbon footprint. Also important to note is the fact that many of the mining facilities are situated in locations where fossil energy is predominantly used for electricity generation, further increasing the carbon impact. While some miners use renewable sources of energy, many are still using the conventional sources, the common being coal and natural gas. In addition to crypto coin mining, smart contracts and decentralized applications (DApps) which operate on the blockchain platforms such as Ethereum consume significant energy. As blockchain continues to enter more sectors from financial to supply and even healthcare industries, the environmental implications are likely to rise as well if no environmentally friendly options are adopted.

## Hardware Requirements and PoW Mechanism

The hardware particularly mining, has a direct influence on the energy usage of blockchain technology. An example of cryptocurrency is Bitcoin mining, which is based on PoW and demands a large amount of computational power and specific hardware, which in turn consumes a large quantity of electricity. Mining is the process of performing calculations to verify or endorse transactions and to create new blocks within a blockchain network. Devices such as ASICs are optimized for mining cryptocurrencies, making them highly efficient but exceptionally power-intensive [11]. The continuous electrical power required by these devices, along with their cooling systems, leads to a further increase in energy demand, making them a significant contributor to extremely high energy consumption. Additionally, the manufacturing and disposal of this equipment also plays a role in the environmental decline owing to the substantial resource extraction and generation of electronic waste. Current PoW models are based on hardware that is powerful, energy consuming, and efficient.

## Non-renewable Resources

A large portion of the energy used in blockchain technology comes from non-renewable sources, such as coal [12]. Mining operations usually run continuously to maximize profit and achieve the highest processing power among competitors, and the energy requirement is fulfilled by non-renewable resources, such as coal. Non-renewable resources cannot be replenished in the near future, causing almost irreversible damage to ecosystems. This reliance on non-renewable energy exacerbates $CO_2$ emissions and has given rise to a critical global impact. Efforts to transition to more sustainable energy practices have also been hindered. Mining operations are often located in regions with low electricity costs, which are typically associated with heavy dependence on fossil fuels. For example, a single Bitcoin transaction can consume more than 600 kW of electricity, resulting in a substantial carbon footprint [13]. Thus, the key factors in blockchain technology, distributed control, and security rely on substantial energy inputs to prevent alterations and ensure legitimate records.

## Carbon Footprint

A carbon footprint considers the seven Kyoto Protocol GHGs: $CO_2$, Methane ($CH_4$), Nitrous oxide ($N_2O$), Hydrofluorocarbons (HFCs), Perfluorocarbons

(PFCs), Sulphur hexafluoride ($SF_6$) and Nitrogen trifluoride (($NF_3)_3$) [14]. Energy consumption in blockchain mining is closely tied to GHG emissions, primarily $CO_2$. A significant computational capacity is required for the mining process, which uses a large amount of energy, particularly energy from hydrocarbon deposits, and produces large amounts of GHG emissions that cause climate change and global warming. High energy consumption and reliance on non-renewable energy sources are the primary reasons for the substantial carbon footprint of blockchain technology. For example, Bitcoin's carbon emissions increased by approximately 43%, from an estimated 63 $MtCO_2$ in 2018 to 90.2 $MtCO_2$ in early 2021, indicating a significant increase in its contribution to global GHG emissions [8]. Owing to the dependency of blockchain technology on non-renewable energy sources for peak performance, there are notable $CO_2$ emissions. Efforts to minimize carbon footprints are hindered by the lack of centralized control over energy-efficient models. Blockchain operations require a more sustainable strategy, as evidenced by the large environmental impact of many transactions and mining activities.

Besides mining, the geographical distribution of blockchain activities also reinforces the environmental challenge. Mining strongly favors areas where electricity costs are low, particularly in regions that heavily depend on coal and other non-renewable energy sources. This leads to seasonal energy shifts for example in areas that heavily rely on hydroelectric power, mining is done during the rainy season for the next season they use carbon sources like coal hence fluctuating $CO_2$ emissions are observed in that region [15]. Besides, the energy required to operate the blockchain nodes that need to be always running and synchronizing with other nodes can incur extra high costs. Every node contains the same information, performs the same operations at different points, and contributes to the duplication of energy consumption even in regions where energy is drawn from non-renewable sources.

Similarly, the legal environment may be equally uncoordinated with little or no regulation regarding energy consumption by blockchains. Since there is no drive or signal for the adoption of renewable sources of power supply, mining operations rely on cheaper opaque carbon-intensive power systems leading to boosting carbon intensity. This decentralization becomes a problem as blockchain adoption increases around the globe because the integration of identical, efficient measures is hampered and the more carbon-infused utility of the industry is solidified. All these factors put pressure on the blockchain industry and it has to look for more sustainable ways to address them and few of them are the use of renewable energy and optimization of the data storage and validation process [16].

Therefore, blockchain technology utilizes large amounts of energy and produces significant $CO_2$ emissions because of factors such as the need for specialized hardware, reliance on non-renewable energy sources, and energy-intensive PoW consensus techniques. These components significantly influence the carbon footprint and broader environmental impacts, including GHG emissions and resource depletion. The swift spread of cryptocurrencies, along with pacing dependence on the latest technologies poses ongoing challenges, especially concerning environmental sustainability and carbon emissions [17]. The recent research on the PoW cryptocurrency approach has listed seven aspects that could affect the environment: resources, energy consumption, carbon footprint, environmental-related social and economic aspects, policy regulation and subsidization, and electronic waste [18]. The creation of electronic waste, sourcing and processing of raw materials for hardware, and the total carbon output from mining facilities collectively degrade the environment. The high energy consumption demand of blockchain technology is associated with high energy and $CO_2$ emissions. To reduce the high-energy requirements of blockchain technology and scandals involving high-energy intake and $CO_2$ emissions, more efficient devices must be installed, renewable energy must be adopted, and sustainable practices must be adopted across the Blockchain revolution. The mitigation of ecosystem impact and the drive towards a sustainable future depend on the adoption of renewable energy sources and alternative consensus mechanisms, such as the Proof of Stake (PoS).

## MITIGATION

The beneficial features of blockchain technology, its decentralized and secured nature, result in frequent energy-intensive operations that contribute to harmful environmental effects. As the use of blockchain technology has spread across various sectors, carbon emissions have increased considerably. For enhancing transparency and accountability, blockchain encourages a green IoT ecosystem that has the unique capability to trace the carbon footprint of products and organizations. The integration of nature-friendly operations with blockchain technology has led to energy-efficient services, which have helped reduce the total carbon footprint.

To reduce the pressure of a high carbon footprint on the ecosystem, several reasons and techniques to overcome them have been investigated over time. Among them, one of the major causes of immense carbon emissions is the use of non-renewable sources of energy for mining operations. Renewable sources of energy, such as solar, wind, and geothermal (which are no longer effective in reducing emissions), have proven to ensure sustainability in blockchain operations, and this shift showcases the industry's efforts and dedication towards sustainable practices [19]. The distributed control of the digital ledger among the users has also helped in minimizing energy usage. The implementation of consensus algorithms such as PoS, the shift towards eco-friendly blockchains (Ethereum 2.0) and unconventional computing have shown great promise in reducing energy consumption.

To maintain sustainable standards and low carbon levels due to blockchain technology, global efforts for combating climate change necessitate the establishment of a transparent and efficient system. Government agencies can initiate policies, legislation, and energy consumption standards and mandate the use of renewable energy sources and carbon offsets during mining. The adoption of these laws will encourage emission reduction as business operations move towards more environmentally friendly technologies. To ensure that the operations follow the standard, blockchain technology makes it easier to monitor carbon credits and offset them.

The combined efforts of developers, miners, environmental organizations, and stakeholders to set up adequate low-carbon technologies and share modern solutions will help mitigate the carbon footprint of a blockchain. Community and organization collaborations lead to the brainstorming of great minds to find solutions for the same problem, thus pointing out new solutions for low-emission technology. The knowledge about the environmental effects of blockchain and strategies to reduce them unfolds from education, awareness, and focus on improving the living space. There should be learning of sustainable practices and green technologies so that developers, miners, and consumers can implement them. There have been new innovative developments that are transforming into new consensus methods such as Proof of Authority (PoA) and hybrid models, as well as ongoing research on energy-efficient technologies that have the ability to balance security, decentralization, and energy consumption [20].

Therefore, the mitigation of the carbon footprint can be addressed by the synthesis of technological advancements, renewable energy adoption, sustainable practices, policies, and industrial collaborations with existing methods. The emission reduction initiatives that integrate blockchain technology with carbon footprint management systems and carbon credit trading platforms also foster transparency and accountability; thus, these alterations do not affect the attractive features of blockchain. As the industry advances, the development of sustainable solutions and environmentally friendly policies to ensure a greener future will become a priority.

## CASE STUDIES

This section provides a showcase of examples of evident concrete strategies and challenges in the sphere of blockchain and digital currencies. These studies employ a technique that provides an understanding of how fragmented districts with blockchain technology can be integrated into different sectors. Blockchain and cryptocurrency mining have been subject to ecological concerns because of their effects on the environment, and more specifically, the carbon traces left behind after executing blockchain and cryptocurrency mining [21]. This series of case studies outlines various strategies through which several projects based on blockchain have attempted to reduce $CO_2$ emissions. The initiatives mentioned in the source of Ethereum's software (PoS) for the use of green energy in the most outstanding areas provide examples that can pioneer the reduction of harm to the environment. Additionally, the efforts of Klima DAO to promote carbon offsetting, the use of blockchain to optimize food supply chains, the Chia Network's unique approach to energy efficiency, the Tezos blockchain's commitment to sustainability, and the evolving landscape of decentralized finance (DeFi) offer diverse perspectives on reducing the carbon footprint.

Other specific examples include the Carbon credit market and environmental management. Blockchain technology is likely to improve the level of transparency and accountability in the markets due to the ease of tracking the flow of carbon credits. This assists the business and government in arranging their strategic carbon offset effectively and laudably, where credibility in the emission reduction is calculated and the duplication of credit is eliminated. Also, the distributed ledger feature of the blockchain technology has also been utilized in tackling the monitoring intensity of the environment where, real-time data on deforestation, pollution, and several other menaces to the natural environment is gathered. The immutability ensures that the data recorded in the blockchain records cannot be altered in any way, this gives authenticity to this data that is advantageous to the regulating bodies as well as the environmental agencies to fight climate change.

Furthermore, the Energy Web Foundation focused on the advancement of the implementation of blockchain in energy markets to promote the use of renewable energy sources. Hence by establishing the concept of P2P platforms where renewable credits are bought and traded as consumed, these platforms aim at decentralizing the consumption process in energy [22]. This helps to make a transition from high-carbon-intensity energy sources to cleaner ones hence reducing the overall carbon cost of blockchain systems.

Nonetheless, it appears that the incidence of a number of barriers that render effective collaboration tools ineffective today exist. For example, when there are no specific global norms or rules on how to develop blockchain, it becomes all but possible to follow sustainable practices when designing several blockchains. Further, some of the blockchain platforms are stricken with scalability issues, which lead to an increase in energy consumption depending on the increase in demand and this erases the advantage of energy-conserving consensus mechanisms like PoS.

It is still a process of addressing how to reduce the negative impact of consumption of blockchain but there is great potential to come up with other sustainable solutions that adopt the decentralized systems without letting go of the major benefits of blockchain in the industries.

Here are a few case studies discussed:

1. **Bitcoin mining:** Bitcoin mining is a power-consuming process that uses electric power produced by burning fossil fuels (non-renewable in nature) [23]. This results in a large carbon footprint, which adversely affects the environment. For example, the Greenidge Generation, a former coal plant in New York, was converted to natural gas and Bitcoin mining began in 2019 [24]. Although the shift from coal to natural gas is beneficial (natural gas is considered a cleaner alternative), Bitcoin mining has drastically increased GHG emissions, thereby affecting climate change.
2. **From PoW to PoS: Ethereum 2.0:** Unlike PoW, PoS is a mechanism in which members or validators perform staking [25]. Staking implies that members lock a certain amount of Ethereum in a smart contract. This amount serves as a security deposit and a source of rewards. Random selection was performed according to an algorithm to add a new block based on various characteristics such as the size of the stake. This is quite different from PoW because the mechanism is computationally and hardware-heavy, making scalability and sustainability difficult. Even though Ethereum 2.0 makes use of PoS, which is more environmentally friendly, it compromises security [26].
3. **Nordic Energy Market:** The energy markets of Nordic countries include Finland, Denmark, Sweden, Norway, and Iceland, where electricity is produced using renewable resources such as hydro, wind, and nuclear power, and the transaction takes place at a price that is fixed in the market. It can be seen that there is a significant potential for this market to be transformed by blockchain technology, where direct energy trading is possible with infused transparency to eliminate intermediaries. In addition, it enables the reduction of $CO_2$ emissions to a minimum because blockchain accurately accounts for renewable resources while encouraging the utilization of green energy and facilitating the implementation of decentralized power resources. This facilitates the smooth flow of energy trade and the selection of cheaper geothermal energy sources, thereby reducing GHG emissions and making the energy market sustainable.
4. **Food supply chain:** Blockchain disrupts traditional food supply chains by

solving problems related to supply chains, food security, and P2P tracing [27]. It lends itself well to real-time automation of the supply and demand of products or services and the accompanying transport and distribution. Factors such as food supply chain transparency, which involves production, processing, distribution, food security, and traceability, are challenges faced by the food supply chain [27]. These problems can be solved by blockchain because the technique is more cooperative and efficient in sharing information, which enables fast tracking of contamination and immediate automation of supply and demand mechanisms [28]. In addition, it helps reduce the environmental impact of the food supply chain through more efficient use of resources, effective waste management, and sustainable practices. This in turn results in improved routing, increased throughput, and reduced fuel consumption, resulting in fewer adverse effects on the environment.

5. **Tezos blockchain:** Tezos is a blockchain-based smart contract platform that implements PoS consensus and allows for the execution of dApps [29]. Compared to PoW, which is used in other cryptocurrencies, PoS is much more environmentally friendly because it uses less energy. In contrast with PoW, PoS aims to eliminate the need for intense computational power, and huge consumption of energy needed for mining activity, PoS chooses validators, which will create new blocks and cooperate in confirming the transactions in proportion to the amount of cryptocurrency, which they are willing to provide to 'stake' [29]. This change in consensus significantly reduces the impact on the environment because the concept of mining for crypto is off the table. Moreover, Tezos's self-amendment feature enables varied changes and improvements in the chain without the occurrence of a hard fork; hence, it does not experience divisions that are common in the blockchain. The ability to upgrade also benefits the network by increasing its durability and flexibility. This network integrates the recent energy-efficient technologies and protocols. Thus, by providing conditions for a more environmentally friendly use of blockchain, Tezos saves its resources and contributes to the creation of a standard that will inspire other projects to think about the same way as nature [29].

6. **DeFi:** DeFi is used for various financial purposes, including trading, borrowing, and lending, based on the blockchain concept. It makes use of smart contracts, most commonly on Ethereum. This enables secure, transparent, and intermediate-free transactions. The evolution of Ethereum 2.0 resulted in a PoS consensus algorithm instead of PoW. Ethereum 2.0 not only improves scalability and efficiency but also plays an important role in reducing the network's environmental impact because it is less computationally heavy, as discussed earlier [30]. This change is part of a larger development in blockchain, which has been going green while also advancing the area of

digital finance.

7. **Chia Network:** This network is a type of blockchain technology that uses the Proof of Space and Time (PoST) mechanism. PoST makes use of unallocated disk space on the blockchain owned by members [31]. Every member contributes some of its space to the network where cryptographic data (plots) are stored. When a new block needs to be added to the chain, the network sends a challenge. The farmers search their plots for the most similar match to the issued challenge. When a farmer finds the closest match, they are rewarded with the ability to add a new block. PoST also ensures that there is a delay between two events. This mechanism is not as computationally heavy as compared to PoW, hence making it more friendly to the environment.

8. **KlimaDAO:** This is a type of decentralized autonomous organization (DAO) that uses blockchain to address climate change issues by aiming to create an efficient carbon market [32]. A carbon market is a system in which countries or other organizations can trade carbon credits (allowances) [33]. These credits represent permits that emit a certain amount of $CO_2$ or other GHGs. The main aim was to maintain carbon emissions in order to control and combat climate change. KlimaDAO tokenizes carbon credits, thereby creating digital assets that represent the carbon offset [33]. This allows the trading of tokens using blockchain while ensuring transparency and traceability. Klima tokens are issued that incentivize organizations to purchase tokenized carbon credits. Thus, the value of carbon credits increases, pushing towards investments in green technologies.

## FUTURE SCOPE

Blockchain is one of the newest innovations and has shown promise in several applications. The long-term conditions of this decentralized technology and its applications can be defined by several potential trends and developments that might be anticipated. The following are important fields in which blockchain technology is expected to advance and have a significant impact:

1. **Scalability and performance improvements:** Another major concern as this technology develops is that the issues that affect scalability in blockchains remain relevant. Expectations are high that new advancements in consensus mechanisms, such as sharding, PoS, PoA, and DPoS, will further improve throughput and achieve much lower latency. In addition, layer 2 solutions, such as state channels and side chains, can provide more throughput and lower costs to make the blockchain more realistic.

2. **Interoperability between blockchain networks:** Future practices are predicted to involve the expansion of the drive to integrate various Blockchains. Demos and APIs, such as Polkadot, Cosmos, and Chainlink,

create bridges for communication between different blockchains. This will make it possible to create new sophisticated dApps and cooperate with different blockchains.

3. **Expansion into New Industries:** Blockchain, although revolutionizing the finance, supply, and healthcare industries, has broader uses than these fields. The blockchain's potential for development includes education, real estate, ownership of rights to intellectual property, and digital identity. Some of these applications include increasing transparency, deprecating fraud, and efficient processing in many fields.

4. **Enhanced privacy and security:** Technologies such as anonymity techniques, zero understanding, homomorphic encryption, and concealed deals are expected to be key elements in the development of blockchain. The following technologies will foster secure and private transactions and improve information privacy. This is particularly notable in industries such as finance, health, government, and services.

5. **Integration with IoT:** The integration of the two has the huge possibility of bringing about changes in the way devices control and exchange information through the use of the blockchain. Thus, it can be concluded that blockchain technology can introduce a reliable distributed database to store IoT activities and increase the degree of security. This can further create prospects for smart cities, automation of supply chains, and smart utilization of energy resources.

6. **Advancements in contracts and dApps:** The development of smart contracts will continue to enhance the use and versatility of dApps. As newer and more effective programming languages and platforms come into operation, developers will be able to deploy enhanced and superior-quality application programs that address different issues corresponding to the multifarious activities of different sectors of society. Additionally, activities in DeFi and non-fungible tokens (NFT) will remain high, presenting new opportunities for growth.

7. **Sustainability and energy efficiency:** As the noise level increases with regard to the adverse environmental influence of blockchain, the required shift towards discovering improved consensus approaches with lower energy consumption will be viewed as high. Thus, alternatives to energy-intensive PoWs, including PoS, PoST, and combined solutions, will gain popularity. In addition, technologies to offset blockchain networks on renewable energy sources and machine learning models to forecast the future potential of bitcoin mining *i.e.*, hash rate, energy consumption, and carbon emissions, will also come to the fore to support sustainability goals in line with maximizing technology [34].

8. **Regulation and governance:** Currently, the legislative environment for blockchains and cryptocurrencies is progressive. In the coming years, it will be

possible to enforce extended regulatory measures to provide a clear vision and stability to businesses and users. These regulations include the AML, KYC, and data protection regulations, all of which affect cryptocurrency use. Decentralized governance structures enable communities to govern themselves and make decisions concerning changes in network protocols and policies.

9. **Digital identity and DAO:** Self-sovereign identity solutions using blockchain are likely to gain popularity because people can own their identities and claim their data. This will allow easy and convenient access to services, guard against episodes such as identity theft, and allow users to own their data. In addition, DAOs continue to improve as a new type of organizational structure that provides decentralized collective organizations and decisions based on transparency.

Consequently, this study finds that the future is bright for the global implementation of blockchain technology. As technology grows and fine-tunes, existing challenges must be addressed, and new opportunities must be opened across various fields and sectors. The maturity and growth of key areas such as scalability, interoperability, privacy, and sustainability will pave the way for the advancement and sufficient use of blockchain in the formation of the digital economy and society.

## CONCLUSION

Blockchain is a relatively new technology with a decentralized and fixed structure that makes it reliable and trustworthy. It has been in the spotlight in many industries, such as finance, health, property, and business because it can preserve ledgers in a transparent manner. Currently, the primary reasons for the increased usability and dependability of blockchain platforms are smart contracts and digital signatures, which provide secure and authentic digital agreements. However, a large amount of power is consumed to offer such facilities; therefore, they release many $CO_2$s. Mining activities using the PoW mechanism should undergo complex exercises and consume a significant amount of energy, which has the propensity to add to the global carbon footprint. In the past several years, to obtain better solutions for energy efficiency, some implementations based on PoS systems have been designed. This proves that there is still room for future work to take the opportunity to harness blockchain technology with no negative impact on the environment. Several cases have been reviewed, including the Chia Network, particularly PoST, and the KlimaDAO carbon credit markets for environmental sustainability through blockchain. These examples are built around uncovered enhanced green power and developing better equipment and environmental awareness. Hence, while acknowledging that blockchain implementation has many advantages, such as security, transparency, and efficiency in its range, it is crucial to point out that sustainability seems to be a very sensitive aspect. With this new trend in the blockchain industry, to ensure it is done in a more sustainable way that does not affect the planet in a very negative way, the services rendered by digital ecosystems are secure, private, transparent, and much faster.

## CONSENT FOR PUBLICATION

We hereby grant consent for the publication of our work titled "The Carbon Footprint of Blockchain: Environmental Impact". We understand and agree that the Publisher has the right to publish, distribute, and make available our work in print, digital, or any other form deemed appropriate. We further acknowledge that the publisher may edit or format the work as necessary for publication, without altering its core content or meaning. We confirm that the work is original, does not infringe on the rights of any third party, and has not been published or submitted elsewhere.

## ACKNOWLEDGEMENT

We would like to express our deep gratitude to Principal, Prof. Dharmender Saini, Head of the Department, Prof. Kirti Gupta, and Associate Professor, Dr. Monica Gupta, Department of Electronics & Communication Engineering for giving us this opportunity.

## REFERENCES

[1]    J.Y. Huumo, D. Ko, S. Choi, S. Park, and K. Smolander, "Where is current research on blockchain technology? —A systematic review", *PLoS One,* vol. 11, pp. 1-27, 2016.

[2]    Z. Zheng, S. Xie, H.N. Dai, X. Chen, and H. Wang, "Blockchain challenges and opportunities: A survey", *Int. J. Web Grid Serv.,* vol. 14, no. 4, pp. 352-375, 2018.
[http://dx.doi.org/10.1504/IJWGS.2018.095647]

[3]    Z. Zheng, S. Xie, H. Dai, X. Chen, and H. Wang, "An overview of blockchain technology: Architecture, consensus, and future trends", *IEEE International Congress on Big Data,* vol. 6, pp. 557-564, 2017.
[http://dx.doi.org/10.1109/BigDataCongress.2017.85]

[4]    L. Ismail, and H. Materwala, "A review of blockchain architecture and consensus protocols: Use cases, challenges, and solutions", *Symmetry (Basel),* vol. 11, no. 10, p. 1198, 2019.
[http://dx.doi.org/10.3390/sym11101198]

[5]    D. Shakhbulatov, A. Arora, Z. Dong, and R.R. Cessa, "Blockchain implementation for analysis of carbon footprint across food supply chain", *IEEE International Conference on Blockchain,* vol. 1, pp. 546-551, 2019.
[http://dx.doi.org/10.1109/Blockchain.2019.00079]

[6]    T. Ali Syed, A. Alzahrani, S. Jan, M.S. Siddiqui, A. Nadeem, and T. Alghamdi, "A comparative analysis of blockchain architecture and its applications: Problems and recommendations", *IEEE Access,* vol. 7, pp. 176838-176869, 2019.
[http://dx.doi.org/10.1109/ACCESS.2019.2957660]

[7]    P.K. Sharma, N. Kumar, and J.H. Park, "Blockchain technology toward green IoT: Opportunities and challenges", *IEEE Netw.,* vol. 34, no. 4, pp. 263-269, 2020.

[http://dx.doi.org/10.1109/MNET.001.1900526]

[8]    V. Kohli, S. Chakravarty, V. Chamola, K.S. Sangwan, and S. Zeadally, "An analysis of energy consumption and carbon footprints of cryptocurrencies and possible solutions", *Digit. Commun. Netw.,* vol. 9, no. 1, pp. 79-89, 2023.
[http://dx.doi.org/10.1016/j.dcan.2022.06.017]

[9]    O. Martynov, "Sustainability analysis of cryptocurrencies based on projected return on investment and environmental impact", *Harvard Extension School,* vol. 1, pp. 1-69, 2020.

[10]   H.P. Winotoatmojo, S.Y. Lazuardy, F. Arland, and A.A. Setyawan, "Environmental impact of cryptocurrency mining: Sustainability challenges and solutions", *J. Sci. Res. Dev.,* vol. 6, no. 1, pp. 118-128, 2024.
[http://dx.doi.org/10.56670/jsrd.v6i1.312]

[11]   A. Jamali, N.I. Ali, I.A. Brohi, N.A. Kanasro, M.U. Murad, and A.A. Jamali, "Exploring relationships among bitcoin's market price, energy consumption and carbon dioxide emissions: A machine learning approach", *IEEE 1st Karachi Section Humanitarian Technology Conference,* vol. 1, pp. 1-6, 2024.
[http://dx.doi.org/10.1109/KHI-HTC60760.2024.10482372]

[12]   S. Chamanara, S.A. Ghaffarizadeh, and K. Madani, "The environmental footprint of bitcoin mining across the globe: Call for urgent action", *Earths Futur.,* vol. 11, no. 10, p. e2023EF003871, 2023.
[http://dx.doi.org/10.1029/2023EF003871]

[13]   C. Stoll, L. Klaaßen, and U. Gallersdörfer, "The carbon footprint of bitcoin", *Joule,* vol. 3, no. 7, pp. 1647-1661, 2019.
[http://dx.doi.org/10.1016/j.joule.2019.05.012]

[14]   A.M.R.D. Cruz, F. Santos, P. Mendes, and E.F. Cruz, "Blockchain-based traceability of carbon footprint a solidity smart contract for ethereum", *International Conference on Enterprise Information Systems,* vol. 2, pp. 259-268, 2020.

[15]   J.I. Ilbanez, and A. Freier, "Bitcoin's carbon footprint revisited: Proof of work mining for renewable energy expansion", *Challenges (Basel),* vol. 14, pp. 1-21, 2023.

[16]   L. Govender, "Cryptocurrency mining using renewable energy. An eco-innovative business model", *Int. Bus. Manag.,* vol. 1, pp. 1-61, 2019.

[17]   R. Mili, A. Trimech, and S. Benammou, "Impact of bitcoin transaction volume and energy consumption on environmental sustainability: Evidence through ARDL model", *IEEE 15th International Colloquium on Logistics and Supply Chain Management (LOGISTIQUA),* vol. 15, pp. 1-8, 2024.
[http://dx.doi.org/10.1109/LOGISTIQUA61063.2024.10571512]

[18]   M. Wendl, M.H. Doan, and R. Sassen, "The environmental impact of cryptocurrencies using proof of work and proof of stake consensus algorithms: A systematic review", *J. Environ. Manage.,* vol. 326, no. Pt A, p. 116530, 2023.
[http://dx.doi.org/10.1016/j.jenvman.2022.116530] [PMID: 36372031]

[19]   S. Kumar, "Review of geothermal energy as an alternate energy source for bitcoin mining", *Journal of Economics and Economic Education Research,* vol. 23, pp. 1-12, 2022.

[20]   H.T. Heinonen, A. Semenov, J. Veijalainen, and T. Hämäläinen, "A survey on technologies which make bitcoin greener or more justified", *IEEE Access,* vol. 10, pp. 74792-74814, 2022.
[http://dx.doi.org/10.1109/ACCESS.2022.3190891]

[21]   S. Tayebi, and H. Amini, "The flip side of the coin: Exploring the environmental and health impacts of proof-of-work cryptocurrency mining", *Environ. Res.,* vol. 252, no. Pt 1, p. 118798, 2024.
[http://dx.doi.org/10.1016/j.envres.2024.118798] [PMID: 38555086]

[22]   K.K. Vaigandla, M. Siluveru, M. kesoju, and R.K. Karne, "Review on blockchain technology: Architecture, characteristics, benefits, algorithms, challenges and applications", *Mesopotamian Journal of Cybersecurity,* vol. 203, pp. 73-84, 2023.

[23]   S. Köhler, and M. Pizzol, "Life cycle assessment of bitcoin mining", *Environ. Sci. Technol.,* vol. 53, no. 23, pp. 13598-13606, 2019.
[http://dx.doi.org/10.1021/acs.est.9b05687] [PMID: 31746188]

[24]   U.Q. Bajra, Ermir Rogova, S. Avdiaj, and E. Rogova, "Cryptocurrency blockchain and its carbon footprint: Anticipating future challenges", *Technol. Soc.,* vol. 77, p. 102571, 2024.
[http://dx.doi.org/10.1016/j.techsoc.2024.102571]

[25]   Y. Chen, L. Yang, Y. Fan, L. Zhang, and L. Tian, "Study on energy efficiency and carbon neutral path of Ethereum blockchain: from PoW to PoS", *International Conference on Energy Materials and Electrical Engineering,* pp. 1-12, 2024.
[http://dx.doi.org/10.1117/12.3015149]

[26]   M. Bilirer, and F. Zeren, "The impact of energy consumption in crypto assets on crypto asset prices and carbon emissions: case of bitcoin and Ethereum", *Financial Studies,* vol. 1, pp. 6-25, 2024.

[27]   J. Joo, and Y. Han, "An evidence of distributed trust in blockchain-based sustainable food supply chain", *Sustainability (Basel),* vol. 13, no. 19, p. 10980, 2021.
[http://dx.doi.org/10.3390/su131910980]

[28]   V. Singh, and S.K. Sharma, "Application of blockchain technology in shaping the future of food industry based on transparency and consumer trust", *J. Food Sci. Technol.,* vol. 60, no. 4, pp. 1237-1254, 2023.
[http://dx.doi.org/10.1007/s13197-022-05360-0] [PMID: 36936108]

[29]   M. Allouche, T. Frikha, M. Mitrea, G. Memmi, and F. Chaabane, "Lightweight blockchain processing. Case study: Scanned document tracking on tezos blockchain", *Appl. Sci. (Basel),* vol. 11, no. 15, p. 7169, 2021.
[http://dx.doi.org/10.3390/app11157169]

[30]   N. Sapra, and I. Shaikh, "Impact of bitcoin mining and crypto market determinants on Bitcoin-based energy consumption", *Manag. Finance,* vol. 49, no. 11, pp. 1828-1846, 2023.
[http://dx.doi.org/10.1108/MF-03-2023-0179]

[31]   B. Cohen, and K. Pietrzak, "The chia network blockchain", *Semantic Scholar,* vol. 1, pp. 1-44, 2019.

[32]   M.A. Sicilia, E. García-Barriocanal, S. Sánchez-Alonso, M. Mora-Cantallops, and J-J. de Lucio, "Understanding klimadao use and value: Insights from an empirical analysis", *Commun. Comput. Inf. Sci.,* vol. 1666, pp. 227-237, 2022.
[http://dx.doi.org/10.1007/978-3-031-22950-3_17]

[33]   M. Jirásek, "Klima DAO: A crypto answer to carbon markets", *J. Organ. Des.,* vol. 12, no. 4, pp. 271-283, 2023.
[http://dx.doi.org/10.1007/s41469-023-00146-w]

[34]   M.Y. Bukhari, A.A. Ansari, M. Yousif, M. Hassan, and U. Hassan, "Current and future implications of bitcoin mining on energy and climate change", *MRS Energy Sustain.,* vol. 11, no. 2, pp. 434-447, 2024.
[http://dx.doi.org/10.1557/s43581-024-00084-4]

# Dissecting Blockchain Technology: An In-Depth Analysis

**Nikhil Kumar**[1], **Richa**[1], **Sweeti Sah**[1,*], **Shweta Sharma**[1,*] and **R. Sujithra Kanmani**[2]

[1] *Department of Computer Engineering, National Institute of Technology, Kurukshetra, Haryana, India*

[2] *School of Computer Science and Engineering, Vellore Institute of Technology, Chennai, Tamil Nadu, India*

**Abstract:** Blockchain is known for being a decentralized ledger with distributed storage. It has changed whole industries across borders by increasing security, transparency, and reliance on intermediaries. Thus, from its initial design for cryptocurrencies like Bitcoin, Blockchain extends its transformative potential for a wide range of fields such as finance, supply chain management, and healthcare. The contribution of this research is an in-depth analysis of blocks, transactions, and consensus mechanisms constituting the anatomy of a blockchain. We have paid particular attention to block-structure research in our work, emphasizing that a block is an indivisible information unit, each containing transactional data and cryptographic hashes that link it to the previous block. One of the most valuable parts of our research consists of an innovative analysis of a consensus mechanism. We explain how different algorithms ensure the validity and sequence of transactions among the network nodes, and review the strengths and weaknesses of algorithms, namely, Proof of Work (PoW), Proof of Stake (PoS), and Delegated Proof of Stake (DPoS). The key highlights in this work are the case studies of well-established blockchain platforms, including Bitcoin and Ethereum. These manifest our insight into their operational efficiencies and mechanisms for security. Further, we demonstrate empirical results on the processing times for transactions and scalabilities of blockchains under different network conditions. Additionally, the challenges of scalability and energy consumption are put forth, for which novel approaches may be proposed for future blockchain development. The study contributes to the further development of blockchain technology by informing future research directions toward solving the existing limitations and exploring new applications within emergent sectors.

**Keywords:** Bitcoin, Blockchain, Consensus mechanisms, Decentralization, DeFi, Distributed ledger, Energy consumption, Ethereum, Mining, NFTs, Proof of stake, Proof of work, Smart contracts.

---

* **Corresponding authors Sweeti Sah and Shweta Sharma:** Department of Computer Engineering, National Institute of Technology, Kurukshetra, Haryana, India; E-mails: sweetisah3@nitkkr.ac.in; shweta.sharma@nitkkr.ac.in

**Monica Bhutani, Monica Gupta, Kirti Gupta, Deepali Kamthania & Danish Ather (Eds.)**
**All rights reserved-© 2025 Bentham Science Publishers**

# INTRODUCTION

First mentioned in 2008 by Satoshi Nakamoto as the underlying technology of Bitcoin [1], blockchain evolved to be more than its core function of leading active innovations for various businesses. Among the strong points brought about by the application of a decentralized and distributed ledger system in blockchain are safety, transparency, efficiency, and partly, reduction of reliance on intermediaries [2, 3]. Due to the presence of these features, blockchain-based industries use it confidently since it is designed for more security and efficiency; thus, it was able to extend its functionality to finance, supply chain management, healthcare, and beyond [4]. The recently attained advances in blockchain technology turned out to be one of the ways to cope with new problems and opportunities in the digital economy. The wider use of DeFi platforms completely changed the current face of financial services by allowing users to do their banking and make more by cutting out the middleman altogether [5]. Another point is that the development of the Non-Fungible Token (NFT) market transforms the creative space and allows artists, musicians, and other individuals to create content for alternative ways of monetizing digital projects, and processes of proving their ownership [6]. The fact that these achievements open a very interesting route for illustrating how capable blockchain can be in reforming the economy and changing individual styles of living and business models. Efficiency and effectiveness in blockchain comprise the blocks, transactions, and consensus mechanisms. These will include immutable blocks containing transaction data and store cryptographic hashes securely linking such blocks to prior ones, hence ensuring data integrity [7]. Transactions represent the life of blockchain, carrying out the role of ensuring that assets or information get transferred from one point of the system to another. The consensus strategy employs different kinds of algorithms that ensure the accuracy and timeliness of transactions, hence arriving at a consensus between different parts [8]. We will go deeper into the internals of various consensus algorithms, such as Proof of Work (PoW), Proof of Stake (PoS), and Delegated Proof of Stake (DPoS), whereby their advantages and disadvantages will be brought out in relation to catering to business queries and network volumes.

# LITERATURE REVIEW

Blockchain technology has drawn interest in recent times from both academia and industry circles as a game-changer across many industries. A lot of research has been done on its fundamentals, applications, and issues with blockchain. This review narrates the development with respect to consensus mechanisms concerning the most important aspects of blockchain technology: reliability, security, and usability. The first application of blockchain technology in Bitcoin used PoW [1]. Although PoW has been tested for safety and reliability in case of network attacks; it is, however, very power-consuming and is limited by capacity. Regardless, it has driven further research into other methods [9].

PoS, electing its validators based on the stake candidates have in the network, has recently been considered a quite promising alternative [10]. This is due to its energy efficiency and potential for improved scalability. In this respect, one of the most significant developments is the ongoing transition of Ethereum into PoS through the Casper protocol [11]. Other consensus mechanisms, such as DPoS, Practical Byzantine Fault Tolerance, and Proof of Authority, have also been proposed and implemented in various blockchain platforms, modulo their trade-offs between security, scalability, and decentralization [12]. Specifically, scalability—the ability to handle an increasing number of transactions without compromising on performance—has been traditionally one of the major challenges for blockchain technology. This has driven many researchers into more scalable and energy-friendly alternatives to PoW [13]. Such transitioning of the PoW to the PoS consensus algorithm will hugely improve Ethereum's scalability while reducing its energy consumption [14]. Layer 2 solutions have shown enormous potential for achieving high performance in blockchain without compromising security or decentralization and at a much cheaper cost of transactions [15].

Security is very critical for blockchain applications, especially in financial and sensitive data management. Although immutability and the crypto-based backbone of blockchain are a prima facie case for security, there are still some vulnerabilities that pertain mostly to smart contracts. This has led to research being directed toward developing strong smart contract auditing tools, which can allow attack simulation that facilitates the identification and mitigation of potential risks [16]. In addition, privacy issues concerning the transparency of public blockchains have also driven the need for research into techniques that offer further layers of privacy, such as zero-knowledge proofs and confidential transactions [17]. Interoperability between the different blockchain networks is one of the top priorities within the growing blockchain ecosystem. Full empowerment of this technology's power requires the seamless exchange of data and assets across chains. These studies led to the realization of cross-chain protocols and bridges like Polkadot and Cosmos that have enabled the communication and collaboration of disparate blockchain networks today [18].

## METHODOLOGY

This section details the experimental design, sources of data, and analysis methods used in studying the basics of components and consensus mechanisms in blockchain technology. We present our methodology in the current pool of research by referencing past studies and pointing out those areas that might require further investigation.

We base our work on previous literature related to blockchain technology such as Byzantine fault tolerance given by Lamport, Shostak, and Pease [19], in addition to which several consensus mechanisms have been designed and developed. The understanding from the different studies performed during Ethereum's transition to PoS helps in improving scalability, reducing energy use, and finding keys for scalability and interoperability-related challenges in blockchain networks [20, 21].

Fig. (1) summarizes the methodology using a flowchart as a case study in the comparison of Bitcoin and Ethereum. This flowchart breaks down the process into different stages, providing a roadmap to understand how the research was conducted and how data was collected, analyzed, and concluded.

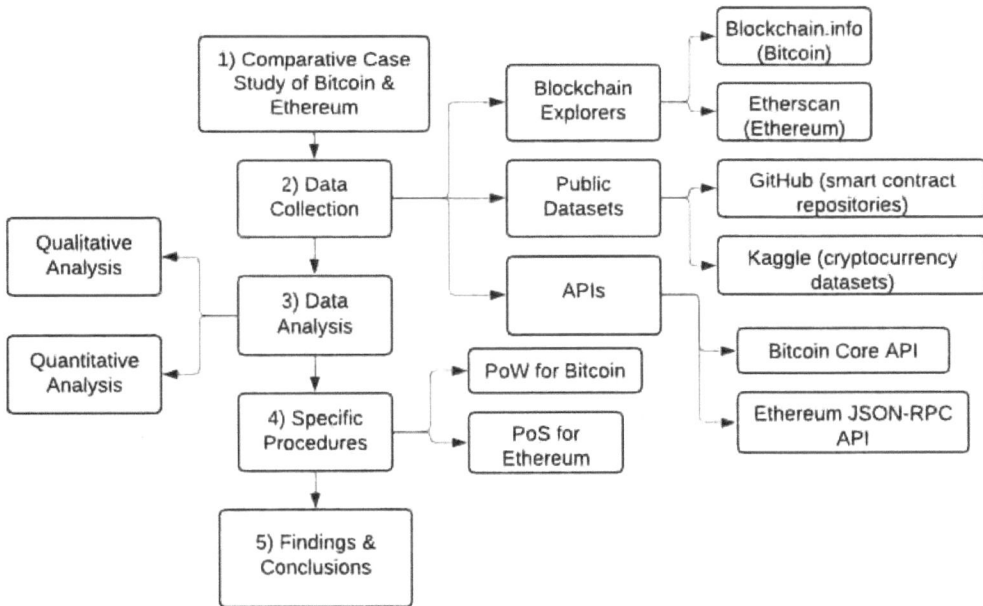

**Fig. (1).** Methodologies involved in the proposed work.

**Comparative Case Study of Bitcoin and Ethereum:** The first stage in the methodology involves a comparative case study of Bitcoin and Ethereum. This serves as the foundation for understanding how these two blockchain platforms function under different consensus mechanisms: PoW for Bitcoin and PoS for Ethereum. It helps to highlight the operational differences between the two platforms in terms of security, scalability, energy consumption, and transaction processing. By analyzing these platforms, the research aims to provide insight into their respective strengths and weaknesses.

**Data Collection:** The second stage of the methodology focuses on the collection of data from various sources, which include blockchain explorers like Blockchain.info for Bitcoin and Etherscan for Ethereum. These explorers provide comprehensive information about block details, transaction history, and network activity. Apart from these online tools, public datasets and APIs like the Bitcoin Core API and Ethereum JSON-RPC API were used to collect real-time and historical data. This data includes block size, transaction count, gas fees, and network congestion levels. The collection of diverse data sources ensures that the research is well-rounded and captures both the technical and operational aspects of Bitcoin and Ethereum.

**Data Analysis:** After the data collection phase, the analysis phase begins. This phase employs both qualitative and quantitative methods. Qualitative analysis is used to identify trends in network behavior such as transaction patterns and network congestion. Quantitative analysis is more detailed using statistical methods to examine metrics like transaction throughput, block times, and gas fees. The use of both approaches allows for a more comprehensive understanding of the blockchain platforms, enabling the research to derive meaningful conclusions from the data.

**Specific Procedures:** Specific procedures are followed to analyze the data using several models, algorithms, or software. Tools such as GitHub were used for smart contract repositories, and Kaggle was used for cryptocurrency datasets, providing us with a robust framework for analyzing blockchain activity.

**Findings & Conclusions:** The final stage compiles all of the analyzed data to form conclusions. It includes drawing comparisons between Bitcoin and Ethereum based on their consensus mechanisms, performance under different network conditions, and overall scalability. The findings also focus on future improvements for both platforms, particularly regarding security, energy consumption, and transaction efficiency.

Next, this work describes both the research design and procedural steps followed in conducting research on core elements and consensus mechanisms of blockchain technology in a comprehensive and systematic manner.

## DATA SOURCES

Data was collected from several sources: blockchain explorers such as Blockchain.info for Bitcoin and Etherscan for Ethereum [22, 23], publicly shared datasets [24, 25] found on Kaggle and GitHub, and APIs [26, 27] provided by the respective blockchain platforms. The data includes block details, transaction histories, network activity, and real-time information about processing times and gas fees for transactions.

This study utilized the following data sources, as detailed in Table **1**. The table provides comprehensive information on each source, including relevant characteristics and their role in the analysis. It contains the block number, timestamp, transaction count, block size, gas used, gas limit, block time, and average gas fee. Each row of the table corresponds to a specific block in the Ethereum blockchain and shows how dynamic the transactions are that get processed on it.

**Table 1. Data source details.**

| Block Number | Time Stamp | Transaction Count | Address | Block Size (bytes) | Gas Used | Gas Limit | Block Time (seconds) | Average Gas Fee (ETH) |
|---|---|---|---|---|---|---|---|---|
| 15348621 | 2024-08-01 14:35:21 | 153 | 0x2a65aca4d5fc5b5c859090a6 | 2,134,671 | 9,876,234 | 10,000,000 | 12 | 0.0123 |
| 15348622 | 2023-08-01 14:35:33 | 160 | 0x829bd824b016326a401d083b | 2,150,980 | 9,900,000 | 10,000,000 | 11 | 0.0118 |
| 15348623 | 2023-08-01 14:35:44 | 157 | 0x3edc7f3b86f3b1e0db3bba9c | 2,145,732 | 9,890,000 | 10,000,000 | 13 | 0.0130 |
| 15348624 | 2023-08-01 14:35:57 | 165 | 0x4d257d8b2cdada5b30d7c3db | 2,160,254 | 9,920,000 | 10,000,000 | 10 | 0.0126 |
| 15348625 | 2023-08-01 14:36:07 | 162 | 0x7fa1f1eb8fc7fef013e2908c | 2,150,120 | 9,930,000 | 10,000,000 | 9 | 0.0129 |

**Block number** is the unique number given to the blocks added to the blockchain. It provides a reference point from which transactions and network activities can be traced. The **timestamp** records the moment when a block was mined or validated. It provides the exact chronological view of how transactions are going over time. This provides the means to monitor performance in a network, which helps in taking appropriate action when transactions fail to get validated on time. A decentralized network requires validation within a given due time.

**Transaction count** simply describes the number of transactions included in a block. It is one way to measure network throughput, illustrating the volume of transactions a blockchain platform is capable of processing within a certain period of time. A higher transaction count means that the platform can handle more, and so it is one of the most important scalability metrics. **Block size** conveys the volume of the overall data in that block. The larger the block size, the more computational resources are required to mine or validate such a block, which has implications for general network efficiency.

**Gas** refers to a measure of the quantity of computational work that must be done on Ethereum to process an operation. The gas limit is the absolute measure of gas that can be consumed to execute all transactions within one block. It sets an upper limit so the network is not overloaded. The **average fee on gas** represents the amount users have to pay in order to get their transactions included in the block. High gas fees might signal network congestion and later become a crucial aspect of examination in transaction cost estimation.

Collectively, these attributes defined by Table **1** outline the complete picture of blockchain operations, including the essential metrics necessary for performance, scalability, and cost efficiency evaluation on blockchain platforms.

Data analysis was done using descriptive statistics in combination with comparative analysis and performance benchmarking. Descriptive statistics shall be deployed to describe and summarize data. Comparative analysis, on the one hand, involved great differences between Bitcoin and Ethereum under different consensus mechanisms. Performance benchmarking techniques are deployed so as to derive results on the scalability and safety of both platforms in variable network conditions. Our research has been based on two of the most adopted blockchain platforms, Bitcoin and Ethereum, considering wider adoption and multiple consensus mechanisms in practice. Data was extracted from various aspects using the following sources:

- *Blockchain Explorers*: Online blockchain explorers provide information with regard to transactions and blocks. In this work, we used Bitcoin—Blockchain.info [22] and Ethereum Etherscan [23]. These websites have enormous amounts of information with regard to block details, transaction histories, and network activities, the basis of higher-order analyses with respect to the behavior of blockchains.
- *Public Datasets:* Publicly available repositories such as Kaggle and GitHub [24, 25] were used for the historical blockchain datasets. These datasets contain the transaction timestamp, block size, miner information, and validator. On these basis, a time-based analysis can be done to identify trends.
- *Application Programming Interfaces (APIs):* We leveraged APIs provided by blockchain platforms to obtain real-time data for our analysis; this research was empowered by APIs, which scoured the most recent information on transaction processing time, network congestion, and how much it would cost in terms of gas fees for making transactions on those platforms. We were thus able to study the current status of these networks and their performances under different conditions. To this effect, very useful were the following: Bitcoin Core API and Ethereum JSON-RPC API [26, 27].

## CONSENSUS MECHANISM ANALYSIS

In this work, we have done a comparative study of two major consensus mechanisms: PoW and PoS. For both consensus mechanisms, there are some major aspects that were considered: energy consumption, security, scalability, transaction speed, method of selection for validators, the initial investment required, environmental impact, resistance to attack, and finally the adoption. Based on these factors, the table of features shows the relative strengths and weaknesses of each mechanism; hence, it gives insight into operating characteristics and suitability with respect to different applications of blockchains. One such comparative analysis of those consensus mechanisms has been presented in Table **2**, and it gives a critical overview of the operational characteristics.

**Table 2. Comparative analysis of consensus mechanisms.**

| Feature | PoW | PoS |
|---|---|---|
| **Block Analysis** | Block sizes and times vary with network difficulty; the distribution of rewards heavily influences miner behavior. | Block validation times are more consistent; staking rewards are distributed based on stake size and network participation. |
| **Energy Consumption** | High energy usage due to intensive computational requirements; significant environmental impact. | Lower energy consumption; validators are chosen based on stake, not computational power, reducing environmental impact. |
| **Network Security** | Vulnerable to 51% attacks; requires immense computational power to compromise the network. | More resistant to 51% attacks; attacking requires owning most of the network's cryptocurrency, making it economically challenging. |
| **Scalability** | Limited scalability; struggles to handle large volumes of transactions efficiently. | Better scalability; capable of processing a higher volume of transactions due to lower resource requirements. |
| **Cost of Participation** | High initial investment in mining hardware and ongoing energy costs; significant financial burden on miners. | Lower economic barriers; requires staking a substantial amount of cryptocurrency, but no need for expensive hardware. |
| **Reward Dynamics** | Rewards fluctuate with block times, network difficulty, and competition; long-term sustainability is a concern. | Staking rewards vary with network participation; they are more predictable and sustainable over the long term. |
| **Network Efficiency** | Block generation can be slow and resource-intensive; network congestion impacts performance. | More efficient transaction processing; lower gas fees, and faster validation times under varying network conditions. |

It examines their performance on various key attributes. The table shall give an overview of how each mechanism treats core facts of blockchain technology such as energy consumption, security, scalability, speed of transaction, validator selection, cost of participation, reward dynamics, and network efficiency. Further, the comparison across these factors shall allow for a critical understanding of how PoW and PoS work in real-world applications with relative strengths and weaknesses. The advantages of PoS are energy efficiency, scalability, and cost, while PoW does remain a rather strong mechanism for network security, yet challenged by high energy demands and the scaling problem.

## PoW

Our contribution includes:

- **Block Analysis:** Block size, block time, mining reward distribution efficiency and scalability of PoW are derived from these factors [1].
- **Energy Consumption:** We estimate energy consumption associated with PoW mechanisms in Bitcoin using data on hash rates and mining hardware power consumption [28]. In this work, we attempt to quantify one perspective on the environmental impact of PoW to contribute to discussions of sustainability.
- **Network Security Assessment**: This work describes the simulated attack against the Bitcoin PoW network, observing resources consumed and approximating the computing power necessary to successfully compromise the network. In this experiment, we could observe how resource-intensive it is to carry out an effective attack in PoW.
- **Scalability**: The research work targets studying scalability issues in the PoW network of Bitcoin, pending on higher volumes of transaction processing without degradation in performance. It has taken into consideration block generation time and the capability of the network to handle high-volume transactions.
- **Cost of Participation**: We estimated investment costs from mining hardware and ongoing energy costs, which can arguably serve as a proxy for economic participation barriers in the PoW network. In fact, this current analysis has placed particular emphasis on unravelling the cost structure and, hence, the financial burden on miners.
- **Reward Dynamics:** We studied reward dynamics that the miners encounter in the Bitcoin mechanism of the PoW. We also saw how mining rewards change dynamically with block time, network difficulty, and competition. From the previous analysis, it is pretty straightforward to get the long-term viability of the PoW mechanism.

## PoS

Our contribution includes:

- **Validator Performance:** Performance tracking of the active validators on the Ethereum network by block validation time and staking rewards, thus enabling the correct and efficient workings of the PoS mechanism at full capacity, was performed [29].
- **Network Efficiency:** We researched the overall efficiency of the Ethereum network. Network under PoS by analyzing transaction processing time and gas fees across a variety of network conditions; this will be very helpful in finding bottlenecks and improvement regions [30].
- **Network Security Assessment**: An experiment was simulated on the PoS network of Ethereum to determine how easy or hard it was for a person to conduct a 51% attack. This experiment focused on the challenges of acquiring a majority stake in the network and what implications such an act has on network security.
- **Scalability**: There have been extensive discussions with respect to the scalability of the Ethereum PoS network concerning efficient handling of large volumes of transactions, congestion on this network, and at what level of performance it could continue during periods of demand.
- **Cost of Participation**: This was the perceived cost that needed to be incurred by validators to participate in the network. In this case, the Ethereum PoS network was concerned with how much cryptocurrency it required for staking in the validation process. This section analyzed access and inclusivity within the context of PoS.
- **Reward Dynamics**: We have seen reward structures available to validators in PoS. Having said this, the dynamics of staking rewards rest on network participation, block validation times, and overall network conditions. In that direction, it would be possible to seek an overview of all address views with regard to the sustainability and equitability of the PoS rewards.

## SCALABILITY AND SECURITY ASSESSMENT

A number of tests have been carried out to assess the scalability and security of Ethereum and Bitcoin by using various consensus techniques. Table **3** depicts the comparison of the security and scalability evaluation of Ethereum and Bitcoin using various techniques of consensus. This also includes how each of these approaches influences resistance to Sybil attacks, double spending, smart contract audit processes, and transaction processing times. The following table compares the security features and performance of Ethereum and Bitcoin in different consensus models, comparing them both under PoW and PoS.

**Table 3.** Scalability and security assessment of bitcoin and ethereum under different consensus mechanisms.

|  | POW | POW | POS | POS |
|---|---|---|---|---|
| Blockchain | Bitcoin | Ethereum | Bitcoin | Ethereum |
| Transaction Processing Time | Moderate | Moderate | High | High |
| Smart Contract Audit | N/A | Moderate | N/A | High |
| Double-Spending Resistance | High | High | Moderate | Moderate |
| Sybil Attack Resistance | High | High | Moderate | Moderate |

The involved key attributes are transaction processing time, auditability of smart contracts, resistance to double spending, and resistance to Sybil attacks. It shows there does exist a trade-off between scalability and security when talking about PoW *versus* PoS. The PoW offers better resistance against security threats of double-spending and Sybil attacks but is less scalable because of slower transaction processing. On the other hand, PoS uses improved scalability and audibility of smart contracts, especially in Ethereum, thus making it more efficient for blockchain applications in modern times, but at some cost due to reduced security.

## PoW

***Transaction Processing Time:*** Solving cryptographic puzzles (Bitcoin and Ethereum) requires a lot of processing power. So, PoW for both Bitcoin and Ethereum exhibits moderate processing durations.

***Smart Contract Audit:*** Ethereum permits limited auditability of smart contracts. under PoW, and Bitcoin often does not support smart contracts, so this factor is not relevant in the case of Bitcoin.

***Double-Spending Resistance:*** Ethereum and Bitcoin both show strong resilience to attacks involving double-spending because higher processing power is required for such an assault.

***Sybil Attack Resistance:*** PoW is very much resistant to this type of attack, as creating multiple identities is costly and resource-intensive.

## PoS

***Transaction Processing Time:*** PoS enables faster transaction processing times for both Bitcoin and Ethereum, as it does not require solving complex puzzles.

***Smart Contract Audit:*** PoS under Ethereum focuses on the importance of smart contracts in case of decentralized applications by providing a high degree of auditability for them, whereas Bitcoin often does not support smart contracts, so this factor is not relevant in the case of Bitcoin.

***Double-Spending Resistance:*** PoS provides a moderate level of protection against double-spending by depending on the stake that validators own rather than computational power, which is normally less secure than PoW.

***Sybil Attack Resistance:*** PoS is moderately resistant to Sybil attacks, relying on economic disincentives rather than computational difficulty to prevent multiple identities.

## EXPERIMENTAL RESULTS

In this research, a comparative case study design has been harnessed to look at two of the most popular blockchain platforms: Bitcoin and Ethereum. The choice of these two platforms was based on the fact that they represent very popular platforms with different consensus mechanisms—PoW and PoS, respectively—and for which extensive data was available. Such a comparative approach allowed for identifying the principal differences and similarities between the two blockchain platforms under study, shedding light on the strengths and weaknesses of each consensus mechanism.

Fig. (2) shows the block data of Bitcoin, with mining difficulties moving in proportion to one another. The PoW consensus of Bitcoin dynamically adjusts mining difficulty for block generation time to remain consistent at approximately 10 minutes. Because of the number of blocks and the timestamps that keep on advancing through mining, it becomes more difficult due to the increase in block size. Therefore, the miners need to solve cryptographic puzzles that become more complex.

For this adjustment, it is crucial that the network stays safe, not dominated by a single miner or a group of miners, hence having control over the blockchain. This is how Bitcoin ensures that its mining process gets more complicated over time-the miners are compelled to renew their hardware and grow in computation power to remain competitive. On the contrary, such a growing mining difficulty has its price. While miners have to use more resources to validate blocks, the PoW mechanism itself does require a large consumption of energy, which raises concerns about the environmental effects of Bitcoin. As the difficulty rises, so does the electricity that is needed to mine each block. Various studies have shown that Bitcoins use as much energy as whole countries utilize. For this reason,

Bitcoins have been a frequent target of criticism regarding the sustainability of blockchain technology.

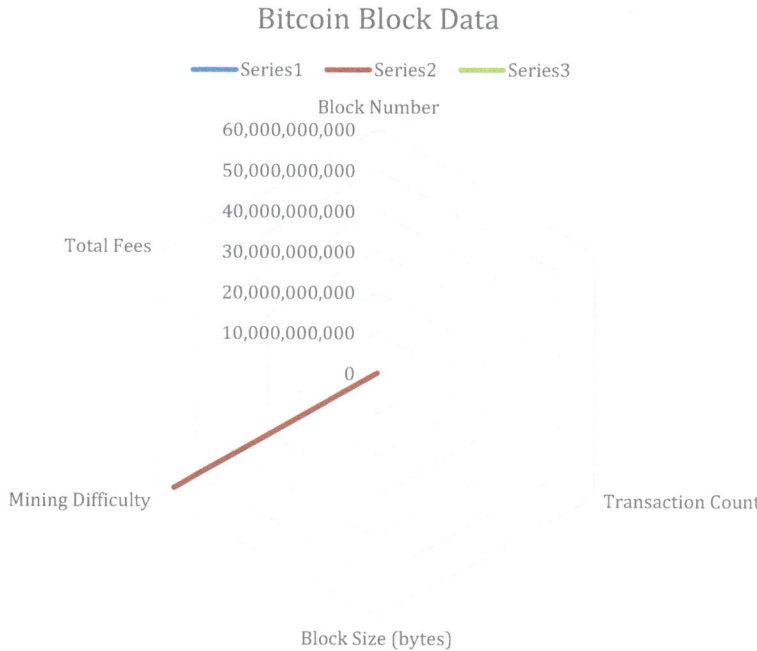

**Fig. (2).** Bitcoin block data *vs.* mining difficulty.

As the number of transactions increase and block size grows, it cannot continue to be sustained with transaction speed being efficient and transaction fees low if energy and computational resources increase in tandem. This is because PoW uses a trade-off between security and scalability, as higher volumes of transactions are not supported by the network because the costs associated with mining increase.

In other words, Fig. (2) summarizes some of the fundamental problems of Bitcoin's underlying PoW system: security provided through computation results in electricity consumption and reduced scalability. PoW is considered an important reason for Bitcoin's security and decentralization. On the other hand, the mechanism of PoW faces more heated discussions because of its environmental impact and inability to scale up easily to allow more users.

The Ethereum Block data table and its attributes are shown below in Table **4**, with six attributes: block number, Timestamp, Transaction count, Gas used, Gas limit, and Block Reward.

**Table 4. Bitcoin block data table.**

| Block Number | Time stamp | Transaction Count | Block Size (bytes) | Mining Difficulty | Total Fees Bitcoin (crypto currency) (BTC) |
|---|---|---|---|---|---|
| 8,10,000 | 2024-08-01 12:00:00 | 2,900 | 12,00,000 | 56,00,00,00,000 | 0.09 |
| 8,10,001 | 2024-08-01 12:10:00 | 2,950 | 12,25,000 | 56,00,00,00,000 | 0.08 |
| 8,10,002 | 2024-08-01 12:20:00 | 3,000 | 12,50,000 | 5620,,00,00,000 | 0.10 |

Table **4**, known as **Bitcoin Block Data**, consists of a number of key properties every block exhibits in the Bitcoin blockchain. These properties are, of course, vital to appreciate the various blockchains regarding their performance and nature in processing the transactions.

The table presents various key attributes like: Bitcoin blocks, including the block number, which uniquely identifies each block of the blockchain, incrementing with each newly mined block. The timestamp denotes the time at which the block was generated and it is about every 10 minutes thereby embracing the frequency at which Bitcoin intended to generate the block. Transaction count reveals how many transactions are included within a given block and if the transactions are more, then the block becomes larger. The value in bytes represents the size of the block and has an effect on how fast it will be transmitted in the network. The mining issue is a measure of how hard it is to mine new blocks where the measure is based on the overall computational power within a network. Finally, the total fees refer to the fees charged by the block users, which are included in the miner's reward and are essential especially when there is congestion in the network.

The table gives a snapshot of how Bitcoin blocks evolve over time in some of the key performance indicators: transaction count, block size, and mining difficulty. These jointly define the efficiency, cost, and scalability of the Bitcoin network.

Fig. (3) shows the relation of Ethereum block data with the number of transactions processed. This figure is important for the study of Ethereum's network performance and helps point out the efficiency of the platform in processing high volumes of transactions. Ethereum relies on a PoS consensus mechanism that secures transactions far quicker and with less energy compared to Bitcoin's PoW. This is mainly an improvement in transaction throughput because of the PoS mechanism where the validators are selected not based on the computational power contributed, but based on the amount of cryptocurrency each validator stakes.

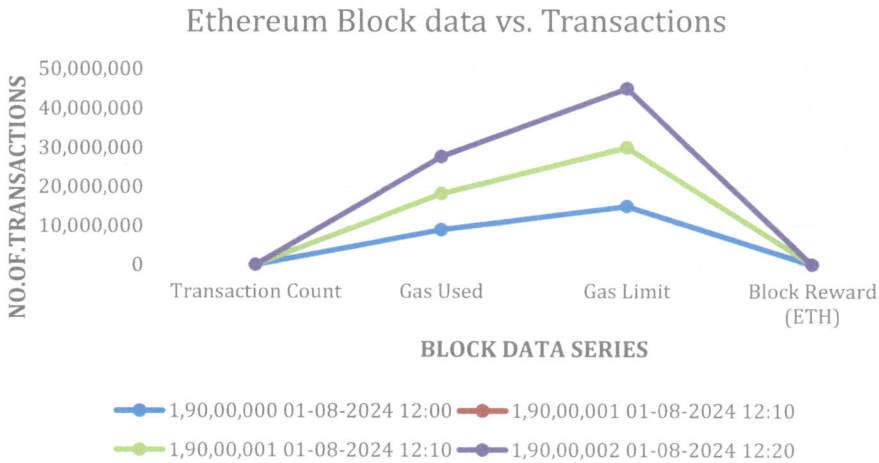

**Fig. (3).** Ethereum block data *vs.* transactions.

The main data used in each block includes: block number, timestamp, transaction count, gas used, gas limit, and block reward. Transaction count is a direct indicator of the number of transactions that get processed within one block and directly reflects Ethereum's scalability and its ability to cope with network congestion. The columns for gas used and gas limit are also very important, as they represent cost and capacity, respectively, for transaction processing. The term gas refers to a measure of the computational work of performing transactions; a gas limit sets an upper boundary on how much gas the network can use in one block. The figure depicts these values dynamically changing depending on the number of transactions to be included so that the efficiency of the whole network can be kept.

It also presents the importance of block rewards in Ethereum's PoS. Moreover, the manner of reward distribution to the validators depends on their stake and frequency of participation in block validation. These are recorded on each block in order for the validator to always have a consistent motive to secure and maintain the efficiency of the network.

Eventually, this figure shows how the Ethereum PoS model increases scalability along with energy efficiency, especially when compared to Bitcoin's PoW. In Ethereum, the whole flow of transaction validation goes smoothly and allows for higher transaction speed and lower fees, and it is more sustainable when coming onto model, the network for modern-day decentralized applications and smart contract executions.

Table **5** contains all the attributes associated with the blocks of the Ethereum blockchain. The information in the table includes the following:

**Table 5. Ethereum block data table.**

| Block Number | Timestamp | Transaction Count | Gas Used | Gas Limit | Block Reward (ETH) |
|---|---|---|---|---|---|
| 1,90,00,000 | 2024-08-01 12:00:00 | 2,000 | 90,00,000 | 1,50,00,000 | 2.0 |
| 1,90,00,001 | 2024-08-01 12:10:00 | 2,050 | 92,00,000 | 1,50,00,000 | 2.1 |
| 1,90,00,002 | 2024-08-01 12:20:00 | 2,100 | 95,00,000 | 1,50,00,000 | 2.0 |

**Block Number:** This is the number that is assigned to every block in the Ethereum blockchain and it continues to grow as new blocks are created through the mining process. This timestamp indicates the time at which the block is created, given that the Ethereum block occurs every 15 seconds affords high rates of transaction processing that is faster than Bitcoin.

The transaction count shows the number of transactions included in the block, so it refers to the block's activity in the transaction processing or smart contract deployment. Gas used shows the total gas consumption in all the transactions within the block or it represents the amount of computational power needed to execute a smart contract or perform a specific transaction. Transaction result specifies the maximum amount of gas that can be used in the process of a certain block; its maximum is set to 15 million gas units and defines the number of transactions that are possible to perform at the same time. Last, the block reward shows how many ETH is given to the miners who verify the block. In recent years, 2 ETH per block was given to miners so that they can continue to contribute to the security of the Ethereum network and not neglect the processing of transactions.

In general, Table **5** shows Ethereum's effectiveness and adaptability. The transaction count, positioned gas usage, and block rewards give an understanding of the network on the execution of smart contracts and further complicated transactions with velocity and efficiency. The elasticity of the gas fee on Ethereum makes it adapt to the different demands on the Ethereum network easily, in contrast with Bitcoin's much simpler approach.

## Bitcoin Descriptive Statistics Table

The descriptive statistics used in this study include the following attributes, as shown in Tables **6** and **7** below.

**Table 6. Bitcoin descriptive statistics.**

| Statistic | Block Size (bytes) | Transaction Count | Mining Difficulty | Total Fees (BTC) |
|---|---|---|---|---|
| Mean | 12,25,000 | 2950 | 56,10,00,00,000 | 0.09 |
| Median | 12,25,000 | 2950 | 56,10,00,00,000 | 0.09 |
| Standard Deviation | 25,000 | 50 | 10,00,00,000 | 0.01 |
| Range | 50,000 | 100 | 10,00,00,000 | 0.02 |

**Table 7. Ethereum descriptive statistics.**

| Statistic | Gas Used | Transaction Count | Gas Limit | Block Reward(ETH) |
|---|---|---|---|---|
| Mean | 9200000 | 2050 | 15000000 | 2.1 |
| Median | 9200000 | 2050 | 15000000 | 2.1 |
| Standard Deviation | 200000 | 50 | 0 | 0.1 |
| Range | 400000 | 100 | 0 | 0.2 |

**Mean:** Average values of block size, transaction count, and processing times.

**Median:** Middle value in the dataset to understand the typical case.

**Standard Deviation:** Measure of the variation or dispersion of the dataset.

**Range:** The difference between the maximum and minimum values in the dataset.

**Frequency Distribution:** Analysis of how often each different value occurs.

From Table **6**, we can get an average and understand the variability of the size of blocks, the number of transactions, mining difficulty, and the total transaction fees in the Bitcoin blockchain. About the block size, the average marked size is 1.225 MB (1,225,000 bytes), which shows how much data is commonly stored by each Block. The median block size is also 1. Fifty percent of the files were found to have a size of at least 225 MB, which indicates a symmetrical bell-shaped distribution with little spread as evidenced by the standard deviation of 25,000 bytes. This implies that the sizes of the blocks within the file across the entire set are relatively uniform, with the largest block of only 50,000 bytes larger than the smallest block hence blocks have relatively decent block performance.

The transaction count of about 2,950 is the number of transactions that happen within each block. The median is also 2,950, indicating that most of the blocks process an equal number of transactions. The variability of 50 transactions demonstrates that the data has the least variability from the mean while the range of 100 indicates that the number of transactions per block does not greatly deviate from each other in the dataset. It is conducive to the unchanging condition of the network, where it can implement transactions according to the number of blocks to be processed.

Mining difficulty is also an important metric for network security and performance with an average value of 56.1 billion, which reflects the computational effort which are required to mine new blocks. The median value matches the mean, showing that mining difficulty is relatively stable. The small standard deviation of 100 million further highlights that the difficulty does not fluctuate significantly between blocks. A range of 100 million indicates that there is only slight variability in mining difficulty, which helps maintain a consistent mining process over time.

Finally, the total fees per block average 0.09 BTC, contributing to the miner's rewards alongside block rewards. The median value is also 0.09 BTC, suggesting that fees are similarly distributed across blocks. The low standard deviation of 0.01 BTC and a small range of 0.02 BTC show that transaction fees are constant, with only minor fluctuations. This stability in fees ensures that miners can predict their earnings from transaction fees, even during varying network conditions.

Overall, the descriptive statistics in Table **6** reveal a high degree of consistency in Bitcoin's block size, transaction count, mining difficulty, and fees, suggesting a stable and efficient blockchain network with predictable performance.

Table **7** presents statistics for key attributes of Ethereum blocks, including the gas used, transaction count, gas limits, and block rewards. The gas used per block averages 9.2 million units reflecting the computational effort required to execute transactions and smart contracts on Ethereum. The median value of 9.2 million units combined with a standard deviation of 200,000 units and a range of 400,000 units suggests consistent gas usage across blocks with minimal variations in computational demand from block to block.

The transaction count per block averages around 2050, which indicates the number of transactions processed within each block. The median is also 2050, implying that transaction volumes are consistent across the network. A standard deviation of 50 transactions and a range of 100 show us that the number of transactions per block varies only slightly, reflecting the network's stable ability to handle a consistent number of transactions.

The gas limit is fixed at 15 million units throughout the dataset, meaning Ethereum enforces a uniform cap on the computational work for all blocks. The absence of variability, with a standard deviation and range of 0, indicates that the network maintains a strict limit on the computational resources that can be used in each block, ensuring predictability and stability in block processing.

Finally, the block reward encourages miners to validate blocks, which makes an average of 2.1 ETH. The median is also 2.1 ETH, showing that block rewards are distributed consistently. A standard deviation of 0.1 ETH and a range of 0.2 ETH suggest that while block rewards may vary slightly, they remain relatively stable, providing reliable compensation to miners for their work.

Overall, Table **7** highlights the steady and predictable nature of the Ethereum blockchain in terms of gas usage, transaction processing, and miner rewards. Low variability across all factors shows Ethereum's reliability in handling transactions and smart contracts, ensuring smooth network operations with consistent computational limits and rewards.

**Analysis of Consensus Mechanisms**, a comparative study between PoW and PoS, is performed through block analysis, with energy estimation in the case of the former, and validator performance concerning network efficiency for the latter. Assessment of scalability and security experiments were used to estimate transaction processing times at different network loads, while the security assessment of both platforms was done using smart contract audits and attack simulations.

## CONCLUSION AND FUTURE WORK

This research provides a comprehensive analysis of the basic elements that make up blockchain technology, such as blocks, transactions, and mechanisms of consensus. The research draws a comparison with the structure and function of blocks as immutable units storing transactional data and cryptographic hashes to ensure data integrity within the blockchain. Another principle is the concept of transactions, which enables the transfer of assets or information on the blockchain. This research focuses on the comparison between different consensus mechanisms such as PoW, PoS, and DPoS. When analyzing the strengths and weaknesses of every mechanism, the factors that will be considered are security, scalability, and energy efficiency, among others. This work adopts a mixed-method approach wherein both qualitative and quantitative analyses have been combined. Case studies of two major blockchain platforms—Bitcoin and Ethereum—are also done, focusing on their operational efficiencies and security mechanisms. This chapter addresses the challenges of scalability and energy consumption of blockchain technology and gives possible solutions and future research directions. It concludes by noting the potential of blockchain technology in effecting transformation in various sectors. In this regard, it stipulated areas that require regulatory and governance reforms to enable it to have wide adoption and growth. This chapter has also participated in the quest to interface blockchain technology with some other emerging technologies, such as artificial intelligence (AI) and the Internet of Things (IoT), underpinning potentiality for unlocking new functionalities that drive innovation in respective fields. This study contributes toward the development of blockchain technology by enhancing the full understanding of its core components and mechanisms of consensus, hence guiding future efforts toward the conquest of existing limitations and the exploration of new applications in emerging sectors.

This area of blockchain research has seen immense growth in the past; still, there are visible gaps and challenges. This pursuit of an ideal consensus mechanism in the pursuit of a balance between security, scalability, decentralization, and energy efficiency is never-ending. Hybrid models of consensus, by fusing different algorithms, offer a plausible future scope of study. It is, moreover, their combination with other emerging technologies—blockchain with AI or IoT—that offers unique opportunities for unlocking new functionalities and driving innovation. Equally necessary conditions for the diffusion of blockchain on a broad scale and its sustainable growth will be meeting the regulatory and governance challenges.

## REFERENCES

[1] H. Tanaka, "Blockchain decentralization: Comprehensive insights into bitcoin, ethereum, and solana", *Adv. Comput. Sci.,* vol. 7, no. 1, pp. 1-5, 2024.

[2] P.O. Shoetan, and B.T. Familoni, "Blockchain's impact on financial security and efficiency beyond cryptocurrency uses", *Int. J. Manag. amp; Entrep. Res.,* vol. 6, no. 4, pp. 1211-1235, 2024.
[http://dx.doi.org/10.51594/ijmer.v6i4.1032]

[3] N. Radziwill, "Blockchain revolution: How the technology behind bitcoin is changing money, business, and the world", *Qual. Manag. J.,* vol. 25, no. 1, pp. 64-65, 2018.
[http://dx.doi.org/10.1080/10686967.2018.1404373]

[4] J. Fan, Q. Wang, and Y. Wang, "The impact of blockchain on the administrative efficiency of provincial governments based on the data envelopment analysis–tobit model", *Sustainability (Basel),* vol. 16, no. 7, p. 2909, 2024.
[http://dx.doi.org/10.3390/su16072909]

[5] F. Schär, "Decentralized finance: On blockchain- and smart contract-based financial markets", *Federal Reserve Bank of St. Louis Review,* vol. 103, no. 2, pp. 1-24, 2021.
[http://dx.doi.org/10.20955/r.103.153-74]

[6] R. Kräussl, and A. Tugnetti, "Non-fungible tokens (NFTs): A review of pricing determinants, applications and opportunities", *J. Econ. Surv.,* vol. 38, no. 2, pp. 555-574, 2024.
[http://dx.doi.org/10.1111/joes.12597]

[7] D. Melo, S.E. Pomares-Hernández, L.M. Rodríguez-Henríquez, and J.C. Pérez-Sansalvador, "DiFastBit: Transaction differentiation scheme to avoid double-spending for fast bitcoin payments", *Mathematics,* vol. 12, no. 16, p. 2484, 2024.

[http://dx.doi.org/10.3390/math12162484]

[8]    G-T. Nguyen, and K. Kim, "A survey about consensus algorithms used in blockchain", *J. Inf. Process. Syst.,* vol. 14, no. 1, pp. 101-128, 2018.

[9]    K. Bala, and P.D. Kaur, "A novel game theory based reliable proof-of-stake consensus mechanism for blockchain", *Trans. Emerg. Telecommun. Technol.,* vol. 33, no. 9, p. e4525, 2022.
[http://dx.doi.org/10.1002/ett.4525]

[10]   A. Hafid, A.S. Hafid, and M. Samih, "Scaling blockchains: A comprehensive survey", *IEEE Access,* vol. 8, pp. 125244-125262, 2020.
[http://dx.doi.org/10.1109/ACCESS.2020.3007251]

[11]   Y. Wang, J. He, N. Zhu, Y. Yi, Q. Zhang, H. Song, and R. Xue, "Security enhancement technologies for smart contracts in the blockchain: A survey", *Trans. Emerg. Telecommun. Technol.,* vol. 32, no. 12, p. e4341, 2021.
[http://dx.doi.org/10.1002/ett.4341]

[12]   L. Zhou, A. Diro, A. Saini, S. Kaisar, and P.C. Hiep, "Leveraging zero knowledge proofs for blockchain-based identity sharing: A survey of advancements, challenges and opportunities", *J. Inf. Secur. Appl.,* vol. 80, pp. 103678-103678, 2024.
[http://dx.doi.org/10.1016/j.jisa.2023.103678]

[13]   Y. Gilad, R. Hemo, S. Micali, G. Vlachos, and N. Zeldovich, "Algorand: Scaling byzantine agreements for cryptocurrencies", *Proceedings of the 26th symposium on operating systems principles,* pp. 51-68, 2017.
[http://dx.doi.org/10.1145/3132747.3132757]

[14]   J. Zhang, J. Chen, Z. Wan, T. Chen, J. Gao, and Z. Chen, "When contracts meets crypto: exploring developers' struggles with ethereum cryptographic APIs", *Proceedings of the IEEE/ACM International Conference on Software Engineering,* pp. 1-13, 2024.
[http://dx.doi.org/10.1145/3597503.3639131]

[15]   M.N.B. Yusoff, and M.A.A. Shams, "Bitcoin layer two scaling solutions: Lightening payment channels network comprehensive review, mechanisms, challenges, open issues and future research directions", *Iraqi J. Comput. Sci. Math.,* vol. 5, no. 1, pp. 25-29, 2024.

[16]   N. Atzei, M. Bartoletti, and T. Cimoli, "A survey of attacks on Ethereum smart contracts (SoK)", *Lect. Notes Comput. Sci.,* vol. 10204, pp. 164-186, 2017.
[http://dx.doi.org/10.1007/978-3-662-54455-6_8]

[17]   E. Ben Sasson, "Zerocash: Decentralized anonymous payments from bitcoin", *IEEE Symposium on Security and Privacy,* pp. 459-474, 2014.

[18]   S.I. Sion, K. Zhang, A. April, and T.M. Lutete, "A comprehensive review of multi-chain architecture for blockchain integration in organizations", *Business Process Management: Blockchain, Robotic Process Automation, Central and Eastern European, Educators and Industry Forum,* vol. 527, pp. 5-24, 2024.

[19]   J. Wang, "A simple Byzantine Generals protocol", *J. Comb. Optim.,* vol. 27, no. 3, pp. 541-544, 2014.
[http://dx.doi.org/10.1007/s10878-012-9534-3]

[20]   R. Auer, B. Haslhofer, S. Kitzler, P. Saggese, and F. Victor, "The technology of decentralized finance (DeFi)", *Digit. Finance,* vol. 6, no. 1, pp. 55-95, 2024.
[http://dx.doi.org/10.1007/s42521-023-00088-8]

[21]   N.B.C. Togoe, S.A. Luca, and C. Pungila, "Towards efficient governance in distributed ledger systems using high-performance computational nodes", *IEEE International Symposium on Symbolic and Numeric Algorithms for Scientific Computing,* pp. 294-301, 2020.

[22]   C. Korkuc, N. Aytas Korkmaz, Y. Genc, A. Akkoc, E. Afacan, and E. Yazgan, "Blockbox: Blockchain based black box designing and modeling", *Concurr. Comput.,* vol. 36, no. 13, p. e8057, 2024.
[http://dx.doi.org/10.1002/cpe.8057]

[23]   Y. Zhou, J. Chen, Y. Wang, Y. Tang, and G. Gu, "Towards understanding crypto-asset risks on ethereum caused by key leakage on the internet", *Companion Proceedings of the ACM on Web Conference,* pp. 875-878, 2024.
[http://dx.doi.org/10.1145/3589335.3651573]

[24]   Available    from:    https://www.kaggle.com/datasets/prasoonkottarathil/ethereum-historical-dataset (Accessed  Jun.  30,  2024).

[25]   Available from: https://github.com/Ugochukwuodinaka/Bitcoin-Historical-Data-Analysis (Accessed Jul. 30, 2024).

[26]   M. Wang, Yang, W. Dai, Y. Liu, Y. Zhang, and X. Fu, "Deanonymizing ethereum users behind third-party RPC services", *IEEE Conference on Computer Communications,* pp. 1701-1710, 2024.

[27]   R. Kiani, and V.S. Sheng, "Ethereum smart contract vulnerability detection and machine learning-driven solutions: A systematic literature review", *Electronics (Basel),* vol. 13, no. 12, p. 2295, 2024.
[http://dx.doi.org/10.3390/electronics13122295]

[28]   A. de Vries, "Bitcoin's growing energy problem", *Joule,* vol. 2, no. 5, pp. 801-805, 2018.
[http://dx.doi.org/10.1016/j.joule.2018.04.016]

[29]   C. Badertscher, U. Maurer, D. Tschudi, and V. Zikas, "Bitcoin as a transaction ledger: A composable treatment", *J. Cryptol.,* vol. 37, no. 2, p. 18, 2024.
[http://dx.doi.org/10.1007/s00145-024-09493-7]

[30]   T. Duong, A. Tuyet, Chepurnoy, L. Fan, and H.-S. Zhou, "Twinscoin: A cryptocurrency *via* proof-of-work and proof-of-stake", *Proceedings of the ACM Workshop on Blockchains, Cryptocurrencies, and Contracts,* pp. 1-13, 2018.

# CHAPTER 9

# Decentralized Identification Systems Using Blockchain and Sovereign Identity

**Rohan Raj**[1] and **Sachin Gupta**[2,*]

[1] *Department of Information Technology and Engineering, Maharaja Agrasen Institute of Technology, Delhi, India*

[2] *Department of Compter Science Engineering (CSE), Maharaja Agrasen Institute of Technology, Delhi, India*

**Abstract:** This chapter focuses on the intersection of self-sovereign identity and blockchain technology. This review encompasses a number of issues: the role of SSI in augmented identity management, the advantages and challenges of blockchain integration, and real-world applications. It looks at how these technologies can make identification processes more efficient, secure, and reliable. The current review elaborates on the impact of SSI and blockchain on identity management with the use of selected papers from previous years. It is here that the main benefits, as well as practical challenges, are identified with the implementation of the technologies. The provided study concludes that SSI and blockchain technology have enormous potential to make identity management an order of magnitude more acceptable for various application domains. This will help shed more light on further research with an understanding of the benefits and challenges of these technologies.

**Keywords:** Authentication, Blockchain, Cryptography, Data integrity, Decentralized identity, Decentralized systems, Digital identity, Distributed ledger, Identity management, Interoperability, Privacy, Protocols, Scalability, Security, Self-sovereign identity, Smart contracts, Trust, User control, Verification systems, Zero-knowledge proofs.

## INTRODUCTION

### Background and Motivation

Conventional systems that are centralized in identity have only one point of control and vulnerability, for which they are enormously capacity-limited to cope with security, privacy, and user autonomy concerns. For example, central systems

* **Corresponding author Sachin Gupta:** Department of Computer Science Engineering (CSE), Maharaja Agrasen Institute of Technology, Delhi, India; E-mail: sachin.gupta@mait.ac.in

**Monica Bhutani, Monica Gupta, Kirti Gupta, Deepali Kamthania & Danish Ather (Eds.)**
**All rights reserved-© 2025 Bentham Science Publishers**

carry single points of failure that attract data breaches and cyberattacks. Identity management systems, especially centralized ones, are ripe for such high-profile incidents, as attested to by the Equifax breach in 2017, where the personal data of millions of individuals was exposed. A graver issue would be that centralized identity systems leave the control in the hands of very few entities; hence, some concerns over user autonomy and data sovereignty arise. Their data usually lies with third parties, who have control over and commercialize personal data without explicit consent. This growing number of digital interactions is the reason why the demand for more secure identity solutions, which are user-centric and privacy-preserving, is on the rise. Much attention goes to decentralized identification systems through the application of blockchain technology principles and self-sovereign identity. Blockchain itself emerges as an inflexible, decentralized structure that provides security, transparency, and tamper-proof identity management. Self-sovereign identity empowers individuals to own, control, and selectively share their personally owned data. They hold the promise of better security, user control, and privacy and are a very appealing model compared to the conventional ones [1]. The shift towards decentralization in identity management is more or less a technological innovation with a fundamental shift in how digital identities should be managed and protected.

## Problem Statement

In addition to this great opportunity, there is now an extensive range of problems associated with the implementation of decentralized systems for identification, including purely technical issues and questions of regulation and conscience. On this basis, perhaps the most significant issue is the capacity of blockchain networks, which must be able to process massive numbers of transactions. It also leaves the point of how these decentralized identity solutions are to interoperate with existing system architecture. Besides, there is one more important aspect; decentralized beings have to negotiate with the rules put in the regulated environment. For example, the General Data Protection Regulation (GDPR) is the regulation of the European Union. Some of them regulate data processing, storage, and user consent, which is quite challenging to reconcile with the principles of blockchain. Protecting users from identity theft, along with ethical considerations and ensuring user obscurity, is crucial for maintaining trust and security in online systems. The integrated 'openness' in the blockchain system can be an issue when it comes to privacy; besides, new approaches will be required to address this issue. The ethical issues of digital identity, like the problem of accessibility and inclusiveness of these technological solutions, must be addressed so that these decentralized systems are equally beneficial to all users.

## Purpose and Scope

In this chapter, an overview of the decentralized identification system applying blockchain technology and SSI is given, including core principles, technical frameworks, regulatory issues, and practical applications. It is based on a number of research works, which gives a rich source of information on the current state of advances and challenges in the field. Furthermore, it identifies the research trends in the subject under discussion and indicates the gaps to be further explored.

## Structure of the Chapter

The chapter will introduce the technology under review in this chapter on blockchain technology and decentralized identity. It starts with an introduction and background, then goes on to state the problem, the purpose, and the scope of the study. Consequently, an overview of blockchain technology, including its key concepts, terminology, benefits, and challenges, is presented. It compares traditional and decentralized identity systems, showing the benefits of decentralized identity, self-sovereign identity (SSI) principles and frameworks, decentralized public key infrastructure, verifiable credentials, and digital identities. The interplay between blockchain and identity is discussed, followed by a discussion of technical architecture and components, security and privacy considerations, regulatory and ethical considerations, legal and regulatory challenges, data protection and privacy laws, and finally, ethical implications and concerns. The chapter then discusses case studies and applications, including real-world implementations and examples, successful case studies, lessons learned, and best practices. Finally, the section on discussion and future directions explores current trends and innovations, open research questions, and potential future developments and concludes with a summary of key findings, implications for research and practice, and future directions.

## OVERVIEW OF BLOCKCHAIN TECHNOLOGY

### Introduction to Blockchain

Blockchain, the greatest creation of Satoshi Nakamoto in 2008 by inventing Bitcoin, is a distributed and decentralized ledger mechanism intended for the safe and immutable recording of transactions taking place over various computers. Each block of this chain features a cryptographic hash of the previous block, along with the transaction data, thereby representing a continuous chain of linked blocks. This structure gives security to the network and makes it tamper-proof so that once a block is added, it cannot be changed retroactively without altering all these subsequent blocks—a process that needs the agreement of a majority of the network. With this inherent immutability and transparency, the blockchain becomes a very solid solution for many other applications, from supply chain management and voting systems to digital identity.

## Key Concepts and Terminology

There are a number of important concepts and terminologies that one should acknowledge first for an understanding of what blockchain technology is:

***Decentralization***: In contrast with traditional centralized systems, blockchain is decentralized. It does not rely on a third party or central authority. This very feature makes it secure and robust since there is not a single point of failure. Every participant in the network holds onto a copy of the whole chain, ensuring that the data is still valid and uncorrupted.

***Consensus Mechanisms***: These are protocols created so network participants can agree on the validity of transactions. The most common consensus mechanisms include:

i. *Proof of Work (PoW)*: PoW is used by Bitcoin, where the miners have to solve very complex problems to validate transactions and add new blocks to the blockchain. PoW, while robust, is energy-intensive.
ii. *Proof of Stake (PoS)*: PoS is used in cryptocurrencies like Ethereum 2.0, where people are required to stake some amount of cryptocurrency to be used in the validation of transactions. Much more energy-efficient than PoW, this promotes a way to hold stakes for network maintenance.

***Cryptographic Hashing***: Here, the data is kept integral with data and data security processes such that digital fingerprints—known as the hashes—are unique to every block. Every change done to the data in a block will bring out a totally different hash, and thus, it is very easy to detect tampering. These are key characteristics for immutability in a blockchain.

***Smart Contracts***: These are self-executing contracts—a grant on terms whose agreements have been written directly into the code. Once required conditions are met, they automatically enforce and execute the agreed terms, hence doing away with the need for intermediaries while complex transactions and DApps are developed.

## Benefits and Challenges

Blockchain technology is handy in quite a few ways:

*Enhanced Security*: Blockchain systems, decentralized by nature, coupled with cryptographic hashing and consensus mechanisms guarantee robust data security and resistance to tampering and fraud. Each block is linked to the previous one, thus constituting a secure chain of data.

*Transparency*: An open ledger within the blockchain ensures transparency. It is the most helpful for any transaction since it gives all the parties involved visibility into the transaction and its verification, hence ensuring trust and accountability. Most importantly, such distribution of data finds wide usage in supply chain management, where information regarding the origin of goods and their distribution is very important.

*Trust*: Blockchain helps build trust among participants by making sure they have no need for a middleman to settle accounts between each other. Smart contracts implement such trusted behavior with auto-execution of agreements without the involvement of any third party.

However, there are also some issues that the technology needs to overcome:

*Scalability*: A blockchain network may encounter a performance problem as the number of transactions and network users increases. Sharding and off-chain transaction technologies are in the process of achieving effective scalability, among other such approaches, but it is still difficult to achieve.

*Energy Consumption*: Several consensus mechanisms, like PoW, are known for their energy-intensive operations and for raising environmental concerns. Alternative mechanisms are available, such as Proof of Stake (PoS), which are working on energy consumption but at a wider scale.

*Regulatory Uncertainty*: In the case of the regulatory framework around blockchain technology, it is all very new. It is challenging to be compliant with data protection rules, financial regulations, and other legal standards that vary from country to country. Such regulatory ambiguity may work against technological progress.

Understanding these benefits and challenges helps stakeholders appreciate the potential of blockchain technology to address obstacles in the widespread adoption of blockchain technology.

## Scope of Blockchain Integration

The implementation of blockchain technology in so many aspects is due to its decentralized, transparent, and secure nature. The potential integration of blockchain technology is huge, extending from the original use case in cryptocurrencies to supply chain management, healthcare, finance, and many more. Blockchains permit organizations to acquire tamper-proof records, make transactions automatically through smart contracts, and maintain data integrity across distributed networks. This is what makes blockchain highly suitable for those environments in which trust, security, and transparency are very critical—voting systems, cross-border payments, and data-sharing platforms. The immutability of records on a blockchain ensures data cannot be tampered with once it is recorded, hence forming a solid base for applications that require a high level of trust and auditability.

The blockchain allows for self-sovereign identity (SSI) with a unique capability that gives control over an identity back to the identity owner, unlike centralized systems. SSI is the idea that people own and control their digital identities, with the information they want to share and with whom they want to share it. Blockchain provides the necessary decentralized infrastructure for SSI, ensuring that identity data is both stored securely and only accessible to authorized parties. Systems of decentralized identity built on blockchain make it possible to create verifiable credentials quite conveniently and make them easily shareable and verifiable across platforms. These systems reduce the risk of identity theft and data breaches because personal information is not stored in a single, vulnerable location. These include Hyperledger Indy, uPort based on Ethereum, and Sovrin. Blockchain technologies are purposely designed to support the SSI and decentralized management of identity. These will be critical for the future of secure digital identity ecosystems.

## DECENTRALIZED IDENTITY

### Definition and Concepts

Decentralized identity systems provide an individual with a self-sovereign way to create, own, and manage their identity without any control from a central authority. This technology is based on blockchain; hence, identity data cannot be corrupted or lost in a decentralized system. In essence, a decentralized identity system works in such a way that a user creates an identifier, often known as a Decentralized Identifier (DID), which is recorded within a distributed ledger. Unlike conventional identifiers, DIDs do not represent any form of centralizing authority and can be proven cryptographically. This paradigm shift will enable individuals to have control over their personal information without having to rely on intermediaries.

A typical decentralized identity system comprises the following elements:

***Decentralized Identifiers (DIDs)***: Unique identifiers made and controlled by the user and registered in a blockchain or other distributed ledger.

***Verifiable Credentials***: These are digital attestations issued by trusted entities that can be presented by a user to prove some attributes or claims without leaking so much personal information.

***Identity Hubs***: Secure storage solutions allowing users to store and manage identity data and verifiable credentials privately.

**Traditional *vs.* Decentralized Identity Systems**

In contrast to decentralized identity systems, traditional identity systems tend to be centralized and controlled by governments or corporate authorities, and there are many failures in the case of a security breach. They also lead the user to have trust in third-party authorities for their validation and management, often with much at stake.

***Single Point of Failure***: Centralized databases are attractive targets for hackers. Breaches can compromise personal information for millions of users, as has happened with numerous high-profile data breaches.

***Lack of User Control***: This kind of control often gets removed from a user in a centralized environment. There is usually limited input by the user in determining how their data may be used. The entities responsible for managing the identity information may also very easily share, monetize, or misuse the said information without the go-ahead of the user.

***Privacy Concerns***: Most centralized identity systems collect very detailed personal information, which may be infiltrated and misused.

However, decentralized identity systems put the power and control back in the hands of users while helping to protect against data breaches and misuse.

***Decentralization***: The data is distributed across a network of nodes. This does away with points of failure in decentralized systems, hence leading to better security and resiliency.

***User Empowerment***: Users are able to self-manage the creation of identifiers, credentials, and information-sharing preferences.

***Selective Disclosure***: It allows users to reveal only the information needed for a transaction or verification, thus ensuring privacy and reducing data leakage.

## Benefits of Decentralized Identity

Decentralized identity systems have a number of benefits, which include:

***User Control***: Such a person has full control over identity data. He can create, own, and present his credentials without relying on any other authorities. This independence is a new dimension in the management of identities.

***Privacy***: Personal data is stored and shared with the explicit consent of the user in a secure manner. In the decentralized identity system, a user can present only relevant verifiable credentials to the verifier—for example, a claim related to a specific request about age or citizenship—and must not reveal any further personal information. This selective disclosure adds to privacy and relieves the risk of identity theft.

***Immutability of Blockchain***: The blockchain ensures data integrity and protects the data from unauthorized access by virtue of its immutability. This very fact, along with cryptographic techniques, in addition to the consensus mechanisms applied, makes it challenging for the attacker to change or temper the data. Moreover, decentralized identity ensures that mass data breaches are drastically reduced since the data is kept on several nodes rather than congregated in one store.

***Interoperability***: Decentralized identity systems can be designed to work on interoperability with other existing platforms and services. It will enable users to have a single digital identity that they can use to access various services and organizations, therefore reducing the burden of multiple identities and providing ease of use.

***Reduced Fraud***: Through tamper-proof and verifiable credentials, decentralized identity systems drastically reduce instances of fraud. This, thereby, authenticates with great security the authenticity of any claim by a user—more so in the financial, health, and e-commerce sectors. Furthermore, the challenges identified with traditional identity systems will be overcome, and the potential of blockchain technology will be harnessed in providing decentralized identity systems an elegant, secure, user-centric, and privacy-preserving solution.

***Compliance***: Decentralized identity systems should enable the ability of organizations to deal with personal data in a transparent and consensual manner, therefore making it possible to comply with data protection regulations like GDPR.

Fig. (1) is the visual representation of decentralized public key infrastructure, highlighting key management without central authorities.

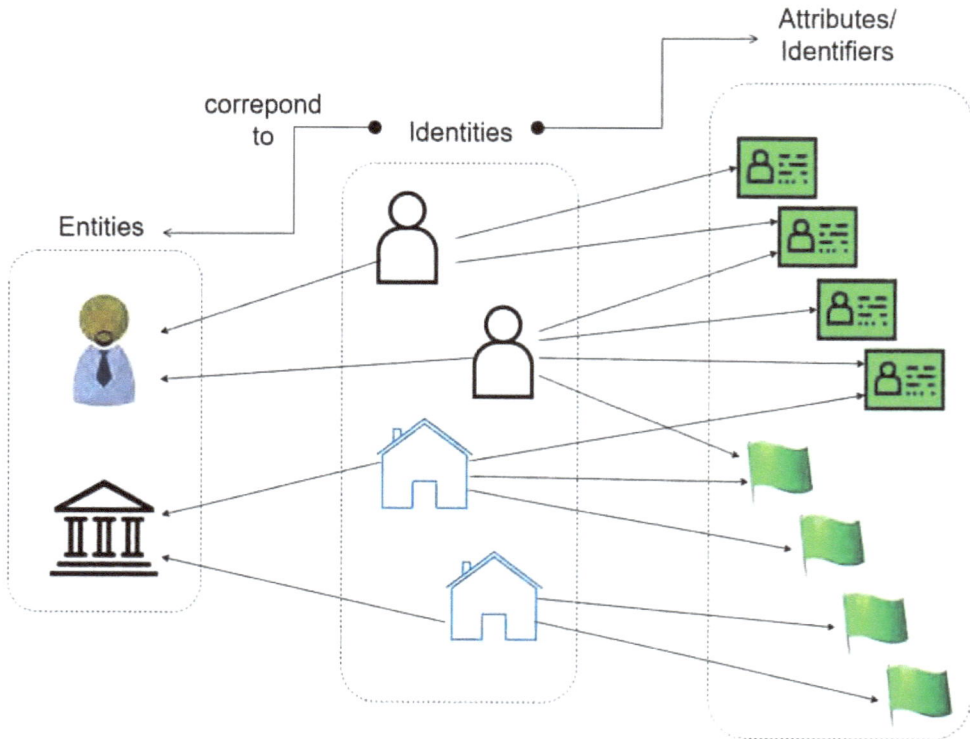

**Fig. (1).** Decentralized public key infrastructure.

## SELF-SOVEREIGN IDENTITY (SSI)

### Principles and Frameworks

Self-sovereign identity is a decentralized form of digital identity in which people own and control their personal information. Therefore, unlike most systems, this places an individual at the center of identity management and, most importantly, with respect to their sovereignty. The major principles of SSI include:

***Decentralization***: It improves security by eliminating a single point of failure; identity data is distributed in a network, not in a central repository. This further enhances security since a single point of failure is eliminated, thereby reducing the risk of a catastrophic data breach. Other components used in this model include decentralized identifiers (DIDs) and distributed ledger technologies (DLTs).

***User Control***: Individuals are able to control and share their ID data. Users create and manage their own cryptographic keys and ID credentials, deciding where, how, and with whom they share their information. This control ensures user privacy and averts third-party access to personal data.

***Interoperability***: The SSI systems are designed for operation on top of different platforms and jurisdictions. This interoperability gives a service where one digital identity can be used in different contexts, allowing users to easily adopt these kinds of solutions at large. For this to happen, a certain level of standardization is necessary for implementation using initiatives like the one from the World Wide Web Consortium (W3C).

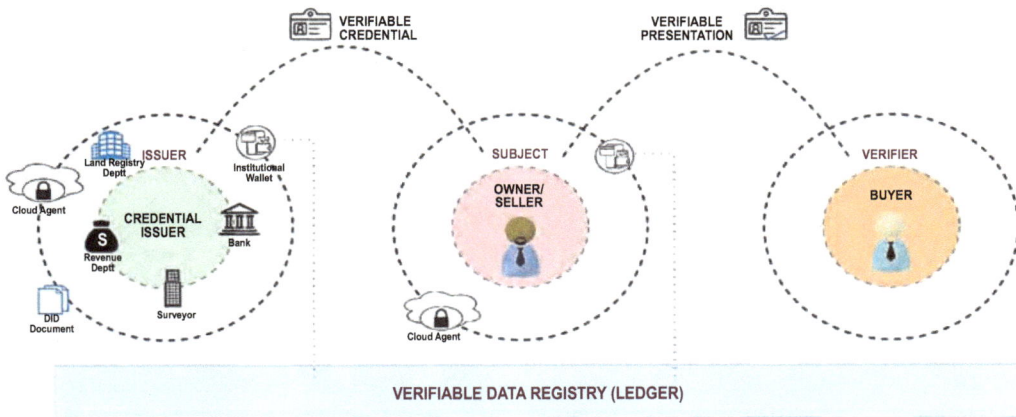

**Fig. (2).** Self-sovereign identity.

## Decentralized Public Key Infrastructure (DPKI)

It provides the basis for self-sovereign identity (SSI), where decentralized public key infrastructure is used in providing cryptographic keys that are securely generated, stored, and managed without a central authority. A DPKI does not rely on centralized hierarchies for the issuance and validation of keys in contrast to traditional PKI systems. This decentralization handles vulnerabilities and trust issues related to centralization.

Key components of DPKI include:

***Decentralized Identifiers (DIDs)***: DIDs are identifiers created and registered by users, so their control of them can be on some distributed ledger, like a blockchain. A DID enables the controller to prove independently verifiable digital identities without a central authority.

***Verifiable Registries***: A Verifiable Registry is a distributed ledger that stores DIDs and their accompanying public keys to support the verification of decentralized identity data. Verifiable Registries allow for ensuring that data concerning an entity is secure, transparent, and tamper-evident.

***Cryptographic Proofs:*** These mechanisms allow users to prove that they own and control their DIDs, together with the credentials, thus ensuring the validity and reliability of the digital.

By decentralizing key management and verification processes, DPKI enhances the security and credibility of digital identities, laying the foundation for robust SSI implementations [1].

## Verifiable Credentials and Digital Identities

Verifiable credentials are tamper-evident digital statements issued to a person by an issuer—a trusted party. A person is able to store these credentials, and then present and share them in a digital fashion, in such a way that the user's privacy is not compromised, when needed, for example, to open a new account. Verifiable credentials are a foundation of SSI and enable secure and private digital interactions. Some key aspects include:

***Issuance***: Trusted authorities, such as government agencies, educational institutions, or employers, issue verifiable credentials to individuals. These credentials contain claims about the individual's identity or attributes, such as age, citizenship, or qualifications.

***Storage***: Individuals store their verifiable credentials in digital wallets or identity hubs. These storage solutions are secure and under the control of the individual, ensuring that personal data is protected.

***Presentation***: Holders can present their verifiable credentials to a third party, if needed, to prove identity or other characteristics. The process is selective and privacy-respecting; thus, the holder is able to disclose only what they wish for any given transaction or interchange.

*__Verification__*: Receivers are able to determine if a received credential is actually authentic by executing cryptographic proofs to relevant public keys registered in the applicable verifiable registries. The verification process authenticates the credentials and ensures that they are not changed.

Reasons why verifiable credentials are being embraced by SSI systems are given below:

*__Greater Privacy__*: People are able to share only some of their attributes without sharing their complete identity or other personal information.

*__Enhanced Security__*: The cryptographic basis of verifiable credentials makes them tamper-proof and virtually forgery-resistant.

*__Improved Trust__*: Involvement of trusted issuers with decentralized verification builds confidence in the truth and integrity of the digital identity [2].

SSI systems allow for secure, human-centric identity management through decentralized principles, user control, and interoperability through verifiable credentials and digital identities.

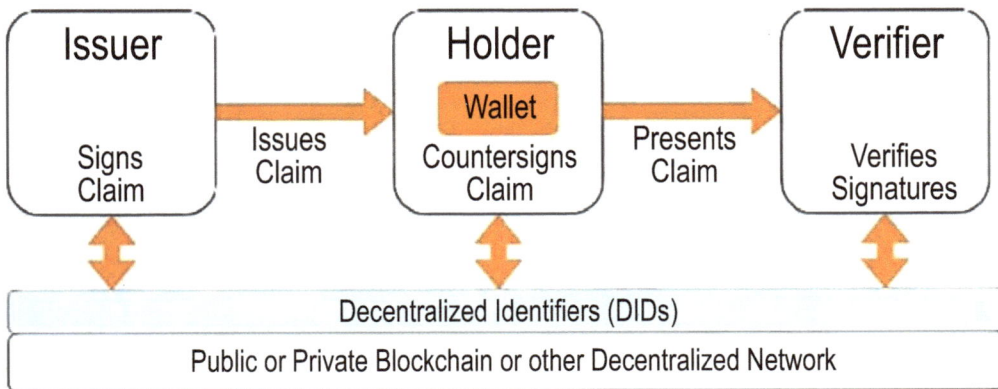

**Fig. (3).** Interaction between blockchain and decentralized identifiers.

## INTERPLAY BETWEEN BLOCKCHAIN AND IDENTITY

### Blockchain as an Enabler for Decentralized Identity

Blockchain is a powerful enabler of decentralized identity systems because it allows the capability of maintaining an unalterable ledger for identity data management securely and privately. Decentralization, transparency, and immutability are key features of any blockchain system. Blockchain supports decentralized identity in several ways.

No-Trust Verification Blockchain creates a trustless environment in which people can verify each other's identity without reliance on a central authority. Some of the ways this can be brought about are through:

***Cryptographic Proofs***: Through the use of cryptographic protocols, mainly digital signatures and hash functions, blockchain ensures the source of identity data and its integrity. These proofs allow identities and credentials to be verified without relying on a central issuer.

***Consensus Mechanisms***: Blockchain makes use of consensus algorithms, like Proof of Work (PoW) or Proof of Stake (PoS), to validate and record transactions. These mechanisms ensure that all nodes in the network agree to the state of the ledger; hence, it provides a trusted foundation for verifying identity.

Data Integrity: Since blockchain is an immutable source, data related to identity taken in cannot be counterfeited or altered. This gives immutability and provides for:

***Reliable History***: All transactions or changes to the identity data get recorded to a block and linked to previous blocks, generating a tamper-proof record of all identity-related activities.

***Tamper-Proof Records***: Cryptographic hashing will see to it that any change in identity data leads to the changing of all successive blocks, which is practically impossible; thus, the data is safeguarded from fraud and unauthorized changes.

Decentralization: Blockchain's decentralized structure eliminates the need for central authorities and, therefore, reduces:

***Single Points of Failure***: By distributing identity data over a network of nodes, blockchain cuts off major risks that come with centralized databases, where one breach or failure of the system jeopardizes the whole.

***Risk to the Security of Data***: The decentralized features of blockchain bolster the security and resilience of the identity systems. Each node keeps a copy of the blockchain, and consistency in data is preserved by the consensus algorithm.

## *Technical Architecture and Components*

Key components of decentralized identity based on blockchain:

***Decentralized Identifiers Definition and Purpose***: This describes names that are created and intended to be DIDs within the global namespace of identifiers constructed on and for use on a blockchain. DIDs are self-generated and self-controlled by human beings or entities, as opposed to the more familiar style of identifier assignment in central agencies. One of the pairs associated with the DID is the cryptographic key — public key and private key. The public key is used to authenticate the DID, and the private key is involved in secure authentication and interactions. DIDs are actually stored on a blockchain, and this will guarantee availability and integrity. DIDs are inherently decentralized, so they will not rely on a single authority, which makes them even more secure and fault-tolerant.

***Verifiable Credentials Definition and Purpose***: Verifiable claims one can make about a subject – such as an entity or individual – are digital files issued by verifiable entities that present their cryptographic proofs. The verifiable credentials live off-chain but can be verified through the blockchain-based DIDs. If a credential holder presents the credential to a recipient, that recipient can easily verify its validity by validating the DID of the issuer and associated cryptographic proofs. Verifiable credentials can find a number of applications in real-life scenarios. The user can provide evidence pertaining to his age, professional qualifications, and even access control. This technology further allows reliance by the individual on the verifier without the need for centralization, which, in effect, increases security and privacy in identity management.

***Identity Wallets Functionalities***: Identity Wallets, in general, are applications or platforms enabling operations of DIDs and Verifiable Credentials for the user. These wallets offer an interface to store, share, and revoke user credentials securely.

### *Features*

i. *Manage & Create DIDs*: Ability to generate and manage decentralized identifiers.
ii. *Store & Share Credentials*: Securely store and share verifiable credentials with trusted parties.
iii. *Control over Privacy*: Users can decide with whom and when to share identity information, significantly enhancing privacy and control.

## *Security and Privacy Considerations*

In order for this to be implemented effectively, there are a few challenges that have to be met, such as:

i. *Security Enhanced Features for Security and Privacy*: Another feature that comes with using blockchain in identity management includes the added security of the records against tampering. It is heavily secure because information that is put in a blockchain ledger about an individual's identity cannot be changed easily in order to not facilitate fraud or other forms of identity alterations. This feature is vital for the management of people's identity information.

ii. *Cryptographic Security*: Blockchain provides protection of identity data in terms of encryption by applying some strong computational mechanisms such as digital signatures and others. These techniques provide a way by which there is assurance that only the relevant users have control and access to their identity information and do not go through the window of breaches.

iii. *Decentralization*: This way, the identity data is distributed across the nodes in a network, making the identity systems more secure and less vulnerable due to blockchain technology. It also removes the risks of a centralized attack because one node cannot threaten the whole decentralized network.

iv. *Selective Disclosure of Privacy*: Decentralized identity can be described as selective disclosure — sharing only such information that would be appropriate for a given incident. For instance, the concept of reputation can be substantiated without disclosing one's date of birth or any other identification data proving one's age.

v. *Data Minimization*: As it shall be seen from the subsequent sections on different decentralized identity systems, the architecture of such system minimizes the amount of data linked to a user's identity that is put on a blockchain to the bare minimum while all other details are put in a 'somewhat more traditional' storage, which is also off-chain. The use of such systems ensures the implementation of the principle of data minimization, thus minimizing the likelihood of a breach of data and any unauthorized access.

vi. *User Control*: Users have complete control over their identity data, including whether, when, and with whom to share information. Privacy in this manner is highly superior, and the chances of misuse of data are very low.

vii. *Key Management Challenges*: Secure management of cryptographic keys guarantees the availability of identity data access to all its users. A user must be sure that his keys do not get lost or are compromised in any way because, without the keys, no access and control will be available over the identity information of the user. Solutions may involve key recovery mechanisms and hardware security modules to help mitigate risks associated with key management.

viii. *Data privacy*: Public blockchains are transparent, thereby bearing high privacy risks for a user. The use of techniques such as zero-knowledge proofs or private/permissioned blockchains can offer a solution to keep user privacy by not allowing everyone to see sensitive information.

ix. *Scalability*: In the case that identity transactions drastically increase, blockchain networks will face the necessity to be scalable. Scalability problems within decentralized identity systems can be solved with solutions such as off-chain storage and scaling techniques of layer two; these are among the enhancements that will be made, helping to reduce the main blockchain load while increasing the number of transactions done per unit time.

Security and privacy concerns in decentralized identity systems are solved using secure, user-centric, and private means of digital identity management. With the help of blockchain technology, these systems increase trust and reliability with regard to the processes of verifying identity.

# REGULATORY AND ETHICAL CONSIDERATIONS

## Legal and Regulatory Challenges

For instance, decentralized identity systems should always be in harmony with the already set legal and regulatory frameworks, such as the General Data Protection Regulation (GDPR) within the European Union. The next are some of the challenges laid by the regulations in relation to data ownership, consent, and the right to be forgotten.

i. ***Data Ownership***: Decentralized identity systems shift control of data from centralized authorities to end-users, deviating from traditional legal frameworks that rely on centralized control. Regulations like the GDPR explicitly define data ownership and control, making compliance in a decentralized setup quite challenging.

ii. ***Consent***: The GDPR mandates that data processing occurs only with explicit user permission. In a decentralized identity system, obtaining and managing consent must be done in a way that aligns with regulatory requirements. Users must be able to provide or withdraw consent at any time and manage their settings, requiring robust systems for tracking and managing consent.

iii. ***Right to be Forgotten***: The GDPR grants individuals the right to request the deletion of their personal information. This is difficult to implement in decentralized systems, where data is stored immutably on the blockchain.

Although solutions like off-chain data storage and pseudonymization are being researched, they need to be developed to meet regulatory requirements.

### Data Protection and Privacy Laws

Decentralized identity systems need to conform to the data protection and privacy laws that will help guarantee secure personal data handling. Vigorous security measures must be put in place by decentralized identity systems to ensure that personal data is safe from unauthorized access and breaches. This shall be achieved by using advanced cryptographic techniques, secure key management practices, and regular security audits to ensure that the data of the users remain integral and confidential.

  i. ***Explicit User Consent***: Data processing in decentralized identity systems should take place with explicit user consent. Clear and transparent consent mechanisms are to be designed, informing the user about the use of their data, which facilitates them being in control of their data-sharing preferences.
 ii. ***Data Minimization and Purpose Limitation***: Privacy laws often require that only the minimum amount of personal data necessary for a stated purpose should be collected and processed. Following are the principles of decentralized identity that any system should follow by enabling selective disclosure and the assurance of data used only for the intended purpose.
iii. ***Data Portability***: Some regulations, like GDPR, give the right to data portability through which a person is able to move personal data among services. The decentralized systems of identity must facilitate data portability in such a way that the user can securely export his identity data and pass the same to any service provider.

### Ethical Implications and Concerns

The issues that have to do with the ethics of decentralized identity systems are mainly to do with guaranteeing access, protecting against misuse, and ensuring user data privacy. The major ethical concerns are:

***Equitable Access***: Design decentralized identity systems in such a way that all people, including the marginalized and those in underserved regions, are guaranteed access. This includes factors such as the digital divide and that the technology reaches and is adequate for all people with different levels of digital literacy and access to resources.

***Preventing Misuse***: The decentralized nature of identity systems increases the risk of misuse, such as malicious individuals creating fake identities or engaging in fraudulent activities. Ethical system design must include mechanisms for detection and prevention, such as strong verification processes and monitoring to identify potentially harmful activities.

***Protecting User Privacy***: Protecting user privacy is fundamental to ethical design. A decentralized identity system should enable users to control their personal data and choose the appropriate privacy settings. Users should be empowered to review and manage their data-sharing preferences, ensuring minimal privacy risks through sound design.

***Transparency and Accountability***: Respectful deployment of decentralized identity requires transparency in how these systems operate and accountability for their impacts on users. This includes clear communication of system functionality, data handling practices, and ways to address user concerns and grievances.

In this respect, decentralized identity systems should be created while taking due consideration of these regulatory and ethical issues so that user rights are upheld. There is conformity to the legal environment, and trust and fairness are built into the digital ID space.

## CASE STUDIES AND APPLICATIONS

### Introduction

The combination of SSI and blockchain technology has been innovative in the solutions applied in every industry to the most critical challenges in identity management and data security. A prominent example is the Sovrin Network, which creates a global decentralized identity network based on the blockchain model. This lays down capabilities for people and organizations to create, own, and operate their digital identities independently of any central authority. It is being practiced in many sectors, such as finance and healthcare, where secure and verifiable digital identities are required for the provision of several services and compliance with privacy and regulatory requirements.

The public sector has initiated a blockchain-based digital identity system in Zug, Switzerland, also known as "Crypto Valley. Therefore, in this manner, citizens will be able to register their identity securely and access all services, including local elections and documents signed with a government institution. Such success stories will serve as role models for other governments when doing preliminary research on blockchain-based identity solutions to prove that public services could gain better transparency, enhanced security, and higher control from users. Another in-the-field application is being affected in the financial sector; for instance, SecureKey Technologies has designed Verified.Me. This blockchain-based digital identity and authentication network enables users to have complete control over their identity information and provides them with a secure way of sharing this critical information with financial institutions and other service providers. Verified.Me helps to prevent identity fraud through its basic technology of blockchain, hence easily facilitating the onboarding of customers for service providers, a process that builds trust with their customers. These are real-world examples that showcase the increasing application of SSI and blockchain to revolutionize how identities are managed and verified across different sectors.

## Real-world Implementations and Examples

### Sovrin Foundation

One of the first to develop a protocol for Self-Sovereign Identity (SSI) based on Decentralized Identity principles is the Sovrin Foundation. The Sovrin protocol was designed to give individuals control over their digital identity by providing them with power on a distributed ledger. Here is how Sovrin's system works:

i. *Decentralized Control*: It uses blockchain technology to enable people to control their identity data free from centralized authorities. Thus, digital identities can be independently created, stored, and controlled by users in a decentralized manner, hence avoiding the associated risks of centralized systems, such as breaches from hacking and cases of stolen identity.
ii. *Identity Verification*: The Sovrin network allows secure identification verification with the use of Decentralized Identifiers and Verifiable Credentials. In this, users can issue, manage, and present identities with guaranteed authenticity and integrity.
iii. *Use Cases*: A wide scope of applications is supported by Sovrin, ranging from online identity verification to even gaining access to a physical space and several services authentication. For instance, Sovrin has been used in pilot projects for enterprise access management to make the process simpler while at the same time increasing the security of online authentication for service provision.

### Hyperledger Indy

Hyperledger Indy is an open-source blockchain framework developed specifically for decentralized identity management. Developed as part of the Hyperledger project, Indy provides a complete infrastructure for creating and managing decentralized identities. Some of the key features are listed below:

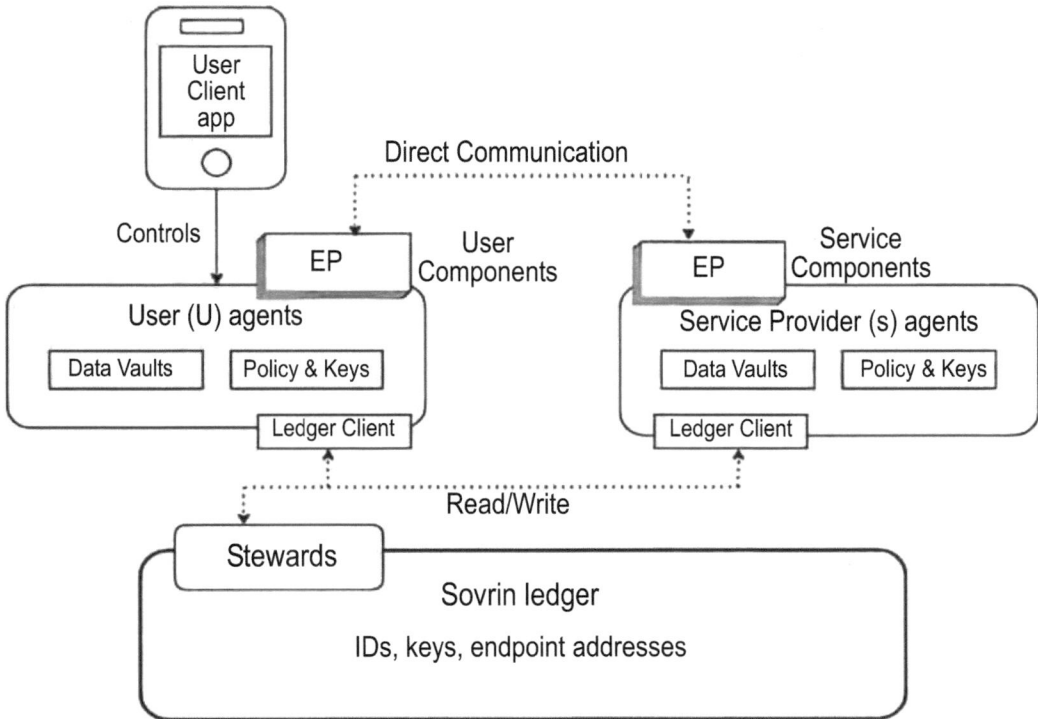

**Fig. (4).** Flowchart of the Sovrin protocol implementation.

i. *Blockchain Infrastructure*: Hyperledger Indy provides a blockchain-based distributed ledger that is specially optimized for identity management. It allows the issuing and verifying of DIDs and Verifiable Credentials in ways that are secure and highly scalable [3].

ii. *Interoperability*: Indy is designed to be used interchangeably with a variety of systems and platforms—broadening its use in numerous applications. This promotes further extensive deployment and adoption through the convergence and frictionless interaction of different identity systems.

iii. *Applications*: Hyperledger Indy has so far been used in a number of projects, including a COVID-19 vaccination credentialing project. The infrastructure behind the project enabled means that were both secure and privacy-preserving to verify the status and form of vaccination [4].

These implementations are a great example of how decentralized identity systems can help overcome numerous weaknesses presented by current identity management systems, such as increased security, privacy, and user control.

## Lessons Learned and Best Practices

The experience mentioned has provided some key lessons learned and best practices:

### Importance of User Education

i. *Educating* Users: Successful implementations place great importance on educating users. Directions in which users can find direction and support will give a clue about how to work with and use decentralized identities for better outcomes. Education on the benefits, risks, and functionalities of decentralized identity systems is critical to gain adoption and minimize errors or misuse [5].

ii. *User Support*: Accessible support channels and resources help build user confidence and support seamless adoption. Responsive support services, user guides, and training materials are fundamental in addressing any concerns raised by the users while creating good experiences from the use of decentralized identity systems [6].

### Strong Security Measures

i. *Strong Cryptography*: Strong security measures should be implemented to protect the data in the identity. This will be achieved by the use of strong cryptographic methods in encrypting and authenticating the data, coupled with safe key management. Regular security audits and updates are necessary to address vulnerabilities and maintain system integrity [7].

ii. *Risk Management*: Identifying and managing potential security risks is integral for retaining user trust. Implementing multi-layered security strategies and proactive risk assessments can help mitigate potential threats, keeping decentralized identity systems reliable [8].

### Value of Standardization in Interoperability

The success of decentralized identity systems relies on interoperability. Standard protocols and frameworks enable easy integration with other systems and platforms. This increases usability and ensures wide acceptance with a corresponding deployment of decentralized identity solutions across various applications and jurisdictions [9].

i. *Collaborate*: Interoperable solutions are best driven by collaborations with other stakeholders and organizations. Industry partnerships and contributions to open standards will go a long way to overcome interoperability challenges on the one hand and, on the other, increase the level of adoption [10].

## *Alignment Regulatory*

i. *Alignment*: Decentralized Identity solutions that must be put in place while ensuring regulatory requirements are upheld. It aligns with data protection and privacy laws, such as GDPR, in dealing with legal aspects and ensuring the rights of users. The implementation of mechanisms for explicit user consent and management of data processing activities is very important for maintaining compliance [11].

ii. *Privacy Features*: These are necessary in decentralized identity systems to ensure proper maintenance of user data. This may include selective disclosure mechanisms, minimizing the collection of data, and control by users over their privacy settings. A system designed with the privacy of its users in consideration forms part of the characteristics that build trust and warrant responsible data handling.

## DISCUSSION AND FUTURE DIRECTIONS

### Current Trends and Innovations

The decentralized identity landscape is being quickly transformed by continuous research and technological advances. Key trends include:

### *Integration with Emerging Technologies*

i. *Artificial Intelligence (AI)*: Combining AI with SSI enhances identity verification through advanced biometric systems and machine learning algorithms, improving fraud detection and authentication.

ii. *Internet of Things (IoT)*: Integrating SSI with IoT securely manages access to interconnected devices, automating identity verification and access control, thereby increasing security and streamlining user interactions [12].

### *Blockchain Interoperability*

i. *Cross-Chain Solutions*: Facilitating the seamless exchange of identity information between different blockchain networks.

ii. *Standardized Protocols*: Developing standardized protocols to ensure consistent operation and reduce fragmentation across different identity systems.

### *Improved User Experience*

i. *User Interfaces with Greater Ease*: Simplifying decentralized identity management to make it more accessible and intuitive.

ii. *Process Simplification*: Reducing the complexity of interactions with decentralized identity systems, optimizing workflows, and leveraging automation.

## *Regulatory and Compliance Solutions*

i. *Privacy-Preserving Technologies*: Using technologies like zero-knowledge proofs to verify identity without revealing sensitive information, aligning with GDPR and preserving user privacy.

ii. *Regulatory Alignment*: Developing mechanisms for managing consent and data processing in compliance with data protection laws.

## Open Research Questions

Important research questions needed to unlock the potential of decentralized identity systems include:

### *Massive Adoption*

i. *Adoption Barriers*: Identifying and overcoming technological, regulatory, and social barriers to adoption. Strategies may include user education programs, adoption incentives, and industry collaboration.

ii. *Sectoral and Regional Differences*: Designing decentralized identity systems to serve the specific needs of different sectors and regions.

### *Scalability*

i. *Scalability Solutions*: Exploring solutions like layer-two scaling techniques, sharding, and off-chain storage to handle massive volumes of transactions and users.

ii. *Performance Optimization*: Improving transaction throughput, reducing latency, and enhancing system efficiency.

### *Regulatory Compliance*

i. *Adaptive Compliance Mechanisms:* Developing mechanisms that accommodate changing regulations while preserving user control and data sovereignty.

ii. *Global Regulatory Frameworks*: Understanding international regulations and aligning decentralized identity solutions with global standards.

### *User Privacy and Security*

i. *Privacy and Security Balance*: Striking a balance between privacy and security while ensuring usability. Managing data privacy, key management, and security threats is crucial.

ii. *Threat Mitigation*: Developing robust security measures to mitigate attacks and unauthorized access.

## Potential Future Developments

Future developments of decentralized identity systems:

### *Global Standards for SSI*

i. *Unified Frameworks*: Establish global standards for self-sovereign identity to enable interoperability, facilitate widespread adoption, and ensure consistency.
ii. *Industry Collaboration*: Engage stakeholders from various sectors to jointly create comprehensive standards that support wide adoption.

### *New Blockchain-Based Identity Solutions*

i. *Innovative Architectures*: Explore alternative blockchain architectures, consensus mechanisms, and privacy-enhancing technologies.
ii. *Enhanced Privacy*: Incorporate advanced encryption methods and privacy-preserving protocols to better secure user data, which is crucial for decentralized identity solutions.

### *Integration with Emerging Technologies*

i. *5G Networks*: Integrate decentralized identity systems with 5G networks for faster and more secure identity verification.
ii. *Edge Computing*: Apply edge computing to increase data processing efficiency and significantly reduce latency.
iii. *Quantum Computing*: Research quantum-resistant cryptographic techniques to protect identity systems from future quantum computing threats.

### *Improved Interoperability and Usability*

i. *Seamless Integration*: Enhance the interoperability of decentralized identity systems and improve usability.
ii. *User-Centered Design*: Develop user-friendly designs with intuitive interfaces, along with support, to maximize user adoption and satisfaction.

## SUMMARY

Blockchain, through its decentralized identification systems enshrined under the principles of SSI, is an evolution from traditional approaches to identity management. This literature review provides an overview of the current research landscape, highlighting the main advances, challenges raised by regulators and ethicists, and potential research lines for the future.

## SUMMARY OF KEY FINDINGS

A number of findings can be summarized from the review:

  i. ***Advantages Over Traditional Systems***: These include massive benefits gained from decentralized identity systems compared to traditional models. Blockchain offers secure, transparent, and self-determined handling of personal data in new ways. The decentralized and immutable features of blockchain can reduce the risks of data leakage or unauthorized access, while SSI can empower individuals with ownership and control of their digital identity.
 ii. ***Issues***: Even with so much promise, decentralized identity systems are open to critical regulatory and ethical issues that could hamper adoption. Conformance to existing legal frameworks, such as GDPR, calls for deliberations surrounding data ownership, consent, and the right to be forgotten. Other considerations that should be taken into account for the responsible deployment of such systems are privacy and ethical issues, equitable access, and prevention of misuse.
iii. ***Current Trends and Innovations***: The current trends and innovations may increase the scalability, interoperability, and user experience of this field very quickly. A promising trend seems to be the integration of SSI with emerging technologies such as artificial intelligence and the Internet of Things, as well as the development of blockchain interoperability solutions. These advances will expand the applicability and effectiveness of decentralized identity systems.
iv. ***Open Research Questions***: Be that as it may, a lot of open research questions remain on how to achieve wide adoption, scalability, and regulatory compliance. That is an important set of things to work on to really unlock the potential and overcome current barriers in decentralized identity systems.

## FUTURE DIRECTIONS

The following are key future developments that promise to add value to decentralized identity systems:

  i. ***Global Standards***: Implementation with global standards on SSI will ensure that there is interoperability between different systems and across jurisdictions, which would allow for an easier adoption and implementation mechanism. Having standard frameworks will result in a better base for implementing solutions using decentralized identities.

ii. ***Blockchain-Based Solutions***: Continuous innovations of blockchain-based identity solutions are likely to offer new ways to do identity management in a functional way, solving some of the issues described.

iii. ***Technological Integration***: Herein, we refer to integrating decentralized identity systems with the aforementioned emergent technologies—5G and quantum computing. This may provide new powers and applications for them, in turn, increasing their effectiveness and usability.

iv. ***Improved Usability***: More effort in the future is likely to focus on user experience; the decentralized identity systems need to integrate smoothly with current systems and workingS. The current frameworks should be accompanied by user-friendly interfaces, robust privacy controls, and ease of use.

## CONCLUSION

Decentralized identity systems are a huge step toward handling digital identifications. Blockchain technology and the principle of self-sovereign identity are now being used, which have a potential far greater than traditional models. As technology continues to develop and mature, it assures different management practices for identities, further helping in enhancements and the guarantee of privacy with respect to securing the globe. All these require continuous research, innovation, and collaboration among various institutions to meet upcoming challenges and fully realize the potential of decentralized identity systems.

## CONSENT FOR PUBLICATION

All contributors to this chapter, including Dr. Sachin Gupta and Mr. Rohan Raj, have given their full consent for its publication. Dr. Sachin Gupta contributed to the research, conceptualization, and structuring of the chapter, while Mr. Rohan contributed to the drafting, illustrations, and literature review. All contributors have reviewed the final version and agree with its content and submission.

## ACKNOWLEDGEMENTS

We would like to express our gratitude to Maharaja Agrasen Institute of Technology for providing us with the opportunity and motivation to engage in challenging research problems and publish our findings.

## REFERENCES

[1]    Available from: https://github.com/WebOfTrustInfo/rwot1-sf/blob/master/final-documents/dpki.pdf

[2]    P. Dunphy, and F.A.P. Petitcolas, "A first look at identity management schemes on the blockchain", *IEEE Secur. Priv.,* vol. 16, no. 4, pp. 20-29, 2018.
[http://dx.doi.org/10.1109/MSP.2018.3111247]

[3]     M.S. Ferdous, F. Chowdhury, and M.O. Alassafi, "In search of self-sovereign identity leveraging blockchain technology", *IEEE Access,* vol. 7, pp. 103059-103079, 2019.
        [http://dx.doi.org/10.1109/ACCESS.2019.2931173]

[4]     M. Finck, "Blockchains and data protection in the european union", *Eur. Data Prot. Law Rev.,* vol. 4, no. 1, pp. 17-35, 2018.
        [http://dx.doi.org/10.21552/edpl/2018/1/6]

[5]     Available from: https://www.hyperledger.org/projects/hyperledger-indy

[6]     S. Nakamoto, "Bitcoin: A peer-to-peer electronic cash system", *Rochester, NY,* p. 3440802, 2008.
        [http://dx.doi.org/10.2139/ssrn.3440802]

[7]     Available from: https://www.manning.com/books/self-sovereign-identity

[8]     O. Rikken, M. Janssen, and Z. Kwee, "Governance challenges of blockchain and decentralized autonomous organizations", *Inf. Polity,* vol. 24, no. 4, pp. 397-417, 2019.
        [http://dx.doi.org/10.3233/IP-190154]

[9]     Available from: https://sovrin.org/library/sovrin-protocol-and-token-white-paper/

[10]    Available from: https://sovrin.org/library/inevitable-rise-of-self-sovereign-identity/

[11]    J. Yli-Huumo, D. Ko, S. Choi, S. Park, and K. Smolander, "Where is current research on blockchain technology?—a systematic review", *PLoS One,* vol. 11, no. 10, p. e0163477, 2016.
        [http://dx.doi.org/10.1371/journal.pone.0163477] [PMID: 27695049]

[12]    G. Zyskind, O. Nathan, and Sandy Pentland, "Decentralizing privacy: Using blockchain to protect personal data", *2015 IEEE Security and Privacy Workshops,* pp. 180-184, 2015.
        [http://dx.doi.org/10.1109/SPW.2015.27]

**CHAPTER 10**

# Exploring the Spectrum of Blockchain: Private, Public, Consortium, and Hybrid and their Applications

**Aparna Singh[1,*], Jaya Sinha[2,†], Tanu Shree[3,†] and Surbhi Sharma[1,†]**

[1] *School of Computer Science Engineering and Technology, Bennett University, Greater Noida, India*

[2] *Department of Computer Science and Engineering, ITS Engineering College, Greater Noida, India*

[3] *Department of Computer Science and Engineering, Galgotias College of Engineering and Technology, Greater Noida, India*

**Abstract:** Blockchain technology, well known for its security and decentralization, has become evident as a revolutionary force among multiple global industries. Initially developed as a foundation for cryptocurrencies like Bitcoin, it is now being used for user authentication, data sharing, record management, access control, and many more. Fundamentally, blockchain is an integration of peer-to-peer networking and cryptography, where each transaction is recorded in the form of blocks. Each block links to the block before the current block through its hash value, thereby forming a chain of blocks. This article delves into the underlying principles of blockchain and its architecture. It also explores the consensus protocols and their application in five key areas: the Internet of Things, finance, healthcare, supply chain management, and the Industrial Internet of Things (IIoT). The four primary forms of blockchain— public, private, consortium, and hybrid —are among the article's main topics of attention.

**Keywords:** Bitcoin, Blockchain, Consensus protocols, Cryptocurrency, Decentralization, Ethereum, Finance, Hash, Healthcare, Hyperledger, Industrial internet of things, Internet of things, Mining, Peer-to-peer network, Private blockchain, Proof of stake, Proof of work, Public blockchain, Smart contracts, Supply chain management.

---

[*] **Corresponding author Aparna Singh:** School of Computer Science Engineering and Technology, Bennett University, Greater Noida, India; E-mail: aparnasingh2211@gmail.com
[†] *These authors have equal contribution.*

Monica Bhutani, Monica Gupta, Kirti Gupta, Deepali Kamthania & Danish Ather (Eds.)
**All rights reserved-© 2025 Bentham Science Publishers**

# INTRODUCTION

Blockchain has become evident as a revolutionary technology in this era of digital applications, significantly transforming how data is generated, transferred, and managed among various industries. Blockchain was initially developed as the underlying technology behind the famous cryptocurrency-Bitcoin, by Satoshi Nakamoto in 2008 [1]. Since then, it has expanded into a significant aid behind applications like healthcare, banking, security, and many other fields. The focal area of blockchain is its distributed ledger system, which, being decentralized, provides enhanced transparency, security, and immutability compared to traditional centralized databases. A recent survey called the Blockchain Hype Cycle survey, done by Gartner, assessed the maturity and ease of acceptance of blockchain technology across a diverse set of industries. It found that while blockchain as a technology had moved past the initial hype, its adoption was still growing steadily, with 60% of enterprises either using or planning to use blockchain in the upcoming two years. The survey also emphasized the shift towards more practical and scalable use cases.

A blockchain is a chain of interconnected blocks, with each block holding a list of transactions. Each block is interconnected to the previous one *via* a cryptographic hash of the previous block, producing a chain that is virtually tamper-proof and immutable. Consensus techniques such as Proof of Work (PoW), Proof of Stake (PoS), or Proof of Burn (PoB) make it even more secure and reliable. "The use of consensus mechanism also ensures that the state of the blockchain is always stable and all the nodes have access to the same chain of blocks" [2]. Additionally, its decentralized nature also portrays that no sole party possesses full authorization, thereby lowering the danger of data breaches or any other interference by an intruder. Each transaction happening in the network is validated by special nodes known as miners.

The increased interest in this ever-growing technology is due to its capability to handle several fundamental difficulties in modern digital systems, such as data security, privacy, and trust. For example, in the banking sector, blockchain aids in the secure and transparent movement of assets without the involvement of middlemen, lowering both costs and risks. Growing financial services without the need for traditional middlemen are provided by Decentralized Finance (DeFi), while Non-Fungible Tokens (NFTs) are moving beyond digital art to include virtual real estate and games. Global research is being done on Central Bank Digital Currencies (CBDCs), which would increase financial efficiency and inclusivity. Interoperability between various blockchains is becoming increasingly important as cross-chain solutions become more prevalent. In healthcare, blockchain can protect the integrity and privacy of sensitive records of patients, allowing for better data storage and management with seamless system interoperability. In addition, blockchain is essential to Web3 and the metaverse, allowing digital ownership and decentralized apps (dApps). To safeguard privacy and control fraudulent activities, security improvements—including cutting-edge crypto-graphic techniques, are also being integrated with blockchain technology. This article examines the core principles of blockchain technology, including its architecture, types of blockchain, the different categories of consensus mechanisms available in it. We also explored its application areas in multiple domains, along with possible future scope and limitations. Section 2 of this chapter explores some of the significant research works done in this field. Section 3 and Section 4 discuss the architecture and its different types. Section 5 throws light on various characteristics of blockchain that make it a revolutionary force in today's world and a prominent part of most of the current and future industries. Section 6 discusses the various applications of blockchain across multiple domains, with the conclusion briefly summarizing the article and also discussing the future scope of blockchain technology.

## LITERATURE REVIEW

This section is used to discuss some of the existing work on this rapidly growing technology, addressing architecture, core components, applications, and associated challenges. The first paragraph covers literature related to surveys conducted on blockchain technology. The second paragraph explores the literature discussing various consensus protocols and the work done, while the third paragraph examines the literature concentrating on blockchain applications in various domains.

Gad *et al.* [3], in their paper, discussed blockchain technology, analyzing existing literature spanning from 2013 to 2020. The paper explored the evolution of blockchain, its current design and state, and its impact on various existing applications. On the same grounds, Dabbagh *et al.* [4], in their paper, conducted an analysis of blockchain technology and provided insight into the existing work on blockchain and its role in enhancing some of the latest technologies. Banerjee *et al.* [5] also presented a survey discussing the integration of blockchain in IoT and explored the available IoT datasets for the same. They highlighted the need for a standard to securely share these datasets and the potential role of blockchain in ensuring dataset integrity and also in making IoT systems more secure. Gorkhali *et al.* [6] provided another comprehensive review of 76 blockchain-related journal publications. It categorized the research into 14 distinct areas, summarizing each category's content and proposing future research directions.

Xu *et al.* [7], in their survey paper, explored the consensus protocols present in the blockchain. They discussed the fundamental basis of these consensus protocols, their working, and also the challenges faced by each of them. On a similar note, Zhang *et al.* [8], in their article, reviewed the consensus protocols based on their strengths, weaknesses, and suitability in different blockchain environments. Their study also emphasized the importance of developing fault-tolerant consensus protocols that align well with the application they are used for. Similarly, Xiao *et al.* [9] presented a survey providing another thorough discussion on various existing blockchain consensus protocols, highlighting the changes incorporated in newer protocols as compared to Nakomato's original one. It introduces five core components of consensus protocols—block proposal, validation, propagation, finalization, and incentives—and uses these parameters to evaluate the performance, vulnerabilities, and suitability of various protocols. Taking the commonly used consensus up a notch, Rebello *et al.* [10], in their article, focused on a consensus mechanism based on quorum as an alternative to Bitcoin's proof-of-work. The study also emphasized the use of Byzantine fault-tolerant protocols, given their robustness against security attacks and intruders. Further discussing Byzantine fault tolerant protocols, Qin and Guan [11] proposed a reputation-based Byzantine Fault Tolerance (BFT) consensus protocol to combat issues of a single source of control and enhance tolerance to failure. The protocol enhances decentralization by selecting function nodes based on reputation and also improves security and efficiency by using a hierarchical model. On a similar note, Taha *et al.* [12] introduced an optimized Byzantine Fault Tolerance (MAC-BFT) protocol concentrating on private blockchains. The developed consensus made use of Message Authentication Codes (MACs) to enhance security. Additionally, the authors managed to decrease the size of the cryptographic operations and communication overhead with the use of shared secret keys to generate MACs. Seeing the popularity of BFT protocols, Borzdov [13] analyzed the effect of Denial of Service (DoS) attacks on these protocols over private blockchains. Their article also highlighted how practical implementations of BFT protocols are vulnerable to such attacks. Further, the authors also discussed the ways to mitigate such attacks and lower their effects in private blockchains.

Coming to the application of blockchain, Singh and Rathee [14], in their research article, addressed the issue of secure identification, integrity, and privacy in e-healthcare resulting from the use of cloud-based services. They introduced a decentralized data storage method by integrating an Interplanetary File System (IPFS) with their proposed model to overcome issues related to centralized management and data unavailability. The authors also made use of attribute-based encryption (CP-ABE), which significantly reduced the key generation time and the storage overhead. Harbi *et al.* [15], in their article, focused on the involvement of blockchain in the Internet of Drones (IoD) network. The author's work also highlighted how blockchain can be used to provide privacy, authentication, confidentiality, integrity, and access control in IoD environments. Kaur and Parashar [16], in their article, focused on blockchain's part in sustainable rural development. The authors conducted a survey of 112 papers from 2010 to 2021, highlighting the aid that blockchain can bring to rural areas, leading to enhanced national development. Blockchain's integration in waste management, e-agriculture, natural hazards, and energy grids is one of the major areas discussed in this research article. Zeba *et al.* [17] discussed the involvement of blockchain in secure data transfer without the intervention of a third party. Their work also highlighted various characteristics of blockchain, like immutability, reliability, and accountability. Olnes *et al.* [18] went on to examine the use case of blockchain technology in governmental processes. The paper highlights the necessity of sound governance models to realize blockchain's potential benefits and also suggests areas for further research on how blockchain can be seamlessly incorporated into e-government-related processes. Javaid *et al.* [19], in their paper, explored the effect of this decentralized ledger on financial services, highlighting its role in enhancing authenticity, security, and risk management. It discusses how blockchain improves efficiency, transparency, and revenue opportunities through smart contracts and blockchain-enabled IDs. The paper also reflects on the future of blockchain in improving credit reporting, reducing costs, and managing financial data with greater precision and customization. Zhang *et al.* [20] proposed a reliable system for data sharing based on blockchain in the environment of the Internet of Vehicles (IoV), addressing challenges related to message distribution, security, and privacy. The proposed model also incorporated a reward mechanism, where vehicles broadcasting the announcement messages and participating in blockchain maintenance were provided incentives, thereby ensuring active engagement and privacy in vehicular communications.

Our analysis indicates that most review-based papers on blockchain technology have focused on specific applications. Only a few recent studies cover numerous application areas. In a study [21], authors analyzed the possible benefits of blockchain, ranging over several domains, including supply chain management, accounting settlement, and smart trading. In another study [22], the authors analyzed the use cases of blockchain in IoT, business, and healthcare, highlighting difficulties and potential. In this article, we not only review existing blockchain architecture in detail but also discuss four major types of blockchain. We also focus on its application in five major areas: IoT, finance, healthcare, supply chain management, and IIoT. Table **1**, given above, lists some of the common blockchain platforms available in the market.

**Table 1. Comparison of blockchain platforms.**

| S.No. | Blockchain Platform | Year | Type of Blockchain | Stateless or Stateful |
|-------|---------------------|------|--------------------|-----------------------|
| 1 | Bitcoin | 2009 | Public | Stateless |
| 2 | Ripple | 2012 | Consortium | Stateful |
| 3 | Ethereum | 2015 | Public | Stateful |
| 4 | IOTA | 2015 | Public | Stateless |
| 5 | MultiChain | 2015 | Private | Stateful |
| 6 | HydraChain | 2015 | Hybrid | Stateful |
| 7 | OpenChain | 2015 | Hybrid | Stateless |
| 8 | Hyperledger Fabric | 2016 | Consortium | Stateful |
| 9 | Corda R3 | 2016 | Consortium | Stateful |
| 10 | Quorum | 2016 | Private/Consortium | Stateful |
| 11 | Sawtooth | 2016 | Hybrid | Stateful |
| 12 | BigChainDB | 2016 | Hybrid | Stateless |
| 13 | Tezos | 2018 | Public | Stateful |
| 14 | Algorand | 2019 | Public | Stateless |
| 15 | Flow | 2020 | Public | Stateful |
| 16 | Avalanche | 2020 | Public | Stateful |
| 17 | Oasis | 2020 | Hybrid | Stateful |
| 18 | Polkadot | 2020 | Hybrid | Stateful |

## ARCHITECTURE OF BLOCKCHAIN

Blockchain architecture is a multi-layered structure that combines multiple components to offer decentralized, secure, immutable, and transparent services. Fig. (1) illustrates the representation of the various layers present in a blockchain ecosystem, with the physical layer being at the bottom, followed by the data & network layer, the consensus & incentive layer, the contract layer, and the application layer.

The physical layer consists of the physical devices, generally referred to as nodes, that form the physical infrastructure of the blockchain network. It also comprises the underlying network connections like the internet that link these nodes together. It can also have the cloud infrastructure/services if applicable. This is followed by the data & network layer, which consists of the peer-to-peer (P2P) network and the immutable blockchain ledger. The Merkle tree is one of the most important data structures that is used here, for verification of the blocks. The core functionality of this layer is transaction propagation and block propagation. Transaction propagation involves the mechanism of broadcasting transactions to all the participating nodes. Block propagation ensures the timely distribution of the newly mined (verified) block to all the nodes.

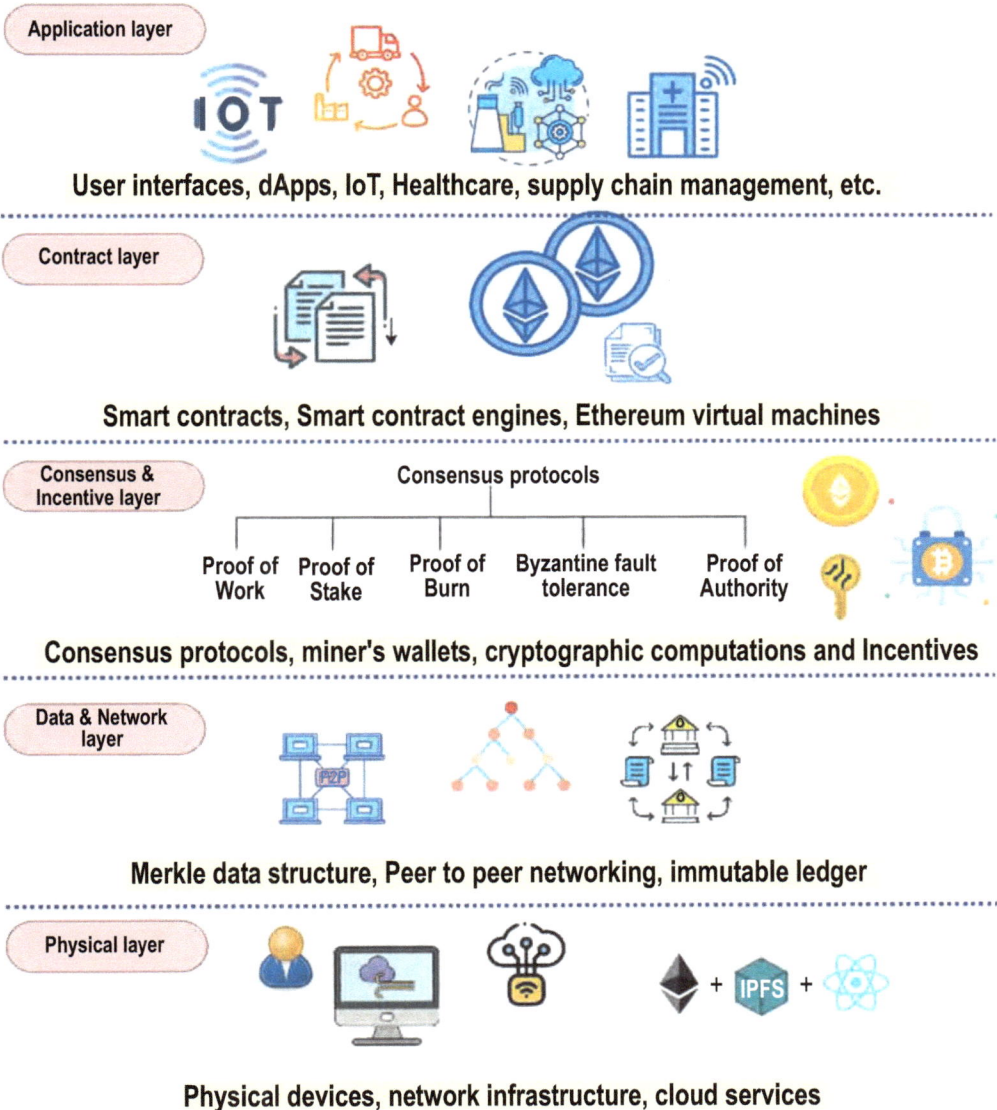

**Fig. (1).** The summarized view of the blockchain ecosystem and the components present at each layer.

Next comes the consensus & incentive layer, which uses pre-defined consensus protocols to verify new blocks and to reach an agreement/consensus on the status of the blockchain. This also includes the miner's wallets and tokens used in the consensus mechanism. This layer has the core functionality of providing network security, along with managing incentives or imposing penalties on the participating nodes.

Generally, cryptocurrencies or any other digital assets are used as a medium of incentives. This layer is followed by the contract layer, which has smart contract engines and Ethereum virtual machines (EVM) that assist in smart contract execution. It also provides the functionality of managing and executing these smart contracts. All the logic and business rules that go behind the creation of a smart contract belong to this layer. Finally, we have the application layer, whose core functionality is to provide the user interface for both the end-users and developers. It also aids in the creation of decentralized applications (dApps).

Below given are some of the core components of blockchain in detail.

## Blocks

A block is the core component of a blockchain. A header and a body are the core sub-components of a block. The metadata related to a block, such as a timestamp and a nonce (random number), are contained inside the header portion. It also consists of the cryptographic hash of the block appearing before the current block in the blockchain, which connects the newly generated block to the previous block, hence creating a chain structure. This chain-like structure is immutable and tamper-proof. The body sub-component contains the list of transactions, where each transaction represents the transmission of data within the network. It is also referred to as the smallest unit of operation within the blockchain network. Each transaction contains information about the sender and receiver and the amount of assets (cryptocurrency, e-assets, digital property, *etc.*) transferred across the network. Each of these transactions is digitally signed by the sender to ensure the authenticity of the transaction and avoid repudiation. Fig. (**2**) illustrates the basic block architecture, its components, and how they form a chain interconnecting with each other.

## Distributed Network and Consensus Protocols

Blockchain makes use of a P2P network organized in a decentralized way, where independent nodes (computers or devices) execute, verify, and validate transactions. Various protocols are used to ensure the consensus between the participating individuals. The chosen mode of consensus protocol is used for the creation of new nodes. It makes sure that most of the nodes participating are on terms with the transaction's validity and the current status of the distributed ledger. Different consensuses offer varying degrees of decentralization, security, and control. Fig. (**3**) illustrates different types of consensus protocols present along with the blockchain platforms that use this consensus mechanism, followed by their brief description below:

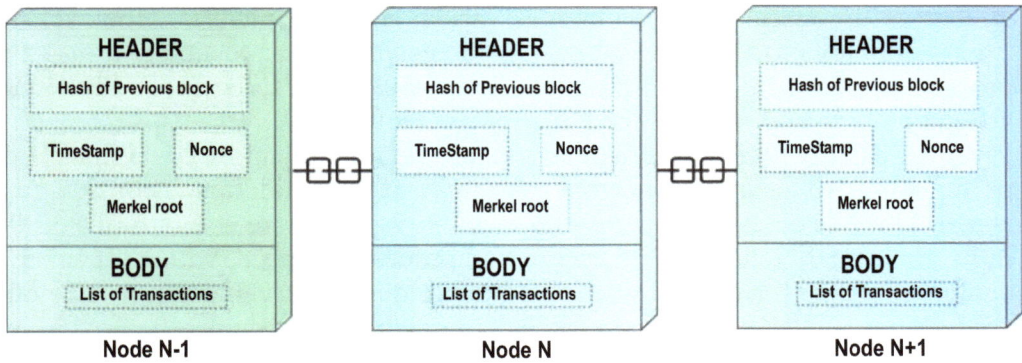

**Fig. (2).** Sample architecture of a block present in a blockchain.

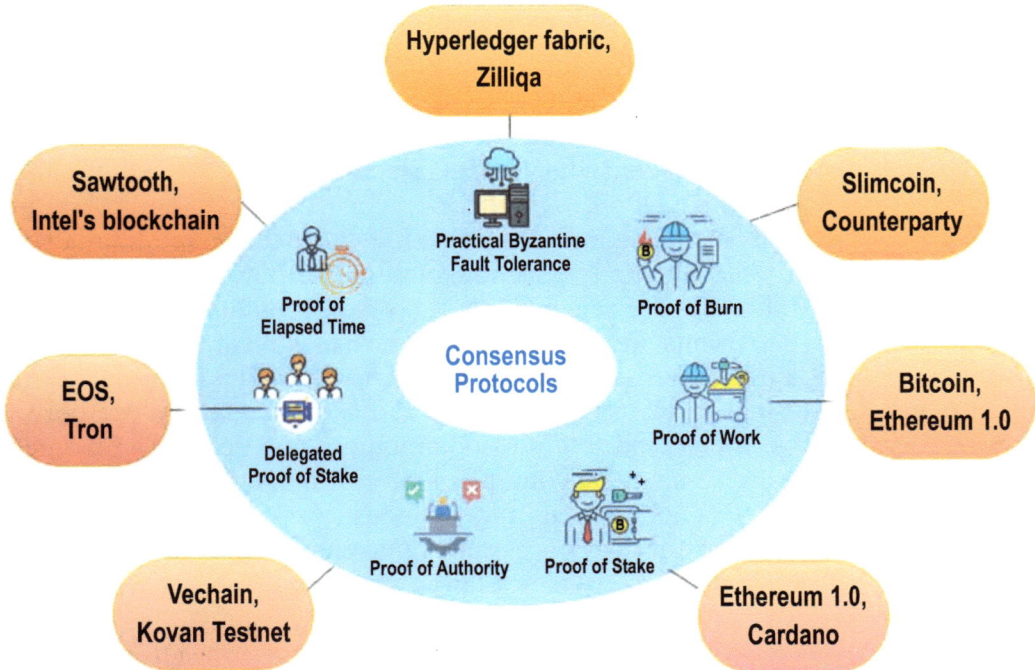

**Fig. (3).** Classification of consensus protocols and the blockchain platforms that utilize them.

- **Proof of Work:** PoW requires the miner nodes to solve complex mathematical puzzles. The miner node who solves the problem is rewarded and also gets to validate new nodes and subsequently add them to the blockchain. Solving complex problems requires an extensive amount of computation power, which becomes a blockage to malicious activities. The core strength of PoW is its higher level of security, given its computational complexity, due to which it is a widely used consensus mechanism in various cryptocurrencies. However, the use of complex puzzles makes it energy-intensive, leading to slower transaction processing and being less environment friendly. Bitcoin, Litecoin, and Ethereum are some of the commonly known platforms that use PoW [15, 23].

- **Proof of Stake:** PoS selects validators based on the count of coins (stake) the participating nodes hold. Since only the stake of the validators is considered, it is a good replacement for energy-intensive PoW. The core strength of PoS lies in its energy efficiency and its transaction processing speed, which is higher as compared to PoW. However, it can lead to accidental centralization if few nodes control larger stakes in the blockchain network. Ethereum 2.0, Tezos, and Cardano are some of the common platforms that use PoS [24].

- **Delegated Proof of Stake:** DPoS allows stakeholders to vote for a set of delegates. This group of delegates will further be in charge of validating transactions and further in the creation of new blocks in the blockchain network. The core strength of DPoS is its higher throughput and scalability. However, given the limited size of the group of chosen delegates, DPoS is not as secure as PoW. Similar to PoS, it can also end up being accidentally centralized if the same group of delegates is selected on repeat. Steem, TRON, and EOS are some of the platforms that utilize DPoS.

- **Proof of Authority:** Similar to PoS, PoA also uses a small group of authorities or validators who will validate transactions and create new blocks within the network. These authorities are selected based on their reputation and feedback, where the stake represents their identity rather than any other digital asset. Similar to DPoS, PoA is also scalable and has higher throughput. It is also more energy efficient as compared to PoW. However, due to the use of a pre-defined group of validators, it can lead to collusion among them. VeChain, Ethereum, and POA networks are some of the common platforms that use PoA.

- **Proof of Burn:** PoB chooses the miner nodes by letting the individual participating nodes burn (destroy) a certain number of cryptocurrencies. The core strength of PoB is that it provides a fairer way to distribute mining power. Burning the cryptocurrencies also reduces the circulating supply, thus managing inflation. However, this burning of cryptocurrencies is wasteful and also requires significant energy. Slimcoin and Counterparty are some of the commonly used platforms that utilize PoB.

- **Proof of Elapsed Time:** PoET uses a pre-defined waiting time to choose the validator node. Here, the participating nodes are randomly allocated a waiting time. The node, whose waiting time expires first, is chosen to validate and henceforth create new blocks. This mode of reaching a consensus is fairer, given the fact that the waiting time is distributed and chosen randomly. It is also energy efficient, given the lack of any complex computational work or burning of cryptocurrencies. However, it does require a trust-based environment to ensure that the allocation of random waiting time is fair. Hyperledger Sawtooth is the most commonly known platform that utilizes PoET.

- **Practical Byzantine Fault Tolerance (PBFT):** Practical Byzantine Fault Tolerance relies on communication between the nodes for deciding the new block. It requires several rounds of voting before reaching a conclusion. Such a consensus is ideal for environments that are susceptible to malicious activities or more prone to node failure. The core advantage of PBFT is its high tolerance to faulty or malicious nodes, which also makes it more secure in the presence of intruders in the network. However, for larger networks, it will need a lot of time to arrive at a consensus, and thus its scalability is limited to moderately sized networks. Hyperledger Fabric and Zilliqa are some of the common platforms that use PBFT [25].

## Node Types

Individual nodes within the blockchain network are the core components of any blockchain infrastructure. These nodes are not only used for verifying transactions based on the chosen consensus mechanism but they are also rewarded with tokens for the same. Different types of nodes perform different functions, like the creation of nodes, their verification, *etc.* These nodes are in continuous contact with each other through a P2P connection.

- **Full Nodes:** They store an entire copy of the current state of the blockchain. They are also used for the validation of blocks. They can also be used to verify the current state and the past state of the blockchain, as they possess a copy of every block within themselves. The verification process is done not just to preserve the integrity and accuracy of the blockchain but also to ensure the prevention of double spending and any other fraudulent activities. Miner nodes, whose task is to validate transactions and also create new blocks within the network, fall under the sub-category of full nodes.
- **Lightweight Nodes:** They store only the block headers or part of the blockchain, due to which they are ideal to be operated through a small handheld device, like your smartphone. They are not involved directly in the validation process and thus depend on the full nodes for the validation process. Compared to full nodes, lightweight nodes are faster and more efficient in terms of their execution. However, given their reliance on the full nodes for verification, they are also less

secure as compared to them.

## Smart Contracts

Developed by Nick Szabo in the 1990s, smart contracts gained popularity with the advent of the Ethereum blockchain. It can be defined as a self-executing line of code (program) that is automatically invoked and executed when certain pre-established scenarios/conditions occur. These pre-established conditions are referred to as triggers. These codes are stored and managed on the blockchain network itself, where each contract has a unique address of its own. Since these contracts are invoked automatically, they do not need the help of any intermediary to execute them. Additionally, they can also be used to control and record major events/transactions running over the blockchain network. They can also be used to create events that can, in turn, trigger other contracts, leading to a snowball effect. The execution of these contracts is approved by the chosen consensus protocol, ensuring that the majority of the participating nodes agree on the outcome and hence rendering the blockchain to a stable state. For instance, a smart contract developed for a crowdfunding campaign can be used to release funds to the owner of the campaign or any other individual once the funds raised exceed a certain limit. If the amount raised fails to meet this limit, it can be automatically returned to the individual contributors [26]. The characteristics given in Fig. (4) make smart contracts popular among blockchain-based applications.

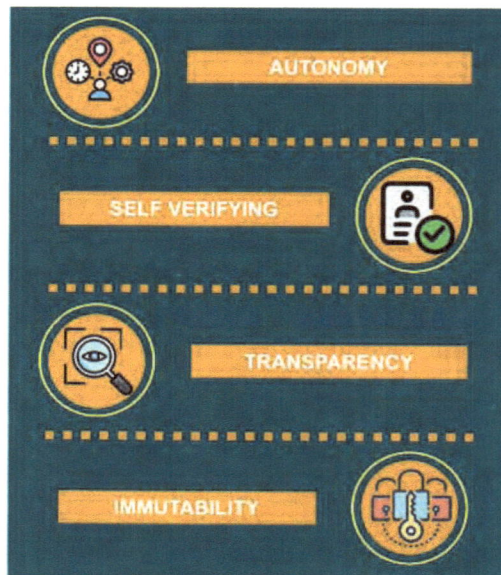

**Fig. (4).** Core characteristics of smart contracts.

Fig. (**5**) illustrates the primary steps involved in operating a blockchain. The entire process starts by initiating a transaction (represented by step 1), which is then broadcast to all participating nodes (represented by step 2). Each receiving node in the network applies the chosen form of consensus mechanism to reach a conclusion (represented by step 3). Once the consensus is reached, a new block comprising verified transactions (represented by step 4) is appended to the existing chain (represented by step 5) and also propagated to all the participating nodes to ensure the stable state of the blockchain (represented by step 6).

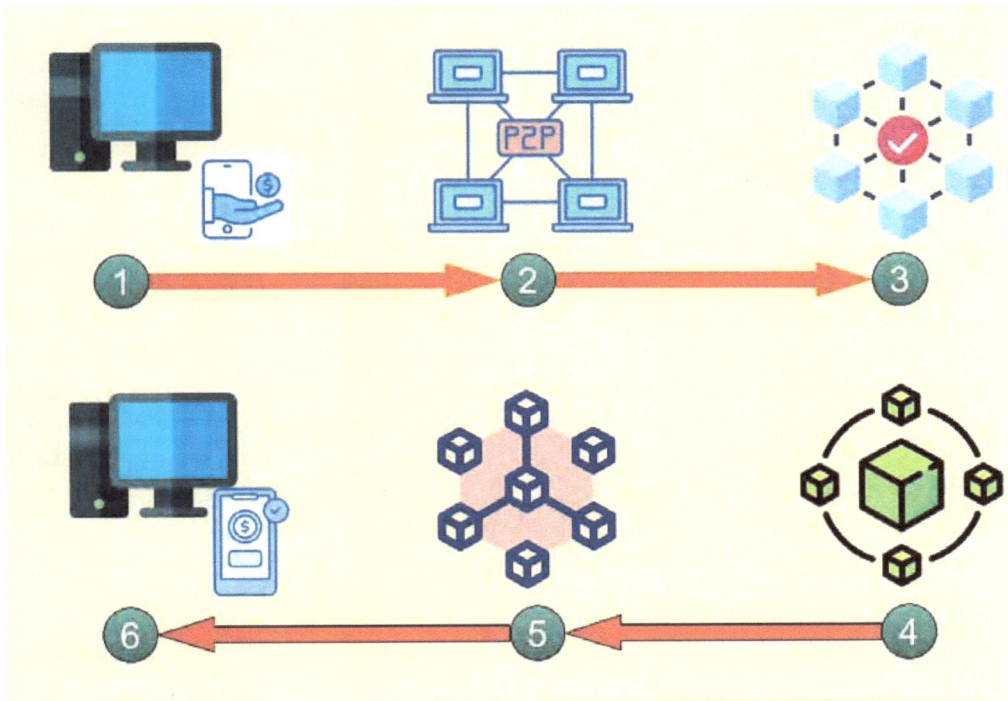

**Fig. (5).** Steps involved in the working of blockchain.

## TYPES OF BLOCKCHAIN

This section elaborates on blockchain types along with discussing their working and existing properties.

Fig. (**6**) illustrates the four categories of blockchain, highlighting their controlling entity. All nodes in red color are permitted to be engaged in the validation process, ensuring decentralized and transparent operations. As discussed in this section, since the public blockchain is open to every node hence, all the nodes are in red color. Similarly, in private blockchain, only one controlling entity

/organization is in charge. In consortium blockchain, multiple nodes or a group of organizations work together to validate transactions, allowing for semi-decentralized control among a trusted network. Lastly, an amalgamation of private and public blockchain, hybrid blockchain is a mix of nodes colored red and white, indicating controlled access, which can also be public.

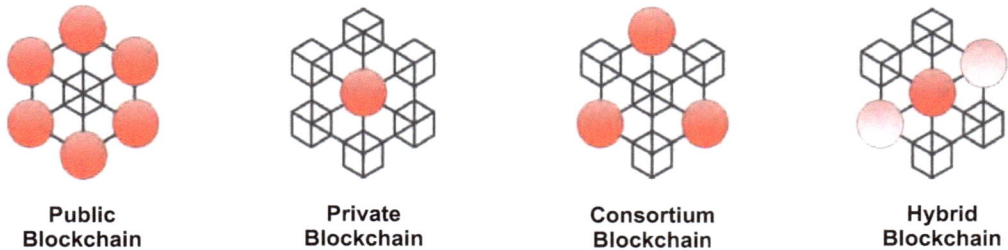

|     Public     |     Private     |    Consortium    |     Hybrid     |
| Blockchain | Blockchain | Blockchain | Blockchain |

**Fig. (6).** Visual representation of different blockchain types.

**Public Blockchain:** Also referred to as permissionless blockchain, it permits any participant to join the network without requiring any prior permission. This blockchain is fully decentralized in nature, allowing all the participating individuals to contribute to consensus, read and transfer transactions, and manage the distributed ledger. "All individuals accessing this blockchain can publish, access, and validate new blocks, allowing them to preserve a complete copy of the Blockchain", as quoted by a study [27]. The network requires computationally intensive consensus mechanisms, like puzzle solving or cryptocurrency investment, to verify transactions added by any individuals accessing this blockchain. Decentralized consensus and hashes prevent manipulation with block contents.

A classic example of such a network where anybody may join and take part in blockchain management is Bitcoin [1]. It is mostly used as a cryptocurrency over a P2P network, which relies on PoW for reaching a consensus. Such blockchains are an ideal choice where decentralization and trustlessness are of utmost importance. Public blockchains offer numerous benefits but also present numerous open research issues. The high number of participants and computationally expensive consensus mechanism make it difficult to achieve higher throughput. Additionally, the complete transparency and open nature of public blockchain can be unacceptable in applications seeking privacy.

**Private Blockchain:** Also referred to as permissioned blockchains, private blockchains are intended for one organization or a group of users. Unlike a public blockchain, in which anyone can participate, here, only selected individuals from an organization are authorized to be part of the blockchain [28]. The restriction on the number of users leads to increased scalability and higher throughput. For businesses where employees are viewed as network nodes and permitted to start transactions, a private blockchain is a good fit. Only employees belonging to the same organization are allowed access to the network. This blockchain network falls under the category of centralization because only the company's employees are permitted to use it. Private blockchains differ from public ones since here, only authorized entities can be part of the network and given rights to add new blocks [29]. Private blockchains are safer and more efficient as compared to public ones since only chosen individuals are allowed to be part of the network. Tampering is also secured by cryptographic hash and participant consensus. However, anonymity can be an issue in private blockchains as nodes are not anonymous in this category.

A popular example of a private blockchain is Hyperledger Fabric [30]. The main use case of Hyperledger fabric is for enterprises and business solutions and is highly recommended for applications requiring customizable transparency, security, and control. Open research challenges in private blockchains include block manipulation and network hacking by authorized players. Additionally decreased decentralization can lead to trust issues with less transparency.

**Consortium blockchain:** Generally referred to as federated blockchain, here, only a group of chosen organizations/authorities share the control of the blockchain. Only the chosen organizations are part of transaction validation and blockchain management. Public users may be permitted to read but not always have access to be a part of the consensus-reaching process, depending on their authorization privileges. As compared to the private category, where the entire responsibility of maintaining the blockchain is on a single organization, here, this responsibility is shared among various participating organizations.

R3 Corda [31] is a popular example of a consortium blockchain. It is mostly used in financial institutions or any other organizational setup where the collaboration of multiple organizations is a key requirement. Since the control is spanned across multiple organizations, it manages to provide a mix of privacy and confidentiality to its underlying application. Despite this advantage, reaching a consensus becomes a tedious task for consortium blockchain. Additionally, the initial phase of establishing such a blockchain-based architecture can be time-consuming, given the collaboration and mutual understanding required to set it up.

**Hybrid Blockchain:** As the name suggests, hybrid blockchain serves as an amalgamation of public and private blockchain. Here, some parts of the transaction can be opened to all, thereby making it public, and some parts can be restricted, similar to a private blockchain. This architecture allows the application using such a blockchain to utilize the advantage of public and private blockchain. This category of blockchain offers transparency and privacy at the same time.

A commonly known example of a hybrid blockchain is Dragonchain, which was developed by Disney [32]. Combining the advantages of both public and private blockchain, Dragonchain keeps the sensitive data private while utilizing the potential of public blockchain. This enables increased interaction with the public nodes while continuing to keep the data private and secret. Like consortium blockchain, establishing a hybrid blockchain is also a tedious process requiring strategic planning and execution.

## CHARACTERISTICS OF BLOCKCHAIN

### Decentralization

According to the decentralization property, P2P transactions can be completed without the requirement of a centralized entity to supervise processing and validation. Each participant has complete access to all of the data, including its history. Without the intervention of a central authority, each user can independently validate every transaction. Using technologies such as distributed consensus, digital signatures, and cryptographic hashes can help decentralize transactions. This functionality can drastically minimize server development and operating expenses while also addressing performance difficulties at the centralized server. Data integrity is safeguarded by the distributed consensus process. Decentralization ensures there is no centralized entity that is vulnerable to security threats [33]. This has been explained well in Table **2**.

### Consistency

Blockchain is designed to be tamper-resistant. Blocks spread around the network contain transaction confirmations and records. It is quite difficult to interfere with. Before being broadcast across the blockchain network, each transaction is validated and approved.

### Security

Blockchain is designed to be secure. Each user has his or her own private and public keys. The transactions are open to anyone on the blockchain network and can be viewed *via* public keys. Hashing is how the blockchain ensures its security. Each block is encrypted using a hash function, and any update to a transaction might cause the hash to change, rendering the block unchainable. The blockchain relies on individuals who participate to validate the transaction and ensure its authenticity, thus keeping transactions in blockchain independent and not dependent on any trusted third party [34].

**Table 2. Factors of comparison between different categories of blockchain.**

| Property | Public | Private | Hybrid | Consortium |
|---|---|---|---|---|
| **Decentralization** | Fully decentralized | Centralized, where the control is with a single entity | Partially decentralized (Mix of public and private control) | Partially decentralized (Controlled by a group of organizations) |
| **Access** | Open to anyone | Restricted to authorized participants | Mixed access (Some parts open, others restricted) | Restricted to consortium members |
| **Transparency** | Full transparency (public ledger) | Limited transparency (private ledger) | Customizable (Public and private elements) | Partial transparency within the consortium |
| **Consensus Mechanisms** | All nodes participate in consensus (*e.g.*, PoW, PoS) | Consensus among a few authorized nodes | Flexible (Can mix public and private methods) | Consensus by pre-selected nodes within the consortium |
| **Speed and Efficiency** | Typically, slower due to the large network size | Faster with fewer participants | Can be optimized for specific use cases | More efficient than public, less than private |
| **Scalability** | Limited scalability due to decentralization | Highly scalable due to controlled environment | Scalable, depending on the design | Moderate scalability depending on network size |
| **Security** | High security, but vulnerable to 51% attacks | Secure within the organization, but centralization can be a risk | Optimizable security based on needs | Secure but vulnerable to collusion and insider attacks |
| **Vulnerable Attacks** | 51% attack, Sybil attack, DDoS attack | Insider attack, Single point of failure, Data tampering | Hybrid attack, Data breach, Coordination attack | Collusion attack, Byzantine failure, Data integrity attack |
| **Power Consumption** | High (due to consensus mechanisms like PoW) | Low | Varies, but typically lower than public blockchains | Low |
| **Traceability** | High traceability | Limited traceability (restricted to authorized participants) | Customizable traceability | Moderate traceability among consortium members |

(Table 2) cont.....

| Property | Public | Private | Hybrid | Consortium |
|---|---|---|---|---|
| **Governance** | Decentralized governance | Organization-oriented governance | Shared between public and private entities | Multi-organization-based governance |
| **Data Privacy** | Low data privacy | High data privacy | Balanced data privacy between private and public data | Moderate data privacy |
| **Common Examples** | Bitcoin, Ethereum | Hyperledger Fabric, Quorum | Dragonchain, IBM Food Trust | R3 Corda, Energy Web Foundation |
| **Use Cases** | Cryptocurrencies, dApps, public record storage | Enterprise solutions, Supply chain management | Government, Finance, Health records | Collaborative industries, Healthcare, Financial services |

## Anonymity

Each peer on the blockchain is assigned a pair of keys, private and public, that serve as their unique identity. During the data exchange between blockchain addresses, everyone who participates has the option of identifying themselves or keeping their identity concealed. The traditional administration can keep track of users and their personal information. Blockchain provides increased privacy [35].

## Traceability

Blockchain technology enables the tracking of transactions. Each transaction is validated and recorded based on a timestamp. You can trace each transaction back to its ancestor. Blockchain improves the data's transparency and traceability.

## Immutability

After the development and subsequent deployment of the smart contracts on the blockchain network, it becomes immutable, *i.e.*, no one can its state or code without creating a new smart contract. Since every smart contract deployed has a unique address of its own, the creation of a new smart contract will require a new address, thus rendering the original contract unmodifiable.

## Transparency and Irreversibility

Since the time a transaction is initiated, it cannot be destroyed, amended, or altered. Blockchain uses computational techniques to ensure that data is recorded on a permanent, chronologically organized database that is available to all network members. Blockchain's immutable nature, along with transparency, ensures that the instant a block is appended, it is impossible to modify or delete it.

## Smart Contracts

These are system-wide instructions that are filed and executed automatically when certain conditions are fulfilled. These contracts offer significant advantages in a variety of sectors, including control of intellectual property, fraud-proof voting, access credentials, and many more.

## APPLICATION AREAS OF BLOCKCHAIN

Fig. (7) illustrates the integration and application of blockchain technology in the top 5 most researched areas.

## Internet of Things (IoT)

In the current scenario of computing, we are all surrounded by smart devices and IoT. According to current data, about 20 billion smartphones and IoT devices are in use. With these smart devices, a person can watch real-time video feeds anytime and anywhere. IoT is successful because of its information-sharing feature with multiple devices, is easily accessible, and can work with many heterogeneous systems. With these benefits, there are some concerns about security, privacy, and trust. Blockchain with IoT proved a significant enhancement in security, privacy, and reliability.

When blockchain and IoT are combined, it results in an improved version of IoT with respect to reliability, security, and privacy. It also comes with inevitable setbacks, like it may have high computation, may result in high energy consumption, may also require higher storage, and can also result in a slow transaction process. A smart city contains various diverse kinds of sensors and equipment that gather and share data about the smart city with the vendor who is providing service to that smart city. This data can be utilized to control smart city assets or to provide citizens with real-time personalized blockchain technologies for IoT services. However, the utilization of data in this manner boosts the efficiency of urban services, including basic services, electricity, and transportation. For smart cities, Intelligent Transport Systems (ITSs) play a vital role. ITS improves the safety and efficiency of citywide transport systems through sensing, communication, analytics, and control.

**Top 5 applications of blockchain**

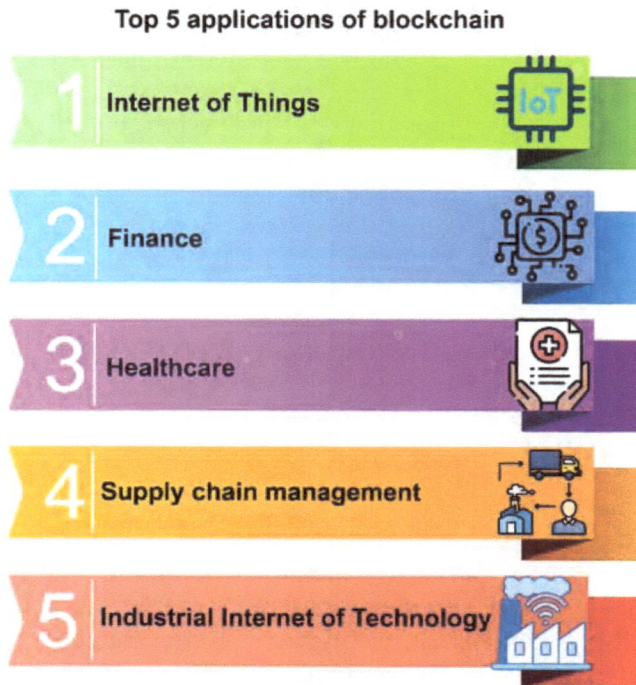

Fig. (7). Top 5 applications of blockchain.

## Finances

For the past ten years, the financial services industry has speculated on the prospects of blockchain. Blockchain is utilized as a database for monetary transactions. Whenever a transaction is initiated, a recorded copy is saved in each ledger due to block propagation (after block creation). It helps to guarantee that transactions are properly documented. Blockchain is practically unalterable and extremely secure since all the participating nodes have a copy of the latest ledger with them. Blockchain fosters reliability among business partners and allows for secure, on-point transactions. It enables the development and deployment of tamper-proof smart contracts that can automate any work, thus improving efficiency and fostering trust.

Blockchain applications in finance are particularly intriguing because digital currencies were the first to be stored on them. For example, an insurance company may make use of smart contracts to automate and assist in the claims process. When a client makes a claim, these contracts automatically assess it.

Blockchain use cases in the banking sector are way simpler and comparatively less expensive. One of the numerous benefits of employing this decentralized technology in banking is the security it provides. Blockchain can be modified to use encryption to secure its transaction ledger, where the data is made visible to peers who possess the right key.

Policymakers might use blockchain technology to explain existing rules and regulations or develop newer ones. This will reduce the dubiety around the potential set of rules of diverse technical use cases, enhancing the trust level of multiple sectors in adopting blockchain-based solutions. Credit reporting, trading platforms, and digital identification-based systems are among some of its widespread use cases.

## Healthcare

Various health applications have the potential to benefit from blockchain technology, as it can address long-existing challenges such as security, data management, and trust [35]. Some of these are:

- Managing Medical Records: By employing timestamps, blockchain can authenticate data generated in clinical trials, therefore ensuring tamper-proof data. Blockchain may streamline the process of recruiting and managing clinical trial volunteers while adding transparency and trust to the recruitment process.
- Clinical Trials and Research: Blockchain can be used for time-stamping and authenticating clinical trials' data, ensuring no one tampers with their findings that should be verifiable to all stakeholders. Blockchain technology simplifies the procedure of recruiting and managing participants in clinical trials, thereby ensuring transparency and confidence in the enrollment process [31].
- Drug Supply Chain Management: Tracing a drug's life cycle from the manufacturer to the end user ensures the removal of counterfeit drugs from the supply chain through blockchain. The blockchain tracks real-time drug stocks for healthcare providers, resulting in minimum wastage and good availability of medication at any point in time.
- Billing and Claims Management: Blockchain technology can automate and protect the claims process, minimizing false claims and ensuring that payments are made accurately and effectively. It can also be used to automate insurance claims, minimizing administrative costs and expediting the claims process by automatically making payments when predetermined conditions are met.
- Telemedicine and telemonitoring: Blockchain can guarantee the security and tamper-resistance of data exchanged between patients and healthcare providers during telemedicine sessions. In telemonitoring, blockchain can securely collect and manage data fetched from IoT devices, ensuring the privacy and accuracy of

patient information.

- Genomics and Personalized Medicine: Blockchain technology enables the secure and controlled sharing of genomic data for research while protecting patient privacy. Blockchain technology can help build personalized medicine technology by securely integrating a patient's genetic information with therapeutic data.
- Medical Insurance: Blockchain can automate the claims process, reduce the likelihood of disputes, and expedite the settlement of insurance claims by utilizing smart contracts that are automatically executed when a pre-defined set of conditions are fulfilled. Blockchain technology can provide secure and authorized transmission of patient data between healthcare providers and insurance companies, increasing claims accuracy and minimizing fraud.

## Supply Chain Management

Applying blockchain innovation in supply chain administration can give a run of benefits:

- System is traceable, straightforward, and trustable: The primary feature of blockchain in the supply chain is to have a pool of data that is a precise, clear, and permanent record of all transactions. This meant having information on data from beginning to end, maintaining integrity, and reducing the chances of data leaks. There will be an improvement in transparency throughout the management of the supply chain; this will impact businesses and show significant improvement as now they can track things and check performance in real time. This can also lead to increased trust among supply chain partners.
- Expanded proficiency leads to speed: By robotizing numerous forms inside the supply chain, blockchain innovation can increase effectiveness and decrease costs. This might incorporate computerizing installments, following stock levels, or streamlining coordination forms. Due to a transparent and automated system, there is a significant increase in speed.
- Diminished Costs: Blockchain eliminated middlemen and lowered the overhead of the administrative section, which resulted in lowering the overall cost. This starts with the planning phase and extends to the development stage, which includes manufacturing, shipping, and arrival back of things. One can take the example of the automotive industry, which can reduce costs by making a reduction in the amount of stock required. Currently, the company is managing its stock level manually for product availability and maintaining its records manually. These companies use computerized forms using blockchain and can see a reduction of cost to a great extent at the administrative level.
- Using blockchain, information can be distributed throughout the whole lifecycle while maintaining its security and integrity, including all the stakeholders of that

company. Stakeholders can be providers, manufacturers, and wholesalers and can access any real-time information. Blockchain technology minimizes the expenses of manual transmission of information, which will be error-free and done during the collaboration of many parties. It will also reduce printing costs, which are managed while the whole supply chain is being managed. Furthermore, the amount of reduced printed material throughout the entire supply chain is great. Moreover, blockchain can help to minimize item advancement costs by offering a secure platform that tracks progress during the planning process and ensures that changes are correctly applied. This may help eliminate delays and errors in the development stage, resulting in a faster time-to-market (TTM).

- Improved Security by Unchanging Nature: Blockchain technology is exceptionally secure due to its distributed architecture and usage of cryptography. One of the most striking characteristics of blockchain is its consistency. By using transmitted records and cryptographic procedures, information saved on a blockchain may be kept perpetually safe and unmodified across time. This makes it exceedingly improbable that hostile actors are able to alter blockchain data or disrupt transaction histories. This nature also enables a traceable supply chain network, as all information is consistent and can be efficiently tracked back to its source. This also increases trust among stakeholders during the supply chain, which, in return, makes it easier for enterprises to stay accountable.

- Superior Client Involvement: Superior client involvement in supply chain management using blockchain alters traditional processes by increasing transparency, traceability, and confidence among all parties. Blockchain technology provides real-time tracking at every stage, allowing clients to follow products from origin to delivery using immutable data. This ensures that clients are informed and involved in crucial decisions like sourcing, inventory management, and delivery dates and provides a clear audit trail to reduce conflicts. Furthermore, smart contracts simplify transactions by automating payments and contractual responsibilities when certain criteria are met, increasing efficiency and client trust. Blockchain strengthens collaborations and improves supply chain performance by giving clients more control, transparency, and real-time data.

## Industrial IoT (IIoT)

IIoT is a common cyber-physical framework where various machines, including computers and other individuals, process high-level mechanical operations using all analytical information available for revolutionizing commerce outcomes. IIoT empowers the integration of remote sensor systems, communication conventions, and web frameworks, empowering clever mechanical operations for checking, examination, and administration. This inter-network of anything within the generation framework setting makes a difference in the computerization of mechanical generation and makes strides in insights, proficiency, and security.

The physical layer, communication layer, and application layer are the three layers of IIoT engineering. The physical layer comprises physical gadgets like sensors, actuators, fabricating hardware, shrewd terminals, and information centers. The communication layer employments arrange innovations, such as actuator and remote sensor systems (WSNs), 5G, and machine-to-machine (M2M) communication, for the integration of different gadgets within the physical layer for mechanical fabricating and automation. The overlayers frame a CPS (Industrial-CPS within the setting of IIoT) to bolster the mechanical and generation application layer utilizing the over advances for the improvement of savvy production lines, supply chains, *etc.* The control, organization, and computing foundations of the cyber frameworks empower the organizing and operation of the generation frameworks.

## CONCLUSION AND FUTURE SCOPE

Centralized networks are not only affected by a single source of failure but are even more susceptible to data tampering, intruders, and denial of service. Decentralized services offered by blockchain can provide better security and efficient solutions to existing infrastructures. This chapter serves as an extensive review of the blockchain architecture, its core components and characteristics, and its use case in the fields of IoT, healthcare, finances, *etc.* The consensus protocols play a pivotal role in the functionality of blockchain and maintaining its operational integrity, ensuring trust and transparency in the network without the requirement of any other party. However, this revolutionary technology also presents its own unique challenges. Issues such as interoperability, scalability, energy consumption, and regulations need to be addressed for better outreach and ease of use. Future researchers continue to find ways to integrate blockchain with artificial intelligence, machine learning, and quantum computing to offer solutions to these challenges.

In conclusion, blockchain's efficiency in offering decentralized, secure, transparent, and immutable services will continue to be a pivotal technology in the future. As the technology matures, its applications are likely to be expanded, driving innovation across various sectors and aiding in the growth of resilient and efficient infrastructures.

## CONSENT FOR PUBLICATION

All the authors approve of the publication.

# ACKNOWLEDGEMENT

The authors express their sincere gratitude to their peers who contributed to the supervision, validation, and review of the final draft.

# REFERENCES

[1]     S. Nakamoto, "Bitcoin: A peer-to-peer electronic cash system", 2008. Available from: https://bitcoin.org/bitcoin.pdf

[2]     Y. Xiao, N. Zhang, W. Lou, and Y.T. Hou, "A survey of distributed consensus protocols for blockchain networks", *IEEE Commun. Surv. Tutor.,* vol. 22, no. 2, pp. 1432-1465, 2020.

[3]     A.G. Gad, D.T. Mosa, L. Abualigah, and A.A. Abohany, "Emerging trends in blockchain technology and applications: A review and outlook", *J. King Saud Univ. Comput. Inf. Sci.,* vol. 34, no. 9, pp. 6719-6742, 2022.
[http://dx.doi.org/10.1016/j.jksuci.2022.03.007]

[4]     M. Dabbagh, M. Sookhak, and N.S. Safa, "The evolution of blockchain: A bibliometric study", *IEEE Access,* vol. 7, pp. 19212-19221, 2019.
[http://dx.doi.org/10.1109/access.2019.2895646]

[5]     M. Banerjee, J. Lee, and K.K.R. Choo, "A blockchain future for internet of things security: A position paper", *Digit. Commun. Networks,* vol. 4, no. 3, pp. 149-160, 2018.
[http://dx.doi.org/10.1016/j.dcan.2017.10.006]

[6]     A. Gorkhali, L. Li, and A. Shrestha, "Blockchain: A literature review", *J. Manag. Anal.,* vol. 7, no. 3, pp. 321-343, 2020.
[http://dx.doi.org/10.1080/23270012.2020.1801529]

[7]     J. Xu, C. Wang, and X. Jia, "A survey of blockchain consensus protocols", *ACM Comput. Surv.,* vol. 55, no. 13s, pp. 1-35, 2023.
[http://dx.doi.org/10.1145/3579845]

[8]     S. Zhang, and J.H. Lee, "Analysis of the main consensus protocols of blockchain", *ICT Express,* vol. 6, no. 2, pp. 93-97, 2020.

[9]     Shijie Zhang, Jong-Hyouk Lee, "Analysis of the main consensus protocols of blockchain", *ICT Express,* vol. 6, no. 2, pp. 93-97, 2020.
[http://dx.doi.org/10.1016/j.icte.2019.08.001]

[10]    G.A.F. Rebello, "In 2022 6th cyber security in networking conference (CSNet)", *IEEE,* 2022

[11]    H. Qin, and Y. Guan, "Joint reputation based grouping and hierarchical byzantine fault tolerance consensus protocol", *IEEE Access,* vol. 11, pp. 90335-90344, 2023.

[12]    M.M. Taha, and M. Alanezi, "In 2023 16th international conference on developments in esystems engineering (DeSE)", *IEEE,* 2023.

[13]    B. Borzdov, M. Minchenok, and Y. Yanovich, "In 2023 XVIII international symposium problems of redundancy in information and control systems (REDUNDANCY)", *IEEE,* 2023.

[14]    A. Singh, and G. Rathee, "FATE: Flexible attribute-based traceable encrypted data sharing scheme using smart contracts in wireless medical sensor networks", *Ann. Telecommun.,* pp. 1-17, 2024.

[15]    Y. Harbi, K. Medani, C. Gherbi, O. Senouci, Z. Aliouat, and S. Harous, "A systematic literature review of blockchain technology for internet of drones security", *Arab. J. Sci. Eng.,* vol. 48, no. 2, pp. 1053-1074, 2023.
[http://dx.doi.org/10.1007/s13369-022-07380-6] [PMID: 36337772]

[16]    P. Kaur, and A. Parashar, "A systematic literature review of blockchain technology for smart villages", *Arch. Comput. Methods Eng.,* vol. 29, no. 4, pp. 2417-2468, 2022.

[http://dx.doi.org/10.1007/s11831-021-09659-7] [PMID: 34720578]

[17] S. Zeba, and P. Suman, *In Distributed Computing to Blockchain.*, pp. 55-68, 2023.*Elsevier,* pp. 55-68, 2023.

[18] S. Ølnes, J. Ubacht, and M. Janssen, "Blockchain in government: Benefits and implications of distributed ledger technology for information sharing", *Gov. Inf. Q.*, vol. 34, no. 3, pp. 355-364, 2017.

[19] M. Javaid, "A review of blockchain technology applications for financial services", *BenchCouncil Trans. Benchmarks Standards and Evaluations,* vol. 2, no. 3, p. 100073, 2022.

[20] L. Zhang, "Blockchain based secure data sharing system for internet of vehicles: A position paper", *Veh. Commun.,* vol. 16, pp. 85-93, 2019.

[21] F. Casino, T.K. Dasaklis, and C. Patsakis, "A systematic literature review of blockchain-based applications: Current status, classification and open issues", *Telemat. Inform.,* vol. 36, pp. 55-81, 2019. [http://dx.doi.org/10.1016/j.tele.2018.11.006]

[22] T. Ali Syed, "A comparative analysis of blockchain architecture and its applications: Problems and recommendations", *IEEE Access,* vol. 7, pp. 176838-176869, 2019. [http://dx.doi.org/10.1109/access.2019.2957660]

[23] A. Gervais, "In proceedings of the 2016 ACM SIGSAC conference on computer and communications security", pp. 3–16, 2016.

[24] P. Gaži, "In 2019 IEEE symposium on security and privacy (SP)", *IEEE,* pp. 139-156, 2019.

[25] M. Abd-El-Malek, "Fault-scalable byzantine fault-tolerant services", *ACM SIGOPS Oper. Syst. Rev.,* vol. 39, no. 5, pp. 59-74, 2005.

[26] S. Bragagnolo, "In 2018 international workshop on blockchain oriented software engineering (IWBOSE)", *IEEE,* 2018.

[27] M.K. Shrivas, and T. Yeboah, "The disruptive blockchain: Types, platforms and applications", *Texila Int. J. Acad. Res.,* vol. 3, pp. 17-39, 2019.

[28] S.B. Lee, A. Park, and J. Song, "Blockchain technology and application", *J. Korea Soc. Comput. Inf.,* vol. 26, no. 2, pp. 89-97, 2021.

[29] J. Kim, "Blockchain technology and its applications: Case studies", *J. Syst. Manag. Sci.,* vol. 10, no. 1, pp. 83-93, 2020.

[30] E. Androulaki, "Hyperledger fabric: A distributed operating system for permissioned blockchains". 2018. [http://dx.doi.org/10.48550/ARXIV.1801.10228]

[31] D. Mohanty, *R3 Corda for Architects and Developers: With Case Studies in Finance, Insurance, Healthcare, Travel, Telecom, and Agriculture.* Apress, 2019.

[32] Y.R. Reddy, V. Karthick, and J. Somasundaram, "In 2022 14th international conference on mathematics, actuarial science, computer science and statistics (MACS)", *IEEE,* pp. 1-4, 2022.

[33] A. Ghazi, "A systematic literature review of blockchain technology", *Int. J. Interact. Mobile Technol.,* vol. 16, no. 10, pp. 97-108, 2022. [http://dx.doi.org/10.3991/ijim.v16i10.30083]

[34] D. Jiang, "A blockchain-reinforced federated intrusion detection architecture for IIoT", *IEEE Internet Things J.,* vol. 11, no. 16, pp. 26793-26805, 2024. [http://dx.doi.org/10.1109/jiot.2024.3406602]

[35] A. Singh, and G.P. Kumar, "Blockchain in healthcare: A comprehensive review of the state of the art", *Health Informatics J.,* vol. 27, no. 4, p. 14604582211037763, 2021. [http://dx.doi.org/10.1177/14604582211037763]

# CHAPTER 11

# MegaETH: A New Era of Real-Time Blockchain Technology

**Kajal Dubey**[1,*] and **Dhiraj Pandey**[1]

*[1] Department Of Information and Technology, JSS Academy of Technical Education, Noida, India*

**Abstract:** MegaETH leads the way in blockchain technology. It created the Real-Time Proof of Stake (RTPoS) consensus method. This new approach tackles regular blockchain networks' main speed and scaling issues in regular blockchain networks. It allows fast transaction processing without giving up security or decentralization. Meg+aETH focuses on high output and can handle thousands of transactions per second (TPS). This opens doors for many decentralized apps (dApps) across different fields. A big plus of the Ethereum platform is how MegaETH fits into the Ethereum ecosystem. It uses smart contract features and works well with the Ethereum Virtual Machine (EVM). This compatibility helps the ecosystem grow and brings new ideas by making it easier for more developers to join in. MegaETH also cares about the environment. Its design uses less energy, meaning it has less impact on nature than proof-of-work systems. MegaETH brings together efficiency, security, and the ability to grow. This sets a new bar for real-time blockchain apps. As a result, it speeds up how the economy takes on decentralized solutions. It also lets developers and companies explore new ways to use this technique.

**Keywords:** Blockchain revolution, Consensus algorithms, Decentralized applications (dApps), Distributed ledger technology (DLT), Ecosystem growth, Energy-efficient, Ethereum virtual machine (EVM), Finance industry disruption, High throughput, Innovation, Interoperability, MegaETH, Proof of stake (PoS), Rapid transaction processing, Real-time applications, Real-time proof of stake (RTPoS), Scalability, Security, Smart contracts, Supply chain management.

## INTRODUCTION

The blockchain space has advanced significantly since its inception, consistently pushing the boundaries of decentralized technologies and digital transactions. Every breakthrough in smart contracts and decentralized finance, from the early days of Bitcoin, has brought us one step closer to achieving the full promise of blockchain technology. Real-time processing is a significant obstacle that has not

---
* **Corresponding author Kajal Dubey:** Department Of Information and Technology, JSS Academy of Technical Education, Noida, India; E-mail: kajal.dubey@jssaten.ac.in

**Monica Bhutani, Monica Gupta, Kirti Gupta, Deepali Kamthania & Danish Ather (Eds.)**
**All rights reserved-© 2025 Bentham Science Publishers**

been fully overcome. We are presenting MegaETH, a ground-breaking invention that has the potential to completely transform blockchain technology. By addressing the crucial need for real-time transaction processing and instant updates, MegaETH is poised to completely transform the industry. MegaETH is built to deliver performance that is both quick and effective, bringing in a new era of real-time capabilities in the cryptocurrency industry. Traditional blockchains, on the other hand, frequently suffer from latency and scalability problems [1, 2].

For the first time in the cryptocurrency industry, Web2-level real-time performance is available thanks to MegaETH, an EVM-compatible blockchain. Our objective is to close the gap between blockchain technology and conventional cloud computing servers by pushing Ethereum L2s' performance to the edge of hardware.

High transaction throughput, a large amount of computing capacity, and—most notably—millisecond-level reaction times even under high demand are just a few of MegaETH's unique qualities. Developers are able to create and construct the most complex apps without limits when using MegaETH.

In this chapter, we will examine how MegaETH is expected to change the real-time blockchain technology ecosystem. We will investigate its novel aspects, evaluate its possible influence on different industries, and comprehend how it is establishing new standards for efficiency in the blockchain field [2]. MegaETH might change industry norms and expand the potential of blockchain technology, marking not simply a technological advance but also a fundamental change in how humans engage with digital systems.

## WHY ANOTHER BLOCKCHAIN? AN OVERVIEW OF MEGAETH'S ROLE AND FUNCTION

### Why is There a Need for New Blockchains?

The creation of new chains, including L1s and L2, is now easier, thanks to the development of blockchain frameworks. As such, a plethora of new chains have surfaced in recent times. As a result, there is currently a boom in the number of blockchain networks, with over 50 L2 projects up and running. Even with this growth of chains, the basic scalability problems remain unresolved by just adding more [2]. The ability of each chain to host decentralized apps (dApps) is still severely limited. As evidenced by the current metrics for gas per second and block timings, significant EVM chains, for instance, have limits regarding transaction throughput and block delays [3].

## Limitations of Current Blockchain Frameworks

Recent gas parameter comparisons show that current EVM chains have major hurdles. Their low transaction throughput is one of the main issues. Even with its remarkable gas rate of 100 MGas/s, opBNB, for instance, is still unable to match the capabilities of contemporary Web2 servers [4]. To put this into perspective, modern database systems can process over one million transactions per second, as demonstrated by the TPC-C benchmark. In comparison, 100 MGas/s is equivalent to about 650 Uniswap swaps or 3,700 ERC-20 transfers per second. There is a noticeable performance disparity here [4]. For example, the table below shows the target gas per second and block time of major EVM chains today (Table **1**).

**Table 1. Comparison of gas parameters across EVM chains in 2024.**

| Select EVM Chains | Gas Per Second | Target Gas Per Block(Supply) | Block Time |
|---|---|---|---|
| opBNB | 100.0 mg/s | 100M | 0.1s |
| BSC | 46.5 mg/s | 140M | 3.0s |
| Polygon | 7.5 mg/s | 15M | 2.0s |
| Avalanche C-Chain | 7.5 mg/s | 15M | 2.0s |
| Arbitrum one | 7.0 mg/s | 1.75M | 0.25s |
| Base | 5.0 mg/s | 15M | 2.0s |
| Optimism Mainnet | 2.5 mg/s | 5M | 2.0s |
| Conduit | 2.5 mg/s | 5M | 2.0s |
| Ethereum L1 | 1.25 mg/s | 15M | 12.0s |

This table (Table **1**) distinctly shows that in many aspects, there are still severe limitations in EVM chains. The lack of computing power for sophisticated applications is another issue. For example, $n = 10^8$ costs about 5.5 billion gas to calculate the n-th Fibonacci number using a standard EVM contract. This calculation in C takes only 30 milliseconds; however, on the opBNB chain, it would take 55 seconds at a rate of 100 MGas/s [5]. This demonstrates the necessity for blockchains to have more processing power, a need that multicore processing can help with by improving performance [5].

Furthermore, the majority of current chains have lengthy block durations, which renders them inappropriate for applications that need instantaneous updates or input. All chains update their statuses at least once every second, except for Arbitrum One [6]. High-frequency trading systems and autonomous worlds that require instantaneous battle simulations, among other entirely on-chain dApps that require real-time interactions, find this delay problematic. Order execution within 10 milliseconds and block intervals of less than 100 milliseconds are necessary for real-time applications to function effectively [7].

## MEGAETH: A SOLUTION TO EXISTING BLOCKCHAIN CHALLENGES

A real-time blockchain such as MegaETH processes transactions and updates instantaneously, providing the high transaction throughput and substantial computational power necessary to maintain a real-time experience even during peak demands [8, 9]. MegaETH's real-time blockchain technology overcomes the traditional constraints of blockchain scalability and performance.

### Solving the Straggler Problem

The "Straggler Problem" harms blockchain networks. It slows down the whole system when the slowest nodes take too long to finish their tasks [10, 11]. This happens in networks with lots of nodes where block finalization depends on all nodes completing their work. Slow hardware, tech issues, or other delays can make the network less productive. To fix the "Straggler problem," MegaETH uses node specialization. This method frees up full nodes from doing transaction execution jobs.

MegaETH works like layer two (L2) blockchains. It uses sequencers and provers along with full nodes. In MegaETH, sequencers organize and run transactions just like in other L2s. To cut down on consensus overhead, MegaETH uses one active sequencer. "Node specialization lets us set different hardware needs for each type of node. This gives us a big advantage."

### Node Specialization Approach

MegaETH tackles the Straggler Problem by using a smart way to make nodes do specific jobs. This plan gives different types of nodes their tasks. In Fig. (**1**), it makes sure each kind of node does its job well, which helps the whole network work better. Here is how MegaETH makes its nodes special:

#### *Sequencers*

These nodes start and carry out transactions. MegaETH uses one active sequencer at a time, which cuts down on the work needed to get everyone to agree [12]. In MegaETH, like in other L2s, sequencers are in charge of organizing and doing transactions.

## *Provers*

These nodes check blocks by looking at the proofs that sequencers give. Nodes must check blocks using proofs from provers.

## *Full Nodes*

In MegaETH, full nodes help build consensus and maintain the blockchain's ledger, but they do not finish transactions. This leads to lower overall node operating costs and makes the network more scalable by allowing full nodes to run on less powerful hardware [13].

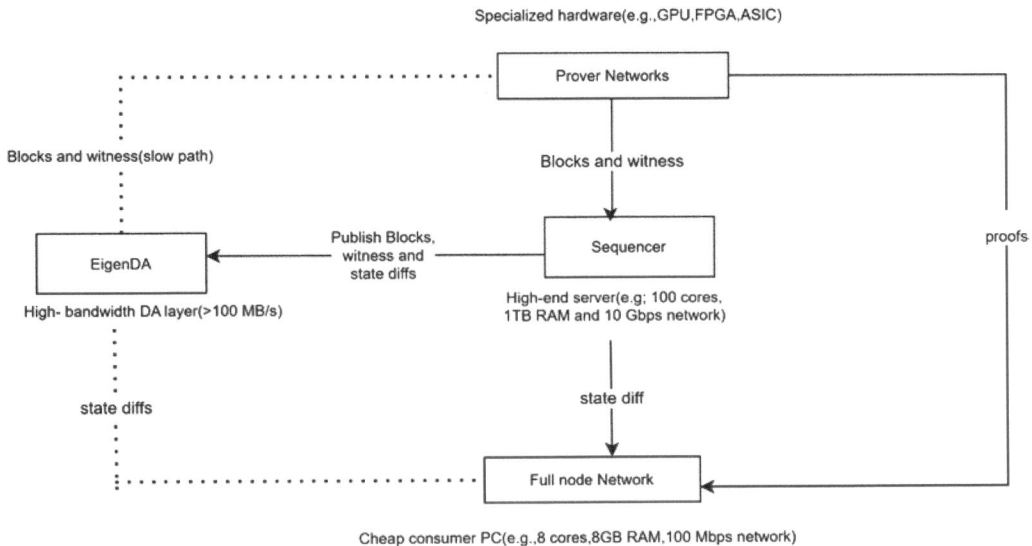

**Fig. (1).** Major Components of MegaETH and their interactions.

The above figure (Fig. **1**) illustrates the basic structure of MegaETH as well as the interaction between its main components.

## *Advantages of Node Specialization*

Node specialization in MegaETH has several key benefits:

***Better Performance:*** High-end servers handle the tough job of managing transaction execution for sequencers. This setup speeds up transaction processing and eases performance bottlenecks. MegaETH removes bottlenecks of performance and accelerates the processing of transactions offloading such bandwidth-intensive operations to specially dedicated servers. With such specialization, the network can execute transactions more quickly and efficiently because of the efficiency at which complex transactions are being processed [14].

*Lower Costs:* In Fig. (1), the full nodes can run on simpler hardware as they do the easier task of proof checking. This cuts down node running costs and gets more people to join the network. This decrease in hardware requirements lowers the cost of maintaining a node. The lower cost of participation thus encourages more people to participate in the network, thereby enhancing more decentralization and inclusion.

*Greater Scalability:* By giving specific tasks to different node types and boosting how they work, MegaETH can deal with more transactions even as the network grows [15]. The network can manage more transactions as it expands with optimized techniques performed by each node and efficient allocations of workload. MegaETH can scale better while still catering to the growing transaction needs without reducing speed. This job splitting will enable the network to process additional transactions when the network increases. By optimizing the operation of each node and by smartly allocating workloads in the most effective way possible, MegaETH scales much better to meet growing transaction needs without compromising on speed.

*Higher Network Efficiency*: The network's quicker block times and overall better performance, with fewer nodes doing transaction execution, tackles the Straggler Problem [16]. The Straggler Problem is addressed by node specialization, where delays in the processing of transactions reason a slowdown in the network as a whole, but the process makes the network overall more reliable by removing block times and improving entire performance with some nodes dedicated to transaction execution.

## CURRENT SCALABILITY ISSUES IN EVM-BASED BLOCKCHAINS

Blockchains based on Ethereum Virtual Machines (EVMs) continue to face numerous scalability problems despite recent advancements in blockchain technology [17, 18]. Triggering factors include interpreter overhead, no parallel execution, and excessive state access latency. By utilizing its novel approach, MegaETH seeks to solve this issue by expediting state access. Compared to database load times, SSD read latency is minimal since the full blockchain state is cached in a large amount of RAM. Still an issue, though, is scalability. The degree to which transactions can be consumed in parallel is limited by their dependencies, and the interdependencies among them influence the potential benefits of parallel processing [19]. Also, the use of non-compute heavy contracts impacts the Revm execution environment and leaves room to boost performance when given the chance. State synchronization poses another challenge for

MegaETH because high transaction volumes can overwhelm network capacity and complicate updates to the chain state root. On top of that, the block gas limit acts as a throttling mechanism that limits transaction throughput while striking a balance between security and scalability [20]. To manage high transaction volumes and maintain the user experience, robust infrastructure becomes even more essential, as shown by the need for efficient RPC nodes and indexers [21].

## ENGINEERING A REAL-TIME BLOCKCHAIN: MEGAETH'S APPROACH

MegaETH's cutting-edge node specialization technique has an influence on performance that goes beyond what standard models offer. This showcases the blockchain technology breakthroughs the company is known for. People often underestimate the research and engineering challenges in MegaETH, even though comparing it to centralized servers helps to understand its potential. To build a real-time blockchain, you need to do more than just enhance the sequencers' hardware and use an off-the-shelf Ethereum execution client.

It is tempting to think of MegaETH as using a souped-up centralized sequencer. However, this view does not do justice to the complex engineering and research behind the project [22]. Creating a real-time blockchain is not just about upgrading hardware. You need to tackle fundamental issues and fine-tune components. Even with a server that has 512GB of RAM, for example, the Reth client can only do approximately 1000 transactions per second (TPS), or 100 MGas/s, while it is in live sync with the latest Ethereum blocks. As updating the Merkle Patricia Trie (MPT) requires computational overhead that is almost ten times more resource-intensive than processing the transactions directly, this represents the main bottleneck in this situation. This problem shows how difficult it is to develop a real-time blockchain and how little can be accomplished by just improving current technology.

In Fig (**2**), the performance experiments with our setup reveal that even with a very powerful server with 512GB RAM, Reth can only achieve about 1000 TPS (and hence about 100 MGas/s) in a live sync on recent Ethereum blocks. As illustrated in the experiment above, Reth's performance is limited due to the overhead of updating the MPT in each block, which is nearly 10 times more computationally expensive than executing the transactions.

## DESIGN PHILOSOPHY AND APPROACH

Resolving performance bottlenecks in blockchain systems calls for more than band-aid solutions. Because it is either not the primary limiting factor or only moves the bottleneck to another location, a single optimization frequently falls short of producing appreciable end-to-end gains [23]. Many initiatives show significant improvements in some areas of performance but often have difficulty converting these improvements into overall system efficiency.

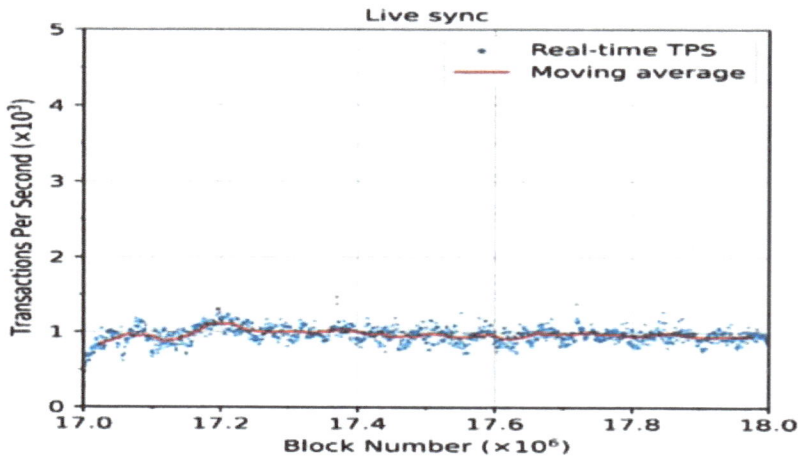

**Fig. (2).** Live sync performance of Reth.

MegaETH conducts its research and development using a comprehensive and moral methodology. The two pillars of our design philosophy are as follows:

**Measure, Then Build**

To identify the true problems with the current systems, we first carry out extensive performance measurements [24]. With these insights, we create all-encompassing solutions that solve all problems at once.

**Push Hardware Boundaries**

We strive for clean-slate designs that push towards the theoretical performance boundaries rather than making small changes to current systems. By taking this approach, the industry can concentrate on other adoption difficulties while minimizing the possibility of future performance enhancements [25].

**TRANSACTION EXECUTION IN MEGAETH**

**Overview of the Transaction Process**

The sequencer, which is an essential part of ordering and executing transactions, is where a user transaction in MegaETH begins [26]. The perception that the performance limits of Layer 2 (L2) solutions based on the Ethereum Virtual

Machine (EVM) are the cause of criticism is not entirely accurate [27]. Many L2 applications can be satisfied with Revm's 14,000 transactions per second (TPS) in a historical sync configuration, according to performance data. Revm is an implementation of the EVM. MegaETH ensures transparent, safe, and effectual transaction processing and contract execution within its distributed network. Security and privacy in MegaETH are maintained by cryptographic hashing, public-private key pairs, and some secure protocols.

The figure (Fig. 3) above describes the process of a user transaction traveling through the system and will be useful in explaining the technical problems discussed later.

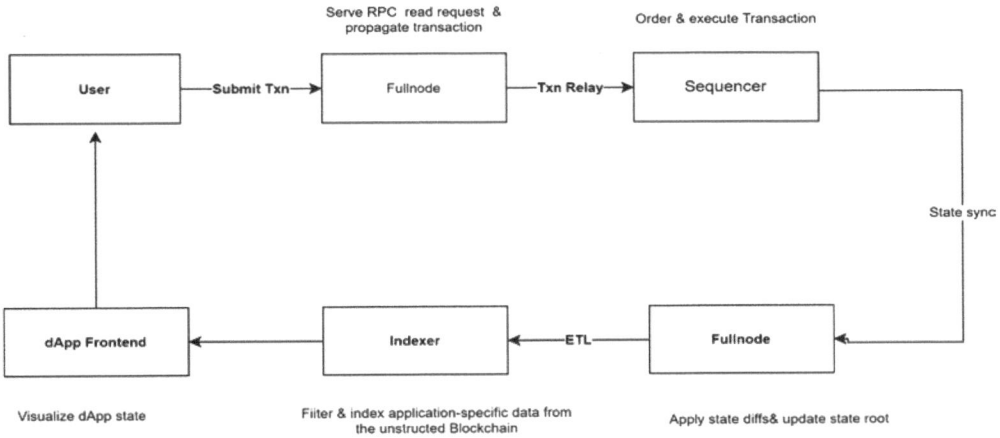

**Fig. (3).** Journey of a user transaction.

## EVM Performance Challenges

The demands of a real-time blockchain such as MegaETH are not fully met by Revm, even though it shows high TPS rates. Typical EVM implementations include several significant inefficiencies, such as:

***Elevated State Access Latency:*** MegaETH reduces SSD read latency by storing the full blockchain state in large amounts of RAM. But difficulties still exist. Despite all this, there are still difficulties. RAM is not enough to eliminate the latency caused by obtaining and processing blockchain state information as a whole, and high state access latency is still in effect. It remains relatively difficult to manage and retrieve state data effectively, especially as the blockchain grows and the complexity of state interactions increases [28].

***Limited Parallel Execution:*** The Block-STM algorithm's attempts to improve parallel execution show that the degree of workload parallelism limits the amount of real speedup. The median parallelism in Ethereum blocks, according to our research, is less than 2, and block batching only slightly raises this number [29]. Block batching has a light effect on the median parallelism of Ethereum blocks. To this end, this constraint in parallel execution impacts the overall performance and efficiency of the EVM because less can be done to hasten transaction processing. Accordingly, these limitations to simultaneous transaction processing limit the scope for potential gains in terms of scale.

*The Overhead of the Interpreter:* Native execution is substantially faster than even the most effective interpreters, such as Revm. Because most contracts have low computational demands, innovations in AOT/JIT compilation, which aim to speed up EVM execution, have not yielded significant improvements in practice. One reason is that most smart contracts have relatively modest processing needs, which makes these optimizations less valuable. This leaves very little room for improvement of speed as the overhead of the interpreter proves to be a performance drawback [30].

**Challenges for Real-Time Blockchains** Real-time blockchains, such as MegaETH, confront additional difficulties not seen in high-performance EVM chains:

*High-Frequency Block Generation:* To achieve real-time needs, blocks must be generated at very high rates, like once every 10 milliseconds [31]. Block creation must occur rapidly to maintain performance and it also ensures the blockchain can manage data flow.

*Transaction prioritizing:* To guarantee that crucial transactions are completed promptly during times of high traffic, the parallel execution engine must provide transaction prioritizing [32]. This can be enhanced by a parallel execution engine by utilizing transaction prioritizing techniques. Such strategies may include the assignment of variable priority levels to the transactions, with their respective weights in importance or urgency, to attain an optimum flow in processing.

## State synchronization

State synchronization is an essential but difficult component of high-performance blockchain systems. It involves updating full nodes with the most recent state changes from the sequencer, a process that is frequently underestimated in its complexity [33]. To demonstrate this difficulty, let's look at ERC-20 token transfers. Since each transfer modifies three values, the estimated state diff size is about 200 bytes. For 100,000 transfers per second, this means that bandwidth is needed for approximately 152.6 Mbps, which exceeds many bandwidth limits. Complex transactions, like Uniswap swaps, which impact multiple storage slots and contract values, can further raise this requirement; for 100,000 Uniswap swaps per second, this equals approximately 476.1 Mbps [34].

Due to several issues, including shared connections across apps, protocol overheads, internet providers' tendency to overestimate speeds, and the requirement for bandwidth for bootstrapping new nodes, a full node's effective bandwidth is frequently less than its maximum capacity in practice. For example, to handle the Uniswap exchanges efficiently, one would need to achieve a 19x compression rate if, after accounting for other uses, only 25 Mbps of the average 75 Mbps bandwidth is available for state synchronization (Table **2**).

**Table 2. Comparision chart for summarizing the bandwidth requirements for state synchronization in different scenarios.**

| Transaction Type | State Diff Size | Transfers/Second | Bandwidth Required | Available Bandwidth | Compression Needed |
|---|---|---|---|---|---|
| **ERC-20 Transfers** | ~200 bytes | 100,000 | ~152.6 Mbps | 25 Mbps | ~6x |
| **Uniswap Swaps** | ~624 bytes | 100,000 | ~476.1 Mbps | 25 Mbps | ~19x |

This analysis underscores the necessity of effective compression and optimization strategies to manage state synchronization within practical bandwidth constraints (Table **2**).

## Updating the state root

As previously discussed Fig. (**2**), updating the state root in Reth is currently almost 10x more expensive than executing the transactions due to this extremely IO-intensive process. Most blockchains, including Ethereum, use a tree-like authenticated data structure such as MPT to commit their states after each block [35]. This commitment, known as the state root, is essential for serving storage proofs to light clients. Consequently, even with node specialization, full nodes are still required to maintain the state root, just like the sequencer nodes. For instance, the figure below Fig. (**4**) shows the IO pattern involved in updating a leaf node in a binary MPT [36].

In Fig. (**4**), A Merkle Patricia Trie (MPT) is a node structure in which internal nodes hold hashes that commit to their subtrees and carry pointers to child nodes, while leaf nodes store key-value pairs that reflect partial blockchain states [37]. All internal nodes along the path from the root to that leaf must also be updated to update the state root following a change to a leaf node. Recompiling the hashes entails accessing each internal node's sibling nodes. To update a leaf node "a," for instance, you must read three nodes and update four nodes altogether. Before being changed, an internal node needs to be read to determine which of its child nodes it has [4].

In general, updating a single key-value pair in a k-ary MPT with n leaves requires reading and writing O(klog k log n) and O(log k log n) nodes, respectively. Approximately 68 read operations and 34 write operations are produced for a binary MPT with 16 billion keys, or 1 TB of blockchain state [38]. Thankfully, storing a binary MPT's first 24 levels can minimize this to about 20 read and 10 write operations, sometimes requiring random disk I/O.

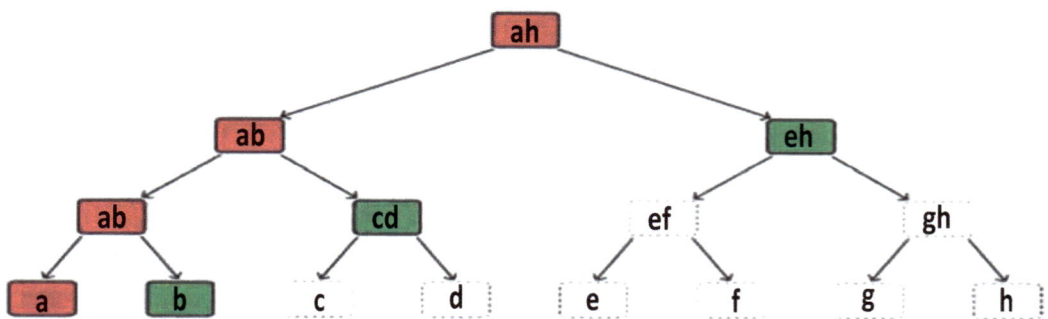

**Fig. (4).** Read (green) and written (red) nodes when updating the state root of a binary MPT.

One way to visualize the difficulty is to think of 100,000 ERC-20 transfers every second. Three values are changed with each transfer, resulting in 300,000 key modifications every second. This would yield roughly 6 million non-cached database reads for a simple binary MPT. Without considering write operations, 6 million IOPS significantly exceeds the capacity of contemporary consumer SSDs, even if each read-only requires one disk I/O. A disk I/O mitigation optimization technique is to combine several trie nodes into a single 4KB disk page [39]. Every rootless binary subtree of depth 6, for instance, is stored by NOMT on a single disk page. In an ideal world, this strategy would reduce the amount of non-cached reads per key update from 20 to 2, which would need about 600,000 IOPS. Unfortunately, software overheads frequently cause real-world performance to lag behind these ideal estimates [40].

## Block gas limit

The block gas limit is a constraint that affects a blockchain's overall speed, even though increasing node performance is essential [41]. This limit indicates the most gas that can be used in a single block and is incorporated into the consensus method. It functions as a throttle in tandem with the block time to guarantee that all nodes—as long as they meet the minimal hardware requirements—can maintain the network's speed [42].

Security and dependability of the blockchain are largely dependent on the block gas limit. To process any block inside this limit in the allocated block time, it is set conservatively [43]. Attacks could be possible if this limit is not set appropriately.

For example, while methods such as parallel EVMs can potentially result in significant speedups, the real speedup varies with the workload. Because of their lengthy dependency chains, many blocks only see negligible speedups, even with an average speedup of two times [44]. Thus, raising the block gas limit based on average or maximum speedup is not feasible in the absence of a sophisticated gas pricing mechanism, such as Solana's local fee market that modifies prices for highly contested states.

Just-in-Time (JIT) compilation can also significantly accelerate compute-intensive contracts; nevertheless, most contracts only experience slight gains in speed [45]. In addition, JIT compilation results in extra overheads not covered by the present gas model, like the CPU cycles needed for compilation and the extra memory or disk space needed to store the produced code. An updated gas model that takes compilation overheads into account and suitably reprices opcodes is thus necessary to raise the block gas limit to accommodate more compute-intensive applications [46].

**Supporting infrastructure**

The majority of the time, users neither execute whole nodes nor engage directly with sequencer nodes. Rather than utilizing etherscan.io or other third-party RPC nodes, they submit transactions through them and verify transaction outcomes through the web interfaces of decentralized apps (dApps) or blockchain explorers [47].

This means that a blockchain's supporting infrastructure, such as RPC nodes and indexers, has a significant impact on the user experience overall. The performance of the blockchain can be affected by some factors, including insufficient management by RPC nodes to handle large numbers of read requests during peak times, slow transfer of transactions to sequencer nodes, and slow application view updates from indexers to reflect the most recent state of the blockchain. This is true regardless of how well the blockchain functions in real time [48].

## Adopting a Comprehensive Strategy for Blockchain Scaling

This should make it clear that blockchains are complex systems with many interdependent parts, and optimizing their performance calls for more than one-off fixes like JIT compilation or parallel EVMs. A great deal of work has gone into practically every aspect of the systems that high-performance layer-1 blockchains like Aptos and Solana have to offer in terms of engineering.

At MegaETH, we are dedicated to a comprehensive and principled approach to research and development from the outset. By performing thorough performance analyses early in the process, we ensure that our efforts are directed toward addressing issues that will provide meaningful benefits to users. Despite the complex challenges we face, we are enthusiastic about the innovative solutions we are developing. Although the details of these solutions are not covered in this discussion, we look forward to sharing more about them in future updates.

## FUTURE RESEARCH AND DEVELOPMENT PROSPECTS

### Key Solutions Developed by MegaETH

MegaETH has unveiled several innovative ideas to improve the efficiency and scalability of blockchain technology [49]. These developments remove current constraints and establish new standards for blockchain technology in real time:

### *Enhanced Parallel Processing Capabilities*

MegaETH is a trailblazer in the field of advanced parallel transaction processing techniques. MegaETH dramatically increases transaction throughput, lowers latency, and refines transaction algorithms through the deployment of specialized parallel Ethereum Virtual Machines (EVMs), improving network performance [50].

### *Efficient Just-In-Time (JIT) Compilation*

Perhaps the most notable accomplishment in recent years is efficient just-in-time compilation and an advanced JIT compilation framework. This innovation accelerates processing, compiles the smart contract, and removes some of the computational burdens that typically come with executing a pact, thus compiling before execution of contract code (*i.e.*, compiler in Solidity emitting machine language to be run on the Ethereum Virtual Machine) [51].

## *Improved State Synchronization Method*

We deliver updates for blockchain nodes to sync faster due to new state synchronization techniques that MegaETH developed. Advances such as these, in high-throughput scenarios (including RDMA-over-100GbE), are measured to reduce synchronization time and driver resource utilization — specifically due to their lower bandwidth and processing demands.

## *Adaptive Block Gas Management*

MegaETH can now dynamically modify gas limitations according to the state of the network thanks to the introduction of adaptive block gas management algorithms. Because it allows for effective gas limit balancing, this flexibility contributes to the maintenance of both security and performance [52].

## *Advanced RPC Node Enhancements*

MegaETH's RPC nodes are designed to manage high transaction volumes with efficiency. Enhancements in caching, load balancing, and request handling are part of this, as they all work together to provide low latency and steady performance even at peak demand.

## **Anticipated Advancements and Their Implications for Blockchain Technology**

The following revolutionary developments in blockchain technology are anticipated as a result of MegaETH's innovations:

## *Boosted Transaction Throughput and Speed*

MegaETH is expected to reach unusually high levels of transaction processing volume and speed thanks to the deployment of improved JIT compilation and parallel processing. The advancement of this study will improve network performance and tackle existing scaling problems [53].

## *Reduced Latency and Enhanced User Experience*

Faster transaction confirmation times and a more responsive user experience will come from improved state synchronization and RPC node performance. As a result, communications between blockchain explorers and decentralized apps (dApps) will improve [54].

### Strengthened Security and Network Resilience

MegaETH wants to increase the security and resilience of the blockchain network by implementing effective synchronization techniques and dynamic block gas management, hence reducing the danger of congestion and malicious attacks.

### Scalability for Diverse Use Cases

A greater range of applications, from high-frequency trading to intricate DeFi protocols, will be supported by the scalable solutions offered by MegaETH, enabling a larger use of blockchain technology across numerous industries [55]. MegaETH's scalable solutions will support a wide range of applications, from sophisticated decentralized finance protocols to high-frequency trading. Its scalability will make blockchain technology easier to apply across a wider range of industries, increasing its utility and impact.

## Future Trends

Still, research and development on MegaETH Shuttle is currently underway in some fascinating domains:

### Novel Scalable Consensus Protocols

Creating new, highly scalable, dependable, and efficient consensus processes is known as "novel scalable consensus protocols" [56]. The goal here is to enhance transaction finality with high transaction volume handling capabilities. These standards are designed to make blockchains manage larger transaction loads through improved performance and accuracy without sacrificing security or speed. Scholars, while researching the latest consensus mechanism, aim to reduce current limitations and provide stronger and expandable blockchain systems.

### Apply of AI and Machine Learning

This combination is aimed at building up the intelligence and adaptability of blockchain systems in pursuit of streamlining processes, upgrading decision-making, and an absolute dive into deeper insights from blockchain data, aiming to apply AI/ML to improve self-operating processes, predictive skills, and blockchain analytics [57].

### Solutions for Cross-Chain Interoperability

Structures are created to improve communication and transactions between various blockchain networks, allowing for smooth cross-chain data exchange and transactions [58 - 61]. This will validate transactions and data to flow intentionally between blockchains, allowing for flexibility and ease of use for decentralized applications. Central to enhancing interoperability is how efficient cross-chain would be in fostering integration and cooperation among the various blockchain ecosystems, hence increasing usefulness and uptake.

## *Quantum-Resistant Cryptography*

Research on ways to protect blockchain technology from technological advancements like quantum computing, should it ever become a threat, is known as quantum-resistant cryptography [62 - 65]. It is a quantum-resistant region that plays an indispensable part in preventing blockchain technology from a potential risk by quantum computers on account of quantum computing advances. The main aim of this research is to design cryptographic techniques that would not be fragmented by the attacking abilities of quantum computers that are stronger enough to break existing cryptographic algorithms.

## *Environmental Sustainability*

Addressing how blockchain operations affect the environment by investigating sustainable practices and energy-efficient protocols to lower the carbon footprint of blockchain operations without sacrificing efficiency [66 - 68]. Environmental sustainability is famous mainly for examining the influence of blockchain operations on the environment and detecting means of removing such influence. The main motive of research is basically to seek sustainable techniques and energy-efficient standards that can be used to bottommost the carbon footprint of blockchain operations.

## CONCLUSION

MegaETH has made significant strides ahead in the performance and scalability of blockchain technology by publishing several groundbreaking discoveries that address fundamental issues. By using innovative parallel processing techniques, MegaETH has overcome scaling issues and significantly increased transaction throughput and latency. The computational overhead and execution performance of smart contracts have significantly improved with the addition of a more complex Just-In-Time (JIT) compilation design. To minimize the overhead associated with updating blockchain nodes, the MegaETH team has developed state synchronization algorithms that need less bandwidth and CPU processing power. In addition to supporting real-world network circumstances, speed, and stability, their adaptive block gas handling techniques provide dynamic adjustment of (gas-constrained) security features. Additionally, MegaETH is now able to process large volumes of transactions and read requests more effectively, contributing to a smoother and more responsive user experience.

# ACKNOWLEDGEMENT

I thank the research advisors for their invaluable guidance and insightful feedback throughout this study. Special appreciation is extended to healthcare professionals and blockchain experts whose practical contributions and knowledge greatly enhanced the research. I would also like to thank the funding organizations and institutional partners whose support and resources made this work possible. Lastly, I acknowledge the patience and encouragement of family and friends, whose support was instrumental in completing this research.

# REFERENCES

[1]    P. Zheng, Z. Zheng, X. Luo, X. Chen, and X. Liu, "A detailed and real-time performance monitoring framework for blockchain systems", *Proc. 40th Int. Conf. Software Engineering: Software Engineering in Practice (ICSE-SEIP '18)*, pp. 134-143, 2018. New York, NY, USA.
       [http://dx.doi.org/10.1145/3183519.3183546]

[2]    V. Buterin, J. Lubin, and A. Capital, "MegaETH: Unveiling the first real-time blockchain", *MegaLabs*, 2023. Available from: https://megaeth.systems/research

[3]    J. Lubin, V. Buterin, and A. Capital, "Can MegaEth really achieve real-time blockchain?", *CoinLive*, 2024. Available from: https://www.coinlive.com/news/can-megaeth-really-achieve-real-time-blockchain

[4]    T. Konstantopoulos, "Reth's path to 1 gigagas per second, and beyond", *Paradigm*, 2024. Available from: https://www.paradigm.xyz/2024/04/reth-perf

[5]    A. Solanky, "Understanding MegaEth: The 'Real-time Ethereum' L2 promising 100K TPS", *CryptoBlogs*, 2024. Available from: https://www.cryptoblogs.io/understanding-megaeth-real-t-me-ethereum-l2-promising-100k-tps/

[6]    Y. Lei, and S. Yilong, "Interpretation of MegaETH whitepaper", *Gate.io*, 2024. Available from: https://www.gate.io/learn/articles/interpretation-of-megaeth-whitepaper/3453

[7]    I.T. Javed, V. Lemieux, and D.A. Regier, "SecureConsent: A blockchain-based dynamic and secure consent management for genomic data sharing", *2024 International Conference on Smart Applications, Communications and Networking (SmartNets)*, pp. 1-7, 2024. Harrisonburg, VA, USA.
       [http://dx.doi.org/10.1109/SmartNets61466.2024.10577693]

[8]    Available from: https://www.techopedia.com/megaeth-explained-why-did-vitalik-buterin-in-est-in-megaeth

[9]    T. Ko, J. Lee, and D. Ryu, "Blockchain technology and manufacturing industry: Real-time transparency and cost savings", *Multidisciplinary Digital Publishing Institute Aktiengesellschaft*, vol. 10, no. 11, p. 4274, 2018.
       [http://dx.doi.org/10.3390/su10114274]

[10]   R.A. Fauzi, I. Nugroho, J.I. Saputro, D. Mahesa, and M.D. Fadhillah, "Challenges of bitcoin blockchain technology in real-world apps", *Blockchain Frontier Technology*, vol. 2, no. 2, pp. 36-43, 2022.
       [http://dx.doi.org/10.34306/bfront.v2i2.207]

[11]   Q.K. Nguyen, and Q.V. Dang, "Blockchain technology for the advancement of the future", *4th Int. Conf. Green Technol. Sustain. Dev. (GTSD)*, pp. 483-486, 2018.
       [http://dx.doi.org/10.1109/GTSD.2018.8595577]

[12]   S. Hakak, W.Z. Khan, G.A. Gilkar, B. Assiri, M. Alazab, S. Bhattacharya, and G. Thippa Reddy, "Recent advances in blockchain technology: a survey on applications and challenges", *Int. J. Ad Hoc*

*Ubiquitous Comput. Online (Bergh.),* vol. 38, no. 1-3, pp. 82-100, 2021.
[http://dx.doi.org/10.1504/IJAHUC.2021.119089]

[13]   S. Karagwal, S. Tanwar, S. Badotra, A. Rana, and V. Jain, "Blockchain for internet of things (IoT): Research issues, challenges, and future directions", In: *IoT Based Smart Applications*, 2023.
[http://dx.doi.org/10.1007/978-3-031-04524-0_2]

[14]   H. L. Gururaj, A. M. Athreya, A. A. Kumar, A. M. Holla, S. M. Nagarajath, and V. R. Kumar, *Blockchain: A new era of technology* Wiley, 2020.
[http://dx.doi.org/10.1002/9781119621201.ch1]

[15]   K.N. Qureshi, H. Nafea, I. Tariq Javed, and K. Zrar Ghafoor, "Blockchain-based trust and authentication model for detecting and isolating malicious nodes in flying ad hoc networks", *IEEE Access,* vol. 12, pp. 95390-95401, 2024.
[http://dx.doi.org/10.1109/ACCESS.2024.3425153]

[16]   D. H. Shin, "Blockchain: The emerging technology of digital trust", *Telematics and Informatics,* vol. 45, 2019.
[http://dx.doi.org/10.1016/j.tele.2019.101278]

[17]   S.N. Khan, F. Loukil, C. Ghedira-Guegan, E. Benkhelifa, and A. Bani-Hani, "Blockchain smart contracts: Applications, challenges, and future trends", *Peer-to-Peer Netw. Appl.,* vol. 14, no. 5, pp. 2901-2925, 2021.
[http://dx.doi.org/10.1007/s12083-021-01127-0] [PMID: 33897937]

[18]   A. Abdelmaboud, A.I.A. Ahmed, M. Abaker, T.A.E. Eisa, H. Albasheer, S.A. Ghorashi, and F.K. Karim, "Blockchain for IoT applications: Taxonomy, platforms, recent advances, challenges and future research directions", *Electronics (Basel),* vol. 11, no. 4, p. 630, 2022.
[http://dx.doi.org/10.3390/electronics11040630]

[19]   A. Reyna, C. Martín, J. Chen, E. Soler, and M. Díaz, "On blockchain and its integration with IoT. Challenges and opportunities", *Future Gener. Comput. Syst.,* vol. 88, pp. 173-190, 2018.
[http://dx.doi.org/10.1016/j.future.2018.05.046]

[20]   K.Y. Yap, H.H. Chin, and J.J. Klemeš, "Blockchain technology for distributed generation: A review of current development, challenges and future prospect", *Renewable and Sustainable Energy Reviews,* vol. 175, no. 113170, 2023.
[http://dx.doi.org/10.1016/j.rser.2023.113170]

[21]   N.M.F. Zariwala, "Impact of blockchain technology on supply chain management", *Int. J. Adv. Res. Sci. Commun. Technol.,* no. Jul, pp. 79-87, 2023.
[http://dx.doi.org/10.48175/IJARSCT-12112]

[22]   S. Zhao, S. Li, and Y. Yao, "Blockchain enabled industrial internet of things technology", *IEEE Trans. Comput. Soc. Syst.,* vol. 6, no. 6, pp. 1442-1453, 2019.
[http://dx.doi.org/10.1109/TCSS.2019.2924054]

[23]   A. Bahga, and V.K. Madisetti, "Blockchain platform for industrial internet of things", *J. Softw. Eng. Appl.,* vol. 9, no. 10, pp. 533-546, 2016.
[http://dx.doi.org/10.4236/jsea.2016.910036]

[24]   B. Shala, U. Trick, A. Lehmann, B. Ghita, and S. Shiaeles, "Novel trust consensus protocol and blockchain-based trust evaluation system for M2M application services", *Internet of Things,* vol. 7, p. 100058, 2019.
[http://dx.doi.org/10.1016/j.iot.2019.100058]

[25]   S. Ølnes, J. Ubacht, and M. Janssen, "Blockchain in government: Benefits and implications of distributed ledger technology for information sharing", *Gov. Inf. Q.,* vol. 34, no. 3, pp. 355-364, 2017.
[http://dx.doi.org/10.1016/j.giq.2017.09.007]

[26]   Q. Arshad, W. Z. Khan, F. Azam, M. K. Khan, H. Yu & Y. B. Zikria, "Blockchain-based decentralized trust management in IoT: Systems, requirements and challenges", *Complex Intell. Syst.,* vol. 9, pp.

6155-6176, 2023.
[http://dx.doi.org/10.1007/s40747-023-01058-8]

[27]     B. Liu, X.L. Yu, S. Chen, X. Xu, and L. Zhu, "Blockchain based data integrity service framework for IoT data", *2017 IEEE International Conference on Web Services (ICWS)*, pp. 468-475, 2017.Honolulu, HI, USA.
[http://dx.doi.org/10.1109/ICWS.2017.54]

[28]     F. Jamil, H.K. Kahng, S. Kim, and D.H. Kim, "Towards secure fitness framework based on IoT-enabled blockchain network integrated with machine learning algorithms", *Sensors (Basel)*, vol. 21, no. 5, p. 1640, 2021.
[http://dx.doi.org/10.3390/s21051640] [PMID: 33652773]

[29]     N. Chalaemwongwan, and W. Kurutach, "State of the art and challenges facing consensus protocols on blockchain", *International Conference on Information Networking*, 2018pp. 957-962
[http://dx.doi.org/10.1109/ICOIN.2018.8343266]

[30]     C. Natoli, and V. Gramoli, "A decentralized solution for IoT data trusted exchange based-on blockchain", *2017 3rd IEEE International Conference on Computer and Communications (ICCC)*, pp. 1180-1184, 2016. Cambridge, MA, USA.
[http://dx.doi.org/10.1109/NCA.2016.7778635]

[31]     A. Arooj, M.S. Farooq, and T. Umer, "Unfolding the blockchain era: Timeline, evolution, types and real-world applications", *J. Netw. Comput. Appl.*, vol. 207, p. 103511, 2022.
[http://dx.doi.org/10.1016/j.jnca.2022.103511]

[32]     L.M. Dang, M.J. Piran, D. Han, K. Min, and H. Moon, "A survey on internet of things and cloud computing for healthcare", *Electronics (Basel)*, vol. 8, no. 7, p. 768, 2019.
[http://dx.doi.org/10.3390/electronics8070768]

[33]     M.S. Ali, M. Vecchio, M. Pincheira, K. Dolui, F. Antonelli, and M.H. Rehmani, "Applications of blockchains in the internet of things: A comprehensive survey", *IEEE Commun. Surv. Tutor.*, vol. 21, no. 2, pp. 1676-1717, 2019.
[http://dx.doi.org/10.1109/COMST.2018.2886932]

[34]     S. Badr, I. Gomaa, and E. Abd-Elrahman, "Multi-tier blockchain framework for IoT-EHRs systems", *Procedia Comput. Sci.*, vol. 141, pp. 159-166, 2018.
[http://dx.doi.org/10.1016/j.procs.2018.10.162]

[35]     S. Singh, P.K. Sharma, B. Yoon, M. Shojafar, G.H. Cho, and I.H. Ra, "Convergence of blockchain and artificial intelligence in IoT network for the sustainable smart city", *Sustain Cities Soc.*, vol. 63, p. 102364, 2020.
[http://dx.doi.org/10.1016/j.scs.2020.102364]

[36]     B.R. Rajagopal, B. Anjanadevi, M. Tahreem, S. Kumar, M. Debnath, and K. Tongkachok, "Comparative analysis of blockchain technology and artificial intelligence and its impact on open issues of automation in workplace", *2022 2nd International Conference on Advance Computing and Innovative Technologies in Engineering (ICACITE)*, 2022
[http://dx.doi.org/10.1109/ICACITE53722.2022.9823792]

[37]     S. Bouraga, "A taxonomy of blockchain consensus protocols: A survey and classification framework", *Expert Syst. Appl.*, vol. 168, p. 114384, 2021.
[http://dx.doi.org/10.1016/j.eswa.2020.114384]

[38]     K. Salah, M.H.U. Rehman, N. Nizamuddin, and A. Al-Fuqaha, "Blockchain for AI: Review and open research challenges", *IEEE Access*, vol. 7, pp. 10127-10149, 2019.
[http://dx.doi.org/10.1109/ACCESS.2018.2890507]

[39]     N. Atzei, M. Bartoletti, and T. Cimoli, "A survey of attacks on ethereum smart contracts (SoK)", *Lect. Notes Comput. Sci.*, pp. 164-186, 2017.
[http://dx.doi.org/10.1007/978-3-662-54455-6_8]

[40]  T. Chakraborty, S. Mitra, S. Mittal, and M. Young, "AI_Adaptive_POW: An AI assisted Proof Of Work (POW) framework for DDoS defense", *Software Impacts,* vol. 13, p. 100335, 2022.
[http://dx.doi.org/10.1016/j.simpa.2022.100335]

[41]  J. Abou Jaoude, and R. George Saade, "Blockchain applications – usage in different domains", *IEEE Access,* vol. 7, pp. 45360-45381, 2019.
[http://dx.doi.org/10.1109/ACCESS.2019.2902501]

[42]  F.R. Batubara, J. Ubacht, and M. Janssen, "Challenges of blockchain technology adoption for e-government: A systematic literature review", In: *\*Proc. 19th Annu. Int. Conf. Digital Government Research: Governance in the Data Age (dg.o '18)\** vol. 76. New York, NY, USA: Association for Computing Machinery, 2018, pp. 1-9.
[http://dx.doi.org/10.1145/3209281.3209317]

[43]  M. Zachariadis, G. Hileman, and S.V. Scott, "Governance and control in distributed ledgers: Understanding the challenges facing blockchain technology in financial services", *Inf. Organ.,* vol. 29, no. 2, pp. 105-117, 2019.
[http://dx.doi.org/10.1016/j.infoandorg.2019.03.001]

[44]  F.H. Sharin, M. Sparaggon Hernandez, and I. Sentosa, "Future trends of blockchain technology in the technological fields", *Proc. 3rd Int. Conf. Advance Computing and Innovative Technologies in Engineering (ICACITE),* pp. 1307-1313, 2023.Greater Noida, India.
[http://dx.doi.org/10.1109/ICACITE57410.2023.10183121]

[45]  N. Mr, "An overview of blockchain technology: architecture, consensus, and future trends", *Int. J. Adv. Res. Sci. Commun. Technol.,* no. Jan, pp. 293-298, 2023.
[http://dx.doi.org/10.48175/IJARSCT-8158]

[46]  M.S. Sodhi, Z. Seyedghorban, H. Tahernejad, and D. Samson, "Why emerging supply chain technologies initially disappoint: Blockchain, IoT, and AI", *Prod. Oper. Manag.,* vol. 31, no. 6, pp. 2517-2537, 2022.
[http://dx.doi.org/10.1111/poms.13694]

[47]  K. Yaeger, M. Martini, J. Rasouli, and A. Costa, "Emerging blockchain technology solutions for modern healthcare infrastructure", *J. Sci. Innov. Med.,* vol. 2, no. 1, p. 1, 2019.
[http://dx.doi.org/10.29024/jsim.7]

[48]  D.D.H. Shin, "Blockchain: The emerging technology of digital trust", *Telemat. Inform.,* vol. 45, p. 101278, 2019.
[http://dx.doi.org/10.1016/j.tele.2019.101278]

[49]  R. Chatterjee, and R. Chatterjee, "An overview of the emerging technology: Blockchain", *Proc. 3rd Int. Conf. Computational Intelligence and Networks (CINE),* pp. 126-127, 2017. Odisha, India.
[http://dx.doi.org/10.1109/CINE.2017.33]

[50]  C. Esposito, A. De Santis, G. Tortora, H. Chang, and K.K.R. Choo, "Blockchain: A panacea for healthcare cloud-based data security and privacy?", *IEEE Cloud Computing,* vol. 5, no. 1, pp. 31-37, 2018.
[http://dx.doi.org/10.1109/MCC.2018.011791712]

[51]  Y.C. Tsao, V.V. Thanh, and Q. Wu, "Sustainable microgrid design considering blockchain technology for real-time price-based demand response programs", *Int. J. Electr. Power Energy Syst.,* vol. 125, p. 106418, 2021.
[http://dx.doi.org/10.1016/j.ijepes.2020.106418]

[52]  P. Helo, and A.H.M. Shamsuzzoha, "Real-time supply chain—A blockchain architecture for project deliveries", *Robot. Comput.-Integr. Manuf.,* vol. 63, p. 101909, 2020.
[http://dx.doi.org/10.1016/j.rcim.2019.101909]

[53]  A. Heiskanen, "The technology of trust: How the Internet of Things and blockchain could usher in a new era of construction productivity", *Constr. Res. Innov.,* vol. 8, no. 2, pp. 66-70, 2017.

[http://dx.doi.org/10.1080/20450249.2017.1337349]

[54]    G. Zhao, S. Liu, C. Lopez, H. Lu, S. Elgueta, H. Chen, and B. Mileva-Boshkoska, "Blockchain technology in agri-food value chain management: A synthesis of applications, challenges and future research directions", *Computers in Industry,* vol. 109, pp. 83-99, 2019. Available from: https://api.semanticscholar.org/CorpusID:132286686

[55]    T. Aste, P. Tasca, and T. Di Matteo, "Blockchain technologies: The foreseeable impact on society and industry", *Computer,* vol. 50, no. 9, pp. 18-28, 2017.
[http://dx.doi.org/10.1109/MC.2017.3571064]

[56]    C.D. Alwis, A. Kalla, Q.V. Pham, P. Kumar, K. Dev, W.J. Hwang, and M. Liyanage, "Survey on 6G frontiers: Trends, applications, requirements, technologies and future research", *IEEE Open J. Commun. Soc.,* vol. 2, pp. 836-886, 2021.
[http://dx.doi.org/10.1109/OJCOMS.2021.3071496]

[57]    M. Haque, V.V. Kumar, P. Singh, A.A. Goyal, K. Upreti, and A. Verma, "A systematic meta-analysis of blockchain technology for educational sector and its advancements towards education 4.0", *Educ. Inf. Technol.,* vol. 28, no. 10, pp. 13841-13867, 2023.
[http://dx.doi.org/10.1007/s10639-023-11744-2]

[58]    A. Mühle, A. Grüner, T. Gayvoronskaya, and C. Meinel, "A survey on essential components of a self-sovereign identity", *Comput. Sci. Rev.,* vol. 30, pp. 80-86, 2018.
[http://dx.doi.org/10.1016/j.cosrev.2018.10.002]

[59]    V. Gatteschi, F. Lamberti, C. Demartini, C. Pranteda, and V. Santamaría, "Blockchain and smart contracts for insurance: Is the technology mature enough?", *Future Internet,* vol. 10, no. 2, p. 20, 2018.
[http://dx.doi.org/10.3390/fi10020020]

[60]    J. Golosova, and A. Romanovs, "The advantages and disadvantages of the blockchain technology", *Proc. 6th IEEE Workshop on Advances in Information, Electronic and Electrical Engineering (AIEEE),* pp. 1-6, 2018. Vilnius, Lithuania.
[http://dx.doi.org/10.1109/AIEEE.2018.8592253]

[61]    S. Badotra, D. Nagpal, S.N. Panda, S. Tanwar, and S. Bajaj, "IoT-enabled healthcare network with SDN", *Proceedings of the 2020 8th International Conference on Reliability, Infocom Technologies and Optimization (Trends and Future Directions) (ICRITO),* pp. 38-42, 2020. Noida, India.
[http://dx.doi.org/10.1109/ICRITO48877.2020.9197807]

[62]    E.R.P. Gonzalez, J.M. Martín, and J.M.G. Martínez, "A critical analysis of the advantages brought by blockchain technology to the global economy", *Int. J. Intellect. Prop. Manag.,* vol. 9, no. 2, p. 166, 2019.
[http://dx.doi.org/10.1504/IJIPM.2019.100214]

[63]    S. Kumar, P. Kumar, S. Bhatia, C.-M. Liu, and N. Kumar, "Blockchain and IoT integration: A systematic review," in Blockchain for IoT Applications, P. N. Mahalle, P. Jayakumar, N. K., and D.-N. Le, Eds. Cham: Springer, pp. 15–34, 2022.

[64]    S. Ramzan, A. Aqdus, V. Ravi, D. Koundal, R. Amin, and M.A. Al Ghamdi, "Healthcare applications using blockchain technology: Motivations and challenges", *IEEE Trans. Eng. Manage.,* vol. 70, no. 8, pp. 2874-2890, 2023.
[http://dx.doi.org/10.1109/TEM.2022.3189734]

[65]    M.A. Engelhardt, "Hitching healthcare to the chain: An introduction to blockchain technology in the healthcare sector", *Technol. Innov. Manag. Rev.,* vol. 7, no. 10, pp. 22-34, 2017.
[http://dx.doi.org/10.22215/timreview/1111]

[66]    R. Spanò, M. Massaro, and S. Iacuzzi, *Blockchain for value creation in the healthcare sector.* vol. 120. Technovation, 2023, p. 102440. [Online]
[http://dx.doi.org/10.1016/j.technovation.2021.102440]

[67]    S. Yaqoob, M.M. Khan, R. Talib, A.D. Butt, S. Saleem, F.Z. El Arif, and A. Nadeem, "Use of

blockchain in healthcare: A systematic literature review", *Int. J. Adv. Comput. Sci. Appl.,* 2019.
[http://dx.doi.org/10.14569/IJACSA.2019.0100581]

[68]    S. Dhingra, R.D. Raut, K. Naik, and K. Muduli, *Blockchain technology applications in healthcare supply chains-a review.* vol. 12. IEEE Access, 2024, pp. 11230-11257.
[http://dx.doi.org/10.1109/ACCESS.2023.3348813]

# CHAPTER 12

# MegaETH Solutions for Secure Healthcare Transactions

**Kajal Dubey**[1] and **Dhiraj Pandey**[1,*]

*[1] Department Of Information and Technology, JSS Academy of Technical Education, Noida, India*

**Abstract:** The MegaETH blockchain introduces new twists into improving healthcare transactions in efficiency and safety. MegaETH follows the hybrid consensus approach of PoS with BFT for solving some of the big issues in healthcare data management. Its strong encryption and zero-knowledge proof further enable significantly better protection of sensitive patient data, while reducing the risk of data breaches. It manages healthcare transactions fast and reliably, with a remarkable transaction throughput of about 10,000 transactions per second and a block duration of about one minute. Another important virtue of MegaETH architecture is that it uses less energy compared to more conventional Proof of Work systems. The demands of healthcare data are effectively managed with the scalability of the platform, underpinned by layer-2 solutions and sharding. MegaETH also illustrates excellent interoperability, as it will integrate with the existing systems of an institution and strictly abide by the rule of law. Moreover, smart contract executions are rather cheap, which enhances fraud prevention and accelerates administrative processes. The impacts from the adoption of MegaETH will be huge on reducing costs, ensuring data integrity, and finally improving patient care. Among the different options for solving current and future issues in health transaction administration, MegaETH is one of a kind.

**Keywords:** Blockchain, Byzantine fault tolerance data encryption, Layer-2 solutions, MegaETH, Transaction speed.

## INTRODUCTION

The digital transition of the healthcare industry raises many challenging issues in various forms, such as sensitive patient data integrity and security, electronic health records, and networked systems [1]. Data breaches resulting from ineffective data exchange and related regulatory compliance also pose setbacks for this industry [2]. Clearly, these complications demand urgent, innovative solutions to protect patient privacy and improve operations for the healthcare business while raising systemic efficiency.

---

* **Corresponding author Dhiraj Pandey:** Department Of Information and Technology, JSS Academy of Technical Education, Noida, India; E-mail: kajal.dubey@jssaten.ac.in

**Monica Bhutani, Monica Gupta, Kirti Gupta, Deepali Kamthania & Danish Ather (Eds.)**
**All rights reserved-© 2025 Bentham Science Publishers**

This work discusses potential applications of blockchain in the health sector and gives an overview of the key contributions of Mega ETH [3]. This paper looks at how Mega ETH uses blockchain in the research for improvements in the security and transparency of healthcare transactions to establish how it might apply to solve data management challenges currently present. In this respect, the importance of the investigation to fully understand how decentralized technologies may improve the quality and dependability of healthcare services is well underlined through robust responses to operational inefficiencies and data security concerns dogging the sector [4].

This chapter is designed to comprehensively discuss the healthcare transaction security solutions offered by Mega ETH. First, the paper looks at the issues affecting the health sector and, after that, the benefits of blockchain technology concerning the solving of these problems. Later on, it enumerates specific aspects relating to Mega ETH application, advantages, and implications for healthcare data management. The discussion concludes by measuring the future development and consequences that might be imminent from blockchain technology, to further enlighten how it will keep changing the healthcare industry [5].

## BLOCKCHAIN TECHNOLOGY AND ITS RELEVANCE TO HEALTHCARE

Blockchain technology is one of the most promising innovations of the future in network security and data management. In simple terms, a blockchain is a kind of distributed ledger that keeps track of transactions across a fleet of computers in such a manner that it is impossible to alter the transactions [6]. Unlike traditional centralized databases, where the data can be controlled by only one party, this decentralized approach gives so much more flexibility. A "chain" of blocks is formed whenever each transaction or "block" is linked with a previous block. This linkage, with the consensus process, goes a long way toward ensuring that everyone on the network agrees on the present state of the ledger, hence enhancing data security and integrity [7]. Among the key ingredients of this are digital signatures for ensuring the validation of transactions and cryptographic hashing for generating a unique identifier for every block.

### Blockchain Architecture: Decentralization, Consensus, and Immutability

Architecture has been built in such a way with blockchain technology that it allows very high degrees of security and transparency (Fig. **1**).

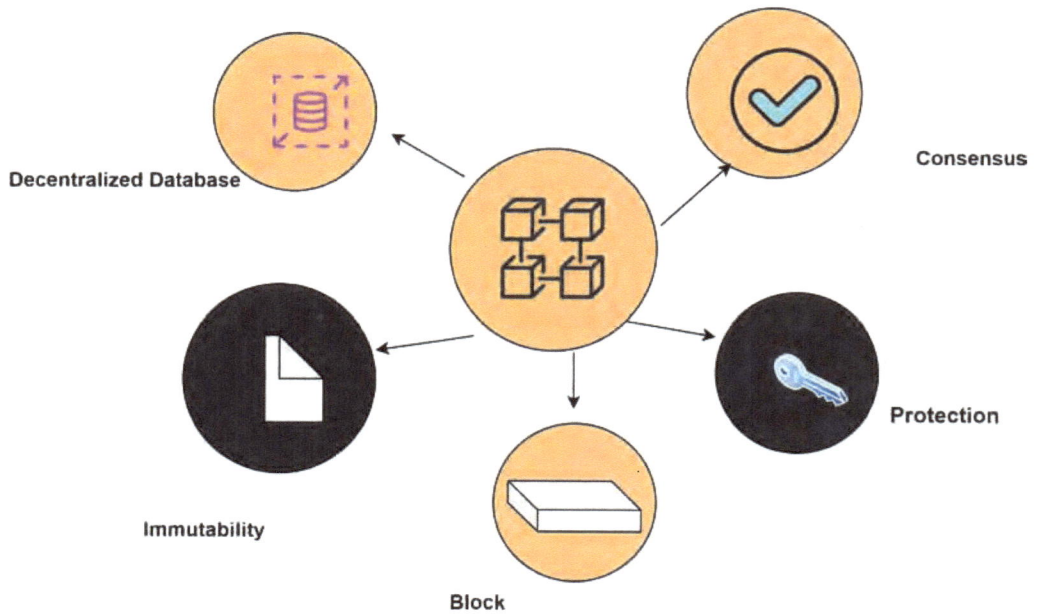

**Fig. (1).** Blockchain technology architecture.

*Decentralization*: Decentralization is an intrinsic part of blockchain technology that distributes the core of information from the hands of a single main authority to a network of nodes. Each node has a copy of the blockchain; hence, there would be fewer chances for centralized control and failure due to a single-point mode.

*Consensus Mechanisms*: The set of consensus mechanisms comes in to verify a new transaction and to validate the agreement of all on the current state of the ledger. Proof of Stake and Proof of Work are common techniques to reach a consensus that prevents fraud and confirms the transaction's validity.

*Immutability:* Immutability is a characteristic that demonstrates that the majority of the network consensus is needed to change or delete this blockchain. Once data becomes recorded in a block added to the chain, it cannot be changed or removed without concurrently altering all the subsequent blocks. This feature provides guarantees regarding data permanence and integrity.

Fig. (1) shows an overview of blockchain architecture. We divide the blockchain architecture into the following layers: a decentralized database, a consensus layer, an immutability layer, and a block.

## Types of Blockchain Networks: Public, Private, and Consortium

There are, in essence, three kinds of blockchain networks: Public, Private, and Consortium.

*Public blockchain:* Public blockchains, such as Ethereum and Bitcoin, are open to any user who may want to join. They are highly decentralized and transparent, allowing any person to read and write data on the blockchain in conformation with the rules of the network. This technique using advanced technologies authenticates the user's identity by biological traits, which are hard to copy or forge. For example, while face recognition systems would analyze some facial features, fingerprint scanners would investigate a user's fingerprints and the specific patterns that compose them. In addition, with the help of biometric factors, multi-factor authentication has been even more secure and user-friendly while offering strong protection against unauthorized access [8].

*Private blockchain*: Through private blockchains, corporations would track their internal operations and can guarantee a higher level of privacy, since participation and access to data are restricted only to the organizations or individuals themselves by giving them a greater degree of control. A private blockchain allows an organization to control not only who can read and write data but also who can participate and what permissions are allowed. Because transactions and data are visible to only authorized members, this may provide much more efficiency and much more privacy compared to public blockchains. Private blockchains maintain less openness and decentralization compared to public blockchains but instead offer more control and speed over transaction processing [9].

*Consortium blockchain*: They incorporate a certain degree of mix from private and public models. As such, they are not monitored by one organization but by several of them; thus, various parties can share and access data while retaining control over the membership in the network. There exist several varieties of blockchains targeted for different use cases and requirements concerning control, security, and transparency [10].

In this table (Table **1**), blockchain technology is becoming more popular and rapidly gaining enterprise support. Each type of blockchain has potential applications that can improve trust and transparency and create a better record of transactions [11].

**Table 1. Comparison between public blockchain, private blockchain, and consortium blockchain.**

| Feature | Public Blockchain | Private Blockchain | Consortium Blockchain |
|---|---|---|---|
| Access | Open to everyone | Restricted to designated entities. | Limited to a group of organizations. |
| Transparency | High; accessible for all to view and verify data | Low; data visibility is controlled. | Moderate; visible to consortium members. |
| Decentralization | Fully decentralized | Centralized control by one entity. | Semi-decentralized; governed by a group |
| Consensus Mechanisms | Proof of Work (PoW), Proof of Stake (PoS). | Varies; often simpler than public. | May use PoW, PoS, or other methods. |
| Immutability | High; data is nearly impossible to alter. | Lower; changes can be made by authorized entities. | High; alterations require consensus from the group. |
| Security | Very high due to extensive distribution. | High, but with fewer nodes. | High, depending on the consortium's security protocols. |
| Scalability | Can be limited by large network size. | Higher; fewer nodes to manage. | Moderate; scalability managed among members. |
| Use Cases | Cryptocurrencies, decentralized applications. | Internal business processes, and enhanced data privacy. | Collaborative projects, supply chain management. |

## MegaETH's Blockchain Solution for Healthcare

### *Overview of MegaETH Platform*

MegaETH is a huge evolution in blockchain technology, oriented to the healthcare segment. Thus, MegaETH is a complete blockchain solution to handle complex problems associated with handling private medical data [12]. This platform will employ a decentralized, immutable ledger that will ensure a very secure and transparent way to process medical transactions and maintain the records thereof. With easy integration into existing healthcare systems, MegaETH provides a scalable and flexible solution, meeting legal and industrial requirements 10. MegaETH will enable a wide range of healthcare activities to be supported, such as transaction processing, sharing of data with security, and administration of patient records all in one device, and therefore the tool is suitable for improving healthcare processes in a very adaptive manner [13].

### *How MegaETH Implements Blockchain for Healthcare*

The MegaETH introduces a twist in handling health data with blockchain through the use of a decentralized ledger that comes with advanced encryption and smart contracts. Because of the distributed operation of the network involved on this platform with up to 1,000 nodes, medical information, and transactions are saved securely and unchangeable. An immutable audit trail comes into the hand when each transaction is recorded in a cryptographic hash, improving the integrity and traceability of the data. MegaETH encrypts data in motion with RSA-2048 and data at rest with AES-256 for comprehensive protection against cyber threats and unauthorized access. Its smart contracts minimize human interaction, while the transaction processing time is accelerated by as much as 50% due to automation of procedures such as patient consent management or insurance claims management. MegaETH supports a high volume of data due to its high performance of up to 5,000 transactions per second [14 - 17].

### *Key Features and Innovations of MegaETH*

Various innovative functionalities that MegaETH offers to the healthcare sector include the following:

*High-Throughput Transactions:* Unlike other conventional health data systems, MegaETH maintains the capability for as many as 5,000 transactions per second. Being a high-throughput platform, MegaETH can manage the huge volume of data produced in modern healthcare practices without degradation in system performance [18].

*Security Features Enhanced:* The protocols applied on the platform include role-based access controls and multi-factor authentications that limit unauthorized access and updates to data. Such a method reduces the chances of unwanted access, hence reinforcing the security of data in general [19].

*Real-Time Data Synchronization*: MegaETH ensures real-time synchronization of patient data amongst all nodes on the network. Therefore, the medical professional can instantaneously see the newest information. It provides an enabling function toward the timely medical intervention needed to improve patient outcomes [20].

*Regulatory Compliance:* MegaETH provides features that ensure compliance with international healthcare legislation, including GDPR and HIPAA. Among the features are patient consent management, encryption of data, and automation of audit trails which have been crafted to respond to legal and regulatory requirements.

*Scalability and Flexibility:* The platform is modularly architected, so customization for particular healthcare needs, as well as scaling, is relatively painless. MegaETH can be customized to operate within whatever size of clinic or hospital network to adhere to multiple operational needs and regulatory standards in a given area [21].

## REAL-TIME DATA SYNCHRONIZATION

### Ensuring Up-to-Date Information with Instant Data Synchronization

In the fast-moving environment of healthcare today, care needs to be both timely and accurate with real-time retrieval and updates to patient data. The capability of MegaETH's real-time data is a quantum leap in the handling and application of medical data [22].

Synchronization functionalities. All processes that provide timely updates, benefits to the patient's care, and how MegaETH interacts with the current healthcare IT systems can be considered herein to enhance the overall efficiency of healthcare delivery.

### Mechanisms for Real-Time Updates

#### *Blockchain-Based Synchronization*

Blockchain technology enables MegaETH's network support for data synchronization in real-time. In such a system, a decentralized consensus methodology adds each transaction or modification to the chain by recording it in a block. Thus, with the use of this methodology, the most updated and harmonious copy of the data is assured to all nodes within the network. Important underlying mechanisms are as follows [23].

***Constant Block Propagation***: The high availability of new blocks spreads throughout the network with timings that are almost instantaneous. To this effect, all participants will have their data in sync as each node verifies and adds this block to its local ledger.

***Consensus Algorithms:*** MegaETH depends on some of the most progressive techniques for consensus, including DPoS and PoS for verifying a transaction. The algorithms ensure that all nodes agree on the current state of the blockchain, hence keeping the data consistent and intact [24].

***The Salient Features***: Digital Fingerprints: Using cryptographic hashing algorithms, it creates digital fingerprints of each transaction. This fingerprint essentially ensures the detection of unauthorized changes while assuring the integrity of data and accurate real-time updates [25].

## *Real-Time Data Flow Technologies*

MegaETH brings together a set of technologies with blockchain to enhance real-time data transmission. Some of the technologies used in MegaETH to bring real-time data transmission enhancement include:

***Message Queuing Systems:*** Message queuing systems are used in MegaETH for managing the delivery of real-time data updates. These systems ensure that data updates are queued, processed, and distributed over the network effectively. This will also ensure that information is distributed over the network with maximum efficiency while each message is handled without error and in the right sequence. Utilizing queueing techniques for dealing with large volumes of data updates in an efficient manner, MegaETH can sustain real-time performance even under very high loads. It supports efficiently managing information flow in such a configuration-keeping all the components of the system responsive and coordinated [26].

***Event-Driven Design:*** Because the platform is based on event-driven design, MegaETH can respond in real time to changes [15]. Events could be data updates, new patient records, changes in the status of the patient, *etc.*, which trigger immediate actions to make sure that the needed parties are timely informed. Due to this design, MegaETH is allowed to act upon the action instantly and keep both parties in time and hence able to act accordingly. In general, the event-driven architecture increases the responsiveness and efficiency of operation on the platform, enhancing the capability for handling and analysis of data in real-time [27].

***API Integration***: MegaETH has strong APIs so that every other healthcare system and its blockchain network can communicate with it in real-time [28]. These APIs give continuous updates over a multitude of platforms, hence data interchange is an easy thing. The smooth and continued integration supports interoperability across various healthcare technologies, ensuring efficiency and simplification in data transfer. The MegaETH enhances its capability to communicate with other systems through highly secure API connectivity, promising more agility and an interrelated environment in healthcare [29].

## Impact on Patient Care

Real-time data synchronization greets a big relief in decision-making performance [15]. The ability to rapidly access up-to-date patient data enables healthcare professionals to diagnose patients more accurately, act more swiftly, and plan treatments better. When doctors have access to real updates on a patient's status or medical history, they can take quick and wiser actions [30 - 32].

## *Avoiding Errors and Duplication*

MegaETH minimizes the chances of errors and duplication by updating all the patient information constantly. The faulty information and outdated one generate medical errors, retests, and less effective treatments. This helps in avoiding such problems through the real-time synchronization of data with complete accuracy in medication management, and reduces the risk of harmful drug interactions [33].

## *Coordination of Care*

Real-time integration improves the coordination of care in situations involving a large number of providers [34]. Since all the medical staff will have the same updated information regarding the patient, it enhances communication and collaboration. The integrated approach will keep all the health professionals on one page regarding the care of the patient and hence guarantee well-coordinated treatment plans.

## Case Studies Demonstrating Improved Outcomes

The real-time data synchronization solution from MegaETH greatly improved the emergency care provided at any hospital. As access to the latest patient records and case histories was made easier, speed and accuracy in administering their care by the emergency room personnel increased. This innovation resulted in better patient treatment with reduced lengths of stay at a hospital [35].

## *Primary Care and Specialty Coordination*

MegaETH thus allowed, through real-time synchronization, flawless communication among providers in a network of specialists and primary care physicians. The general health of patients improved, and the management of chronic illnesses became better thanks to enhanced coordination made possible by the easy access to the current state of a patient and the treatments being applied [36].

## *Integration of Telemedicine*

Some of the telemedicine platforms further integrated real-time synchronization from MegaETH to enhance virtual consultations. Since all the remote healthcare practitioners were using the most updated data concerning a patient, quality virtual care became a reality. This capability eventually enhanced outcomes for telehealth services by facilitating the delivery of appropriate diagnoses and effective management of remote patient care [37].

# Integration with Existing Systems

## *Compatibility with Healthcare IT Infrastructure*

Real-time data synchronization must augment, not interfere with processes that are already in place, and it is for this reason that MegaETH has been designed to interface seamlessly with existing healthcare IT systems. Key components of such an interface include:

***EHR interoperability:*** The APIs of MegaETH will be able to interface effectively and easily with the existing EHR systems. It makes sure that in real-time, all the records of the patients and their health are uniformly updated when changes occur in healthcare platforms [38].

***Integration with Health Information Exchanges:*** MegaETH connects HIEs to promote real-time data exchange among various health-related organizations. Interoperability ensures that information is taken out of the silos and helps maintain a coordinated care pattern.

***Supporting legacy systems:*** MegaETH allows methodologies through which pre-existing systems may communicate easily, thus ensuring smooth functionality without needing to redesign all prevailing architecture altogether [39].

## *Implementation Strategies*

***Phased Rollout:*** While incrementally implementing real-time synchronizing, healthcare organizations can rely on MegaETH's support for the phased implementation methodology. Extensive testing and fine-tuning are possible with minimal disturbances by using this approach [40].

***Training and Support:*** It offers detailed training programs to make sure the medical personnel are using every feature of MegaETH for real-time synchronizing. This also includes ongoing support to quickly resolve any integration issue.

# SECURITY PROTOCOLS

Data protection in healthcare is an obligation not only legally but also for the assurance of safety and confidence among patients. MegaETH provides a strong set of security and protection [41].

These are security measures against breaches, unauthorized access, and other security vulnerabilities in healthcare data [16]. This section discusses important elements of the security architecture at MegaETH: incident response and recovery plans, procedures for authentication and authorization, and data encryption standards [9].

## Data Encryption Standards

### *Types of Encryption Used*

MegaETH works at a multi-layered encryption level to make sure that any critical medical data is kept well-guarded throughout the life of a person. Some of the most important methods of encryption it uses include:

***Symmetric Encryption:*** MegaETH uses symmetric encryption algorithms, the AES using 256-bit keys. Using this, large amounts of data can be encrypted very fast, and AES-256 is a well-renowned powerful encryption standard that works very well for both in-transit as well as at-rest data [42].

***Asymmetric Encryption:*** Symmetric encryption methods in MegaETH enable secure data transfers and authentication, utilizing methods such as elliptic curve cryptography and RSA. In asymmetric encryption, a pair of keys is used, whereby a digital signature enables secure communication and authentication; the public key provides for encryption, and decryption is performed using the private key.

***Hash Functions:*** In MegaETH, cryptographic hash functions, such as SHA-256, are used to ensure the integrity of data. The unique data of fingerprints through hashing allows for the verification of the validity of data and its unauthorized changes in it [43].

### *Effectiveness of Encryption*

The security mechanisms of MegaETH work appropriately within the realm of:

***Ensuring Confidentiality:*** Sensitive patient information is kept secret and unavailable to unauthorized parties by encryption. Data cannot be decrypted without the right decryption keys, even if it is intercepted or accessed illegally [44].

***Data Integrity Preservation:*** This technology behind cryptographic hashing helps in the detection of data manipulation. Modification in any hash value alerts about changes, hence guaranteeing the integrity of data with accuracy.

***Securing Secure Data Transmission:*** Asymmetric encryption guards data in transmission between systems, ensuring that information across networks is not only encrypted but also accessible to an intended party alone.

## Authentication and Authorization

### *Multi-Factor Authentication (MFA)*

However, multi-factor authentication increases the aspect of security in MegaETH, since accessing systems and data requires several verification techniques. These include:

***Knowledge-Based Factors:*** This is the initial layer of verification wherein the users are required to put in the password or the PIN [45]. In most cases, this involves typing a password or Personal Identification Number. These credentials, because they are the first tier of defense against unauthorized access, should be complex and unique. Therefore, it is suggested that users create strong and unique passwords, which are hard to guess or crack to make this layer much more secure [46].

***Possession-Based Factors:*** An additional form of verification can be in the form of a smart card, a mobile application generating OTPs, or even a hardware token. The examples commonly known include smart cards, physical cards with encrypted information, and mobile applications that generate One-Time Passwords. It also concerns hardware tokens-small, physical devices generating a time-bound code. This method makes it secure because even if the password is compromised, the entry of unauthorized users cannot be effectuated without the additional physical token, as it requires entering a code or authenticating one's identity by a possession factor [47].

***Biometric Factors:*** Advanced biometric techniques utilized for fingerprint or facial recognition provide the third layer of protection for sensitive data. Therefore, the approach leverages special technologies to validate the user's identity through biological traits that are difficult to forge or replicate. While face recognition systems will evaluate certain facial features, fingerprint scanners analyze the unique patterns of a user's fingerprint. By adding biometric elements, MFA becomes even more secure and user-friendly, hence an effective way of repelling unauthorized access [48].

In the below table (Table **2**), the authentication systems already in place employ an enormous number of sensors allowing a user to be identified. In the following chapter, we elaborate further on the MFA-suitable factors corresponding to market-available sensors and associate challenges along with more details on the ones that are to be potentially deployed in the near future. Besides MFA, MegaETH provides several other safe ways of logging in. Some of them are:

**Table 2. Multi-factor authentication (MFA).**

| Authentication Factor | Description | Examples |
|---|---|---|
| Knowledge-Based Factors | Requires the user to supply the information they know. | Password, PIN |
| Possession-Based Factors | Requires the user to present something they own. | Hardware token, mobile app for OTPs, and smart card. |
| Biometric Factors | Requires the user to provide a physical characteristic. | Fingerprint scan, and facial recognition. |

*Password Complexity Policy:* The creation of a password by a user should be intuitively complex, including a mix of letters, numbers, and special characters to avoid unauthorized access attempts. This makes it much harder for unauthorized users to access through brute-force attacks or password guessing. MegaETH ensures that the user account is better protected against potential breaches by insisting on the following complexity requirements [49].

*Session Management:* MegaETH monitors and manages user sessions to avoid unwanted access. Suspicious or inactive sessions are logged out automatically. MegaETH continuously monitors user sessions to detect and manage suspicious or abnormal activities. By default, sessions are automatically closed if they are deemed idle for a long time, or show activity that is harmful to the users. In case of forgotten left-open sessions or session hacking, proactive ways ensure the system does not allow unwanted access. MegaETH's active session management is very helpful because it provides access to only authorized users [50].

*Role-Based Access Control:* It controls access through systems and information by giving restrictions, according to the different user roles and functions. It, therefore, minimizes the risk of leakage since one is sure that the users cannot access information that does not fall under the scope of their role. This approach minimizes the occurrence of data loss or unlawful access because users can neither view nor change any information that exceeds their scope. RBAC ensures that a user works within a clearly defined and constrained access framework that assists in maintaining data integrity and security.

## Incident Response and Recovery

***Incident Response and Recovery:*** MegaETH has adopted an incident response and recovery strategy that best suits the handling of security breaches. Incident Detection and Reporting: Events that could potentially lead to a security breach are detected in real-time through continuous monitoring systems. The automated alert system sends suspicious activity notifications to the Incident Response Team [51].

***Incident Response Team:*** The team would include forensic analysts, communication specialists, and cybersecurity experts. In breach incidents, the IRT identifies the severity of the security breach, isolates systems affected, and blocks further unauthorized access. Eradication and Containment: Security breaches are eliminated as quickly as possible. It involves segregating compromised systems, removing malicious code, and patching exploited vulnerabilities.

***Recovery and Restoration:*** After containment, MegaETH focuses on activities such as restoration of data from safe backups, verification that restored systems are reliable, and quickly getting back to normal operations [52].

***Post-event analysis:*** In case of any event, a thorough analysis is done to identify the cause, how effective our response was, and what needs improvement. Knowledge so acquired is applied to improve security protocols and to enhance defenses against a possible attack.

### Communication and Transparency

Communication at the time of, and following, a security incident is extremely important. MegaETH ensures timely information related to the breach, its consequences, and actions taken for mitigation are provided to all parties concerned, including patients and healthcare providers. This builds confidence and exhibits care about patient data protection.

## BENEFITS, IMPACT, AND CHALLENGES

MegaETH presents a new paradigm for healthcare transaction security, which has optimized operational efficiencies and, more crucially, patient care [53]. However, it is equally important to consider the challenges of its implementation. This section undertakes an in-depth review of the extent to which MegaETH optimizes the domains of patient outcomes and operational effectiveness while confronting typical challenges.

### Enhancing Patient Safety

### Reducing Errors and Enhancing Decision-Making

MegaETH provides secure real-time data syncing, which greatly reduces the risk of medical mistakes. MegaETH makes it possible for medical personnel to make more correct diagnoses and take swift action based on the latest information by rapidly making access to the most current information about the patient. The sophisticated encryption and authentication mechanisms ensure data integrity and minimize any chance of an error due to obsolete or corrupted data. The aftermath increased precision in decision-making with improved health outcomes and heightened patient safety [54].

## *Streamlining Operations*

### ***Boosting Efficiency in Data Management and Communication***

MegaETH further streamlines communication and management of data processes in health. There is no duplication of files, as all nodes on the network are updated in real time. This reduces latency in accessing this most valuable information. Overall productivity increases because healthcare providers need not to spend much time on administrative issues but focus on patient care due to increased efficiencies [55]. The mega ETH is further easily integrated with the existing healthcare systems to ensure maximum sharing and coordination among various departments and stakeholders.

### ***Cost Savings***

Health institutes can reap significant financial benefits from the solutions provided by MegaETH. The cost savings would be viewed as quite huge, factoring in the efficiencies that come with streamlined management of data and reduced administrative activities. This is aside from the reduction of errors and costs associated with medical errors, such as additional testing or extended hospitalization. Buying MegaETH enhances efficiency and ensures value for money by reducing costs and better resource management.

### **Challenges and Solutions**

There are some technical difficulties in integrating MegaETH with currently installed healthcare IT systems, mainly on data migration and system compatibility issues [56]. These legacy systems may require modifications or even upgrades themselves to be compatible with blockchain-based solutions developed on MegaETH. Such obstacles can be overcome by careful planning and testing during integration [57]. These healthcare organizations should liaise well with the technical support of MegaETH to ensure integration is smooth, that it is easy in terms of data migration processes, and there will be interoperability between the systems.

## Navigating Healthcare Regulations and Standards

The healthcare industry has to work through an exceptionally complex regulatory environment as it implements new technologies. MegaETH supports organizations in such resources and guidance on compliance, frequent updates on compliance, and support for regulatory audits. With legally protected patient information used in their operations, MegaETH has to comply with various regulations such as HIPAA and GDRP [58].

## Strategies for Training and Encouraging Use Among Healthcare Professionals

MegaETH deployment can only be successful with the acceptance of healthcare professionals. Moreover, a lot of barriers may appear regarding the efficient application of the MegaETH solution: reluctance to adapt or lack of experience in approaching new technologies [59]. In this respect, MegaETH provides detailed training courses with continuous support for healthcare workers to get used to the new system. This can go a long way in smoother adoption by early involvement of key stakeholders and highlighting useful advantages to them. Ongoing feedback and support are given to the users so that any problems that arise may quickly be overcome and the user can continue to stay confident in using the system.

## FUTURE DIRECTIONS

### Emerging Technologies

There will be a variety of new developments in technology that will impact the future of MegaETH within healthcare. New technological advances, such as quantum computing, machine learning, and AI, can enhance blockchain solutions applied by MegaETH [60]. Machine learning and AI may have the potential to automatically provide predictive analytics and data management. Quantum computing could transform data security and encryption to a whole new level. MegaETH is committed to integrating such advances into service, so it keeps its status as a leader in healthcare technology and constantly improves.

As the leakages of healthcare data have grown, so it needs better security. The future of this domain incorporates advanced encryption methods, decentralized options for storing data, and real-time threat detection systems. MegaETH observes these trends with great concern and corrects its approach whenever it is necessary so that its solutions would withstand new risks and remain compliant with the changing law requirements.

## Long-Term Vision For Megaeth

The long-term vision of MegaETH also involves the expansion of its influence within the healthcare sector through the following strategic goals:

### *Scalability*

This would mean scalability of the blockchain systems for handling the growing volume of healthcare data and increasing users in general. The blockchain infrastructure shall be optimized to manage large datasets and a high number of transactions without any loss of efficiency. Due to this scalability, MegaETH is in a position to support a strong healthcare ecosystem in which data will be managed and stored effectively in the growth of the network. This job splitting enables the network to manage more transactions as it expands. Each node will operate optimally about workload distribution, which allows scaling for MegaETH to be much more efficient at handling higher transaction demands while maintaining the same speed.

### *Interoperability*

Interoperability means compatibility with a wide range of different health technologies and systems in such a way that smooth integration and interchanging of data, for example, would be easily facilitated. That would ensure the ability of MegaETH to easily combine and share information on several platforms used in healthcare organizations. Generally, high interoperability means that for better coordination among practitioners and an overall higher quality of care, standards, and protocols must be developed that allow the sharing of data between diverse health information systems.

### *Global Reach*

MegaETH's solutions are scaled into other markets for them to handle global healthcare issues and adapt to other regulatory regimes. The MegaETH project aspires to address numerous health concerns, among many others, on a worldwide scale by extending its blockchain technology. This way, MegaETH will be able to provide global solutions, increase accessibility, and fill the gaps in healthcare needs around the world.

### *Innovation*

Active and continuous pursuit of new ways and technologies can enhance general efficacy, safety, and efficiency in the domain of healthcare transactions. Advanced technologies and methods should be researched to enhance effectiveness, security, and speed in general healthcare systems. MegaETH wants to lead the healthcare industry at the frontline of technology, ensuring that its blockchain solutions are innovative and state-of-the-art to solve new problems [61].

## CONCLUSION

The powerful solutions offered by MegaETH have revolutionized healthcare security into safe transactions, real-time data synchronization, and enhanced patient safety, bringing tremendous advancement. Improvement in patient outcomes and operational efficiency is based on key benefits like multi-factor authentication, enhanced encryption, and optimized operations. The scalability of MegaETH's solution into the existing health systems and its impact on the sector are shown by the fact that it is scalable into mainstream adoption. Its involvement inproviding the solutions of major issues related to data security and operational efficiency involves the disruption of this very sector. MegaETH not only enhances general healthcare delivery but also sets a new benchmark for safety and efficiency in general healthcare transactions by enhancing patient safety and cost savings. In this respect, with the growth in technology, it will be very important for MegaETH to keep pace with innovation and adaptation in developing security systems within the healthcare domain to support emergent threats and ensure that these infrastructures remain robust and efficient.

## ACKNOWLEDGEMENT

I extend my heartfelt thanks to my Head of Department for his invaluable guidance and insightful feedback, which were crucial in shaping this chapter on MegaETH Solutions for Secure Healthcare Transactions. I am also deeply grateful to my senior colleagues for their support and expertise throughout this process. Additionally, I would like to thank my family for their unwavering encouragement and understanding during this work. Your collective support has been instrumental in bringing this chapter to completion. Thank you all for your significant contributions and encouragement.

## REFERENCES

[1]     P. Shojaei, E. Vlahu-Gjorgievska, and Y.W. Chow, "Security and privacy of technologies in health information systems: A systematic literature review", *Computers,* vol. 13, no. 2, p. 41, 2024.
[http://dx.doi.org/10.3390/computers13020041]

[2]     J. Vora, P. Italiya, S. Tanwar, S. Tyagi, N. Kumar, M.S. Obaidat, and K.F. Hsiao, "Ensuring privacy and security in e-health records", In: *in Proc. International Confrence. Computer, Information and Telecommunication Systems (CITS)* Colmar, France, 2018.
[http://dx.doi.org/10.1109/CITS.2018.8440164]

[3]     S. Mbonihankuye, A. Nkunzimana, and A. Ndagijimana, "Healthcare data security technology: HIPAA compliance", *Wireless Communications and Mobile Computing,* vol. 2019, pp. 1927495-1927495, 2019.

[http://dx.doi.org/10.1155/2019/1927495]

[4]    M. Attaran, "Blockchain technology in healthcare: Challenges and opportunities", *Int. J. Healthc. Manag.,* vol. 15, no. 1, pp. 70-83, 2022.
[http://dx.doi.org/10.1080/20479700.2020.1843887]

[5]    Z. Zheng, S. Xie, H. Dai, X. Chen, and H. Wang, "An overview of blockchain technology: architecture, consensus, and future trends", *2017 IEEE International Congress on Big Data (BigData Congress),* pp. 557-564, 2017.
[http://dx.doi.org/10.1109/BigDataCongress.2017.85]

[6]    B. Shrimali, and H.B. Patel, "Blockchain state-of-the-art: architecture, use cases, consensus, challenges and opportunities", *J. King Saud Univ. - Comput. Inf. Sci.,* vol. 34, no. 9, pp. 6793-6807, 2022.
[http://dx.doi.org/10.1016/j.jksuci.2021.08.005]

[7]    F. Hofmann, S. Wurster, E. Ron, and M. Böhmecke-Schwafert, "The immutability concept of blockchains and benefits of early standardization", In: *2017 ITU Kaleidoscope: Challenges for a Data-Driven Society.* ITU K: Nanjing, China, 2017, pp. 1-8.
[http://dx.doi.org/10.23919/ITU-WT.2017.8247004]

[8]    S.K. Panda, A.K. Jena, S.K. Swain, S.C. Satapathy, Ed., *Blockchain technology: Applications and challenges.* Springer, 2021.
[http://dx.doi.org/10.1007/978-3-030-69395-4]

[9]    K.N. Qureshi, H. Nafea, I. Tariq Javed, and K. Zrar Ghafoor, "Blockchain-based trust and authentication model for detecting and isolating malicious nodes in flying ad hoc networks", *IEEE Access,* vol. 12, pp. 95390-95401, 2024.
[http://dx.doi.org/10.1109/ACCESS.2024.3425153]

[10]   D. Alves Batista, "Enhancing transparency and accountability in public procurement: exploring blockchain technology to mitigate records fraud", *Rec. Manage. J.,* vol. 34, no. 2/3, pp. 151-170, 2024.
[http://dx.doi.org/10.1108/RMJ-10-2023-0054]

[12]   T. Suleski, "A review of multi-factor authentication in the Internet of Healthcare Things", 9, Jan. 2023.
[http://dx.doi.org/10.1177/20552076231177144]

[13]   V. Buterin, J. Lubin, and A. Capital, "MegaETH: Unveiling the first real-time blockchain", *MegaLabs,* 2023. Available from: Available: https://megaeth.systems/research

[14]   A. Solanky, "Understanding megaETH: The 'real-time ethereum' L2 promising 100K TPS", *CryptoBlogs,* 2024. Available from: https://www.cryptoblogs.io/understanding-megaeth-real-time-ethereum-l2-promising-100k-tps/

[15]   J. Lubin, V. Buterin, and A. Capital, "Can MegaETH really achieve real-time blockchain?", *CoinLive,* 2024. Available from: https://www.coinlive.com/news/can-megaeth-really-achieve-real-time-blockchain

[16]   R. Zhang, R. Xue, and L. Liu, "Security and privacy for healthcare blockchains", *IEEE Trans. Serv. Comput.,* vol. 15, no. 6, pp. 3668-3686, 2022.
[http://dx.doi.org/10.1109/TSC.2021.3085913]

[17]   M.S. Arbabi, C. Lal, N.R. Veeraragavan, D. Marijan, J.F. Nygård, and R. Vitenberg, "A survey on blockchain for healthcare: Challenges, benefits, and future directions", *IEEE Communications Surveys & Tutorials,* vol. 25, no. 1, pp. 386-424, 2023.
[http://dx.doi.org/10.1109/COMST.2022.3224644]

[18]   Rahman, Md. H., Yeoh, W., & Pal, S, "Exploring factors influencing blockchain adoption's effectiveness in organizations for generating business value: A systematic literature review and thematic analysis", *Enterp. Inf. Syst.,* vol. 18, no. 8, 2024.
[http://dx.doi.org/]

[19]   T. McGhin, K.K.R. Choo, C.Z. Liu, and D. He, "Blockchain in healthcare applications: Research

challenges and opportunities", *J. Netw. Comput. Appl.,* vol. 135, pp. 62-75, 2019.
[http://dx.doi.org/10.1016/j.jnca.2019.02.027]

[20]   L. Ismail, H. Materwala, and S. Zeadally, "Lightweight blockchain for healthcare", *IEEE Access,* vol.
7, pp. 149935-149951, 2019.
[http://dx.doi.org/10.1109/ACCESS.2019.2947613]

[21]   M. Mettler, "Blockchain technology in healthcare: The revolution starts here", In: *in 2016 IEEE 18th
International Conference on e-Health Networking, Applications and Services (Healthcom)* Munich,
Germany, 2016, pp. 1-3.
[http://dx.doi.org/10.1109/HealthCom.2016.7749510]

[22]   P. Zhang, M.A. Walker, J. White, D.C. Schmidt, and G. Lenz, "Metrics for assessing blockchain-based
healthcare decentralized apps", In: *in 2017 IEEE 19th International Conference on e-Health
Networking, Applications and Services (Healthcom)* Dalian, China, 2017, pp. 1-4.
[http://dx.doi.org/10.1109/HealthCom.2017.8210842]

[23]   I. Yaqoob, K. Salah, R. Jayaraman, and Y. Al-Hammadi, "Blockchain for healthcare data
management: opportunities, challenges, and future recommendations", *Neural Comput. Appl.,* vol. 34,
no. 14, pp. 11475-11490, 2022.
[http://dx.doi.org/10.1007/s00521-020-05519-w]

[24]   Z. Alhadhrami, S. Alghfeli, M. Alghfeli, J.A. Abedlla, and K. Shuaib, "Introducing blockchains for
healthcare", *2017 International Conference on Electrical and Computing Technologies and
Applications (ICECTA),* 2017
[http://dx.doi.org/10.1109/ICECTA.2017.8252043]

[25]   A. Tandon, A. Dhir, A.K.M.N. Islam, and M. Mäntymäki, "Blockchain in healthcare: A systematic
literature review, synthesizing framework and future research agenda", *Comput. Ind.,* vol. 122, p.
103290, 2020.
[http://dx.doi.org/10.1016/j.compind.2020.103290]

[26]   B. Zaabar, O. Cheikhrouhou, F. Jamil, M. Ammi, and M. Abid, "HealthBlock: A secure blockchain-
based healthcare data management system", *Comput. Netw.,* vol. 200, p. 108500, 2021.
[http://dx.doi.org/10.1016/j.comnet.2021.108500]

[27]   X. Yue, H. Wang, D. Jin, M. Li, and W. Jiang, "Healthcare data gateways: Found healthcare
intelligence on blockchain with novel privacy risk control", *J. Med. Syst.,* vol. 40, no. 10, p. 218, 2016.
[http://dx.doi.org/10.1007/s10916-016-0574-6] [PMID: 27565509]

[28]   A.P. Singh, N.R. Pradhan, A.K. Luhach, S. Agnihotri, N.Z. Jhanjhi, S. Verma, U. Kavita, U. Ghosh,
and D.S. Roy, "A novel patient-centric architectural framework for blockchain-enabled healthcare
applications", *IEEE Trans. Industr. Inform.,* vol. 17, no. 8, pp. 5779-5789, 2021.
[http://dx.doi.org/10.1109/TII.2020.3037889]

[29]   S. Badr, I. Gomaa, and E. Abd-Elrahman, "Multi-tier blockchain framework for IoT-EHRs systems",
*Procedia Comput. Sci.,* vol. 141, pp. 159-166, 2018.
[http://dx.doi.org/10.1016/j.procs.2018.10.162]

[30]   M.S. Ali, M. Vecchio, M. Pincheira, K. Dolui, F. Antonelli, and M.H. Rehmani, "Applications of
blockchains in the internet of things: A comprehensive survey", *IEEE Commun. Surv. Tutor.,* vol. 21,
no. 2, pp. 1676-1717, 2019.
[http://dx.doi.org/10.1109/COMST.2018.2886932]

[31]   L.M. Dang, M.J. Piran, D. Han, K. Min, and H. Moon, "A survey on internet of things and cloud
computing for healthcare", *Electronics (Basel),* vol. 8, no. 7, p. 768, 2019.
[http://dx.doi.org/10.3390/electronics8070768]

[32]   M.A. Rahman, M.M. Rashid, M.S. Hossain, E. Hassanain, M.F. Alhamid, and M. Guizani,
"Blockchain and IoT-based cognitive edge framework for sharing economy services in a smart city",
*IEEE Access,* vol. 7, pp. 18611-18621, 2019.
[http://dx.doi.org/10.1109/ACCESS.2019.2896065]

[33]   D. Dhagarra, M. Goswami, and G. Kumar, "Impact of trust and privacy concerns on technology acceptance in healthcare: An indian perspective", *Int. J. Med. Inform.,* vol. 141, p. 104164, 2020.
[http://dx.doi.org/10.1016/j.ijmedinf.2020.104164]

[34]   D.C. Nguyen, P.N. Pathirana, M. Ding, and A. Seneviratne, "Integration of blockchain and cloud of things: Architecture, applications and challenges", *IEEE Commun. Surv. Tutor.,* vol. 22, no. 4, pp. 2521-2549, 2020.
[http://dx.doi.org/10.1109/COMST.2020.3020092]

[35]   M. Ejaz, T. Kumar, I. Kovacevic, M. Ylianttila, and E. Harjula, "Health-blockedge: Blockchain-edge framework for reliable low-latency digital healthcare applications", *Sensors (Basel),* vol. 21, no. 7, p. 2502, 2021.
[http://dx.doi.org/10.3390/s21072502] [PMID: 33916700]

[36]   A.N. Gohar, S.A. Abdelmawgoud, and M.S. Farhan, "A patient-centric healthcare framework reference architecture for better semantic interoperability based on blockchain, cloud, and IoT", *IEEE Access,* vol. 10, pp. 92137-92157, 2022.
[http://dx.doi.org/10.1109/ACCESS.2022.3202902]

[37]   D. Saraswat, P. Bhattacharya, A. Verma, V.K. Prasad, S. Tanwar, G. Sharma, P.N. Bokoro, and R. Sharma, "Explainable AI for healthcare 5.0: opportunities and challenges", *IEEE Access,* vol. 10, pp. 84486-84517, 2022.
[http://dx.doi.org/10.1109/ACCESS.2022.3197671]

[38]   N. Taimoor, and S. Rehman, "Reliable and resilient AI and IoT-based personalised healthcare services: A survey", *IEEE Access,* vol. 10, pp. 535-563, 2022.
[http://dx.doi.org/10.1109/ACCESS.2021.3137364]

[39]   S. Vitabile, M. Marks, D. Stojanovic, S. Pllana, J.M. Molina, M. Krzyszton, and I. Salomie, "Medical data processing and analysis for remote health and activities monitoring", In: *High-Performance Modelling and Simulation for Big Data Applications: Selected Results of the COST Action IC1406 cHiPSet.* Springer International Publishing: Cham, 2019, pp. 186-220.
[http://dx.doi.org/10.1007/978-3-030-16272-6_7]

[40]   D.C. Nguyen, P.N. Pathirana, M. Ding, and A. Seneviratne, "BEdgeHealth: A decentralized architecture for edge-based IoMT networks using blockchain", *IEEE Internet Things J.,* vol. 8, no. 14, pp. 11743-11757, 2021.
[http://dx.doi.org/10.1109/JIOT.2021.3058953]

[41]   K. Zala, H.K. Thakkar, R. Jadeja, P. Singh, K. Kotecha, and M. Shukla, "PRMS: Design and development of patients' e-healthcare records management system for privacy preservation in third party cloud platforms", *IEEE Access,* vol. 10, pp. 85777-85791, 2022.
[http://dx.doi.org/10.1109/ACCESS.2022.3198094]

[42]   L. Chen, W.K. Lee, C.C. Chang, K.K.R. Choo, and N. Zhang, "Blockchain based searchable encryption for electronic health record sharing", *Future Gener. Comput. Syst.,* vol. 95, pp. 420-429, 2019.
[http://dx.doi.org/10.1016/j.future.2019.01.018]

[43]   H. Zhao, P. Bai, Y. Peng, and R. Xu, "Efficient key management scheme for health blockchain", *CAAI Trans. Intell. Technol.,* vol. 3, no. 2, pp. 114-118, 2018.
[http://dx.doi.org/10.1049/trit.2018.0014]

[44]   X. Yang, T. Tian, J. Wang, and C. Wang, "Blockchain-based multi-user certificateless encryption with keyword search for electronic health record sharing", *Peer-to-Peer Netw. Appl.,* vol. 15, no. 5, pp. 2270-2288, 2022.
[http://dx.doi.org/10.1007/s12083-022-01345-0]

[45]   L. Zhang, T. Zhang, Q. Wu, Y. Mu, and F. Rezaeibagha, "Secure decentralized attribute-based sharing of personal health records with blockchain", *IEEE Internet Things J.,* vol. 9, no. 14, pp. 12482-12496, 2022.

[http://dx.doi.org/10.1109/JIOT.2021.3137240]

[46]   M. Wang, Y. Guo, C. Zhang, C. Wang, H. Huang, and X. Jia, "MedShare: A privacy-preserving medical data sharing system by using blockchain", *IEEE Trans. Serv. Comput.,* no. Jan, p. 1, 2021.
[http://dx.doi.org/10.1109/TSC.2021.3114719]

[47]   T.L. Tan, I. Salam, and M. Singh, "Blockchain-based healthcare management system with two-side verifiability", *PLoS One,* vol. 17, no. 4, p. e0266916, 2022.
[http://dx.doi.org/10.1371/journal.pone.0266916] [PMID: 35421184]

[48]   X. Yang, T. Li, R. Liu, and M. Wang, "Blockchain-Based Secure and Searchable EHR Sharing Scheme", *2019 4th International Conference on Mechanical, Control and Computer Engineering (ICMCCE),* 2019.
[http://dx.doi.org/10.1109/ICMCCE48743.2019.00188]

[49]   Yue, Xiao & Wang, Huiju & Jin, Dawei & Li, Mingqiang & Jiang, Wei, "Healthcare data gateways: Found healthcare intelligence on blockchain with novel privacy risk control", *J. med. syst.,* vol. 40, p. 218, 2016.
[http://dx.doi.org/10.1007/s10916-016-0574-6]

[50]   A.D. Dwivedi, G. Srivastava, S. Dhar, and R. Singh, "A decentralized privacy-preserving healthcare blockchain for IoT", *Sensors (Basel),* vol. 19, no. 2, p. 326, 2019.
[http://dx.doi.org/10.3390/s19020326] [PMID: 30650612]

[51]   G.G. Dagher, J. Mohler, M. Milojkovic, and P.B. Marella, "Ancile: Privacy-preserving framework for access control and interoperability of electronic health records using blockchain technology", *Sustain Cities Soc.,* vol. 39, pp. 283-297, 2018.
[http://dx.doi.org/10.1016/j.scs.2018.02.014]

[52]   N. Andola, R. Prakash, S. Venkatesan, and S. Verma, "SHEMB: A secure approach for healthcare management system using blockchain", *2019 IEEE Conference on Information and Communication Technology,* pp. 1-6, 2019.

[53]   A.A. Siyal, A.Z. Junejo, M. Zawish, K. Ahmed, A. Khalil, and G. Soursou, "Applications of blockchain technology in medicine and healthcare: challenges and future perspectives", *Cryptography,* vol. 3, no. 1, p. 3, 2019.
[http://dx.doi.org/10.3390/cryptography3010003]

[54]   T.K. Mackey, T.T. Kuo, B. Gummadi, K.A. Clauson, G. Church, D. Grishin, K. Obbad, R. Barkovich, and M. Palombini, "'Fit-for-purpose?' – challenges and opportunities for applications of blockchain technology in the future of healthcare", *BMC Med.,* vol. 17, no. 1, p. 68, 2019.
[http://dx.doi.org/10.1186/s12916-019-1296-7] [PMID: 30914045]

[55]   F. Alam Khan, M. Asif, A. Ahmad, M. Alharbi, and H. Aljuaid, "Blockchain technology, improvement suggestions, security challenges on smart grid and its application in healthcare for sustainable development", *Sustain Cities Soc.,* vol. 55, p. 102018, 2020.
[http://dx.doi.org/10.1016/j.scs.2020.102018]

[56]   S. Dash, P.K. Gantayat, and R.K. Das, "Blockchain technology in healthcare: Opportunities and challenges", *Intelligent Systems Reference Library,* pp. 97-111, 2021.
[http://dx.doi.org/10.1007/978-3-030-69395-4_6]

[57]   T. Ahram, A. Sargolzaei, S. Sargolzaei, J. Daniels, and B. Amaba, "Blockchain technology innovations", In: *in 2017 IEEE Technology & Engineering Management Conference.* Temscon: Santa Clara, CA, USA, 2017, pp. 137-141.
[http://dx.doi.org/10.1109/TEMSCON.2017.7998367]

[58]   P. Dutta, T.M. Choi, S. Somani, and R. Butala, "Blockchain technology in supply chain operations: Applications, challenges and research opportunities", *Transp. Res., Part E Logist. Trans. Rev.,* vol. 142, p. 102067, 2020.
[http://dx.doi.org/10.1016/j.tre.2020.102067] [PMID: 33013183]

[59]   S. Ramzan, A. Aqdus, V. Ravi, D. Koundal, R. Amin, and M.A. Al Ghamdi, "Healthcare applications using blockchain technology: Motivations and challenges", *IEEE Trans. Eng. Manage.,* vol. 70, no. 8, pp. 2874-2890, 2023.
[http://dx.doi.org/10.1109/TEM.2022.3189734]

[60]   P. Pandey, and R. Litoriya, "Implementing healthcare services on a large scale: Challenges and remedies based on blockchain technology", *Health Policy Technol.,* vol. 9, no. 1, pp. 69-78, 2020.
[http://dx.doi.org/10.1016/j.hlpt.2020.01.004]

[61]   J.Z. Zhang, W. He, S. Shetty, X. Tian, Y. He, A. Behl, and A.K.V. Veetil, "Understanding governance and control challenges of blockchain technology in healthcare and energy sectors: a historical perspective", *J. Manag. Hist.,* vol. 30, no. 2, pp. 219-242, 2024.
[http://dx.doi.org/10.1108/JMH-12-2022-0086]

# SUBJECT INDEX

## A

Access Control   109–110
Account Abstraction   20
Accountability   115
Adaptive Blockchain Architectures   6
Address Formats (Base58, Bech32)   20
Agriculture Supply Chain   63–64
AI Integration   2, 83
  AI-driven fraud detection   115
  AI-powered smart contract auditing   83
  AI-enhanced scalability   118
Anti-Money Laundering (AML)   115
Applications of Blockchain   12–13, 41–42, 65, 83, 112
  banking sector   88–90
  education sector   98–100
  governance & voting   94–96
  healthcare sector   72–75
  insurance sector   101–102
  logistics sector   62–64
  pharmaceutical sector   76–78
  real estate   97–98
  waste management   104–106
Architecture of Blockchain   5–6
Asymmetric Cryptography   6, 108
Asset Management   45
Asset Tokenization   46–47, 84
Atomic Swaps   89
Auditability   7

## B

Backup Strategies   109
Banking Applications   88–90
Base Layer Protocols   1–4
Big Data Integration   83
Bitcoin   3–4, 20
Bitcoin Lightning Network   20
Block Explorer   7
Block Propagation   6
Block Size Debate   118

Block Structure   6–7
Blockchain   1–4, 35–38
  adoption barriers   120
  adoption lifecycle   120–121
  architecture   5–6
  auditing potential   7
  characteristics   8
  governance models   115
  history   2–3
  hybrid blockchain   5
  impact on finance   88
  permissioned blockchain   4
  permissionless blockchain   4
  regulation   115–116
Blockchain-as-a-Service (BaaS)   42
Bridge Protocols   113
Business Continuity   113
Business Process Automation   42, 86
Byzantine Fault Tolerance   9

## C

CBDC (Central Bank Digital Currency)   92–93
Chain Interoperability   113
Chaincode   3
Chain Reorganizations   109
Challenges of Blockchain   14, 120–121
Compliance Requirements   115
Consensus Algorithms   8–11
  Casper   10
  HotStuff   10
  Nakamoto Consensus   8
  Raft   10
  Tendermint   10
  all Proof-based models (see individual entries)
Consensus-as-a-Service   11
Consensus Layer   8
Cryptanalysis   108
Cryptocurrency   3–4, 19, 93
  custody solutions   93

**Monica Bhutani, Monica Gupta, Kirti Gupta, Deepali Kamthania & Danish Ather (Eds.)**
**All rights reserved-© 2025 Bentham Science Publishers**

    decentralized exchanges   89
    hot wallets   20
    cold storage   20
Cryptography   6, 108
    elliptic curve cryptography   108
    hash functions   6–7
    Merkle Trees   6
Crypto Wallets   20, 93
    multi-signature wallets   20
    hardware wallets   20

**D**

DAO Governance Models   3–4
Data Anonymization   114
Data Breaches   109
Data Encryption   109
Data Provenance   12
Data Privacy   114–115
Decentralization   8, 40, 87
Decentralized Applications (dApps)   82–83
Decentralized Exchanges   89
DeFi   88–90
    yield farming   89
    liquidity pools   89
    stablecoins   89
    DEX aggregators   89
Digital Identity   50–51, 91
Distributed Consensus   8–10
Distributed Ledger Technology (DLT)   1
Double-Spending Problem   8

**E**

Eclipse Attack   109
Education Applications   98–100
Edge Computing   68
Electronic Health Records   72–73
Elliptic Curve Digital Signature Algorithm
    (ECDSA)   108
Energy Consumption   14, 119
Enterprise Blockchain Solutions   41
Ethereum   3–4, 20
Ethereum 2.0 (Eth2)   20
Ethereum Virtual Machine (EVM)   20
Evolution / Timeline   2–3
E-Voting   94–96
Exploit Mitigation   109

**F**

Federated Learning   83
Fiat-to-Crypto Gateways   89
Finality (Transaction)   9
Flash Loans   89
Fraud Prevention   109, 115
Front-running Attacks   109
Future Scope   15

**G**

Gas Fees   20
General Data Protection Regulation (GDPR)
    114
Governance Frameworks   115–116
Green Blockchain Initiatives   119

**H**

Hard Forks   20
Hash Functions   6–7, 108
Healthcare Applications   72–75
Health Data Interoperability   74
Health Record Sharing   73
Hyperledger Fabric   3–4
Hyperledger Sawtooth   3–4
Hyperledger Besu   3–4

**I**

Identity Management   50–51, 91
Immutability   6
Industry 4.0   68
Insurance Applications   101–102
Interoperability   14, 113
InterPlanetary File System (IPFS)   11
IoT Integration   13, 68–70
IoT Security with Blockchain   69

**K**

Key Management   109
Keyless Signature Infrastructure   109

**L**

Latency Issues   118
Layer-2 Scaling Solutions   118

Ledger Synchronization   6
Legal Compliance   115
Lightning Network   20
Liquidity Mining   89
Logistics & Transportation   62–64

# M

Merkle Trees   6
Metamask   20
Metaverse Integration   86
Mining Pools   8
Multi-Chain Ecosystems   113
Multi-Signature Schemes   20

# N

NFT Marketplaces   85–86
Node Types   6
Nonce   6

# P

Permissioned Blockchain   4–5
Permissionless Blockchain   4
Pharmaceutical Supply Chain   76–78
Phishing Attacks   109
Plasma Chains   118
Privacy Coins   93
Privacy Preserving Computation   114
Private Keys   20
Proof of Authority   9
Proof of Personhood   10
Proof of Space-Time   10
Public Keys   20

# R

Real Estate   97–98
RegTech Solutions   115
Replay Attacks   109
Reputation Systems   10
Risk Management   118
Rollups (Optimistic, ZK)   118

# S

Scalability   14, 118
Security Audits   109

Security Tokens   84
Self-Sovereign Identity   91
Sharding   118
Sidechains   118
Slashing (PoS)   8
Smart Contracts   1–3, 12, 39, 82
    auditing   82
    use cases   39, 83
    vulnerabilities   109
Stablecoins   89
Supply Chain   12–13, 59–62, 74
    agri-food traceability   63
    cold chain management   76
    logistics tracking   62
Sybil Attack   109

# T

Token Economy   84–85
Token Standards   20
Traceability   12–13, 60, 75
Transaction Fees   20
Transaction Malleability   109
Transparency   12–13, 75
Trusted Execution Environments (TEE)   9
Types of Blockchain   4–5

# V

Validator Nodes   8
Vault Security   109
Voting Systems   94–96

# W

Wallet Security   109
Waste Management   104–106
Web3   87
Whale Tracking   89

www.ingramcontent.com/pod-product-compliance
Lightning Source LLC
Chambersburg PA
CBHW050811220326
41598CB00006B/181